Reconstruction and Cold War in Germany

Modern Economic and Social History Series

General Editor: Derek H. Aldcroft

Titles in this series include:

Exchange Rates and Economic Policy in the 20th Century
Edited by Ross E. Catterall and Derek H. Aldcroft

Britain and the Economic Problem of the Cold War
The Political Economy and the Economic Impact of the British Defence Effort, 1945–1955
Till Geiger

Studies in the Interwar European Economy
Derek H. Aldcroft

Arms and the State
Sir William Armstrong and the Remaking of British Naval Power, 1854–1914
Marshall J. Bastable

Whatever Happened to Monetarism?
Economic Policy Making and Social Learning in the United Kingdom Since 1979
Michael J. Oliver

Disillusionment or New Opportunites?
The Changing Nature of Work in Offices, Glasgow 1880–1914
R. Guerriero Wilson

Raleigh and the British Bicycle Industry
An Economic and Business History, 1870–1960
Roger Lloyd-Jones and M.J. Lewis

Battles for the Standard
Bimetallism and the Spread of the Gold Standard in the Nineteenth Century
Ted Wilson

The British Footwear Industry
Peter R. Mounfield

Reconstruction and Cold War in Germany

The Kreditanstalt für Wiederaufbau (1948-1961)

ARMIN GRÜNBACHER

Routledge
Taylor & Francis Group
LONDON AND NEW YORK

First published 2004 by Ashgate Publishing

2 Park Square, Milton Park, Abingdon, Oxfordshire OX14 4RN
52 Vanderbilt Avenue, New York, NY 10017

Routledge is an imprint of the Taylor & Francis Group, an informa business

First issued in paperback 2020

A Library of Congress record exists under LC control number: 2004048256

ISBN 13: 978-0-8153-9136-4 (hbk)
ISBN 13: 978-0-367-59389-6 (pbk)

Contents

Contents

List of Tables

Acknowledgements

This book is based on my thesis which was accepted for a PhD at the University of Birmingham. As every PhD candidate knows, a work like this can only come about with the help and support of other people. Although not all of them can be named here, it is an obligation which I am following willingly, to acknowledge all their help and support.

First, I want to express my gratitude to the staff of the various archives in which I conducted my research. Here I want to mention in particular the staff of the Historisches Archiv der Deutschen Bundesbank, who were extremely kind and helpful despite their workload during the preparation for the Bundesbank's 50th Anniversary. The staff of my favourite archive, the Bundesarchiv Koblenz, also have to be mentioned. Their friendly help and good humour brightened up many research days. My thanks goes also to Frau Dr Köchling of the Historisches Archiv der Kreditanstalt für Wiederaufbau. Despite her massive workload and her busy schedule in preparing the Kreditanstalt's 50th Anniversary, she patiently produced all the files and documents for me and supplied me with various 'Hausmaterialien' related to the topic and which proved to be most useful. Our discussions, sadly too few due to her busy schedule, provided me with much insight into the structure, task and history of the Kreditanstalt für Wiederaufbau.

On the institutional side I have to express my thanks to the University of Birmingham which provided me with a grant under its 'German Initiative' scheme, and to the School of Historical Studies at the University of Birmingham, which extended the grant.

Much of my research could be only done because good friends offered me their hospitality. Without their kindness I would not have been able to spend so much time in the archives for my primary research and this book would not be what it is. My warm thanks goes to Evi Halbich, Nils Mayer, Claire Mason and Dom Williamson. They always had an open door for me and made me feel welcome and never showed how bored they were when I told them about my research.

I feel much obliged to, and want to express my thanks to Dee Fellows, Katherine Dixon, James Williams and John Washbourne.

I am also indebted to Prof. Scott Lucas, who, despite his very busy schedule, always had time for a chat and provided important information and details on American policy both in occupied Germany and the wider context of the Cold War. I am most grateful to the best supervisor I could possibly have. Dr Sabine Lee guided me through my topic with constructive criticism, suggestions and encouragement which has meant a lot to me. She always found time for discussions and because these were often controversial and stimulating for my research they became a source of inspiration, particularly in some 'dark hours'. Dr

Lee's dedication to her PhD student went well beyond the call of a supervisor's duty and will always be a source of motivation and inspiration for me now that I am supervising students myself. Our discussions and her advice found once more its expression in this book and it is my pleasure to say thanks to her yet again.

Finally, I want to thank my family who provided me with a safe home base whenever I needed one. Above all else, my love and gratitude goes to my partner Juliane Schwarz. How much she endured and how much patience she needed with me during the years she alone knows.

List of Abbreviations

AA	Auswärtiges Amt
ABC	Allied Banking Commission
ABP	Arbeitsbeschaffungsprogramm
AHC	Allied High Commission
AIL	Auxiliary Investment Law
AKA	Ausfuhrkredit AG
APuZ	Aus Politik und Zeitgeschichte
AVBRD	Akten zur Vorgeschichte der Bundesrepublik Deutschland
BA	Bundesarchiv
BDA	Bundesverband deutscher Arbeitgeberverbände
BdL	Bank deutscher Länder
BDI	Bundesverband der Deutschen Industrie
BEWAG	Berliner Elektrizitäts-und Lichtwerke AG
BfAA	Bundesanstalt für Arbeitsvermittlung und Arbeitslosenversicherung
BGBl	Bundesgesetzblatt
BiB	Bipartite Board
BIB	Berliner Industriebank
BiCO	Bipartite Control Office
BMBes	Bundesminister/ministerium für wirtschaftlichen Besitz des Bundes
BMELF	Bundesminister/ministerium für Ernährung, Landwirtschaft und Forsten
BMF	Bundesminister/ministerium für Finanzen
BMP	Bundesminister/ministerium für den Marshallplan
BMVk	Bundesminister/ministerium für Verkehr
BMWi	Bundesminister/ministerium für Wirtschaft
BMwiZ	Bundesminister/ministerium für wirtschaftliche Zusammenarbeit
BMWo	Bundesminister/ministerium für Wohnungsbau
BoD	Board of Directors
BoM	Board of Managers
BTPA	(Deutscher) Bundestag, Parlamentsarchiv
CCCG	Combined Coal Control Group
CDU	Christlich Demokratische Union
CFM	Conference of Foreign Ministers

CSCG	Combined Steel Control Group
DBBHA	Deutsche Bundesbank, Historisches Archiv
DGB	Deutscher Gewerkschaftsbund
DIHT	Deutscher Industrie und Handelstag
DKBL	Deutsche Kohlenbergbauleitung
DKV	Deutscher Kohlenverkauf
DM	Deutsche Mark
DrS	Drucksache
ECA	Economic Corporation Act/Administration
ECSC	European Coal and Steel Community
EDC	European Defence Community
EEC	European Economic Community
EPU	European Payments Union
ERP	European Recovery Program
FDP	Freie Demokratische Partei
FGI	Federation of German Industry
FO	Foreign Office
FOA	Foreign Operations Administration
FRUS	Foreign Relations of the United States
GARIOA	Government Appropriations for Relief in Occupied Areas
GATT	General Agreement on Trade and Tariffs
GCI	Gross Capital Investment
GDP	Gross Domestic Product
GDR	German Democratic Republic
HA	High Authority
IAR	International Authority of the Ruhr
ICA	International Cooperation Administration
IKB	Industriekreditbank
Jb	Jahresberichte
JCS	Joint Chiefs of Staff
JEIA	Joint Export Import Agency
KfW	Kreditanstalt für Wiederaufbau
KfW HA	Kreditanstalt für Wiederaufbau, Historisches Archiv
KPD	Kommunistische Partei Deutschlands
kWh	Kilowatt hour
MEFO	Metallforschungsgesellschaft
MSA	Mutual Security Agency/Act
MSB	Military Security Board
MW	Megawatt
NA	National Archives
NATO	North Atlantic Treaty Organisation
NWDR	Nordwestdeutscher Rundfunk

OEEC	Organisation for European Economic Co-operation
OMGUS	Office of the Military Government, US, in Germany
PAAA	Politisches Archiv des Auswärtigen Amtes
PLI	Prohibited and Limited Industries
POW	Prisoner of War
PRO	Public Record Office
RG	Record Group
RM	Reichsmark
RWE	Rheinisch-Westfälische Elektrizitätswerke
SPD	Sozialdemokratische Partei Deutschlands
StEG	Staatliche Erfassungsgesellschaft für öffentliches Gut
StSek	Staatssekretär
SVR	Siedlungsverband Ruhrkohlenbezirk
TOP	Tagesordnungspunkt
US/UKCCG	United States/United Kingdom Coal Control Group
UVR	Unternehmensverband Ruhrbergbau
VEBA	Vereinigte Elektrizitäts-und Bergwerks AG
VELF	Verwaltung für Ernährung, Landwirtschaft und Forsten
VEW	Vereinigte Elektrizitätswerke
VfF	Verwaltung für Finanzen
VfW	Verwaltung für Wirtschaft
VIAG	Vereinigte Industriewerke AG
VfZ	Vierteljahrshefte für Zeitgeschichte
VW	Volkswagen
VWG	Vereinigtes Wirtschaftsgebiet
WVEIS	Wirtschaftsvereinigung der Eisen- und Stahlindustrie
ZT	Zins und Tilgung

Modern Economic and Social History Series General Editor's Preface

Economic and social history has been a flourishing subject of scholarly study during recent decades. Not only has the volume of literature increased enormously but the range of interest in time, space and subject matter has broadened considerably so that today there are many sub-branches of the subject which have developed considerable status in their own right.

One of the aims of this new series is to encourage the publication of scholarly monographs on any aspect of modern economic and social history. The geographical coverage is world-wide and contributions on the non-British themes will be especially welcome. While emphasis will be placed on works embodying original research, it is also intended that the series should provide the opportunity to publish studies of a more general thematic nature which offer a reappraisal or critical analysis of major issues of debate.

Derek H. Aldcroft
University of Leicester

Dedicated in loving memory to my mother

Introduction

The history of the Cold War has been extensively researched by a large number of historians, mainly with a focus on political history. Usually these books have dealt with the antagonism between the USA and the USSR, with some looking at the impact of the Cold War on Europe, or on the role individual European countries played within it. Similarly, a large number of books and articles have been written on West Germany's economic recovery after the Second World War. While most authors mention the impact of the Cold War on the creation of West Germany they do so mainly in the broadest political terms to explain how American thinking influenced developments in Germany. In the case of Germany's involvement in the Marshall Plan the importance of the Cold War is sometimes stressed more than in the purely 'political' field but a wider analysis of German and Allied decisions on the country's reconstruction within the context of the Cold War – apart from individual case studies, mainly on foreign trade – is still missing. This book contributes towards closing this gap by investigating how West Germany acted and reacted to the challenges – real or imagined – of the Cold War by looking at a key institution in the reconstruction process up to 1961, the Kreditanstalt für Wiederaufbau (KfW). The Kreditanstalt is a very German institution in the sense that it has its roots in German corporatist and statist tradition. That the Kreditanstalt für Wiederaufbau was and still is a very successful organisation is perhaps best demonstrated by the fact that it is older than any other German post-war institution still in existence. It outlived even the much admired and treasured Deutsch Mark which disappeared with the introduction of the Euro currency in 2002. The Kreditanstalt, with its unique set up, remit and organisational and operational structure, allows – like no other institution – an insight into developments in Germany and into decisions taken by German authorities during the country's reconstruction in the Cold War period.

On 5 November 1948, four and a half months after the currency reform in the western zones of occupation, a new phase in this reconstruction process began with the establishment of the KfW. The creation itself, a law enacted by the German authorities, which was partly inspired by the Americans and British occupying powers, attracted little interest at the time. The Kreditanstalt usually has kept out of the limelight and although today it is one of the biggest banks in Germany, it is scarcely known. But this can hardly explain the lack of attention it has received from historians and economic historians.

This book intends to be more than just another *Firmengeschichte* (company history). Instead its aim is to show the impact of social and political decisions and /or political events – both external and domestic – on the work of the Kreditanstalt from its foundations until 1961 and the repercussions it had on the economy. The significance of 1961 in German history can hardly be adequately appreciated. Usually, only the building of the Berlin Wall comes to mind. While the Wall symbolised ultimately the political split of Germany and Europe, it also had social and economic significance for West Germany. It terminated the continual stream of East Germans fleeing to the West and consequently the West German economy, still expanding, lost its supply of mainly young, well-trained and highly motivated workers. Two other events in 1961, the revaluation of the German currency and the completion of the sixth million new dwelling built since 1949 – significant in the Cold War propaganda between the two German states – marked the definite end of the reconstruction era. The new strength of the Mark on the international money markets showed the extent to which the economic recovery had succeeded. Much less publicised but of great importance for the work of the Kreditanstalt für Wiederaufbau was its redefined role as West Germany's Development Aid Bank. The new task, another indication for the country's new economic strength, changed its work like no other event before or after. Here again, the Cold War played a major role in the developments. For the next decade roughly half the Kreditanstalt's funds, about DM 1 billion annually, were spent on development aid projects.

Part one of the book shows that the influence of foreign political interests on the work of the Kreditanstalt für Wiederaufbau began even before its establishment with the Anglo-Americans deliberations on banking policy in Germany.

Part two is concerned with the Kreditanstalt's funding and with the influence the various parties involved in this process had on the bank. Direct US interference, of particular significance during the years of the European Recovery Program, the Marshall Plan, continued in various forms up to 1960. American requirements against West Germany during these years, like the demanded end to exports to Eastern Europe, were motivated once again by the Cold War and it is one intention of this book to show the impact and results of these demands. This involves an investigation of American influence on the Bonn government and their direct influence on the operations of the Kreditanstalt. This entails an investigation of how successful the German government and the Anstalt were in their attempts to avert American interference. This question is of special interest since the Germans intended to regain a place within the international community due to the country's economic performance. As will be shown, for the Kreditanstalt für Wiederaufbau the struggle for independence also meant – at least to some degree – independence from direct governmental interference in its business as well.

Part three investigates the utilisation and use of Kreditanstalt money within the reconstruction process. Here it will be shown that the German authorities had three main political intentions which influenced the work of the KfW. The early aim was to counter American influence and interference in German affairs as much as possible. The second objective was to obtain a proper tool for West Germany's involvement in US Cold War policy. It will be shown that the Kreditanstalt was just this instrument. Well beyond this, the effects of a West

German foreign policy doctrine of its own, the Hallstein Doctrine, and on German domestic level, the impact of the ideological confrontation with the GDR on the operations of the Anstalt will be shown. Finally, the Kreditanstalt's activities and involvement in *Wirtschaftslenkung* in some of the economic key sectors or those of social importance like housing construction will demonstrate that during the time under consideration, *Soziale Marktwirtschaft* was both less social and less market oriented than the myth which was created around it wants to make us believe.

A wide range of sources was accessible for researching this topic. The most important of the archives was of course that of the Kreditanstalt für Wiederaufbau itself. Ironically, despite the mass of information gathered there, it was also of all the archives visited the one which had the toughest restrictions in place. Due to German archival laws, information such as the minutes of the Board of Managers or the files containing the names of borrowers are treated as banking secrets and remain closed for 80 years. Due to a loophole in the law, some of these names and figures, usually concerning big companies, could be found and used without legal impediments in other archives, mainly at the Historische Archiv der Deutschen Bundesbank. However, because of the law it was not possible to obtain figures on losses the Kreditanstalt experienced for example due to bankruptcy of clients or due to fraud. Such figures could have provided additional information on the efficiency of the KfW's work.

The Bundesarchiv Koblenz holds the files of the German Bizonal administration, which are of major importance to establish the different stages in the legal process in the setting up of the Kreditanstalt. After September 1949, the files of the Economics Ministry, Finance Ministry, of the Chancellery and of the Ministry for the Marshall Plan provide a great deal of information on the political impact of the work of the Kreditanstalt. The files of the Ministry for Housing have recently been examined in detail by Schulz and Wagner and both produced excellent studies on housing policy. Files of the Office of the Military Government, US, (OMGUS) which are largely available at Koblenz gave an insight in American ideas and planning and showed occasionally the influence and impact of British thinking. Those documents were supplemented by records held at the US National Archives in Washington, DC. The Politisches Archiv des Auswärtigen Amtes keeps plenty of material on the Kreditanstalt für Wiederaufbau for the second half of the 1950s, both in regard to export finance, especially on the Indian case, and on the establishment of the Anstalt as Development Aid Bank.

Unfortunately, the private papers and archive of Hermann Josef Abs were after his death in February 1994 incorporated into the Deutsche Bank Archiv and will officially remain closed until 2014. However, Lothar Gall was allowed to carry out research for a biography on Abs which is due to be published in 2004. It will certainly shed some light on this most important man and his actions and motives, but unfortunately its publication will be too late to be considered for this book.

In addition to the German archives, interesting material could be found in the Public Record Office at Kew. Foreign Office files proved to be a valuable source on British occupational policy as well as on British attitudes towards the Federal Republic during the Korean War and on British reactions regarding Germany's re-emergence on the export market.

The archival research could be supplemented with a wide range of printed and edited sources which gave an insight into the various aspects of Allied and German intentions and politics in the late 1940s and the 1950s. One of the sources, however, the *Jahresberichte der Kreditanstalt für Wiederaufbau* sometimes proved to be a delicate source. Though the *Jahresberichte* in general provided a good account of the economic (and occasionally even of political) developments and supplied usually good tables, the latter proved sometimes to be inconsistent from year to year. Since it was not always possible in such cases to draw on other sources, some of the tables and figures in this book have therefore to be regarded, and are marked, as estimates.

Surprisingly, only two major pieces of work dealing with the Kreditanstalt itself appeared before 1998, when the bank's official history was published. The first by Erich Schmidt, published in 1966, is a doctoral thesis in law and is concerned with the legal position of a *öffentlich-rechtliche Anstalt*. The second by Manfred Pohl is the only historical account of the Kreditanstalt's work to date. It covers only the years until 1952-53 and as such only deals with the first years of the KfW's existence. Nevertheless, it provides a good summary of early operations, a basic insight into the bank and, most important, a good appendix containing the various laws on the Kreditanstalt and its statutes. However, the book disregards most of the political influences on the work of the Kreditanstalt and – though well-informed – the author turns the story on the KfW into one of praise for its most important figure, Hermann Josef Abs.

Although economics obviously plays an important role in this book, it is not intended as research into the economic situation of West Germany. Instead, the aim is to show how economic power was used to influence political decisions (as can be best seen in the cases of the European Recovery Programme and aid to India), and how political decisions (for example Erhard favouring the consumer goods industries) influenced the economy. Although there is a wider choice of economic sectors it is believed that those investigated in parts three and four demonstrate most clearly the events in those sectors. They show best the political reasons for the KfW's participation in the reconstruction process, in export expansion and the political subsidies for West Berlin. It will be shown that the Kreditanstalt für Wiederaufbau in all the cases acted as a link between economy and politics and that it was (and still is) an effective tool in the hands of the government to intervene quietly into the economy; so quietly in fact that the 'sacred' reputation of Erhard's social market economy remained untouched.

Part I
Setting the Scene

Chapter 1

The Cold War Developments and the Political and Economic Situation in Germany 1947-1948

While it is impossible to put a firm date on the 'outbreak' of the Cold War, it is clear that the 12 months from July 1946 to June 1947, which saw a change in tone of politics in Washington, were decisive in the development of the East-West tensions and had considerable impact on developments in (West) Germany. Following George F. Kennan's Long Telegram, the USA began to adopt the Policy of Containment while the Soviet Union became increasingly frustrated by the failure to treat occupied Germany as an economic unit (mainly by the French), which was in clear breach of the Potsdam Protocol[1]. Perhaps in an effort to get things moving again they announced during the Paris Conference of Foreign Ministers in July 1946 that they were considering the possibility of re-uniting Germany. This speech by Soviet Foreign Minister Molotov increased American fears that the Soviets wanted to take over the whole of the country. The Americans knew that they could not offer anything similar to the Germans without Soviet consent while, on the other hand, they could hardly block a serious Soviet attempt in this direction. In other words, in 1946 Stalin held the key to German unification and he knew this. Although there was still no clear US policy on Germany at that time, a united Germany under Soviet control certainly threatened American interests in Europe. The famous speech given by US Secretary of State Byrnes in September 1946 in Stuttgart in which he promised Germany's reconstruction was therefore much more a direct response to Molotov and directed against Russia than John Gimbel suggests[2]. Byrnes' speech was the first clear sign of a change in US policy and demonstrated American willingness to integrate at least parts of Germany into the Western sphere of influence in Europe.

Whereas in 1947 the reconstruction in many western European countries was well under way and production figures were again reaching pre-war levels, the situation in Germany was entirely different[3]. This was not least because of the

---

[1] Wilfried Loth, *The Division of the World 1941-1955*, London 1988, pp. 106 ff.

[2] John Gimbel, 'Byrnes' Stuttgarter Rede und die amerikanische Nachkriegspolitik in Deutschland' in: *Vierteljahrshefte für Zeitgeschichte* (henceforth *VfZ*), vol. 20 (1972), p. 42.

[3] Alan Milward, *The Reconstruction of Western Europe 1945-1951*, London 1984, pp. 8 ff.

country's division into four zones of occupation, all separately run by their respective Military Governors. In 1945 the Americans had hoped for a quick revival of German industrial production to pay with export proceeds for much needed food imports, but recovery remained at a very slow pace – particularly in comparison with the other European countries. The zonal division had created four separate economic areas, with the zonal borders as effective trade barriers. The British zone was most severely hit by this artificial division. The densely populated industrial areas of the Ruhr could only be kept viable with food supplies from Britain after its former agricultural hinterland in the east of Germany had been cut off. Under the Geneva Convention occupying powers had to take care of the civilian population under its control but with the United Kingdom itself struggling to support its population and the Treasury unable to provide the necessary funds to pay for the food supply of its former enemy as well, the British were desperate for a solution to this impasse. So the United Kingdom welcomed a proposal for merging their zone of occupation with the American zone, which would give them the chance to share the burden. In December 1946 the Bevin-Byrnes Agreement was signed and on 1 January 1947 the two zones became the Combined Economic Area, commonly known as the Bizone. Although the other two occupying powers were invited to join the Anglo-American Bizone as well, its creation increased the Cold War sentiments. From the Soviet point of view the establishment of the Combined Economic Area appeared to confirm that the USA was attempting to dominate Western Europe and exclude the USSR from any economic benefits. Thus, the emerging Bizone had a significant impact on the course of the Cold War.

Of course, the Americans were hardly motivated by altruistic reasons for their decision to create the Bizone, which led to an increase in their occupation costs. They feared that the German population, facing a desperate economic situation, might begin to sympathise with the Soviet Union, in particular after Molotov's Paris speech.

By early 1947 the small economic improvements, which had been achieved had come to an abrupt end because of the severe weather conditions of the 1946-47 winter which caused serious setbacks in production. This so-called 'stagnation crisis' which occurred as a result of too low an output of the basic industries, caused by a lack of transport, made the Allies aware that disruption originating from war damage was still severe in Germany[4]. It was not so much the destruction of roads, railways, bridges and waterways, which caused havoc, for most of these had already been repaired in 1945-46[5]. It was the lack of rolling stock and barges in operation, which caused a breakdown in the transportation system. It was not before the summer of 1947 and after the Allies had put considerable effort into

---

[4]Werner Abelshauser, *Wirtschaftsgeschichte der Bundesrepublik Deutschland 1945-1980,* Frankfurt/M 1983, pp. 34, 36, 40.

[5]See for example Lucius D. Clay, *Decision in Germany,* Westport, Conn. 1950, 2nd edn. New York 1970, pp. 188 f.

transport and the basic industries, particularly into coal, that the German economy could recover and regain its 1946 production figures[6].

By that time the Americans had realised that in Germany they could achieve the political and economic successes necessary for their Cold War purposes only with the co-operation of the Germans themselves[7]. To secure German participation in the decision-making and administrative process, a semi-autonomous German administration, the Economic Council or *Wirtschaftsrat*, was established in Frankfurt in 1947-48[8]. Although responsible for only two of the four zones, it was for the first time after the war that a preliminary German central governmental body was created. To keep French and Soviet criticism at a minimum and to stress its provisional, non-governmental character, the name 'Economic Council' was chosen. Nevertheless, the Economic Council would eventually become the core of the future West German government and with its legislation paved the way for the establishment of the Federal Republic in 1949.

In the accelerating Cold War the Western Allies realised that if they wanted to successfully integrate at least parts of Germany into their sphere of influence, they had to do more than to establish a German administrative body under their control. The revival of economic life became the paramount task but also a task which would encounter massive difficulties. The population of the territory of the future Federal Republic had increased by nearly 20 per cent compared to 1939, due to the influx of refugees and people expelled from the former German territory in the East. There was a low rate of productivity combined with a high rate of unemployment and hidden unemployment, even without these refugees[9]. Furthermore, the refugees were concentrated along the eastern border of the Anglo-American zone. These mainly agricultural areas in Schleswig-Holstein, Lower Saxony and eastern Bavaria could offer hardly any employment. Because of the destruction of housing in the industrial centres, there was no immediate prospect of resettling these people to places with better employment opportunities. By 1947 the destruction and lack of housing was one of the biggest social problems in Germany and it seemed likely to remain a long-term problem. Experts estimated that it would take 25 to 30 years at pre-war construction rates to eradicate the housing shortage in West Germany.

---

[6]Abelshauser, *Wirtschaftsgeschichte*, pp. 42f., 34.

[7]John Gimbel, 'Amerikanische Besatzungspolitik und deutsche Tradition', in: Ludolf Herbst (eds) ***Westdeutschland 1945-1955. Unterwerfung, Kontrolle, Integration,*** München 1986, p. 147.

[8]See Tilmann Pünder, *Das Bizonale Interregnum,* Waiblingen 1966, which is still the best work on the establishment and the work of the Economic Council.

[9]Since money had lost its value, many employees were officially kept in employment and receiving payment in more or less worthless Reichsmarks thus covering up the real extent of unemployment. Following the currency reform and the re-establishing of money value, many of these employees lost their jobs.

Whilst having no immediate effect on the bleak situation, the establishment of the Bizone on 1 January 1947 signalled the beginning of an economic and political reconstruction, which, fuelled by the intensifying Cold War, developed during 1947 with increasing pace. For the economy, 1947 marked the beginning of West German's real recovery while significant political developments and decisions helped to support the process.

On 10 March the Moscow Conference of Foreign Ministers (CFM) began. It was the last attempt by all the former war Allies to look seriously for a mutual political settlement in Europe but its success was more than doubtful right from the beginning. On 12 March the US President in a speech before Congress announced a new policy, which was to become known as the Truman Doctrine. In April the Moscow CFM finally ended in failure because of the American refusal to supply reparations from Germany to the Soviet Union. On his way back to Washington, US Secretary of State Marshall had a confidential meeting in Berlin with General Clay, the US Military Governor in Germany, which was to have a significant impact on further developments in Germany[10]. Following Marshall's speech at Harvard on 5 June in which he announced the European Recovery Program (ERP), better known as the Marshall Plan, the US Military Government in Germany on 11 July received new directions on how to run affairs in Germany. JCS 1067, the Joint Chiefs of Staff directive in place since April 1945, had prevented the pragmatic Clay from taking active steps towards German economic recovery[11]. Now, the new directive JCS 1779 allowed and even encouraged those steps. The new directive was of considerable political importance. In terms of US domestic policy it was a victory for the State Department and the US Military Government (OMGUS) over the remaining 'Morgenthau Boys', hard-line members in the US administration close to Treasury Secretary Morgenthau who wanted a punitive settlement in Germany, and a signal that the top-level executives in Washington had accepted the course which OMGUS proposed. In terms of US foreign policy it was the last sign that Cold War considerations were now completely determining American thinking.

About six weeks later, by the end of August, the three western Military Governors agreed on an increased level for strictly controlled German industrial output, although the dismantling of industrial plants in the French and British zones continued[12]. This kind of contradiction, reconstruction running parallel to dismantling, would go on until 1951 when the British at last gave it up. But the decisions taken during the summer of 1947 made sure that the German economy could finally take the road to recovery – and as Abelshauser has convincingly shown did so long before the Marshall Plan – although at first at a slow pace[13].

---

[10]Clay, *Decision,* p. 174.

[11]Beate Ruhm von Oppen (ed) *Documents on Germany under Occupation 1945-1954,* London, New York, Toronto 1955, pp. 13 ff.

[12]Ruhm von Oppen, *Documents,* pp. 238 ff.

[13]Werner Abelshauser, *Wirtschaft in Westdeutschland 1945-1948,* Stuttgart 1975.

The conditions for an economic recovery were indeed not as bad as one might have expected in the aftermath of the bombing war. While residential areas had been hard hit by Allied carpet-bombing, the impact on industry as a whole was less severe and even less on industrial machinery[14]. The Nazi re-armament programme had had a huge impact on Germany's industrial structure. The Gross Fixed Assets (GFA) value of machinery in the Bizone area had risen by about 75 per cent in real terms of 1936 money between 1936 and 1945[15]. In this process the age structure of the machinery and the equipment, obviously improved as well, so that by 1945 more than half the machinery was less than ten years old. Neither the results of the Allied bombing, nor the dismantling or the lack of investments could reverse wartime expansion so that by 1948 the GFA was still 11 per cent higher than in 1936[16]. This extended and improved machinery would provide the material basis for the reconstruction, while the unemployed, and amongst them in particular the expellees and refugees, provided a large reserve of skilled and semi-skilled labour, keen to work even for relatively low wages. Although they had to be regarded as a liability to the national economy in the short term and would have to be resettled into the industrial areas at high costs before they could enter the labour market, the refugees were one reason for the rapid economic reconstruction in 1950s Germany.

However, various developments adversely affected the reconstruction process. In the British zone in particular the question of whether or not some industries should be transferred into public ownership was still looming. The Americans were strictly against such schemes for reasons of principle. With rising anti-Communist and anti-Socialist sentiments in the USA the American administration already found it hard to swallow the nationalisation of industries in Britain. They had certainly no intention of losing a second big European economy to what they regarded as socialist experiments. This was clearly demonstrated in 1946, when General Clay suspended the socialisation of big industries in Hesse, although the population had voted in favour of the nationalisation by a majority of over two-thirds[17]. The American position in Germany *vis-à-vis* the British improved markedly in their favour after the revised Bizonal Agreement of

---

[14]United States Strategic Bombing Survey (Report # 3) *The Effects of Strategic Bombing on the German War Economy,* Washington, DC 1945, reprinted New York 1976, pp. 44 f. The report stresses that there may have been damage to the factories but only slight damage to the machine tools. Even in the particularly hard hit ball bearing industries only 15 per cent of the machinery was damaged or destroyed.

[15]Abelshauser, *Wirtschaftsgeschichte,* p. 20; Rolf Krengel, *Anlagevermögen, Produktion und Beschäftigung der Industrie im Gebiet der Bundesrepublik von 1924 bis 1956,* Berlin 1958, pp. 12 ff, tables pp. 94 ff.

[16]Krengel, *Anlagevermögen,* pp. 12 ff., 49 ff., esp. pp. 52 f.

[17]Rolf Steininger, *Deutsche Geschichte 1945-1961,* Frankfurt/M 1989 (2nd edn.), vol. 2, p. 323.

December 1947. Because of British economic and financial weakness the Americans agreed to pay for most of the occupation costs in the Bizone, which had previously been split equally between the two countries. In return for this financial support the British had to surrender their equal say in the running of the Combined Economic Area. Thus the Americans managed to postpone the question of nationalisation of German industries, which was strongly favoured by the British Labour government for an indefinite period. Furthermore, they made clear that they would try to prevent any such attempts in future. Nevertheless, as long as there was the slightest chance of nationalisation, German business leaders remained very careful with regard to any investments.

Apart from the uncertainty over the economic future caused by these politically motivated quarrels, there was an important economic reason for the slow reconstruction process. The German capital market was a shambles. As a result of the Nazi war finance a huge money surplus had arisen[18]. The Allies had kept in place tough price and wage controls in order to prevent open inflation, but money had lost its value nevertheless. Low morale at the workplace, with a high level of absenteeism, and black market business determined the German economy and the 'Ami', American cigarettes, had nearly replaced the Reichsmark as a means of payment. Therefore, a currency reform to re-establish a proper currency-commodity balance was inevitable.

Although the Americans had developed a plan for a currency reform as early as 1946, it took two more years for it to be implemented. As a first step, the Bank deutscher Länder (BdL) was established on 1 March 1948 as the Bizone's new central bank. The Land central banks of the French zone joined in on 28 March[19], establishing the first Trizonal institution. This was followed by the currency reform itself on 20 June 1948. With the currency reform, 90 per cent of the old Reichsmark value was taken out of circulation and the rest replaced by the new Deutsche Mark (DM). But contrary to German proposals for the reform, there was no sharing of burden, or *Lastenausgleich,* in the American plan to compensate the holders of money against the holders of material assets and real estate. This of course would strongly determine the economic system towards one favoured by the Americans since it was very much to the benefit of those social groups, which held non-money assets and supported a market economy.

However, both the establishment of the BdL and the currency reform have to be seen not only in the context of German reconstruction despite, or even because of, the importance American planners attached to Germany in the context of East-West tensions. Both measures were vital pieces for the success of the European Recovery Program and the political aims behind it.

---

[18]Between 1932 and 1945 the amount of money in circulation increased nearly fifteen-fold, bank and saving accounts rose by a factor of eight and the Reich's debt increased more than thirty-fold, see Abelshauser, *Wirtschaftsgeschichte,* p. 46.

[19]Monika Dickhaus, *Die Bundesbank im westeuropäischen Wiederaufbau,* München 1996, p. 49.

The BdL was set up nine months after Marshall's Harvard speech as a necessary precondition for the currency reform. The essential requirement to make the ERP work in West Germany was a functioning monetary system based on a sound central bank and only if West Germany could participate successfully in the Marshall Plan was its success possible on the European level[20]. American experts had realised that without economic recovery in the three western zones, the whole Marshall Plan was doomed to fail in the rest of Europe as well, thus endangering US containment policy and Cold War strategy. Thus, once the decision for the Marshall Plan had been taken, the establishment of the BdL and the subsequent currency reform were the next logical steps.

The currency reform had an immediate psychological and a long-term economic impact in West Germany, the latter mainly due to the economic policy of Ludwig Erhard, the Director for Economics in the *Verwaltungsrat des Vereinigten Wirtschaftsgebietes,* the Executive Council of the German administration. The short-term effect was full shop windows the day after the currency reform. Psychologically, this was of paramount importance for the success of the reform and it established the myth of the currency reform as the basis of the *Wirtschaftswunder*, the economic miracle. However, the rise of production figures in the third quarter of 1948 by a staggering 30 per cent compared to those of the second quarter was mainly due to the previously deliberate underestimation of production statistics. Therefore, it is difficult to estimate the real impact of the currency reform on the economic growth in 1948-49[21]. The post reform boom caused an inflationary tendency. Money in circulation reached the figure of 14.3 billion marks by the end of 1948, thus more than doubling the amount of less then 6 billion marks at the currency reform while bank loans soared from nil to 5.2 billion marks[22]. The inflation was a profit inflation, for Erhard, in order to stabilise the exchange rate of the DM, had given up price controls[23]. Only coal, steel, electricity, fuel and rents remained under price control as did wages, the latter until November 1948. Because of the increasing gap between wages and prices, two votes of no confidence were tabled against Erhard in the Economic Council. Both failed, the

[20]For the importance of the German economy for trade in Western Europe, see for example, Winfried Kretzschmar, *Auslandshilfe als Mittel der Außenwirtschafts- und Außenpolitik,* München 1964, p. 189.

[21]For the debate on the importance of the currency reform see Abelshauser, *Westdeutschland,* and Albrecht Rischel, 'Die Währungsreform von 1948 und der Wiederaufstieg der deutschen Industrie', in: *VfZ,* vol. 33 (1985), pp 136-165 and Werner Abelshauser, 'Schopenhauers Gesetz und die Währungsreform', in: *VfZ,* vol. 33 (1985), pp. 214-218.

[22]Abelshauser, *Wirtschaftsgeschichte,* p. 53.

[23]Jens Hölscher, *Entwicklungsmodell Westdeutschland. Aspekte der Akkumulation in der Geldwirtschaft,* Berlin 1994, p. 27.

second only by a small margin, otherwise West Germany's economic development might have turned out quite differently.

But Erhard's policy had not only these negative social effects it also altered the longer-term economic structure of the reconstruction. In the aftermath of the 1946-47 stagnation crisis the Allies had tried to put all available resources into basic industries, in particular coal mining. This was to change after the introduction of the DM and the reforms Erhard initiated with it. He believed in economic growth via consumer goods industries and exports and regarded the abolition of price controls in these sectors as essential for a growing market economy. At the same time he insisted on fixed (and low) prices for the products of basic industry in order to provide the consumer and export industries with cheap resources. This doctrine was to cause serious problems. With the prices for basic commodities fixed and those for consumer goods free, it became more profitable to invest in consumer goods industries, because these promised higher and faster returns of profits. Consequently, the basic industries, and again coal in particular, lost out. Because of Erhard's priorities they could get neither the desperately needed long-term loans from the capital market nor could they finance the necessary investments via profits as long as prices were controlled. Dangerous gaps in investment in the basic industries resulted from this development, with a serious long-term impact on the whole reconstruction process. For example, if the coalmines of the Ruhr could not produce enough coal because of a lack of investment, the shortage of Ruhr coal could jeopardise not only the recovery of Germany but also that of the rest of Western Europe, which depended on these supplies. If there were not enough long-term investment funds to pay for housing construction in Germany, the refugees living in cramped conditions in camps and emergency accommodation might try to affiliate themselves with the Communists to find deliverance from their plight. This kind of scenario would seriously threaten US anti-Communist policy and therefore had to be prevented.

But worse was to come. In early 1949 deflation was developing due to the lack of consumer spending and the lack of exports. With the capital market still not recovered from the currency reform and the Allies sticking to a policy of high taxes, not allowing tax exemption for the companies' self-financing, the reconstruction process slowed down because it lacked investment capital. It would become one of the main tasks of the Kreditanstalt für Wiederaufbau to provide the money to fill the gap.

Chapter 2

The Foundation of the Kreditanstalt and its First Action

The Allied Prelude

When the Kreditanstalt für Wiederaufbau was set up on 5 November 1948, the discussion about its existence, let alone its shape, had been going on for nearly 18 months. The major West European countries participating in the war had already set up their own national reconstruction banks. They had been inspired by the idea of the International Bank of Economic Development and Reconstruction – the World Bank – which had been agreed on at the Bretton Woods Conference in 1944[1]. So the KfW was neither a genuinely German idea nor was its spiritual father the banker Hermann Josef Abs, as has previously been claimed[2]. As a matter of fact the Anstalt was a result of the Anglo-American dispute over banking policy in the Bizone.

The American point of view was that the German system of central banking and even more so the German system of universal banking had supported the Nazis and enabled them to stage the war. Since they regarded German banking as an ultra-conservative, cartelistic stronghold opposed to democracy they intended to crush and decentralise both the central bank, the Reichsbank, and the big banks[3]. With different opinions in the US Treasury, the Department of War and the State Department over the policy in Germany in general, the reorganisation of the German banking system seemed to be the only point where all three were in

---

[1]Wilhelm Hankel, *Die zweite Kapitalverteilung. Ein marktwirtschaftlicher Weg langfristiger Finanzierungspolitik*, Frankfurt/Main 1961, pp 153 ff. There were banks in France, in the Netherlands, and Italy. In Britain, the Finance Corporation for Industry was set up on a private basis to help small and medium-size industry. For details on the Finance Corporation see Michael Collins, *Money and Banking in the UK*, London et al., 1988, p. 446 and Richard Coopey, Donald Clarke, *3i: Fifty Years Investing in Industry*, Oxford, New York 1995.

[2]Manfred Pohl, *Wiederaufbau. Kunst und Technik der Finanzierung 1947-1953*, Frankfurt/Main 1973, p. 21; and Abs' own claim in: Hans-Peter Schwarz (ed) *Die Wiederherstellung des deutschen Kredits. Das Londoner Schuldenabkommen*, Rhöndorfer Gespräche (vol. 4), Stuttgart 1982, p. 78.

[3]Theo Horstmann, *Die Alliierten und die deutschen Großbanken. Bankenpolitik nach dem Zweiten Weltkrieg in Westdeutschland*, Bonn 1991, passim.

agreement. Otherwise US occupation policy was inconsistent at least until late 1947. The Treasury still favoured the Morgenthau Plan and a complete decartelisation of the whole German economy, while the War Department wanted the Army to hand over responsibility to some other agency as soon as possible. The State Department, with their Cold War outlook and because they wanted to prevent the whole of Germany falling under Soviet influence had the most pragmatic view. It was their idea to re-establish and utilise the German economy as a bulwark against Communism within the democratic and peaceful framework of Western Europe.

British policy, although some points of dispute remained, had been agreed upon in principle by the ministries involved as early as 1944. It was intended to utilise German economic strength for the reconstruction of war-damaged Europe. For this the British aimed to use the German administrative machinery and in particular the central bank system. With the Reichsbank working roughly in the same way as the Bank of England, the planners in London saw no need to abolish a working system they were familiar with. By late 1945 they had established a *Reichsbank-Leitstelle* at Hamburg which took over the old Reichsbank's tasks within the British zone of occupation[4]. With the fusion of the Anglo-American zones of occupation and the establishment of the Bizone, on 1 January 1947 the British, due to their growing economic dependence on the US, had to relinquish many of their ideas about reshaping Germany. It was as part of this process of increasing American dominance that the US Military Government in Germany, in a paper dated 10 June 1947, asked their British counterpart for support of the US decartelisation policy which was soon to be discussed quadripartily[5]. The proposal, headlined 'Joint Banking Board and Central Budget' suggested that a study on these matters should be presented at the next meeting of the Bizone's Anglo-American administrative body, the Bipartite Board (BiB). During the meeting on 12 June the Finance Advisers to the Military Governors were directed to investigate the feasibility of a Joint Banking Board, an institution which was eventually to become the Bank deutscher Länder[6].

One month later, at the 13th meeting of the Bipartite Board held on 11 July, a British paper was presented. As well as the approval for the Bizonal budget the paper contained three points: the first stressed the acceptance of the Joint Banking Board. The second point demanded the creation of a Loan Corporation along the guidelines given in an appendix to the paper. The third point made the establishment of both these institutions a condition for the decentralisation of the banking system in the British zone of occupation, which should take place simultaneously with their introduction. The British justified their request on the grounds that:

---

[4]Horstmann, *Alliierten*, pp. 32 ff.; pp. 70 ff.

[5]Public Record Office, Foreign Office files 944 355, BiB/P(47)58, henceforth quoted as PRO FO and file number.

[6]PRO, FO 944 355, BiB/P(47)77.

> ...the establishment of a Loan Corporation would provide machinery for attracting long-term funds from both zones and diverting them to needy areas or objects, an essential object which the Joint Banking Board by itself would be unable to achieve. The dangers of the financial vacuum arising in any industrial area would then be minimised[7].

Indeed, the danger of a financial vacuum in the British zone, with its huge war damaged industrial centre in the Ruhr, was a serious threat to British reconstruction plans. Other than the cost of food supplies the British were faced in particular with large-scale subsidies for the coalmines. The paper was eventually submitted to the Americans but the fact that it was done only on the day the meeting took place suggests that the British were determined to push through their idea of the Loan Corporation by taking the Americans by surprise. General Clay, the US Military Governor, realised that the proposed corporation would, at least to some extent, counter US attempts to decentralise the German banking system. With some justification he accused the British of bringing forward new conditions for the decentralisation whenever it was discussed. Clay added that he would rather consider the setting up of a Loan Corporation on its own merits and not as a condition for banking decentralisation[8]. Indeed, as early as 1946 there were ideas in the American Military Government to set up a new bank, modelled on the Reconstruction Finance Corporation of the New Deal, which should provide revolving loans for Germany's reconstruction. However, this idea was not developed further[9]. The most likely reason was the influence of Morgenthau partisans.

From the American point of view, Clay's anger was justified not only by the late submission of the draft. Following the British proposals for the 'Corporation for Reconstruction Loans', as given in the appendix of the paper, its Board of Directors would be appointed by the Joint Banking Board, giving the latter additional influence over the new institutions by modelling them on the old centralised Reichsbank system. Two of the eight board members of the corporation were to be, *ex officio*, the Bizonal Directors for Finance and Economics. The remaining six members were to be representatives of the Combined Zones (three from each zone) from banking, industry, and the Land Finance Ministries. The Board of Directors of the corporation would be allowed to appoint its own chairman and to nominate subject to the approval of the Joint Banking Board a president and other management officials[10]. It was intended that the task of the

---

[7]Ibid.

[8]PRO, FO 1005 81, BiB/M(47)9.

[9]National Archives, Washington DC, Record Group 260, OMGUS Finance Adviser, box 107, folder 4, henceforth quoted as NA RG and file description.

[10]It was roughly this system, which was later used for the Zentralbankrat and the Bank deutscher Länder.

corporation was to provide long-term credits for reconstruction both to enterprises and public bodies on conditions devised under its own authority, thus providing it with very wide-ranging powers. The phrase '... in cases where general market conditions justify it [i.e. long-term credits] ...' [11] describes the role which the Kreditanstalt für Wiederaufbau eventually took on: giving money to reconstruction projects which were or seemed to be important to the reconstruction process but were unable to obtain loans on the free market.

It appears that the Americans paid little attention to the whole project during the remainder of 1947. In the following BiB paper concerned with the topic, dated 3 October 1947 they continued to work along the guidelines set out by the British[12]. In December the British sent the Americans a draft law, which had been prepared by German members of the former Reichsbank[13]. The draft also included a statute for the envisaged corporation and contained two striking features. First, there was no limit set for loans which could be given, neither an upper limit for individual loans nor one for the total sum of lending. Only the corporation's capital was set at 100 million Reichsmarks (section 8) and there was a limitation on the issuing of debentures to 20 times the capital (section 4). This limitation was a result of the advice of Otto Niemeyer, Governor of the Bank of England, given to Sir Eric Coats, the British Finance Adviser to the Military Government. In Niemeyer's opinion, which he did not elaborate any further, the corporation itself should not raise loans but only pass on money put at its disposal by the Economic Council[14]. The capital sum itself appears to be high compared with the sum of DM 1 million, which later became the nominal capital. But one has to keep in mind that the Reichsmark was a currency completely devaluated as a result of the Nazis' war finance. In fact, the currency reform which was already looming by the end of 1947 or early 1948 took some 90 per cent of the currency out of circulation so if one considers this reduction the British proposal was not too far off the mark[15].

The second feature of the bill was even more important. It proposed that the supervision of the corporation should be completely in the hands of the Germans, not of the Allies. It was to be administered by the Länder Union Bank (the name proposed at first for the Bank deutscher Länder), which was to appoint a Plenipotentiary (section 2). With the Corporation's chairmanship exercised by the President of the Länder Union Bank (section 11) the influence of this institution would have risen sharply, in strong contrast to the American ideas of a decentralised banking system, especially as the British would also allow the corporation to establish branch offices (section 1).

[11]PRO, FO 944 355, BiB/P(47)77, Annex A. The annex is also in the Bundesarchiv Koblenz, BA Z 45F/2/95-4, 3. fiche, henceforth BA and file description.
[12]PRO FO 944 355, BiB/P(47)77/1, paper submitted by US-member. BiB/P(47)77/2 only repeats that 'A Loan Corporation shall be established'.
[13]BA Z 45 F/2/154/4, 2. fiche, the draft law in Z 45 F ABC-12/3.
[14]PRO, FO 944 355, letter from Sir Coats, 14 August 1947 to Hampshire, FO, German Section.
[15]Abelshauser, *Wirtschaftsgeschichte*, p. 50.

The British accepted the far-reaching German proposals because these were very much in line with their own ideas. But the American reaction to the draft law presented by the British was a sharp one. In a memorandum to Richard Aikin, chief of the Finance Institution Branch of the US Military Government (OMGUS) dated 19 February 1948 the dangers of establishing '... a new superbank in a vertical (branch banking) and in horizontal (universal banking) sense ...' were raised. Even more, the whole US-banking policy in Germany was at risk if the bill was to be passed or if the former Reichsbank personnel who worked for the British were allowed to continue their work. The memorandum pointed out that the British were going to create a new bank (preamble and section 1 of the draft) in order to bypass banking decentralisation, which was in contrast to an agreed Bipartite Board paper. It criticised the capital of 100 million Reichsmarks, which would make the corporation 'a subsidiary of the Bank deutscher Länder'. It was feared that the amount of 2 billion Marks, which could be issued in bonds would prevent rather than enable the utilisation of private capital for reconstruction. The capital market in the Bizone, it was stated correctly, was extremely tight and certainly in no shape to take such an amount of money so that the central banking system would have to fill the gap. Above all, it was feared that once again a centralised German banking system could be run by men opposed to Allied policy and the attempts to democratise Germany. The memorandum saw the proposed corporation as the cornerstone of this new centralised system and thus the Americans feared that the story of the Weimar Republic would be repeated[16].

By early 1948 these voices were silenced. US Military Government intensified their efforts to find a solution to the problem of long-term credits for reconstruction. In their attempt they, too began to seek the advice of German experts. In a letter to OMGUS, Finance Division, dated 20 March 1948, Otto Veit, President of the Land Central Bank of Hesse and member of the BdL's Central Bank Council, proposed the division of long-term financing for industry, agriculture and housing construction alongside traditional German lines with the establishment of special banks for each of these sectors and tax relief for that purpose[17]. It is most remarkable that Veit as a key figure in German banking did not mention the creation of a Kreditanstalt für Wiederaufbau[18]. This and some other German attempts made later (and which are described below) suggest that the Germans were trying to find additional ways to re-establish their old banking system and finance the reconstruction process in the face of Allied opposition.

By April 1948 a new draft spoke only of a 'nominal capital', which indicates that BiCO was already planning for the currency reform[19]. At this time the Americans had also enhanced their influence in the combined administration of

[16]BA Z 45 F/ABC 12/3 Memorandum to Mr Aikin, 19 February 1948.

[17]Ibid., letter by Otto Veit to OMGUS, Finance Division, 20 March 1948.

[18]See, for example, Pohl, *Wiederaufbau*, p. 21 where he states without source that H.J. Abs had proposed this to the Americans already in September 1947.

[19]BA Z 45 F/2/154/4, 2. fiche, letter by K. Anderson to Jack Bennet, 8 April 1948.

Germany through the revised Bizonal Agreement, which was in part the result of a change in politics in Washington[20]. Morgenthau's plan had long been scrapped and anti-Communist sentiments now determined decisions in the USA. Germany had become an important asset in American Cold War diplomacy. As a result, US occupation policy in Germany became more focused on reconstruction. Due to their economic superiority over Britain or rather due to Britain's growing dependence on the USA in particular in financing the occupation (by the end of 1947 the US paid for most British food imports into their zone) it became easier for OMGUS to push through their ideas. This can be seen in the 'Principles for the Reconstruction Loan Corporation', the name under which the Kreditanstalt would be called by the Allies. These principles were laid down by BiCO's Finance Advisers in a Bipartite Board paper dated 26 May 1948[21]. The proposal was to be presented at the next Bipartite Board meeting on 2 June and had strong curbs on British ideas for the KfW. The institution's capital was cut to DM 1,000,000 and no branches or agencies were to be authorised. The supervision was to lie completely with the Bipartite Control Office (BiCO), not with German authorities, allowing strong Allied – or for that matter, US – influence. As members of the Board of Directors, the paper named the Directors of the Administration of Finance and Economics together with a representative of the Bank deutscher Länder, two from industry, two of the Land Finance ministers and one each from the Commercial and the Saving banks. The paper further requested the Economic Council, in co-operation with the BdL, to prepare the Kreditanstalt's work by re-establishing two old financial institutions, the Deutsche Industriebank and the Deutsche Bau- und Bodenbank.

When the 28th Bipartite Board meeting took place on 2 June some of the old disputes re-emerged. The British Military Governor, General Robertson, was opposed to extensive supervision by the Military Government. He argued that the Anstalt should be formed under German legislation and therefore German government supervision would be appropriate and sufficient. General Clay strongly disagreed with him. With the Kreditanstalt being only a quasi-public body he hoped to prevent excessive influence from the German government. After meeting such strong resistance on the matter from Clay, Robertson withdrew his objections[22]. Apart from this dispute the Bipartite Board meeting brought another alteration to the first draft. The composition of the Board of Directors was now much more vaguely described as being made up of representatives' ... in proper proportion of government, banking, business, and Land governments'[23]. When the Americans internally considered the disputed points further in a paper by the Finance Adviser dated 14 June, the issue of Board membership and of branches were set aside only to be inserted again later. The task of the future Kreditanstalt für Wiederaufbau

[20]Werner Abelshauser, *Der Ruhrkohlenbergbau seit 1945. Wiederaufbau, Krise, Wiederanpassung*, München 1984, p. 51.

[21]PRO, FO 944 336, BiB/P(48)76.

[22]PRO, FO 944 336, BiB/M(48)10.

[23]PRO, FO 944 336 BiB/P(48)76/1.

itself was not under dispute from either side. The KfW should provide long-term loans by channelling private savings into areas of capital deficit. In this way important projects ought to be assisted, in particular when a lack of finance would otherwise restrict the reconstruction process. The Anstalt's Board of Directors, in concurrence with the BdL, was to be allowed to give short-term loans in exceptional cases and was entitled to accept securities other than mortgages if they regarded these as adequate[24]. With the Allies having reached agreement on the principles of the Kreditanstalt, the task to work out the legal details was handed over to the Germans.

The Bizonal Legislation

The setting up of the Kreditanstalt für Wiederaufbau gave the Germans the chance to regain some legislative power from the Military Government. Under US Proclamation No. 5 and British Ordinance No. 88 respectively, both dated 10 June 1947, the powers and the tasks of the Economic Council were laid down. The Allies allowed the *Wirtschaftsrat* to enact bills regarding public finance, currency and financial matters as well as bank and property controls. But in the British Ordinance No. 126 and US Proclamation No. 7, taking effect on 2 February 1948, the Allies withdrew the Economic Council's authority for finance, credit, and banking bills[25]. At a meeting of the Economic Council's Finance Committee with Generals Clay and Robertson held on 14 April 1948 the German representatives pointed out the impact of these restrictions and tried to convince the Military Governors to reverse them again[26]. But there was no intention on the Allied side to allow the Germans to regain general control on these matters. Economic affairs were seen as too important by the Americans to leave it to the Germans. Consequently, when the Economic Council's Finance Committee on 24 June requested the Administration of Finance to draft bills regarding the establishment of the Deutsche Industriebank, the Rentenbank Kreditanstalt and an institute for the building industry, this was vetoed by BiCO on the grounds that the Economic Council had no authority to do so under Proclamation No. 7 – Ordinance No. 126 thus stressing to the German administration that the Allies retained control of economic and financial matters. Nevertheless, the Military Government agreed that it would give some consideration to the German plans[27].

---

[24]BA Z 45 F/ABC 12/3; *Wörtliche Berichte und Drucksachen des Wirtschaftsrates des Vereinigten Wirtschaftsgebietes 1947-1949*, eds. Institut für Zeitgeschichte and Deutscher Bundestag, Wissenschaftliche Dienste, edited by ChristophWeisz and Hans Woller, 6 vols., München, Wien 1977, vol. 4, Drucksache (DrS.) 386, (henceforth *Wörtliche Berichte* and volume number).

[25]Reprinted in: Pünder, *Interregnum*, pp. 370 ff, pp. 377 ff.

[26]BA Z 13/667, Tagesordnungen und Protokolle des Ausschusses für Finanzen April 1948-January 1949, undated copy of the minutes.

[27]BA Z 13/667, minutes of the Finance Committees meeting on 24 June; minutes of the

In June and even in July 1948, the Allied authorisation, which had been given for the establishment of the KfW by BiCO on 24 June, was still exceptional but the Germans took the chance and acted quickly. On 8 July the Administration of Finance had sent a draft bill to the Finance Committee of the second chamber, *Länderrat*, which represented the interests of the German states. The draft was discussed by the Bizonal Executive Committee, the regular meeting of the Directors of the various Administrations, on 13 July. Informing the *Länderrat* about a piece of legislation in preparation before the Executive Committee itself discussed it was a normal part of the Bizonal legislative process[28]. At its 19th meeting the Executive Committee discussed the utilisation of GARIOA[29] funds for the new institution and then passed the bill on to the various administrations for further considerations and co-ordination. At its 23rd meeting on 3 August the Executive Committee decided to send the draft for consideration to the *Länderrat* and the Economic Council at the same time, a procedure used only for urgent matters[30]. Attached to the draft was a note which mentioned the possibility of altering the method of raising capital at a later stage so that private companies could participate in the Kreditanstalt[31]. This idea was eventually dropped completely to prevent a delay in the KfW's work because complications were expected in a process in which capital was raised at the same time by public and private bodies. But it also meant that the influence of private business on the Kreditanstalt was limited to influence via the Board of Directors, indicating that the KfW was still considered to become a semi-governmental tool.

The first reading of the bill in the Economic Council took place on 17 August 1948. It was introduced by the Director of the Administration for Finance, Alfred Hartmann. His brief explanation of the draft was followed by a short debate on the issue. The CDU, the SPD, and the FDP all welcomed the establishment of a reconstruction bank. For them it meant the beginning of Germany's restoration, with the help of the Americans, and a move to reduce the threat of Soviet influence. Only the Communists opposed it as they saw it as a way of '... Wall Street

---

meeting on 12 August 1948, BiCO letter 9 August 1948.

[28] *Akten zur Vorgeschichte der Bundesrepublik Deutschland 1945-1949*, eds. Bundesarchiv and Institut für Zeitgeschichte, edited by Christoph Weisz et al., 5 vols., München, Wien 1983, vol. 4, p. 675, footnote 17 (henceforth *AVBRD* and volume number); BA Z 13/1173, note by Herbert Martini regarding the Directors' meeting on 13 July 1948; Pünder, *Interregnum*, p. 193.

[29] Government Appropriations for Relieve in Occupied Areas. This was a special fund of the US Department of the Army, set up under the Geneva Convention to prevent starvation, disease and unrest in occupied territories. The money was administered by the US Military Governor and played an important role for German reconstruction before Marshall-Plan money was available.

[30] *AVBRD*, vol. 4, p. 675. The draft is reprinted in: *Wörtliche Berichte*, vol. 4, DrS. 434. Normally, the *Länderrat* received draft bills before the Economic Council did. See Pünder, *Interregnum*, p.193.

[31] BA Z 13/647, *AVBRD*, vol. 4, p. 709.

establishing control over the German economy'[32]. After the debate the bill was passed on to the Standing Committees for Finance and Economics for further consideration.

The German draft bill was in most points close or even identical to the Allied principles submitted to the Chairman of the Executive Committee. But in addition to minor alterations and adoptions to the German way of banking and administration there were two major alterations introduced. First, the Germans wanted to keep the new institution's supervision to themselves, the second regarded the Kreditanstalt's own borrowing. The German draft explicitly allowed the utilisation of counterpart funds. This was a crucial alteration, which would determine the KfW's future business. The only feasible explanation why BiCO had not introduced this clause before is that they expected to raise enough money from German sources, a hope which turned out to be unworkable for some years to come. The ensuing discussion in the Standing Committee for Finance and Tax introduced some important changes. First of all, the description of the Kreditanstalt's tasks was changed and enhanced so that more ways of action in potential economic key sectors became possible. Now loans could be given not only to banks but also to '... all sectors of the economy ...'[33]. This clause would allow the granting of funds as direct loans and for special projects. The liabilities were named more precisely and the membership on the Board of Directors was increased. Representatives of the Co-operative Banks (*Genossenschaftsbanken*) got a seat as well as institutions dealing with industrial credit, the latter being a clear victory for the industrial lobby. The Trades (*Handwerk*) also received a seat, for although mainly small- and medium-sized in Germany, they traditionally had a strong influence on German politics and economy. In face of the huge destruction of dwellings and the urgent need to house an increased population, it is not surprising that a representative of the construction industry also got a seat on the board[34]. Finally, a concession was made to the Social Democrats who held the majority in the *Länderrat*. Three members of the trade unions now received seats on the Board in order to get the SPD's agreement to the bill. Already during the first reading in the Economic Council they regarded a single trade union member on the Board as merely a token gesture and announced that they were going to fight for more influence[35]. But the fact that a trade union representative was considered at all for board membership of a reconstruction bank signifies the importance and influence of the trade unions in the first place. They were seen as one of the few

[32] *Wörtliche Berichte*, vol. 2, pp 772 ff.
[33] *Wörtliche Berichte*, vol. 4, DrS. 502.
[34] The draft at the first reading of the bill spoke of only three members whose background had to be agriculture, industry, banking or from the construction industry. The German word 'Bauwirtschaft' (construction industry) was replaced by 'Wohnungsbau' (housing construction) and this word eventually by 'Wohnungswirtschaft' (roughly translated as housing industry) which has a much broader meaning. This would later cause some trouble with the different interest groups involved.
[35] *Wörtliche Berichte*, vol. 2, p. 775.

groups, which had not been discredited during the Nazi period and were regarded as an important political force, even by the Americans. Especially the trade union's leadership was seen as fairly moderate and could thus help to limit the influence of any more radical left-wing movement in West Germany.

The second and third readings of the proposed bill in the Economic Council took place on 31 August[36]. The Communists now used different tactics to oppose the bill. They argued that the proposed capital of DM 1 million was too low and not even the DM 1 billion scheduled for lending would have any significant impact on the Bizonal economy. By playing the 'All-German' card they refused to accept the idea of a bank solely for the Bizonal area and demanded a state bank for the reconstruction of all four zones of occupation[37]. As before, the speakers of the other main parties all welcomed the establishment of the Kreditanstalt. So in the final vote the bill passed with only 12 deputies abstaining and three voting against it[38].

On 10 September the *Länderrat* gave its statement and demanded some amendments to the bill[39]. The *Länderrat* sought a direct say in the selection of the chairman and deputy chairman of the Anstalt's Board of Directors as well as the final say in the appointment of the Board members chosen by the Executive Committee. Furthermore, the *Länderrat* argued to increase the number of its representatives on the Board to four to balance the membership of the Director for Labour, which the *Länderrat* wished to see on the board as well. Finally, the *Länderrat* demanded a say in the drawing up of the KfW's statutes. In justification of its demands, the second chamber spoke with very strong reservations about the idea of the Kreditanstalt für Wiederaufbau. This may be surprising, for in the long run during the reconstruction period, the *Länder* would gain most from the KfW's establishment. The *Länder*-chamber tried to justify the demand for additional influence by stressing the need to co-ordinate the reconstruction process.

The *Länderrat's* claims must be seen as a twofold tactical reaction. First of all, it showed the struggle of the *Länder* to keep to and defend federal principles and to maintain or even enhance their influence against the 'central' administration of the Economic Council. But it was also an inter-party and maybe even an intra-party conflict. While the SPD was in opposition in the Economic Council the party held power in six of the eight *Länder* and could thus determine the second chamber's policies. Although three of these six *Länder* governments were coalition governments including the CDU many Christian Democrats in these *Länder*

---

[36]Ibid., pp. 851 ff. All amendments and alterations of the bill so far are reprinted in: *Wörtliche Berichte*, vol. 4, DrS. 502 and DrS. 519.

[37]*Wörtliche Berichte*, vol. 2, pp. 854 f.

[38]Ibid., p. 858. The 'nos' certainly came from the Communists but it is not mentioned in the minutes who abstained. There were only three 'no' votes since two of the six Communist deputies were ill and one excused for the meeting, see Deutscher Bundestag, Parlamentsarchiv 2/178, 20. Vollversammlung des Wirtschaftsrates, Anwesenheitsliste, (henceforth BTPA and file description).

[39]*Wörtliche Berichte*, vol. 4, DrS. 536.

belonged to the party's left-wing, most notably Karl Arnold in North Rhine-Westphalia[40]. The *Länderrat's* offer to balance the fourth member it demanded on the KfW's Board with the Director of the Administration for Labour was also motivated by an ulterior political goal. Anton Storch, who held the office was a member of the CDU's trade union wing. Because of his position – even more so because of his trade union background – he would have been in favour of a work creation programme financed by the KfW. Such a programme would help to ease the financial burden the unemployed posed on the *Länder*. Ludwig Erhard, whose first priority was the expansion of productivity had so far blocked all attempts the *Länderrat* had made for the implementation of such a scheme[41]. The effort to get Storch on to the Board can therefore be seen as a manoeuvre to bypass Erhard's influence and actively fight the unemployment problem.

The *Länderrat's* statement and petition was dealt with by the Economic Council during its 23rd general assembly on 9 October[42]. Although the CDU's left-wing supported the membership of the Director for Labour on the Kreditanstalt's Board the whole petition was rejected[43]. With the rejection of the *Länderrat's* demanded changes the bill had passed all legislative hurdles on the German side and was transferred to BiCO for approval. This was granted by BiCO in letters to the President of the Economic Council, to the Chairman of the *Länderrat* and to the Chairman of the Executive Committee all dated 1 November. In the letter, BiCO's Joint Secretary stressed the necessity that all the Board members should be responsible for the whole of the Bizone and its entire population, not only to the group whose interests they were chosen to represent[44]. It would take less than two month before BiCO's pessimistic premonition became reality and the first clash of group interests took place.

Somewhat surprisingly the law received Allied approval despite the fact that it handed supervision of the new institution to the Germans. It is even more surprising since, in face of previous American insistence on Allied control over the Kreditanstalt, BiCO's Finance Group had in minute detail compared the Allied principles against the German draft as early as September 1948[45]. The memo, signed by a British member, Miss Milne, contains a table of the differences. But while minor distinctions like the capital supply or the share taken out of the profits to establish a reserve fund were properly listed, the deviation on supervision is not mentioned at all. It seems strange that the Americans, who were opposed to such a solution in the first place, did not raise the issue again either, before they accepted

[40]For the exact events and reasons for the SPD decisions see Pünder, *Interregnum*, p. 112; the three *Länder* were Hesse, North-Rhine-Westphalia, and Lower Saxony, see: Gerhard A. Ritter, Merith Niehuss, *Wahlen in Deutschland 1946-1991*, München 1991, p. 147.
[41]*Wörtliche Berichte*, vol. 4, DrS. 536.
[42]*Wörtliche Berichte*, vol. 3, pp. 1068 ff.
[43]The Finance Committee had a petition brought in to refuse the *Länderrat's* motion, see *Wörtliche Berichte*, vol. 5, DrS. 655.
[44]BA Z 13/1174, *Wörtliche Berichte*, vol. 5, DrS. 674, *AVBRD*, vol 4, p. 919, footnote 20.
[45]PRO, FO 1005 167, BiP FIN/Memo(48)229.

the bill[46]. This negligence would cause some inconvenience and embarrassment for the Allies in the near future. But since they wanted the KfW operational as soon as possible so that it could support the Marshall Plan's political and economic reconstruction aims they had little choice but to accept the German draft. Such an explanation would be well in line with Gimbel's view that the US had to rely heavily on German co-operation[47].

After BiCOs approval the bill became law with its publication in the Bizonal law gazette on 5 November 1948[48]. On 16 November BiCO US Secretariat sent a letter to the Executive Committee indicating that the British Military Governor had given the legislative power to the Economic Council to enact an ordinance to establish a Loan Corporation. These powers were to be made retrospectively from 2 June 1948 in order to authorise German legislation which they did not have under British Ordinance No. 126 and US Proclamation No. 7 respectively[49].

Personnel Policy, Party Policy and the Struggle for Independence

If one accepts Abelshauser's interpretation that the reconstruction process in post-war Germany had already taken off in 1947 and was well on its way in 1948 instead of being a result of currency reform and the Marshall Plan as the traditional school claims – the story of the Kreditanstalt für Wiederaufbau has to be looked at in a different way. For under these circumstances the KfW was not only a means to accelerate – or even initiate – the reconstruction process but a mainly political tool to direct economic developments, similar to the former Reichskreditgesellschaft and both institutions would have much more in common then just personnel[50]. Thus the appointment of the Board of Directors (BoD), its Chairman and Deputy Chairman and the Board of Managers (BoM) became very important indeed since it would have a strong influence on the KfW's policy and operations. Some months before the law on the Kreditanstalt came into effect, there were speculations about the potential candidates. On 11 September the daily *Frankfurter Rundschau* named as candidates for the Board of Managers Franz Blücher, Eberhard Wildermuth and Otto Neubaur. For the chairmanship of the Board of Directors, Otto Schniewind was named, with Hermann Josef Abs as his deputy[51].

---

[46]BA Z 45 F/2/154/4, 1. fiche, letter to Jack Bennet, OMGUS Finance Adviser, 23 October 1948.

[47]See Gimbel, 'Besatzungspolitik'.

[48]*Gesetzblatt der Verwaltung des Vereinigten Wirtschaftsgebietes* 1948, Nr. 25, reprinted in: Pohl, *Wiederaufbau*, pp. 160 ff.

[49]BA Z 13/1174.

[50] Walter Hofmann, *Private Bank in öffentlichem Besitz. Kleine Geschichte der Reichs-Kredit-Aktiengesellschaft*, Mainz 1980, is the only book on the topic. Although mainly narrative, it still provides a good insight into the task of the RKG.

[51]BA Z 13/1173, Pressenotitz. Franz Blücher (1896-1959), before the war bank director in Essen, 1946-47 Finance Minister in North Rhine-Westphalia, 1947-49 chairman of the FDP

On 3 November the Executive Committee deliberated the appointments officially for the first time. Here too, Schniewind and Abs were named as chairman and deputy chairman. Although a discussion took place about whom the Executive Committee should appoint for the BoD, a decision was officially postponed but the meeting more or less anticipated the eventual result[52]. The nomination and later confirmation of Ferdinand Schunck as the representative of the housing industry was a clear indication of this[53]. The case of Schunck is of particular interest because it is the first one in which party politics and ideology, as well as personality, played a decisive role in the decision for the appointment of a BoD member. As a matter of fact, it is more the story of the man who succeeded Schunck than his own but it highlights all the issues about party politics and their underlying ideologies.

Schunck was nominated for the Board of Directors by the Association for Housing Affairs, Urban Development and Planning (*Verband Wohnungswesen, Städtebau und Raumordnung*) as a representative for the non-profit housing associations (*Gemeinnützige Wohnungsbaugesellschaften*) outside the trade unions. His competitors were Julius Brecht, who represented the trade unions' Co-operative Building Societies, a Herr Grockenberger who was a nominee from the construction industry, and Johannes Handschumacher, President of the Association of Private House and Property Owners (*Verband der privaten Haus- und Grundeigentümer*)[54]. Handschumacher stood for a 'market-only' solution to the existing housing problem while Brecht stood for the opposite side favouring mainly co-operative and social housing[55]. The last two candidates stood for the opposing sides of the ideological battleground over housing policy in post-war Germany. Schunck was therefore an excellent compromise candidate who was also a good mediator during difficult negotiations. A member of the CDU left-wing, he saw the need for a policy of careful deregulation in the housing sector where rents were still fixed at 1936 levels, combined with a social housing programme. Another reason for Schunck's appointment was certainly the fact that Hermann Pünder was honorary president of the association Schunck represented and that they knew each other well[56].

---

group in the Economic Council, 1949-54 FDP federal Party Chairman, federal minister 1949-57; Eberhard Wildermuth (1890-1952), 1925-28 Reich Ministry for Labour, from 1928 board member of the Bau-und Bodenbank, 1947 Economics Minister in Württemberg-Hohenzollern, federal minister 1949-52; for Neubaur see chapter 3.

[52]BA Z 13/1175, Direktorialkanzlei, Banken, KfW, November 48-April 49; *AVBRD*, vol. 4, p.919.

[53]BA Z 13/1175, Direktorialkanzlei, Banken, KfW, November 48-April 49, Vermerk betr. Bestellung der Vorstandsmitlgieder, 29 November 1948.

[54]Ibid., Vermerk betr. Bestellung der Vorstandsmitglieder, 29 November 1948.

[55]Günther Schulz, *Wiederaufbau in Deutschland. Die Wohnungsbaupolitik in den Westzonen und der Bundesrepublik von 1945 bis 1957*, Düsseldorf 1994, pp. 85 ff.

[56]BA Z 13 / 492, letter of invitation by the association.

At least two months before the final decision on the candidates was taken Handschumacher was looking for allies to get himself appointed. In a letter to the President of the Central Bank Council, Karl Bernard, on 13 September he complained bitterly about the 'excessive' influence of the co-operative building societies, which might lead to their representation on the KfW's board. He asked Bernard to support a change on this matter[57]. In early 1949, after the choice had been made already, Handschumacher intensified his campaign. In a letter to important CDU members he threatened that the party would suffer the consequences at the ballot box in the forthcoming federal election if the CDU was not prepared to meet his association's demands to appoint him to the board. The association's three million members and their family members made up about ten million voters and therefore amounted to a very considerable political force[58]. Then events took a sudden turn. On 27 December 1949 Schunck died[59]. Within a week Handschumacher had written to Chancellor Adenauer who was now in charge of appointments for board membership. He called Schunck's appointment a mistake and demanded to become his replacement[60]. The other possible candidates were again Brecht for the Co-operatives and Weisser nominated from Schunck's association. Despite the fact that this association withdrew its candidate and supported Brecht, Handschumacher was appointed. The decision infuriated the trade unions and they protested sharply to Adenauer, fearing that this decision would prevent any large-scale future public and cooperative housing projects[61].

When in December 1950 Handschumacher's position came up for re-appointment as part of the BoD's membership rotation Hermann Pünder took the opportunity and wrote to Adenauer[62]. He asked him not to re-appoint Handschumacher and justified his decision in the Executive Committee because of his rude manners and his completely uncooperative behaviour[63]. It appears that Adenauer never replied. Handschumacher's appointment and his subsequent re-appointments (he was a board member until his death in October 1957) marked the

---

[57]Deutsche Bundesbank, Historisches Archiv, B 330/3152 (henceforth qouted DBB HA and file description), letter to Bernard, 13 September 1949.

[58]BA Z 13/1175, Direktorialkanzlei, Banken, KfW November 1948-April 1949, letter by Franz Etzel to Hermann Pünder, dated 22 January 1949, in the annex Handschumacher's letter to Etzel. Schulz also mentioned letters to Pünder and Holzapfel, the CDU chief whip in the Economic Council, Schulz, *Wiederaufbau*, p. 85, footnote 245.

[59]*Jahresberichte der Kreditanstalt für Wiederaufbau*, 1949, p. 10, (henceforth *Jb* and year).

[60]BA B 136/2332, letter Handschumacher to Adenauer, 3 January 1950. Although the letter was more modest in tone compared to the one to Etzel, it is still impolite, threatening and written in the language of class war.

[61]Ibid., letter Martini to Kanzleramt, 31 January 1950; letter KfW Verwaltungsrats-vorsitzender to Bundeskanzleramt, 8 February 1950; draft letter, Bundeskanzler to KfW-Verwaltungsrat Vorsitzenden, 20 May 1950; letter DGB Vorstand to Adenauer, undated, presumably late June 1950.

[62]Every year one-third of the board members had to leave the board, with their reappointment possible. The pattern of the rotation was set in the first two years by lot.

[63]BA B136/2332, letter Pünder to Adenauer, 14 December 1950.

first success of an interest group on the BoD for these ideological reasons and because their aims were more in line with Adenauer's own ideas. Perhaps more significantly, it was the first step in the ideological battle over housing policy, which led to the success of the private housing advocates.

Just before the Executive Committee took its final decision on the nominations Adenauer unsuccessfully tried to replace the chairman designate, Schniewind, by Erich Köhler, President of the Economic Council despite Schniewind being the much more qualified candidate[64]. It is not quite clear whether Adenauer tried to push a potential rival on the way to the chancellery to one side, or if he was to hold down Schniewind, who was a close personal friend of Hermann Pünder, thus weakening the latter's influence. The first appears more likely for Köhler was a stronger contester for the Chancellery than Pünder. On 8 December 1948 at its 40th meeting, the Executive Committee finally agreed on all the members of the Board of Directors it was entitled to appoint and the members nominated by the other authorities were accepted as well. According to the law, the Executive Committee appointed next to the Chairman and Deputy Chairman, one board member each for trade, industry, agriculture and the housing industry as well as three representatives for the trade unions. The Directors of the Administrations for Finance, Economics and Agriculture became *ex officio* members. The Bank deutscher Länder appointed its own deputy and one each for the Saving Banks (*Sparkassen*), the Co-operative Banks (*Genossenschaftsbanken*), and the Mortgage Banks (*Realkreditinstitute*). The Board was completed by three members chosen by the *Länderrat*[65].

The Board of Directors of the Kreditanstalt für Wiederaufbau held its initial meeting on 21 December 1948. Two weeks before Otto Schniewind had been appointed Chairman by the Executive Council. He would hold the post until his retirement in 1958[66]. Schniewind was born in 1887 and had entered the Reich's Treasury in 1919. He moved to the Disconto-Gesellschaft bank and from there in 1925 into the Prussian Ministry of Commerce where his task was to organise trade with Scandinavia and Great Britain. After some years abroad he became Reich Commissioner at the Berlin Stock Exchange from where he transferred to the Reich Ministry of Economics, only to become a member of the Reichsbank Directorate in 1937. One year later he resigned because of his opposition to Nazi financial policy. Due to his connections to Karl Goerdeler's resistance circle he was arrested after the plot of 20 July 1944 and was taken to a Concentration Camp. In 1947, when the Marshall Plan was launched he became *Marshallplan-Berater* (adviser) for the Bizonal Administration[67].

With Hermann J. Abs as Deputy Chairman the dominant and most powerful figure in the post-war German economy was chosen for the job. With all his

---

[64]*AVBRD,* vol. 4, p. 957, footnote 30.
[65]*AVBRD,* vol. 4, p. 994.
[66]*Jb* 1958, p. 15.
[67]Pohl, *Wiederaufbau,* p. 40.

influence in politics and business he was perhaps even more important than Ludwig Erhard. Born in 1901 he had started a banking apprenticeship in 1920. He went to the Netherlands and Britain in 1923 where he received special training in foreign currency trade. Business then took him to the USA and Latin America. In 1929 he became attorney in the private banking house of Delbrück, Schlicker & Co and in 1935 he was made a partner. In January 1938 Abs was made a member of the Board of Managers of the Deutsche Bank responsible for the Foreign Department[68]. A practising Catholic he was never a Nazi party member but his activities and posts during the Nazi era multiplied. He held more than 30 board memberships during the war years, including one at IG Farben although the Nazis had introduced a law limiting the number of seats held by one person to 20. According to US investigations, he '... cooperated hand-in-glove ... with the leading political personalities in government, industry and party circles'[69]. Abs seems to have had contact with the resistance via Adam von Trott zu Solz and he once attended a meeting of the Goerdeler-circle, but was never really involved in the conspiracy. Shortly before the end of the war, Abs left Deutsche Bank's Berlin headquarters to establish new regional headquarters in Hamburg as part of Deutsche Bank's planning for the post-war era. Although all top-level bank personnel were immediately suspended and interrogated by the Western Allies, the British Military Government Banking Branch was seeking his advice from as early as 8 May 1945[70]. Even more, Abs received help and protection from old friends in the British Banking Branch against American attempts to prosecute him in the war-crimes trials[71]. Despite British protection American pressure finally won over and in January 1946 Abs was arrested and detained for three months[72].

During 1947 even the Americans had realised Abs' extraordinary understanding of the banking business and in September 1947 Richard Whitehead, Special Envoy of President Truman, discussed with Abs the use of Marshall Plan funds in Germany[73]. In spite of this meeting, American resentment remained, which is evident in the appointments of the new Bank deutscher Länder chief executives. Although Abs was elected President of the BdL-Directorate and Schniewind

[68]Ibid.

[69]DBB HA B330/1 Report of Investigation by Allied Authorities, 20 February 1947. As Lothar Gall has recently shown none of the political allegations against Abs and his activities under the Nazis other than his economic activities could be substantiated and he was exonerated on all accounts, see Lothat Gall, 'A Man for All Seasons? H. J. Abs in the Third Reich', in: *Financial History Review*, vol. 6 no. 2 (1999).

[70]Harold James, 'The Deutsche Bank and the Dictatorship 1933-1945', in: Lothar Gall et al *The Deutsche Bank, 1870-1995*, London 1995, pp. 351, 356, 370 ff.

[71]Horstmann, *Alliierten*, pp. 70 ff.

[72]Carl Ludwig Holtfrerich, 'The Deutsche Bank 1945-1957: Military Rule and Reconstruction', in: Gall et al., *The Deutsche Bank*, pp. 374 f.

[73]Ibid., p. 443. This meeting is wrongly seen by Pohl as the Kreditanstalt's hour of birth.

President of the Central Bank Council respectively, they were rejected for political reasons by the Allied Bank Commission (ABC)[74].

When Abs accepted the post at the Kreditanstalt he immediately took a central role. At the first meeting of the Board of Directors he was delegated to the Board of Managers[75]. The possibility of delegating a member of the BoD to the BoM was not included in the first draft bill by the Administration of Finance, dated 12 June 1948. It seems to have only been introduced at the Executive Committee meeting on 3 August. Pohl argues that this right for delegation was introduced specifically to make Abs accept the job at the KfW[76]. But since he and Schniewind had actually helped to draw up the bill, it is likely the clause was invented by them in the first place[77]. Following Abs' delegation the BoD the letter of the KfW law was violated for the first time. As a member of the BoM all of Abs' rights as a member of the BoD should have been suspended automatically[78]. Instead he became Chairman of four and Deputy Chairman of the other two standing committees the BoD had established (committees for industrial credit, agricultural credit, housing construction credit and a committee for credit permission)[79].

Abs' influence can also be judged by the obituary the Kreditanstalt für Wiederaufbau gave him after his death in February 1994: 'Er schuf die Grundlage für die Kreditanstalt, die ... nach seinen Vorstellungen... gegründet wurde ...'[80] which stresses not only his influence on drafting the bill, but also on his everyday work. Outside the KfW Abs held several posts and special commissions. While officially retired from the (then decentralised) Deutsche Bank he still acted as one of its official advisers until 1952 when he became Spokesman of the Süddeutsche Bank, one of Deutsche Bank's successor banks. When Deutsche Bank was reunited in 1957, he took over the same job there[81]. Abs was head of the German delegation during the negotiations at the London debt agreement, 1951-3 and for the

[74]DBB, HA, B 330/1, Protokoll der 3. Sitzung, were in a statement by Joe Fisher Freeman, US-Finance Adviser it is said that Abs is '... aus verschiedenen Gründen nicht tragbar.'; Protokoll der 4. Zentralbankrat-Sitzung on 2 April 1948. See also Holtfrerich, 'Military Rule', p. 433. Pohl's claim that the two candidates were not appointed because of the demands they put forward is not sustainable, Pohl, *Wiederaufbau,* pp. 21 f.

[75]Kreditanstalt für Wiederaufbau, Historisches Archiv, Prot 10-1, Protokoll der 1. Sitzung des Verwaltungsrates, TOP 4, (henceforth KfW HA and file description).

[76]BA Z 13/1174, Banken, KfW, Juni 48-Oktober 49; *AVBRD*, vol. 4, p. 709, footnote 3; Pohl, *Wiederaufbau*, p. 29. Pohl is again incorrect when he calls this 'lex Abs'. In reality, 'lex Abs' was a law introduced in the 1960s which limited board memberships to 15 seats.

[77]Heinrich Harries, *Wiederaufbau, Welt und Wende. Die KfW- Eine Bank mit öffentlichem Auftrag*, Frankfurt/Main 1998, p. 14.

[78]Kreditanstaltsgesetz vom 5.11. 1948, § 6 (2), quoted henceforth as 'KfW-Gesetz' and date of issue.

[79]KfW HA Prot 10-1, Protokoll der 1. Sitzung, TOP 9; Pohl, *Wiederaufbau*, pp. 44 f. The Committee for Credit Permission was set up only in early 1950.

[80]*Jb*, 1993, Obituary. 'He created the foundation for the Kreditanstalt ... which was established according to his ideas' (translation AG).

[81]Holtfrerich, 'Deutsche Bank', pp. 425, 467, 485.

negotiations on German assets frozen in the US during the Second World War[82]. He was also a member of the *Kleiner Kreis des Bundeskanzlers für Wirtschaftspolitische Fragen*, introduced by Adenauer himself in late 1949 as well as being a member of the so called *Küchenkabinett*, initiated in 1953 by Adenauer's friend, the banker Robert Pferdmenges[83].

Abs' influence during the 1950s not only in industry and commerce where he held about 30 seats on different Boards of Directors but also in politics can hardly be overestimated. Adenauer himself named him repeatedly as candidate for ministerial posts including Foreign Minister, Defence Minister and Minister for Economics and Finance[84]. However, the nominations can also be seen as political tactics by Adenauer to show his ministers that there was always a high-calibre replacement for them. Nevertheless, by the end of the 1950s he had become so powerful that draft bills were written according to his ideas and he was even able to alter the minutes of cabinet meetings[85]. Abs is perhaps best characterised as a financial genius with a photographic memory for figures whose first loyalty always remained with Deutsche Bank, which was a kind of traditional trade mark of all board members there. Politically an arch-conservative he strove to reach for the best solution for the common good or what he thought that was. Abs himself never seemed to have had ministerial ambitions; he preferred the role of the *éminence grise* to the people in the limelight since it offered a less visible and therefore a less challenged influence.

During its first meeting the BoD chose, apart from Abs, the other members of the BoM. But with the designated candidate, Otto Neubaur, ill Abs offered an interim solution. He proposed to appoint Walter Tron, a former Deputy Director of Deutsche Bank, for the period of six months[86].

It became clear at the first meeting of the BoD that BiCO had made a significant mistake when, in their comment on the KfW bill, they did not mention the shift of supervision over the KfW. The board members under the leadership of Abs and Schniewind refused American attendance at the meeting[87]. Not all of the Board members seemed to have shared this view, but with the legal argument that the KfW was not under Allied control, a vote was taken against US participation.

---

[82]For a detailed account see: Hermann J. Abs, *Entscheidungen 1949-1953. Die Entstehung des Londoner Schuldenabkommens*, München, Mainz 1991, 2nd edn.

[83]BA B 136/4800 Kleiner Kreis.des Bundeskanzlers für Wirtschaftspolitische Fragen; DBB, HA, B 330/2011 Korrespondenz Vocke. Other members of the circle were ministers Blücher, Erhard, Schäffer, BdL president Wilhelm Vocke, the chairman of the Central Bank Council, Bernard and Pferdmenges. The other members of the kitchen cabinet were Vocke, BDI president Fritz Berg, AEG chairman Friedrich Spennrath, Blessing and Pferdmenges. In particular Berg used this circle to openly agitate for the BDI's interest.

[84]*Der Spiegel*, 1954, Nr. 24, p. 5; 1955, Nr. 1, p. 6.

[85]See: *Die Zeit*, Nr. 9, 50. Jg. (1995). For the draft bills see Holtfrerich, 'Deutsche Bank', pp. 474 ff.

[86]KfW HA, Prot 10-1, Protokoll der 1. Sitzung, TOP 4.

[87]Ibid., TOP 1.

Instead the Americans were offered 'friendly co-operation and information after the meeting'[88]. The Americans had no choice but to give in. If they had insisted on their rights as supreme occupational power, they would have alienated the Board and lost its co-operation, which was politically vital in the process of reconstruction.

When the second Board meeting took place on 8 January 1949, the Americans demanded an additional scrutiny of the Board members by a political vetting party. This was refused by Abs and again the matter was settled in favour of the Germans. On 24 January Hermann Pünder wrote to Erich Köhler, President of the Economic Council, that BiCO was now prepared to accept denazification certificates only and would not insist on additional political vetting[89]. Despite this new American retreat the matter simmered until early April 1949, when at a press conference Otto Schniewind threatened the resignation of the entire BoM if the political vetting was not stopped. The men working for the KfW, he argued, had to be regarded as banking staff and not as civil servants, thus there was no need to screen their political backgrounds[90].

While the row over personnel continued, BiCO also tried to receive business reports and internal information from the Kreditanstalt. In a letter to the BoD, dated 11 February, BiCO's Joint Secretary requested a list of internal reports including the minutes of all Board and Committee meetings. BiCO justified this with its supervisory rights based on the principles of BiCO letter BiB/P(48)376 of 24 June 1948, in which the KfW's establishment was requested. Again, the Americans met with strong resistance from the Anstalt and the Executive Committee and on 25 February a letter was sent to the KfW that the information was no longer demanded in the same quantity[91]. On 26 March talks took place between BiCO's Finance Group and KfW representatives. These talks brought forward a new list of reports and information, which was accepted by the Finance Group because it was '... submitted ... by the RLC in a spirit of co-operation after informal discussions'[92]. As a matter of fact, the new list offered by the KfW was similar to the one previously demanded by BiCO. Although it called for less information it nevertheless included minutes of both Board meetings. By a simple trick, Abs and Schniewind stopped the handover of the minutes of the Board of Manager. They stated that so far – by mid April 1949 – there had been no BoM meetings and thus no minutes existed[93]. The BoD minutes on the other hand were written in such a way that outsiders could

[88]KfW HA, Prot 10-1, Protokoll der 1. Sitzung, TOP 1; Pohl, *Wiederaufbau*, p. 47.

[89]KfW HA, Prot 10-1, Protokoll der 2. Sitzung, TOP 2; KfW HA, VS 65, Handakte Schniewind, copy of the letter for Schniewind.

[90]KfW HA, VS 66, Handakte Schniewind, note from 5 April 1949 regarding a press conference on 1 April 1949.

[91]KfW HA, VS 38, BiCO/Sec(49)74.

[92]BA Z 45 F/Fin-4/8, 2nd Fiche, letter BiCO, Finance Group to BiCO, Joint Secretariat, 18 April 1949.

[93]Ibid., letter from Abs and Schniewind to BiCO, Finance Group, 12 April 1949. The letter is annexed to Finance Group's letter to BiCO, Joint Secretariat.

gain very little information. However, Pohl alleges that there was an informer within the BoD who supplied BiCO with information about the Board meetings. Since this was possibly Abs himself it has to be seen as a token gesture to please the Americans[94]. It is unlikely that he would have told them any important internal information.

Still, it appears to be more than doubtful that no meetings of the BoM had taken place. Running a bank like the Kreditanstalt needed more than a few meetings of its own supervisory body. There must have been decisions taken by the Board of Managers. Again, this incident together with the quarrels over personnel policy showed the strong position the KfW's chief executives held against the Americans. The Americans depended on a co-operative German organisation and administration if they wanted the Marshall Plan to succeed in Germany. West German reconstruction as the cornerstone of European reconstruction had become vital to the American effort to fight the Cold War in Europe. People like Abs with their enormous international experience and connections must have seen this very clearly. It is therefore hardly surprising that the first action taken by the KfW's executive was to try to achieve independence from the Allies. Only in this way could the KfW become the special tool to direct the German economy in its traditional ways and with the old elite in charge, contrary to American ideas. The policy the US intended for the German economy, i.e. its democratisation and the removal of the old elite was a failure; it was eventually abandoned because of the Cold War.

Further Legislation until 1961

The remarks made by the Communists during the reading of the draft bill, that one billion DM was not sufficient to supply the West German economy with capital, were soon proved correct. By June 1949 the Economic Council was presented with an amendment to the law. Apart from some minor changes regarding the easier and smoother administration of the KfW, an attempt was made to increase the total sum of money to be borrowed from the Kreditanstalt to 3 billion DM and to allow not only securities under the mortgage law, but also securities of shipping-mortgage banks (*Schiffs-Hypothekenbanken*). The new bill was debated over a very short space of time. All three readings took place during the 38th general assembly of the Economic Council on 23 and 24 June and it was passed unanimously[95]. Apart from the obvious reasons for the increase of the sum lent by the Anstalt, the desperate need for capital in West Germany, the acceptance of securities from shipping-mortgage banks would have offered the chance to finance the expansion of the crippled German coastal and fishing fleet. By doing so, the Germans tried to

[94]BA Z 45 F/2/154/7, 2. fiche, memorandum by Holgate and March, 1 March 1949; Pohl, *Wiederaufbau*, p. 47.
[95]*Wörtliche Berichte*, vol. 3, p. 1848, vol. 6, DrSn. 1341, 1383.

by-pass at least to some extent the Allied refusal of the extension of the shipping-mortgage law, which the Germans had tried to introduce earlier that year[96]. After internal debate BiCO agreed to the increase in money available for lending, but opposed the acceptance of the shipping-mortgage banks securities[97]. A likely reason for the Allied refusal was to prevent German competition on the seas and in shipping construction and to prevent the re-emergence of new German naval capacity although the construction of small vessels had just been authorised again. BiCO's Joint Secretariat informed the President of the Economic Council and the Chairman of the Executive Committee that the ordinance could not be amended in the way the Germans had hoped for. In order to save at least the increased sum for borrowing the Economic Council acted quickly. Just three days after the refusal at the 40th general assembly they passed a changed draft, which did not include shipping mortgage banks. The altered draft became law on 18 August 1949 having been accepted by both the *Länderrat* and BiCO[98].

In December 1951 the second amendment of the *Kreditanstalts-Gesetz* was passed. It was not only a process of cosmetic adaptation, replacing the names of Bizonal authorities and offices with those of the new republic. It also granted an extension of the KfW's tasks and authority. From now on the Kreditanstalt für Wiederaufbau was no longer dependent on the agreement of the Bank deutscher Länder if it intended to give short-term credits. The decision was now only with the BoD, a clear sign that the men in charge in West Germany no longer feared inflationary pressure caused by a lack of (short-term) credit control. On the contrary, the Korean Crisis, which had passed its peak by that time showed that it was partly the lack of investment capital which prevented the expansion of production and thus caused the rise in prices. The KfW became entitled to give loans to finance West German exports, a measure which significantly improved German competitiveness on world markets. Once more the total sum, which could be borrowed from the Anstalt was increased. It was raised from DM 3 to DM 8 billion, demonstrating the success of the institution and the extent of German economic recovery[99]. Shipping mortgages were now accepted as securities by law and not only in the bank's statutes, after the first attempt was blocked by the Allies two years previously. With effect from 1 January 1952, the Board of Directors was enlarged by eight members[100]. Walter Tron, who left the Board of Managers on 31 March 1951 became the representative of the Credit banks. In order to promote the reconstruction and improvements of the communities and of the infrastructure, the local authorities were given a seat as well. The number of trade union deputies on

---

[96]Pünder, *Interregnum*, p. 209

[97]PRO, FO 1005 168, BIPFIN/Memo(49) 241, letter by BiCO Finance Group, 9 July 1949.

[98]BA Z 13/1174, letter BiCO, Joint Secretariat 5 June 1949; *Wörtliche Berichte*, vol. 3, pp. 1984 f., vol. 6, DrS. 1628; *Wirtschaftsgesetzblatt* 1949, Nr. 32, reprinted in Pohl, *Wiederaufbau*, pp. 166 f.

[99]*Bundesgesetzblatt* 1951 (I), Nr 56, (henceforth *BGBl* and year and number of issue), Art. 1 No. 2a, d.

[100]*Jb* 1952, Bericht des Verwaltungsrates.

the board was increased to four in order to balance a second board membership for industry and two more members for the *Länder* balanced the intake of the Federal Ministers for the Marshall Plan and for Transports. However, it was only a numerical balance because the Federal Government increased its influence by making all the ministerial seats permanent ones, *ex officio,* thus taking them out of the rotational process for other members. In addition, the ministers were allowed to deputise their state secretaries to the meetings[101].

After the 1957 general election and Finance Minister Fritz Schäffer's consequent replacement an extensive legislative process began which brought new tasks for the Kreditanstalt. In an internal paper by the Finance Ministry it was stressed that an amendment to the law would be inevitable because much of the KfW's work was carried out in a legal 'no-man's- land' [102]. The ideas circulating in the Finance Ministry would bring about a large capital expansion and if possible the removal of at least one trade union representative from the Board of Directors. Altogether, the influence of the Federal Government was to increase and transform the Kreditanstalt für Wiederaufbau even more than before into the government's tool by granting special permission to conduct any kind of business, which the government deemed necessary or appropriate[103]. The KfW was also designated to become Germany's Development Aid Bank, a move which came about partly because of fierce American pressure for German funds as part of the 'western defence' in Third World countries. This was strongly opposed by Erhard who did not like the thought that exports or export finance should be used for political propaganda in such countries. When the new bill finally became law on 16 August 1961 it brought so many changes and amendments that its passing marked the final landmark in the West German reconstruction process[104]. This is most clearly visible in the new Article 1 of the law. While the old regulation spoke of the KfW's foundation as a means of supporting reconstruction, this phrase was dropped from the amendment and appeared only amongst the other tasks. The KfW's capital was increased from DM 1 million to 1 billion of which only 15 per cent had to be paid in and it lost its previous *Bund-Länder* balance. Now the Federal Government provided 80 per cent of the capital. This shift in influence was also reflected on the Board of Directors where the Foreign Minister's new permanent seat was not balanced by a sixth representative for the *Länder*. Instead a deputy for Commerce (*Handel*) was appointed[105].

---

[101] KfW Gesetz 1951, Art 1, No. 5a, b.

[102]BA B 126/7451, Vermerk Referat V A 3 an Finanzminister, 6 August 1959.

[103]BA B 126/7451, passim.

[104]*BGBl.* 1961 (I), Nr. 67.

[105]Ibid., Art. 1(2), Art. 7(1) Nr.2 and Nr. 6. After the termination of the European Recovery Programme the Minister for the Marshall Plan kept his seat on the Board, but with his title altered to 'Minister für Wirtschaftliche Zusammenarbeit' BMwiZ, (Minister for Economic Cooperation) and then in 1957 to 'Minister für Wirtschaftlichen Besitz des Bundes' BMBes (Minister for Federal Commercial Assets).

The biggest change affecting everyday work appeared in Article 2, titled 'Aufgaben und Geschäfte' (Tasks and Business). The Anstalt's task was now defined first and foremost as to supply loans for reconstruction or for the support of the German economy if other institutions could not provide the necessary means. Although the word 'reconstruction' was still used the main emphasis had now shifted to support. This was stressed by the fact that export financing developed a more prominent role and was put under Article 2(1) No. 2 instead of section four as previously. Article 2(2) now expressly allowed the financing of development aid or any similar tasks '... [die] im besonderen staatlichen oder wirtschaftlichen Interesse der Bundesrepublik Deutschland liegen'.

While section three prohibited any other business for the Kreditanstalt unless it was related to the ones named in section one or two, section four allowed all kind of exceptions if '... es sich um ein Geschäft handelt, an dem ein staatliches Interesse der Bundesrepublik Deutschland besteht und das der Anstalt im Einzelfall von der Bundesregierung zugewiesen wird'[106]. With this phrase the Federal Government created for itself a highly sophisticated tool indeed, enabling all kind of deals within existing legislation or as in the case of the financing of Tornado fighter planes for Jordan in the 1980s even outside it. With this clause any kind of economic or political interests could be served. It follows clearly from the change of business focus, which is expressed in this amendment that the government itself regarded the reconstruction as completed. From now on the attention of economic policy had shifted to Third World development aid, which during the second half of the 1950s had become a new focal point for the Cold War.

[106]Ibid., Art. 2(1) Nr.1; Art. 2(2) '[which] were of special political or economic interest for the Federal Republic of Germany' (translation AG); Art. 2(4) '... as long as they are deals in which the Federal Republic of Germany has a special political interest and which will be assigned to the Corporation by the Federal Government in each individual case' (translation AG).

Chapter 3

Task, Senior Staff, Internal Structure and Ways of Operation

The Kreditanstalt für Wiederaufbau was established as a financial institution which would be able to promote Germany's reconstruction by providing medium and long-term loans to all sectors of the economy in order to enable businesses to carry out important reconstruction projects, which could not be financed by other credit institutions. The KfW also had to help balance regional differences in capital formation according to capital requirements. Finally, the Kreditanstalt was obliged to involve other banks in the lending process and not to give its loans directly to applicants. Exceptions to this last rule, however, were allowed with special permission given by the Board of Directors. Short-term loans were allowed only in exceptional circumstances and required the approval of the Bank deutscher Länder, a measure which was devised to prevent inflation[1].

Despite the significant expansion of money supply in the aftermath of the currency reform long-term loans for the rebuilding of infrastructure, housing and basic industries were in short supply. The banks, themselves short of cash and assets, preferred to give short-term loans to those businesses which promised fast and secure return of interest. For the banks, long-term, large scale commitments which were necessary for many reconstruction projects were simply not profitable enough, or carried too great a risk[2]. The dissolution of three of the former six 'big banks' by the Allies and the splitting up of the other three banks into institutions with only regional permission of operation, which was part of the American drive to decentralise German business and industry, obviously did not improve the situation at the capital market[3]. The establishment of the KfW thus signified a direct state intervention into the financial market to improve the prospects of reconstruction. As an organisation under public law (*Körperschaft des öffentlichen Rechts)*, the Kreditanstalt would be able to grant loans, which were too risky for the private banks thus balancing some of the flaws on the capital market, which had arisen due to Erhard's preference for consumer goods industries and due to the general situation the capital market was in. Counter-measures were necessary

[1]KfW-Gesetz, 1948, § 3 (1).

[2]*Jb*, 1949, pp. 24, 42.

[3]Eckhard Wandel, *Die Entsehung der Bank deutscher Länder und die deutsche Währungsreform 1948*, Frankfurt/M. 1980, p. 49. The three were the Bank der deutschen Arbeit, Reichskreditgesellschaft and the Berliner Handelsgesellschaft.

because the imbalance on the capital market created bottleneck sectors in industrial sectors vital to the reconstruction.

The limitation of the KfW's task to cases where no loans from private banks could be obtained was a concession to the private banking sector. It had been stressed already during the legislative process that the KfW should not become a public competitor to them. Instead, the Anstalt should be a body directing the capital flow (*Kapitalleitstelle)*, which is why the name 'Kreditanstalt' and not 'bank' was chosen[4]. It had been of some importance to the Executive Council not to alienate banking when the bill was drafted. This is also evident in the clause, which stated that the KfW had to give its loans via other banks so that they could keep their direct relationships with their clients. It was clearly Abs' influence during the drafting of the bill, which guaranteed that they would not face renewed competition in form of a state bank similar to the former Reichskreditgesellschaft, which had been a strong rival for business banks[5]. Apart from the fact that the KfW, due to its structure, would have been in no position to manage all the expected applications for loans on its own, the clause brought an additional benefit: the banks could claim a fee for their involvement, which normally ranged between 0.5 and 1 per cent of the interest rate[6]. This generated a small profit for the banks and therefore additional money for the national economy. In spite of the clause, most of the money given by the KfW until 1951 was given as direct credits.

In the first instance, all loans had to be secured by material assets or by bonds issued from credit institutions in accordance with the regulations of the mortgage bank law. However, here too exceptions were possible. If the Board of Directors agreed, bonds without the regulations of the mortgage bank law could be accepted. Furthermore, if the BoD decided that a requested loan was of special importance to the reconstruction process, it had the right to accept any other securities[7]. Of course, this passage in effect allowed all kinds of securities, even those, which were no securities in a proper financial sense. Loans to the expropriated coalmines in 1949-51 in particular were given on the Allies' word that the KfW would be the first to be allowed to claim a mortgage on the pits as soon as these were released from Allied control[8].

Although the KfW was requested to help balance regional differences in capital formation, in other words to carry out structural policy, in the first years of its existence the Kreditanstalt gave most of its money to the Ruhr area and some other industrial centres. Only in the mid-1950s was money given to improve regional infrastructure, mainly public utilities on a significant scale[9].

---

[4] *Wörtliche Berichte,* vol. 2, p. 772.
[5] Harries, *Wiederaufbau*, p. 20.
[6] Pohl, *Wiederaufbau*, pp. 59 ff.
[7] KfW-Gesetz 1948, § 3(2).
[8] *Jb.* 1951, p. 53.
[9] See *Jb.*, various years.

Under Article 3 (3) the law allowed the Kreditanstalt to take on medium and long- term guarantees for loans given by other credit institutions. Although the limit to the guarantees was set to a total of DM 1 billion they were hardly used by clients before the mid-1950s[10].

On 15 July 1949 the Board of Directors passed the statutes for the Kreditanstalt für Wiederaufbau, which had been drafted by the Board of Managers, according to Article 8 of the KfW law. The way and the wording in which the statutes were drafted made them another example for German or at least KfW attempts to circumvent Allied restrictions. By introducing these clauses into the statutes, for example the acceptance of shipping mortgage bonds as securities also without having to ask the BoD's permission, the KfW could bypass without much difficulty any Allied veto placed on German legislation. For this matter, they could operate within a much wider framework than even the German legislation allowed[11].

The second amendment of the KfW law in December 1951 brought an expansion of the Anstalt's task. The authorisation of guarantees for other banks' loans helped to extent the capital market. It was also a farsighted decision since it would later allow the KfW to become involved in the repurchase of bonds, which had been issued by German banks in the 1920s, mainly on the American market[12]. The involvement of the KfW in this kind of business was important for the West German national economy in two ways. The repurchase strengthened Germany's credit worthiness and it helped to prevent foreign companies buying these bonds, which would then have allowed them direct influence on German business.

The most important amendment for the KfW in 1951 was clearly the permission to finance exports deals[13]. This legalised not only a sometimes fairly dubious practice which was carried out for political reasons motivated by the Cold War, it also constituted a subsidy for German exports, which were important for the country's economic reconstruction and its political rehabilitation and reintegration into the world markets.

The ultimate change in the KfW's defined task came in 1961 when an amendment to the law established the Anstalt as Germany's development aid bank. Once more, the law was only changed to adapt to reality, for the Kreditanstalt had been directly involved in foreign aid since 1958. But the amendment went further than just supplying money for development projects in Third World countries. It was stressed explicitly that the KfW could alter the terms of debts of foreign debtors, both private and public, to assist German creditors when necessary[14]. Such

[10]KfW-Gesetz 1948, Art. 4(2); Guarantees had a volume of DM 84 million in 1953 and rose to DM 396 million in 1955, see *Jb.* 1955, p. 45.

[11]KfW-Gesetz 1948, Art. 8; Statutes, Art. 14a, and, indirectly Art. 2(1)4; statutes reprinted in: Pohl, *Wiederaufbau*, pp. 180 ff.

[12]KfW-Gesetz 1951, Art 3(3). See, for example, DBB HA B 330/337, Rückkauf der Rentenbank-Kreditanstalt $-Anleihe.

[13]KfW-Gesetz 1951, Art. 3(4).

[14]KfW-Gesetz 1961, Art. 2(2).

a clause is obviously a major interference in the market and therefore highly political. While it did further strengthen the position of German exporters its origins were again found in the Cold War. The impact and implications these changes had will be shown in Chapters 10 and 11.

The support of 'special public or economic interests' of the Federal Republic abroad also became the Kreditanstalt's concern. This meant that from now on the KfW could be used legally as a governmental tool in economic and Cold War policy mainly abroad but also at home. In a wider context the clause signified the end of the reconstruction process in West Germany since it showed that the country had become a capital exporter.

Another important change with a long-term impact came into effect with the 1961 amendment. Since it was the Federal Government which would have to step in if the KfW ever made losses, the clause regarding profits was altered. The first law and its previous amendments stated that the net profit had to go into a reserve until it reached 10 per cent of the capital and the liabilities. From then on the *Länder* and the Federal Government would share the profits on equal terms. Now, in order to cover for possible losses in development aid, profits exceeding the 10 per cent share would go into a special reserve. By 2001 this special reserve had grown to EUR 3.273 billion or DM 6.39 billion[15].

When Schniewind and Abs were appointed Chairman and Deputy Chairman respectively of the KfW's Board of Directors on 8 December 1948 most of the other posts had not yet been officially decided on[16]. However, with the old networks of politics and business still functioning, the decision who would sit on the Board of Managers had been taken unofficially at least since September 1948[17]. One of the chosen men was Otto Neubaur who would become the senior figure amongst the BoM's members. Born in 1891 he had been educated in a Prussian Cadet School to become an army officer. After military service in World War I, he took an apprenticeship at a Berlin bank (from 1919 to 1922) while at the same time studying for a degree in Economics. After holding various posts with several banks he joined the Reichskreditgesellschaft in 1927 where he became a member of the Board of Managers in 1932. In 1939 he joined the board of the Vereinigte Industriewerke AG (VIAG), which he left at the end of 1942 when he became a board member of a chemical company. In 1945 he was suspended by OMGUS and interned for 15 months[18]. Although he was a member of the Nazi party, he was

[15]KfW-Gesetz 1948, 1951, 1961, Art. 10; *Jb.* 2001, p.126.

[16]KfW-HA VS 65, confidential memorandum by von Ilberg, 11 December 1948; *AVBRD*, vol. 4, p. 994. No document on the decision making process for the posts seems to exist. No names other than those of Abs and Schniewind were mentioned in the records and while there were consultations on the matter during the 37th meeting of the Executive Council, the 40th meeting on 8 December just presented the results. This strongly suggests that the decision was taken informally.

[17]KfW-HA VS 72/II, Schniewind's farewell address for Tron, 31.3.1951.

[18]This was due to his leading post in the Reichskreditgesellschaft, which, as a state bank, was heavily involved in the 'Aryanisation' of Jewish business and Nazi war financing.

cleared of all charges in 1948 by a denazification appeal court and even accepted by the Americans for the vice presidency of the BdL. In spite of being elected for the post by the Central Bank Council, Neubaur refused to take it. Instead he wrote a farsighted paper on 'Thoughts on the Foundation of the Reconstruction Loan Corporation' (Gedanken zur Gründung der Kreditanstalt für Wiederaufbau). A first draft dated 10 September was followed by a revised version on 10 November which already had references to the KfW law, although this was only made public ten days later, which indicates that Neubaur had received inside information[19].

However, due to bad health Neubaur could not take up his post with the Anstalt at its establishment. Only after he had recovered was he appointed to the Board of Managers during a meeting of the BoD on 24 June 1949. Following Abs' resignation from the BoM on 31 March 1952, Neubaur became his successor as the Board's spokesman. He held this position until he himself retired from the Board on 30 June 1958[20].

Otto Schniewind also retired as Chairman of the Board of Directors that year and Abs was to take the position. However, the actual events were somewhat absurd and farcical. Abs, still the strong man within the KfW, was certainly the first choice for the job and consequently Neubaur was designated Deputy Chairman. But by the end of October Staatssekretär Ludger Westrick of the Economic Ministry had written to the Chancellery that Neubaur should become Chairman and Abs only his deputy and that both men had agreed on this. On 29 October the Cabinet decided in this way[21].

On 14 November, in a letter to Westrick, Neubaur withdrew his willingness to take the KfW's chair. He justified his decision by claiming poor health, including attacks of dizziness caused by the emotional strain, which resulted from his fear of carrying the responsibility, which the job of chairman might bring. He therefore suggested appointing Abs as Chairman. This is, of course, a very peculiar statement for a top manager, who at this time held more than half a dozen other posts as supervisory board member, including two as chairman and two more as deputy chairman[22]. The real reason for Neubaur's decline has to be seen as an

---

[19]DBB-HA B 330/3367 Neubaur's CV is on the back of a note pad. A slightly different CV can be found in the Bundesarchiv in BA B 136/2332, note 3 November 1958 for a Cabinet meeting on 5 November 1958; B 330/001, minutes of the 3rd meeting of the Zentralbankrat; Wandel, *Entstehung*, pp. 75 f. No reason is given why Neubaur declined; KfW-HA VS 67/I.
[20]KfW-HA Prot 10-1, Protokoll der 7. Sitzung, TOP 1; *Jb* 1952, Bericht des Verwaltungsrats; *Die Kreditanstalt für Wiederaufbau - 1948 bis heute*, Frankfurt/M. 1997 (2nd. edn.), p. 15; KfW-HA VS 184, Bescheinigungen über Zeichnungsvollmacht; *Jb.* 1958, Bericht des Verwaltungsrates.
[21]BA B 136/2332, letter StSek. Westrick to StSek. Globke, 13 September 1958; letter StSek. Westrick to StSek. Globke, 23 October 1958; letter Abs to Adenauer, 6 December 1958. However, it is possible that the cabinet meeting was only on 5th November, the day the cabinet received Neubaur's CV.
[22]BA B 136/2332, letter Neubaur to StSek. Westrick, 14 November 1958. For his posts see *Leitende Männer der Wirtschaft*, Darmstadt, Berlin, Essen, 3rd edn. 1955, 8th edn. 1960.

attempt to put Abs back into the chairmanship. Abs had been refused the post by Finance Minister Etzel during a talk with Adenauer in mid-October. Although Etzel gave as the reason for his decision the concentration of power, which lay with Abs, there were certainly personal feelings involved as well. After Abs had been rejected by Jean Monnet as head of the German delegation for the Schuman Plan negotiations in 1950 he became the strongest critic of the treaty. In this way he also became a critic of, and came in opposition to, Etzel who was a convinced European and Vice President of the High Authority of the European Coal and Steel Community (ECSC). However, after the Economics Ministry suggested a change of posts, the cabinet finally agreed to appoint Abs as Chairman and Neubaur his deputy[23].

In 1948, Neubaur's illness had caused some trouble for the establishment of the KfW's executive, for another candidate had his support withdrawn[24]. To fill the gap and get the Anstalt operational, Abs proposed taking on Walter Tron as an interim solution. Tron was a former senior vice president of the Deutsche Bank and the managing director of the bank's Leipzig branch, and as such an old colleague of Abs. Tron was taken onto the BoM on 21 December 1948, but even before that date he was already involved with the KfW's early organisational difficulties prior to its official start. On 9 December Tron took part in a first meeting, which dealt with organisational, personnel and accommodation problems and the viewing of a suitable accommodation for the bank the following day. Tron's contract, which ran at first for six months was extended until the end of 1949. After another extension he eventually left the BoM in March 1951 to become a member of the Board of Directors for the Credit Banks[25].

During the meeting a further discussion developed on the question of whether another managing director with experience in the field of mortgage loan banking (Realkreditbanken) should be appointed. Eberhard Wildermuth was named again. The other possible candidates were Helmut Wolf, Herbert Lubowski and Johannes Perdelwitz. The BoD could not reach an agreement but several members

---

The German word for dizziness, Schwindel, means also cheating or swindling, so that the words are often used for jokes and puns.

[23]BA B 136/2332, letter Abs to Adenauer, 6 December 1958; Henning Köhler, *Adenauer,* Berlin, Frankfurt/M 1994, p. 608; BA B 136/2332, letter BMWi to StSek Bundeskanzleramt, 29 December 1958 and letter StSek Bundeskanzleramt to the various ministries, 9 January 1959.

[24]See Schniewind's farewell address for Tron although no name is given there; also Pohl, *Wiederaufbau*, p. 43.

[25]Presumably Johannes Perdelwitz,Chairman of the Rheinische Hypothekenbank, Mannheim, a specialist in mortgage banking ; Pohl, *Wiederaufbau,* p. 43; Holtfrerich, 'Deutsche Bank', p. 434; KfW-HA Prot 10-1, Protokoll der 1. Sitzung, TOP 4., KfW-HA VS 65, confidential memorandum by von Ilberg, 11 December 1948; KfW-HA Prot 10-1, Protokoll der 7. Sitzung, TOP 1; KfW-HA VS 72/II, Schniewind's Farewell Address; *Jb* 1951, Bericht des Verwaltungsrats.

favoured Perdelwitz[26]. Only at the third meeting of the Directors on 4 February 1949 was Abs authorised to negotiate with Perdelwitz about him joining the KfW's Board of Managers. However, the latter declined the offer. From the start, Lubowski was out of the question for the Board, despite his qualifications. He was a member of the SPD which made the conservative bankers suspicious of him[27].

A fourth man who was eventually appointed managing director, Herbert Martini, was the first without a banking background. Born in 1903 he went into the Civil Service where he reached the rank of *Ministerialdirigent.* Under the Bizonal administration he held a post in the *Direktorialkanzlei* (Office of the Chairman of the Executive Council) where he became Schniewind's deputy as adviser for the Marshall Plan. Martini was the official responsible for the drafting of the KfW law. He also participated in the KfW's preliminary meetings, which were held to organise operations. Martini was appointed to the Board of Managers in late 1949 and started work at the Kreditanstalt officially on 1 January 1950[28]. His appointment proved very helpful at this stage because he provided important connections to the ministerial bureaucracy. Nevertheless, with the dissolution of the *Direktorialkanzlei* imminent after the founding of the Federal Republic, he had to be regarded as a classic *Versorgungsfall* since only one quarter of the personnel were taken over into the federal administration. His case is a good example to demonstrate how old networks were still operating. It can be presumed that the close relationship Martini had developed with Schniewind in the Marshall Plan office helped him to get the post.

Within the Kreditanstalt für Wiederaufbau Martini became responsible for loans to the construction industry, agriculture, public utilities and the shipping industry. Furthermore, he was in charge of the Board of Managers' affairs, personnel, legal affairs and the most important ERP-Committee. He also dealt with

---

[26]KfW-HA Prot 10-1, Protokoll der 1. Sitzung, TOP 4. Herbert Lubowski, born 1898, President of the Preußiscche Landespfandbriefanstalt; Helmut Wolf, born 1901 of the Süddeutsche Bodenkreditbank München; Johannes Perdelwitz, born 1900, Chairman of the Rheinische Hypothekenbank Mannheim.

[27]KfW-HA Prot 10-1, Protokoll der 3. Sitzung, TOP 1; KfW-HA VS 72/II, Schniewind's Farewell Address. Schniewind stated that Perdelwitz thought the BoD too big and not able to operate properly; Heinrich Tröger, *Interregnum. Tagebuch des Generalsekretärs des Länderrats der Bizone 1947-1949,* ed. by Wolfgang Benz and Constantin Goschler, München 1985, pp. 96, 100.

[28]KfW-HA VS 185, Handakte Martini, VfF letter 14 February 1949, addressed to Herbert Martini, Direktorialkanzlei des Verwaltungsrates des VWG. But in another letter dated 18 November 1948 with attached minutes of a meeting he was named a member of the VfW; Pünder, *Interregnum,* p. 241. Some of the surviving documents bear his initials, see BA Z13/1174; DB PA 2/373; also Harries, *Wiederaufbau,* p. 14; KfW-HA VS 65, confidential Memorandum by von Ilberg, 11 December 1948; KfW-HA Prot 10-1 Protokoll der 7. Sitzung, TOP 1. The minutes speak of the intention to take Martini on to the Board in the second half of 1949. The information given by Pünder, *Interregnum,* p. 248 and *AVBRD,* vol. 4, p. 995 footnote 24, are wrong. See also KfW-HA VS 184, Bescheinigung über Zeichnungsberechtigung, which gives Martini's joining date as 1 January 1950.

a lot of the ministerial contacts. Following Neubaur's retirement from the Board in 1958 Martini became his successor as the Board's spokesman. It is not without some irony that Martini, who in 1948 spoke vehemently against the utilisation of counterpart funds for the KfW, became the bank's longest serving spokesman[29].

August 1954 saw the third permanent extension to the Board. Before, another former Deutsche Bank manager, Richard Gdynia was taken on the Board as a deputy member in 1951 to fill the coming vacancy of Tron leaving the Board. Gdynia became a full member in October 1953 but would retire in 1956 when he reached the age limit[30]. The new managing director in 1954 was Klaus Dohrn who joined the KfW in August and became responsible for loans to the coal mining, iron and steel industries and later on also for long-term export financing[31]. Born in 1905, Dohrn came to attention in 1947 when the US Military Government in Bavaria refused to accept him as a custodian for the Commerzbank in Bavaria[32]. In 1950 he entered the Bayrische Hypotheken- und Wechselbank where he became managing director before he joined the KfW. Apart from the 'interim solutions' Abs and Tron, Dohrn was the only member of the Board of Managers (including the deputy managing directors) who left the KfW before he reached retirement age. In particular the Economics Ministry, where he was quite unpopular, was glad about his departure because he had given internal information to the press and had initiated several big deals without informing the responsible ministries or his KfW colleagues[33].

The most important institution of the Kreditanstalt für Wiederaufbau in the early years was the Board of Directors. It had to appoint the Board of Managers and was responsible for the supervision of business conduct, the passing of statutes and it had to check the annual closing of the accounts[34]. To make the work of the BoD as efficient as possible, the establishment of various committees was

---

[29]KfW HA, Sammlung des HA der KfW , Innere Organisation 1951-1960; for ministerial contacts see correspondence in KfW-HA VS 162; KfW-HA VS 2, letter Martini to Schniewind, 2 July 1948, Martini calls the reason for his opposition too delicate ('zu heikel') to be written down. Harries vaguely names the 'relationship to other banks' as a reason, Harries, *Wiederaufbau*, p. 14. Martini served 13 years until 1971, see *Die KfW - 1948 bis heute*, p. 15.

[30]KfW-HA Prot 10-1 Protokoll der 19. Sitzung TOP 1; *Jb 1953*, Bericht des Verwaltungsrats; *Jb* 1956, Bericht des Verwaltungsrats; KfW-HA VS 184, Bescheinigungen über Zeichnungsberechtigung.

[31]KfW HA VS 184, Zeichnungsberechtigung.; *Jb* 1954, Bericht des Verwaltungsrats; Klaus Dohrn, *Meine Zeit*, Pfullingen 1991, p. 205, where he states that he joined the board to replace Otto Neubaur but the latter only retired in 1958. It is more likely that he replaced Gdynia, who is not mentioned in Dohrn's colourful autobiography. The 1955 internal KfW structure names him as responsible for Public Utilities and food industries.

[32]*OMGUS-Handbuch. Die amerikanische Militärregierung in Deutschland 1945-1949*, ed. Christoph Weisz, München 1994, p. 268, footnote 285. No reason for the decline is given.

[33]BA B 102/25352, internal BMWi letter to the Staatssekretär, 10 June 1960; Harries, *Wiederaufbau*, p. 26.

[34]KfW-Gesetz 1949, 1951, Art. 7, 8, 9.

anticipated in the law and in its first meeting on 21 December 1948 the Board had established such committees[35]. One detail about these Committees for Industrial Credit (*Industriekreditausschuß*), Agricultural Credits (*Agrarkreditausschuß*), the Committee for Credits to Housing Construction (*Wohnungsbaukreditausschuß*), the Committee for Credits under Public Law (*Öffentlich-rechtlicher Kreditausschuß*) and the most important Committee for Credit Approval (*Kreditbewilligungsausschuß*) is of special interest; this is the fact that Abs was chairman or at least a member of all of them. In direct violation of the law the BoD had given its consent that Abs should be entitled to be on the committees, although it was explicitly stated that when a member of the BoD was delegated to the BoM, his membership rights of the BoD should be suspended[36]. The blatant breach of the law showed once more Abs' importance and central position within the Kreditanstalt.

According to the statutes the committees were entitled to grant loans to a single debtor amounting to DM 10 million. In this way the committees acted as a bridging link between the Board of Managers, which was entitled to give loans up to DM 3 millions on its own to an individual debtor and the plenary meetings of the BoD, which had to agree on all loans beyond the DM 10 millions limit[37]. The fact that out of 43 meetings, the BoD held until the end of 1961 12 took place in 1948-49 and another six in 1950 showed that the KfW and its *Verwaltungsrat* were certainly not idle and useless, as the Americans at one point complained[38]. The Germans countered these allegations in a press conference on 2 April where they claimed that the delays in the KfW's operations were only due to the Allied practice of political scrutiny of potential KfW staff [39]. Most of Clay's complaints were exaggerated. When he made his accusation, the Kreditanstalt was just finishing its draft for the 'at once programme', in spite of the very few staff it had. Furthermore, it was never intended to build up an apparatus similar to an ordinary bank[40]. Right from the beginning, it had been planned that the banks of the credit seeking companies would carry out all the applicants' financial scrutiny. There were several reasons for this procedure: the banks should keep close contacts with old clients but would be liable to the KfW for the loans they were passing on to their customers so it was in their interest to forward only sound applications. The KfW's task was only to review the banks scrutiny and not to do their own

[35]KfW-Gesetz 1949, Art. 7(6), Statues Art. 9; KfW-HA Prot 10-1, Protokoll der 1. Sitzung, TOP 9.

[36]See Pohl, *Wiederaufbau*, p. 44; KfW-Gesetz 1949, Art. 6(2) 2, 3.

[37]Statutes, Art. 2(3), Art 9(1).

[38]KfW-HA VS 65 Handakte Schniewind, various notes 31 March 1949 regarding an interview given by General Clay, in which he called the KfW incompetent because it had so far only eight employees, that so far it had not acquired any money and that it was only greedy for counterpart funds.

[39]BA Z 3, Anhang 7, Handakte Köhler, note on press conference, 5 April 1949.

[40]By the end of 1950, there were still only 105 people employed by the KfW and this figure included all secretarial personnel as well as auxiliary workers like drivers and caretakers, *Jb.* 1950, p. 60.

investigations in every single case. They carried out only a certain number of random sample checks so that the small number of staff could deal with its 'real' task, the directing of funds into the needy areas. Most of the money, which was distributed by the KfW in its first few years was given in a relatively small number of direct loans compared to a much larger number of 'regular' credits which were relatively smaller in size[41]. The latter were handled by the companies' banks, leaving the KfW time to deal with the direct loans, which were usually of greater importance to the national economy.

Loans given by the Kreditanstalt für Wiederaufbau in this period can be divided into three types. Direct loans, as the name suggests, were given directly to the applicants although in many cases the loans had been prepared by the companies' banks. Direct loans were given to avoid liabilities for the banks in cases where no securities could be offered and where there was a risk that the loan could turn bad. Indirect loans, on the other hand, were given either as 'normal' loans (which should have been the standard procedure) or as 'global loans' (*Globalkredite*). In a normal loan an applicant approached the KfW by the use of its bank or via its bank and the apparatus behind it. In such a case up to three levels of the banking apparatus could be involved in processing a loan before it reached the applicant[42]. Although the banks gave the loans under their own obligation and had to check the credit worthiness and the securities offered by the applicant before any application could be sent to the Kreditanstalt, it reserved the right to check on the applicants for solvency and agreed use of the money[43]. In the case of *Globalkredite*, the KfW gave a lump sum of money to one bank, usually the Industriekreditbank (IKB) at Düsseldorf, which then was responsible for distributing it as personal loans (*Kleinkredite*) to its clients. In such a case the KfW only specified to the IKB the conditions under which the loans were to be given, such as the types of projects for which the money was to be used or the maximum size of an individual loan[44].

The rate of interest made the loans extremely attractive for borrowers and has to be seen as an additional stimulus to the reconstruction industry. Rates were usually 7 or 7.5 per cent for industrial investments, well below the normal market rate. The KfW paid a rate of 5.5 per cent for the money it borrowed from the

[41]KfW-HA VS 158, Gesetzgebungsausschuß, Protokoll der 1. Sitzung, where Neubaur gave the proportion of direct loans to indirect ones as DM 550 millions to DM 128 millions, at a time when there were about 4000 loans to trade and small business alone, see *Jb* 1949, Anlage 4. To compare the figure, by the end of 1951, when the KfW was already well established, there were 570 loans to the coal mining industry amounting to DM 534 millions. 90 per cent of these loans were given as direct loans, see *Jb* 1951, pp. 52 ff.

[42]*Jb* 1949, Anlage 7, 8-12. For example a farmer applied at his local *Kreditgenossenschaft* for a loan (local level), the bank handed it on to the *Ländliche Zentralkasse* (regional or *Länder* level), which forwarded it to the *Deutsche Genossenschaftskasse* (national level), which then sent it to the KfW.

[43]See for example *Jb* 1949, p. 41; *Jb* 1950, pp. 59 f.

[44]*Jb* 1949, p. 31; *Jb* 1950, pp 56 f.

Counterpart Special Accounts and the banks were allowed to keep the difference in the interest rates as processing fees. The profits for the banks were therefore not very large, especially if two or even three banks were involved in a loan and they had to share the 1.5 or 2 per cent margin. But it was a form of money creation, which helped not only the banks but the whole economy. In years in which the basic rates were lower than average, as in 1958-59, the KfW cut its own basic rates to support small and medium sized business which had no access to the capital market[45].

While the KfW's basic rates of 5 to 5.5 per cent were low enough for borrowers in trade and industry to guarantee both repayment and a profit out of the investment, the situation in agriculture and housing construction was quite different. Because of the long-term, low yield engagements in these sectors special arrangements were required. But in spite of the obvious necessity for a lower interest rate, the US Military Government and the ECA Administration insisted on the same basic rate of 5.5 per cent for all as a matter of principle and refused to lower it for housing and agriculture[46]. Only from mid-1950 onwards, after the Federal Republic took over the administration of the Special Accounts following the signing of the Bilateral Agreement in December 1949 was the KfW able to cut the rates for housing construction from 6.25 per cent for the borrower to 5 per cent as a rule and to 3 per cent for housing construction for refugees. Similar cuts and changes in the conditions of loans already given were made in agricultural finance, too[47].

When the KfW eventually paid out a loan to an applicant – that is a loan which was not a *Globalkredit* – in particular when it was a large credit, it was usually done in instalments instead of one lump sum[48]. There were several reasons to operate in such a way. Since the money was paid out only in accordance with the progress of the project, money scheduled for the final phase of a scheme could be used in the meantime to finance short-term credits. Furthermore, the KfW had better control of the money, both in regard to the final borrower and the banks involved. It was easier for a borrower to secure a loan if a project was defined in phases and the KfW could prevent banks from keeping money idle for themselves for too long a time. Apart from the aspect of control the paying out in instalments enabled the Kreditanstalt to promise more money to the economy than it actually had[49]. This allowed the commencement of more reconstruction projects, which in

---

[45]*Jb* 1949, pp. 24 f ; the BdL's discount rate in 1949/50 varied between 4 and 6 per cent, the rate for loans on securities (*Lombardsatz*) between 5 and 7 per cent, so that a normal borrower's rate was well above 10 per cent. In 1959 the rates fell to 2.75 per cent and 3.75 per cent respectively, see *Deutsches Geld- und Bankenwesen in Zahlen 1876-1975*, ed. Deutsche Bundesbank, Frankfurt 1976, p. 276; *Jb* 1959, p. 39.

[46] Pohl, *Wiedraufbau*, p. 55.

[47]*Jb* 1949, p. 29; *Jb* 1950, pp. 53 f; KfW-HA BA Sch 5, Vermerk Schölzel, 26 January 1954.

[48]*Jb* 1949, p. 23.

[49]*Jb* 1949, p 37.

turn put pressure on the Americans to supply more counterpart funds for the completion of the projects.

Part II
Raising Capital

Chapter 4

American Money: Counterpart Funds and ERP Special Assets

Chapters two and three have shown that on matters concerning personnel policy, organisational outlines and even supervision, the Germans and not the Allies called the shots, which was for several reasons. The Allies needed German expertise in the running of the country, especially since the Allied armies were quickly demobilised after the war had ended. This had a considerable impact on the manning levels and quality of personnel of the Military Governments, which were generally lacking staff, especially legal and financial experts. At the same time, especially in the case of the British, they wanted to limit their civilian manpower necessary to control German administration. If the Americans wanted to turn the western zones of occupation into a bulwark against Communism they needed to reconstruct the country and for this they needed all the help they could get, even from people who had been involved with the Nazis. Despite this disadvantage, the Americans still had one major tool with which they could influence German decisions, which was their economic power. Most of the Kreditanstalt's money during its first decade of operation originated from what was called 'counterpart funds' which originated from (mainly American) aid programmes. To illustrate this point, until the end of 1950, DM 3.2 billion had been provided for the Kreditanstalt to be given as loans to the economy. Only DM 762 millions of this money, less than a quarter had been provided from German sources, the rest came from counterpart funds[1]. Nothing demonstrates more clearly the significance of the counterpart funds than the fact that it was not before 1959 that the share of the ERP-Special Assets, (which consisted of the original counterpart funds and the interests raised on it), was surpassed by any other source of KfW refinancing[2].

Before the main sources of the counterpart funds and their political and economic significance are investigated, it is necessary to explain their origin and legal framework. The counterpart funds were first established in 1946/47 following a severe crisis. In 1945 the Americans had hoped to revive Germany's economy in a short period of time so that German exports could pay for the country's necessary imports, mainly foodstuff. In 1946 it had become clear that economic recovery was

---

[1]*Jb* 1950, p. 33.
[2]*Jb* 1959, p. 41.

still a remote prospect and the Americans realised that they had to provide food and other essentials to prevent starvation and disease. The scheme they set up for this purpose was the GARIOA programme. Although GARIOA was to provide survival aid it was not free. The German administration or German importers had to pay the equivalent of the dollar value in Reichsmarks (RM) and after 20 June 1948 in Deutsch Mark (DM) into special accounts held in the name of the Military Governors[3]. With the establishment of the Bank deutscher Länder in March 1948 these accounts were centralised at the new bank. When the Marshall Plan began in 1948 the same system was applied. From 1949 onwards the KfW was allowed to use the money in these funds for the financing of investment projects. Naturally, the Allies, namely the Americans, gained a strong influence on the German economy by controlling these funds. For example, the withholding or the release of money could significantly influence a reconstruction scheme. At the same time both money or projects could be used for Cold War purposes such as propaganda, as will be shown in later chapters.

On 15 December 1949 the Federal Republic signed its first treaty with a foreign power[4]. The treaty was the Agreement on Economic Co-operation, commonly known as the Bilateral Agreement. That it also became a federal law in January 1950 was only due to American pressure. Since the official title was 'agreement' and not 'treaty' the German government had hoped to avoid any further parliamentary process[5]. American insistence on this matter was due to the far-reaching impact the agreement had. Under articles IV and V, the counterpart funds, which had so far been kept under the name of the Military Governors, were to be handed over to the Federal Republic, which had to establish separate special accounts, both for the GARIOA and the ERP funds. Although the counterpart funds, now under the name of *Sondervermögen* or Special Assets thus came under German administration, American approval was still necessary for any kind of utilisation of the funds. The agreement was highly praised by West Germany's Minister for the Marshall Plan, Franz Blücher, because it would give the Germans access to the funds; but the Americans gained extensive rights of interference into the German economy at the same time[6]. West Germany was required to subsidise Berlin's western sectors economically (Art. VII), although the city was not part of the Federal Republic. Furthermore, in accordance with American wishes, the German government had to put particular effort into the coalmining sector (Art. II).

---

[3]Dieter Carstens, *Der Bund als Finanzier. Kredite, Leistungen und Bürgschaften des ERP-Sondervermögens*, Bad Godesberg 1960, p. 202. Because the British had their own much smaller aid programme, the UK Contributions, both Military Governors had a say on the matter but with a clear American dominance.

[4]Gerd Hardach, *Der Marshallplan*, München 1994, p. 121.

[5]*BGBl* 1950 (I), p. 9 ff.; *Kabinettsprotokolle der Bundesregierung*, ed. for the Bundesarchiv by Hans Booms, vol. 1, 23. Sitzung, pp. 202 ff. (henceforth *Kabinettsprotokolle* and volume). Under German law an agreement can be enacted by the government a treaty needs parliamentary approval.

[6]Hardach, *Marshallplan*, p. 121.

German coal was the key to European recovery since not only Germany, but also most of its neighbours, most notably France, depended on it. Thus coal supply was not only an economic but also a political issue. The treaty also demanded the delivery of such German goods or materials to the USA which were already in short supply in America or for which there was a potential for short supply. Furthermore, the Federal Republic had to guarantee a minimum supply of such goods to the USA (Art. VI). Legally the American say in matters regarding counterpart funds established a state which allowed the USA to terminate any further aid if the Germans disobeyed or refused any American demand regarding counterpart funds[7]. In other words, the Germans had to comply with all these clauses and possibly other US wishes or risk losing the aid. Although the Adenauer government knew about the importance of German reconstruction for US policy, they were unable to profit from this knowledge and refuse any American demands because they would have put the aid at risk altogether. At this time, it would have been a very difficult task to explain to the German public why the government had lost American aid for the sake of political principles. During a Cabinet meeting it was therefore stressed that despite these clauses the Federal Republic had to sign the agreement in order to receive counterpart funds at all[8]. Despite Blücher's public praise, when the bill that transferred the Bilateral Agreement into law in West Germany was discussed in the Bundestag, all official German enthusiasm about the ERP had gone, not least because of these clauses. Nevertheless, they had to pass the law if they wanted to receive any aid at all[9].

In 1949-50 American interference was limited to 'first generation' funds. 'Second generation' funds, that is, interests gained from them and all repayments which returned to the accounts, could be used by the Germans without any American intervention but only for such projects for which other US aid had already been scheduled. This meant that most new projects to be supported with 'second generation' funds had also to get – indirect – American approval.

Proceedings followed this rule until mid-1952, when an amendment to the Economic Cooperation Act, the Mutual Security Act of 1952 (the so-called Zablocky Amendment), was introduced. The amendment, which was followed by an even tougher one in 1953, determined that all interests and repayments were now also subject to direct American control. Both amendments have therefore to be seen in the context of increased Cold War tensions since they increased US influence over the utilisation of the funds.

The 1952 extension of American control over the funds was somewhat unexpected, as the amendments were made at a time when the negotiations on

[7]Wolfgang Becker, *Das ERP-Sondervermögen. Entstehung und Verwaltung*, Göttingen 1968, p. 29.
[8]*Kabinettsprotokolle*, 28. Sitzung, pp. 240 f.
[9] Hardach, *Marshallplan*, pp. 121 ff.

German foreign debts in London were well under way in 1952 and completed in 1953 when the second amendment was enacted. Although West Germany in the agreement acknowledged all pre-war debts of the Reich and took on the responsibility for repaying post-war aid (including Marshall Aid) as well, the Americans now had full control of the funds, including the interest which had been paid by German lenders[10]. Even if American approval had become a formality by the mid-1950s their official participation on decisions on counterpart funds ended only on 30 December 1960 following an exchange of notes between the US and the West German government[11].

On 31 August 1953, the law concerning the administration of the ERP-Special Assets (*Gesetz über die Verwaltung des ERP Sondervermögens*), which was now the official name of the funds, was enacted. This was a step in line with German administrative habits[12]. The law had become necessary because German budget regulations demanded legal separation between the budget and Special Assets. The Bilateral Agreement had turned the counterpart funds into such a federal special asset (*Sondervermögen des Bundes*)[13]. The most important regulations of the *Verwaltungsgesetz*, given in Article 4, were that the Special Assets, although administrated by the Ministry of the Marshall Plan, had to be kept separate from all other federal assets. They had to be preserved in their existence so that usually only interest-bearing loans were given. Both interests and repayments had to return to the Special Assets so that an ever-increasing revolving fund would be created (Art. 5)[14]. This clause was a result of a demand the ECA had already made in 1949 and which had to be adopted for legal reasons in accordance with the Bilateral Agreement. Thus, the law guaranteed the long-term survival of a special fund outside the normal budget and therefore outside the normal budget debates[15]. The German government could use it to intervene in the economy or to provide money for financial projects, which had special political significance without detailed parliamentary approval. And for the KfW the Special Assets meant a safe source from which it could refinance its own lending.

Therefore, at least in this way, the Kreditanstalt für Wiederaufbau gained from the American demands to establish the counterpart accounts as a revolving

---

[10]For details on the debts and the conference see: Abs, *Entscheidungen.*

[11]Becker, *ERP*, pp. 30 f., 35.

[12] Eric Owen Smith, *The German Economy*, London 1994, p. 130; *BGBl* 1953(I) pp.1312ff.

[13]*BGBl* 1950 (I), p. 8.

[14]By the end of 1983 the Special Assets had risen from approximately DM 6 billion to DM 13.9 billion, see Zóltan Jáckli, *Vom Marshallplan zum Kohlepfennig.Grundrisse der Subventionspolitik in der Bundesrepublik Deutschland 1948-1982*, Opladen 1990, p. 67. For the size of the Special Assets at its beginnings, various figures were given, see Dietrich Dickertmann, *Öffentliche Finanzierungshilfen*, Baden-Baden 1980, p. 293. In 1997 the Assets had reached DM 23 billion, see Susan Stern, *The Marshall Plan 1947-1997. A German View*, Frankfurt/Main 1997, p. 5.

[15]However, since it was a federal asset, a special ERP budget (Wirtschaftsplan des ERP Sondervermögens) had to be enacted by Parliament every year, see *BGBl* 1954 ff. (II).

fund. It was Finance Minister Schäffer in particular who had wanted to incorporate at least the interest and if possible even the repayments of loans from the funds into the normal budget to close budget gaps and to repay German foreign debts[16]. However, Schäffer's intention was blocked in the Cabinet due to the American clause for a revolving fund and because of Abs' strong intervention to retain the Kreditanstalt's most important source of money[17].

The application for funds to the Americans, usually carried out by the Ministry for the Marshall Plan, was made by drafting a main programme (*Rahmen- oder Hauptprogramm*) which the ECA and its successor organisations respectively, had to agree on before the money was released in instalments known as 'tranches'. After the release, the German government could transfer the money into *Hauptverteilungskonten* (main distributing accounts) with the BdL. From there, the Ministry of the Marshall Plan could disburse the money to the three main lending institutes (*Hauptleihinstitute*), the Berliner Industriebank (BIB), the Lastenausgleichsbank and, most importantly, to the Kreditanstalt für Wiederaufbau. The *Hauptleihinstitute*, however could release the money to a lender only after the ECA had agreed to the individual project. In this way the USA gained a two-fold control over the West German economy under the Marshall Plan, first by deciding over exports under the ERP and secondly, by determining the use of the counterpart funds for investment finance. German officials, in practice only had the right to propose certain projects[18].

The following sub-chapters will take a closer look at the two main sources of the counterpart funds, their peculiarities and significance.

4.1 GARIOA

According to the 1907 Hague Convention any occupying power was obliged to retain administration and civil order in the occupied territory. This included the prevention of starvation, disease and civil unrest amongst the local population. During the winter of 1945-46 the food supply in Germany was close to collapse with people dying of starvation. This proved American planning for the occupation of Germany, which had hoped for German exports proceeds to pay for the cost of occupation and the import of foodstuffs, futile and the US Military Government had to provide aid. Other than the legal reasons arising from the Hague Convention, the Americans were motivated by humanitarian concerns and political implications. There was a real fear that if they were not able to feed the population Germans

[16]BA NL 168/33 (Nachlaß Schäffer), letter from Schäffer to Staatssekretär Hartmann, 26 September 1952. I am grateful to Frau Dr. Gerda Bracker née Schäffer for her kind permission to use her father's papers in the Bundesarchiv.

[17]Abs, *Entscheidungen*, p. 263.

[18]See Carstens, *Bund*, passim; Becker, *ERP*, pp. 33 f.

might drift towards more radical solutions offered by Communism. In particular in the big urban centres there was a rise in membership of the Communist Party during 1946-47, though not a dramatic one. Consequently, the GARIOA programme was introduced into the budget of the US Army in 1946-47. Under the programme all sorts of commodities which could help to improve basic living conditions in the American and British zones of occupation were imported by OMGUS, in particular foodstuffs, medicine, seeds, fertilizers and fuel. Table 4.1.1 shows the size of the programme, which had also wider implications. Since the aid came from the army budget Clay was able to bypass any remaining Morgenthau supporters in the US-administration and he could lay the foundation for a future (counterpart) aid programme, even in defiance of JCS 1067, since the funds were under his direct control.

Table 4.1.1
GARIOA Imports and Services to the Bizone
(in million $)

Goods and Services provided	1.7.46 - 30.6.47	1.7.47 - 30.6.48	1.7.48 - 30.6.49	1.7.49 - 31.3.50	Total
Foodstuffs	179.61	406.31	423.71	163.25	1172.88
Fertilizers, seeds	6.20	48.60	49.99	0.04	104.83
Fuel	10.71	27.75	26.06	5.18	69.80
Medicine	0.06				0.06
Transport costs	46.61	69.00	50.65	20.57	186.83
Information and education	1.29	4.38	6.93	0.31	12.91
Various Admin. costs	18.60	24.05	21.21	9.03	72.89
Total	263.08	580.19	578.55	198.38	1620.20

Source: Manfred Knapp, 'Deutschland und der Marshallplan', in: Hans-Jürgen Schröder (ed.), *Marschallplan und Westdeutscher Wiederaufstieg*, Stuttgart 1990 p. 44.

Without the GARIOA imports of foodstuffs, which made up nearly three-quarters of all deliveries there would have been widespread starvation in western Germany in particular in 1947, the year so crucial for the reconstruction process[19]. Therefore, the impact of the programme has to be seen first and foremost as one of aid, not reconstruction, despite the fact that it actually was $100 million bigger than the famous Marshall Plan. Its wider significance lay in the fact that the USA was prepared to provide the aid, thus showing a commitment to German reconstruction.

[19]Abelshauser, *Wirtschaftsgeschichte*, pp. 40 ff.

GARIOA also helped the American farmers who were able to sell their surplus stocks at normal market prices although much of the stuff was hardly any longer suitable for human consumption[20]. This fact was addressed in a speech by Johannes Semmler, Erhard's predecessor as the Bizonal Director for Economics (Direktor für Wirtschaft) in January 1948. He complained about the low quality of the foodstuffs and called it *Hühnerfutter*, chicken feed. German importers, he went on, had to buy it at high prices and the German administration even had to be thankful for this. Following the speech, Semmler was suspended as Director for Economics by the Military Governors for 'untruthful claims' and replaced by Ludwig Erhard[21].

Imports under the GARIOA programme were called 'category A' imports as against 'category B' imports which were industrial products, including raw materials which had to be paid for with German export proceeds[22]. As already stated, German importers had to pay for the 'A' imports the commodities' value in German currency into the Military Governors counterpart accounts. However, the money which had been paid into the accounts in Reichsmarks before the currency reform and which made up the largest part of all GARIOA aid was lost during the currency reform. The actual DM amount paid into the GARIOA accounts could not be established but because the Allied Joint Export Import Agency (JEIA) used about a dozen different exchange rates for the various imports[23].

With GARIOA counterpart funds as part of the army budget under General Clay's control, he had a strong tool for West German reconstruction to which he was deeply committed, not only since Secretary of State Marshall's confidential talks with him in Berlin in April 1947[24]. The way Clay saw himself and his role as 'proconsul' was not always in line with general US policy, in particular on the question of industrial dismantling or the re-establishment of the German economy where he favoured a pragmatic approach of reconstruction. His relationship with the ECA would be even more tense since he saw them interfering in his sphere of influence. Because he prioritised German reconstruction over ECA attempts to promote intra-European trade, serious rifts appeared between him and the Administration.

To promote reconstruction Clay asked members of the Bizonal administration on 30 July 1948 to apply immediately for counterpart funds for reconstruction purposes. In a letter to BiCO, dated 4 August 1948 Hermann Pünder

---

[20]Abelshauer, *Wirtschaftsgeschichte*, p. 30.

[21]Wolfgang Benz, *Die Gründung der Bundesrepublik Deutschland. Von der Bizone zum souveränen Staat*, München 1989 (3rd edn.) p. 72.

[22]*Monthly Report of the Military Govenor, OMGUS*, no. 38 (August 1948), p. 45, (henceforth *Monthly Report* and number).

[23]Egon Baumgart, *Investitionen und ERP Finanzierung*, Berlin 1961, p. 27. Baumgart speaks of DM 778 million but this seems to be a typing error and should read $.

[24]Wolfgang Krieger, *General Lucius D. Clay und die amerikanische Deutschlandpolitik 1945-1949*, Stuttgart 1988 (2nd edn.), p. 241.

did this and requested the release of DM 2 billion from the GARIOA funds[25]. The money was destined for the KfW although the legal process to set up the bank had hardly begun at that time. During a meeting on 13 August the British Deputy Military Governor MacReady briefed members of the German administration that the finance advisers to the Military Governors were considering Pünder's request. Three days later, on 16 August, they agreed in principle on the release of the funds to the KfW[26]. Naturally this increased German hopes. In the first reading of the KfW bill on 17 August, Director for Finance Alfred Hartmann expressed his hope to get some hundred million DM for the first half year of operation[27]. But political events dashed these high hopes and GARIOA money had to be utilised in a much more urgent case of Cold War policy. The Berlin Blockade and the airlift had just begun and General Clay had to find ways to reduce its mounting costs for American taxpayers. In the end the transportation costs alone would amount to $ 200 million. In a meeting with the Minister Presidents of the Bizonal *Länder* on 30 September General Clay announced that the cost of all goods to Berlin, regardless of whether food or coal, had to be paid for in DM out of the GARIOA counterpart funds. While this helped the Bizonal budget it reduced money available for investment financing. In addition to the costs of goods, GARIOA funds were used to cover parts of the Berlin budget deficit of DM 53 million per month, which arose as a result of the blockade[28]. Under these circumstances it was no surprise that General MacReady had to tell the Bizonal administration that there was hardly any money left in the counterpart accounts and that the little there was would be needed to assist Berlin. In spite of this, Ludwig Erhard asked for the immediate release of DM 100 million from the funds for the use of the KfW and tried to reach an agreement that all future 'category A' counterparts should automatically go to the Kreditanstalt[29].

The end of 1948 saw the fading of the economic boom, which had been caused by the currency reform and the inflationary trend turned into a depression. German productivity was still not sufficient and the little money that was available for investment finance went much too frequently into projects with little value for reconstruction and the national economy, for example the reconstruction of a consumer goods plant instead of investment in basic industries[30]. OMGUS estimated the difference between the necessary capital formation and the available funds to be DM 3.5 to 4 billion for 1949 alone[31]. In this situation the Military

[25]KfW HA VS 38, note 7 December 1948; BA Z 4/552, letter Pünder to BiCO, 4 August 1948, enclosure no. 3 to a *Länderrat* Finance Committee meeting on 12 August 1948.
[26]BA Z 3, Anhang 1, note regarding the meeting with BiCO on 13 August 1948, TOP 2,3; *Monthly Report* no. 38 (August 1948), p. 39.
[27]*Wörtliche Berichte*, vol. 2, p. 772.
[28]BA Z 3, Anhang 1, minutes of the meeting on 30 September 1948; Benz, *Gründung*, p. 30.
[29]BA Z 3, Anhang 2, minutes of a preliminary meeting with BiCO on 10 December 1948; *Monthly Report* no. 42 (December 1948), p. 58.
[30]Hardach, *Marshallplan*, p. 253; *Jb* 1949, pp. 14, 16 f.
[31]*Monthly Report* no. 43 (January 1949), p. 75.

Governors ordered BiCO and the KfW to outline an immediate investment programme to finance specific projects in order to counter the extensive mis-investments. Already in a first meeting on 7 January plans were drawn up for investments of DM 400 million. DM 170 million was scheduled for the energy sector, 75 million each for mining and transport and 80 million for other industries. The following day Hermann Pünder informed the KfW's Board of Directors of General Clay's confirmation of the release of GARIOA funds for that purpose[32]. But since the economic and political situation constantly changed the planning continued. In an internal letter to the KfW's credit committee, dated 20 January 1949 some important changes to the first draft were laid out. Now agriculture should benefit with DM 5 million from the programme and the share of mining was increased to DM 80 million, both at the expense of the other industries. The Kreditanstalt also complained to the Military Government about the lack of funds for housing construction and asked for more money for that purpose in an attempt to get more funds overall. By mid March the KfW was prepared to provide DM 90 million for housing construction out of the 'at once' programme as the scheme was to be called[33].

BiCO too, continued planning and developed a different approach to the reconstruction than the Germans. In a letter dated 15 February 1949, BiCO, Joint Secretariat told the KfW about an intended energy programme for which the bank should provide DM 220 million in 1949. BiCO also increased the funds for mining to DM 135 million and stated that none of the money should be used for the construction of miners' housing which the KfW had hoped would have helped to recruit new miners[34]. This demonstrates the importance BiCO, in contrast to the Germans, put on coal production within the framework of the reconstruction process. For the Americans, coal meant electric energy and electricity meant higher productivity. In spite of clear Allied demands, the Kreditanstalt's Board of Directors in its fifth meeting on 31 March still hoped to utilise at least some of the funds for miners' housing to ease the housing shortage in the Ruhr[35]. In a second letter BiCO announced that the proposed funds for transport were cut down to a mere DM 5 million for the reconstruction of inland water transports only. The cut

[32]KfW HA VS 38, letter form the KfW to Joe Fisher-Freeman (OMGUS Finance Adviser), 28 January 1949; KfW HA Prot 10-1, Protokoll der 2. Sitzung, address by Pünder.

[33]KfW HA VS 65, letter to the Kreditausschuß, 20 January 1949; FO 944 799, BiB/P(49)21, 11 February 1949, Annex 'A'; ibid., RECO/M(49)2, 22 March 1949. However, there is no sign of any changes in the schedule of the remaining 'at once' programme, which suggests that already by then an extension beyond the DM 400 million was intended. The term 'at once programme' was used in the KfW's correspondence with BiCO to translate the German 'Sofortprogramm'.

[34]KfW HA BA 1, BiCO/Memo(49)13, to KfW, 15 February 1949; KfW HA VS 65, BiCO/Memo(49)32, 30 March 1949.

[35]KfW HA Prot 10-1, Protokoll der 5. Sitzung, TOP 5.

was possible because a loan for the national railway, the Reichsbahn had been taken out of the programme and had been given as a direct loan, instead. Altogether, the Reichsbahn received direct loans from GARIOA funds totalling DM 360 million, money the KfW would miss dearly[36].

When the 'at once' programme was finally agreed on 31 March, both Allies and Germans had made significant amendments to their first drafts. BiCO insisted on giving DM 220 million to the power industry and DM 135 million to the coalmines. The Germans suggested additional DM 228 million to the original programme, to benefit housing construction (DM 90 million), agriculture (53 million), transport (5 million) and the other industries (80 million)[37]. While BiCO limited the programme to DM 555 million, there was only one project, which was vetoed by the Military Government[38]. A loan of 2 million to the ball bearing industry was prevented with no reason given but it was most likely on grounds of security, either real fears or just as a gesture towards France, to show that there would be no aid for the production of strategic materials. This is quite probable since the draft letter to the KfW merely requested further information on the project. It was only during the following BiCO meeting on 23 March that the loan was stopped while the proposed DM 5 million for transport was taken out of the KfW's care. In the end only electricity and coal mining escaped any cuts due to the programme's limitation to DM 555 million, which confirmed once more the importance BiCO placed on these sectors[39].

The position of the KfW during its negotiations with BiCO was relatively strong for the Bizonal Executive Committee had agreed to give the Kreditanstalt the authority to negotiate directly with the Military Government on all matters concerning the 'at once' programme[40]. Other than strengthening the KfW's position vis-à-vis BiCO the authorisation had the further advantage of cutting out unnecessary bureaucratic delays making the work of the Kreditanstalt much more flexible.

The loans to the mining industry were processed and paid out within just three months but the loans to the power industry had to follow the progress of the reconstruction works. The other sectors requested their loans very slowly, mainly because of insufficient knowledge by clients and banks about the whole new procedure. But even this delay turned out to be an advantage for the KfW since in summer 1949 only DM 265 million were left in the GARIOA accounts, not enough to cover all planned projects. Nevertheless, in order to continue with the scheduled investments the KfW was forced to borrow the missing sum in anticipation of the expected release of ERP money[41].

[36]KfW HA VS 65, BiCO/Memo(49)33, 30 March 1949; Baumgart, *Investitionen,* p. 41.
[37]Pohl, *Wiederaufbau*, p. 54.
[38]KfW HA VS 65, BiCO/Memo(49)33, 30 March 1949.
[39]NA RG 260, OMGUS, BiCO, records of the US Secretariat, box 117, folder 5, draft of BiCO/Memo (49)33; on the meeting see ibid., BiPFin/Memo(49)113; *Jb* 1949, p. 21.
[40]KfW HA VS 65, letter Pünder to the Finance Advisers, 4 February 1949.
[41]KfW HA VS 7, table 'Die Inanspruchnahme von Freigabe aus counterpart funds', undated,

Although the 'category A' import accounts were held in the name of both Military Governors, it was obvious that it was Clay who really had the final say when he authorised the release of funds. The Lovett-Strang-Agreement of December 1947 had shifted the balance of the burden and responsibility for the Bizone further to the American side, so the General's influence had been increased as well[42]. For Clay this was also a basis to strengthen his influence in occupied Germany against the ECA. Clay did not like the idea of sharing power in the Bizone in the first place, not even in the field of economic policy. When the Marshall Plan in Germany began more slowly than expected and did not produce a significant impact in 1948, Clay saw the responsibility for this with the ECA and decided to take action for the reconstruction by means he commanded. The Military Governor's intention in late 1948 and early 1949, to release the GARIOA counterpart funds stood in sharp contrast to the ECA's policy. By that time, the agency's main concern was to prevent a further increase in inflation, which had appeared with the post currency reform boom. Even a complete neutralisation of all counterpart funds, at least for some time, had been considered by the ECA. However, Clay had a better feeling for the economic developments, which proved to be right when the economic boom and the ensuing inflation began to falter and soon began to cause deflationary pressures. His release of the funds matched the economic situation much better than the ECA's response. For the Germans Clay's decision must have been a ray of hope, especially since the Marshall Plan began extremely slowly and had no visible impact by late 1948. Clay's action showed the German administration that the Americans were really committed to the reconstruction process and the release of the funds had an important psychological impact despite GARIOA's relative small size. Furthermore, long-term planning could begin, for with the release of the first counterpart funds there was a certain pressure on the Americans to continue and support the investments with ERP counterpart funds.

While GARIOA money did not play a decisive role in terms of size in the KfW's investment programme because of its relatively small volume, it certainly had a catalytic role for the release of the other counterpart funds. Furthermore, Clay's decision to release the funds for reconstruction purposes and thus initiating the process has to be seen as one of supreme importance, perhaps more psychologically than in economic terms. Beyond its small but significant part in the reconstruction process the GARIOA accounts were to play a role in the Cold War, too. According to an agreement within the US administration, which had been

but presumably January or February 1950; KfW HA VS 40, Aktenvermerk 22 August 1949; ibid., note 'Betreffs Übernahme des GARIOA Defizits' dated 15 November 1949; *Jb* 1949, pp. 22, 24. Due to some internal restacking the shortfall could be reduced to DM 273 million. The description of the matter given by Pohl is somewhat inaccurate, Pohl, *Wiederaufbau*, pp 54 f;

[42]Krieger, *General Clay*, p. 318.

reached in spring 1950, 25 per cent of all ECA/MSA counterparts had to be transferred into the GARIOA accounts. Here they were under the control of the US High Commissioner and could be used very much in the way he saw fit. The importance of these funds, which amounted to approximately DM 700 million, will be discussed later.

4.2 The European Recovery Program

American Cold War policy made it inevitable that Europe was to be rebuilt and integrated into a western block, both in military and in economic terms. The defence of Western Europe without Germany, or without Germany as the first line of defence, would have been very difficult not least because of its geo-strategic position. Furthermore, the economic reconstruction of Europe without Germany, the country which had been the biggest importer and exporter of European goods and services before the war, would have been close to impossible. Therefore, the Marshall Plan had to fulfil three crucial tasks: first, it had to pave the way for (West) German reintegration into the emerging post-war western economic system – in spite of some very heavy resistance from its neighbours, most notably France[43]. Secondly, the European Recovery Program had to bring about European economic co-operation, and at a later stage perhaps even a kind of political union. The need for co-operation would also show the Europeans that the USA was no longer prepared to act as Europe's 'horn of plenty' to which the Europeans could turn to get all their economic wishes fulfilled. The ERP became thus the first co-ordinated attempt to rebuild war torn Europe. A side effect of the programme was also that it guaranteed the level of US exports to Europe to remain high, even in face of a severe dollar shortage, which existed on the Old Continent[44]. Economic co-operation and the American role as the great benefactor, thirdly, were used for a large-scale propaganda campaign on behalf of the USA in Europe.

Publicity was of utmost importance to the Americans. The Economic Cooperation Administration (ECA), the administrative body of the scheme, for example demanded that all construction sites in Germany, which received ERP counterpart funds had to display signs advertising that they were part-financed with Marshall aid. It was not least due to such signs that the Marshall Plan remained in the German public memory to the present day and helped to create the myth of the Marshall Plan. The result of Marshall Plan propaganda was better and longer lasting than hoped for. The vast number of all kinds of literature, which dealt with the plan and the number of historical conferences and celebrations to mark its 50th anniversary in 1997 are clear proof of that[45]. The Marshall Plan and the propaganda

---

[43]See Milward, *Reconstruction.*

[44]See Ute Daniel, *Dollardiplomatie in Europa. Marshallplan, Kalter Krieg und US-Außenwirtschaftspolitik*, Düsseldorf 1982.

[45]Hardach, *Marshallplan*, p. 13. Already by 1953 nearly 5000 books, articles and newspaper

around it made people forget that more than half of all American aid given between 1945 and 1952 was given before the European Recovery Program had begun[46].

But Marshall Plan counterpart funds were used for Cold War purposes in more direct ways. According to article IV (4) and V (2c) of the Bilateral Agreement 5 per cent of all payments into counterpart accounts, nearly DM 300 million in the German case alone, had to be provided for US 'administrative purposes'. This innocent phrase hid the fact that the money was actually used to finance the Central Intelligence Agency's activities in the participating countries[47].

The organisational structure of the ERP made it inevitable that West Germany played a part in the Organisation for European Economic Co-operation (OEEC), set up to coordinate the European planning for the Marshall Plan. While the Military Governors signed for the Bizone's membership in the OEEC in April 1948 and German experts at first were only there as 'advisers' for their Allied representatives, the economic integration was the first step to Germany's reintegration into international organisations[48].

The western zones of occupation and later on the Federal Republic of Germany were nevertheless treated differently within the framework of the Marshall Plan. Because of the Occupation Statutes the Americans were in a stronger position to impose their policy on West Germany than on the other European countries, which were much more concerned about their national sovereignty. For example, when the Bilateral Agreement, both the first on 14 July 1948 and the second on 15 December 1949, were signed, it was clearly stated that all aid for the western zones would constitute a claim against Germany[49]. This sentence did not appear in a contract with any other country. The official American explanation was that the clause had to be introduced because of the Russians. With it the Americans could argue that West Germany did not receive any gifts for its reconstruction[50], which might have exacerbated East-West tensions. However, this was only half the truth. Public opinion in France would also have been outraged by the thought that the former enemy would be treated on equal terms and the US had to take the French political situation into consideration. Finally, the claim clause provided a strong source of influence on German economic development.

A second source of influence, and one of even more significance derived from the counterpart clause. While the Foreign Assistance Act demanded the establishment of counterpart funds only for grant related aid Germany, in contrast

---

reports had been written on the programme.

[46]Daniel, *Dollardiplomatie*, p. 30.

[47]Burton Hersch, *The Old Boys. The American Elite and the Origins of the CIA*, New York 1992, pp. 235 f. My thanks to Professor Scott Lucas for pointing out this fact.

[48]Benz, *Gründung*, p. 96.

[49]BA Z 14/173 letter by the BdL to Schniewind and Martini, 28 September 1948 (with a handwritten correction by Martini to 29 September 1948); *BGBl* 1950 (I), pp. 9 ff.

[50] BA Z 14/173, passim.

to the other European countries, had to pay for all its aid into the counterpart accounts[51]. With the final say on the release of the funds, the US was in a position to quietly control and direct the process of reconstruction in economic and social fields and as a consequence, politics as well[52].

The Economic Cooperation Administration

Expectations of the ERP were very high in the Bizone in 1948 and 1949 not only among the population but also in administrative circles. This is best demonstrated by Erhard's statement in early 1948 that all the money for capital formation necessary for the reconstruction could be raised from Marshall Plan counterpart funds[53]. The reality was quite different. The slow process of the Marshall Plan imports during 1948 forced Schniewind in his capacity as *Marshallplan Berater* to write two reports at the end of the year, an 'official' one for the public and a confidential one for the administration, which gave the real, disappointing figures of the plan so far[54]. Even after some disillusionment during 1948 and early 1949 caused by the slow progress of the program and its handling by the Americans, ERP money remained central to German planning. This caused General Clay to call the existence of the counterpart funds the biggest evil for the German economy since he had not seen one German proposal for reconstruction which was not based on counterpart funds[55]. However, the persistent German demands for counterparts were only one side of the story. To prepare the Marshall Plan the State Department had organised a '90 days programme' for the period of April to June 1948, paid for by ERP funds, which should ignite the European reconstruction process. Bizonia was to receive $109 million for the import of raw materials, with another $ 20million for the French zone of occupation. Since the delivery of the goods was so sluggish, the amounts of DM paid into the accounts accumulated very slowly so that the first ECA counterparts were released only in September 1949 when the Agency agreed to pay DM 57 million to the French zone of occupation and DM 94 million to the Bizone[56]. The use and the significance of these DM 94 million will be discussed below but it is important to note that the Allies named individual projects for which the money had to be used and that it was given to the KfW as a gift and not as a loan[57].

In contrast to the late release definite planning and instructions to the Germans were in place from as early as March 1949, when BiCO sent a letter to

---

51 Economic Assistance Act of 1948, printed in *Europa Archiv*, 6 July 1948, pp. 1385 ff.
52 Abelshauser, *Wirtschaftsgeschichte*, p. 59.
53 Abelshauser, *Wirtschaftsgeschichte*, p. 54.
54 Hardach, *Marshallplan*, pp. 111 f., 255 ff., 262 f.
55 KfW HA VS 65, note on a meeting with the Military Govenors on 13 April 1949.
56 *Jb* 1949, p. 23; Hardach, *Marshallplan*, pp. 210, 274.
57 KfW HA Prot 10-1, Protokoll der 10. Sitzung, TOP 2; BA Z 45 F/ABC-8/3, 3. fiche, ECA letter to KfW and Abs, 3 October 1949.

both the German administration and the KfW. It contained the 'Principles for Basis on which counterpart funds will be made available to or through the Reconstruction Loan Corporation'[58]. KfW planning for the investment of ERP money took place during spring. In a reply to a BiCO request on how the estimated DM 1.2 billion, which were expected during the 1949-50 budget year were going to be spent, the Kreditanstalt outlined an investment plan[59]. The total of its proposal exceeded the scheduled 1.2 billion by DM 145 million, which was justified with expected cancellations and delays in processing the loans. There was some concern within the KfW whether BiCO would agree on DM 50 million for the shipbuilding industry, since it was expected that Britain would try to prevent the re-emergence of German competition in the field for as long as possible. For the sectors of industry other than electricity, mining, agriculture, public utilities and the steel industry the KfW had scheduled DM 150 million which stood in sharp contrast to the recommendation of DM 700 million which was made by Erhard's Verwaltung für Wirtschaft (VfW). This deliberate over-subscription by the VfW had been heavily criticised by the KfW on previous occasions because it caused high expectations and then disappointments with individual firms when they had to be declined and because it prevented a proper financial planning in the companies[60]. For Erhard, however, it was more important to build up a psychological momentum of trust into the reconstruction by pretending investment money was available.

In spite of all German planning and the release of the DM 94 million in September the first big release of ECA money only took place in mid-December. Considering the desperate need for investment funds but even more the high hopes which the Germans had attached to the Marshall Plan this was quite some time. The delay can be partly explained with the task the ECA was faced with. The reconstruction of Europe and the political situation under which it had to take place often forced the Agency to act in a very un-coordinated way. Once again political considerations with regard to France played a role, as did the ECA's overall economic policy of monetary stability in Germany[61]. Furthermore, the Americans demanded German efforts to raise money on the capital market, an endeavour the KfW tried unsuccessfully in September. ECA counterpart funds were finally released after the signing of the Bilateral Agreement on 15 December thus giving the US an internationally binding agreement, which allowed them to intervene into Germany's economic and social and thus political affairs.

The first release of these so-called ECA tranches to the KfW amounted to DM 1036 million, of which DM 600 million were released in a first step, the rest

---

[58]KfW HA VS 65, appendix 'A' to BiCO/Sec(49)112 1 March 1949; BiCO/Sec(49)122, 9 March; see also DBBHA B 330/3367.

[59]KfW HA VS 38, KfW draft letter to BiCO, 3 May 1949.

[60]KfW HA Prot 10-1, Protokoll der 8. Sitzung, TOP 8; Protokoll der 9. Sitzung, TOP 6.

[61]Milward, *Reconstruction*, pp. 155 f; KfW HA VS 7, letter by R.M. Hanes (Chief, ECA Special Mission) to Minister Blücher, 13 December 1949.

could be withdrawn by the Germans on a monthly basis with an advanced notification to the ECA of two weeks[62]. But not all of the money could be used for new projects as the KfW had to cover the deficit of DM 273 million which had arisen from the 'at once' programme, due to the lack of GARIOA funds. Furthermore, 10 per cent of all funds, in this case DM 98.4 million, had to go to the aid of West Berlin with its special needs as the Cold War's forefront. This money was only passed through by the Kreditanstalt. By the end of 1950 the money, which was processed by the KfW some DM 937 million, was spent with only a mere DM 12 million not yet paid out[63].

The release of the second ECA tranche in late June 1950 coincided with the outbreak of the Korean War but because the projects had already been chosen the hostilities had no impact of the fund's distribution – for now. ECA II amounted to DM 1166 million of which DM 111.7 million went to West Berlin, so that the KfW was to handle DM 1054.3 million. More than half the sum had to be used to finance previously begun programmes leaving only DM 516 million for new projects. Compared to ECA I, the second tranche spread the money to more sectors of the economy, including small and medium sized refugee businesses and granted subsidies for agriculture and research of nearly DM 100 million. The distribution of the funds in this way has to be seen as the psychologically important incentives Erhard had wanted, demonstrating to small businesses that they were not forgotten in the reconstruction process.

ECA III, the launch of which the Germans had hoped for in the autumn of 1950, was not released until March 1951[64]. Originally, the Germans had expected to receive DM 1.7 billion with the third tranche but pressure from the US Congress after the outbreak of the Korean War had already reduced the sum to 1.5 billion[65]. Some members of the Kreditanstalt's Board of Directors saw this cutback as politically motivated in order to make the Germans comply with American demands, but this was denied at a board meeting by Abs in order to calm and reassure his colleagues[66]. The reason for the delay was ECA's demand for a second German work creation programme (*Arbeitsbeschaffungsprogramm*, ABP), worth about DM 1 billion[67]. In face of an unemployment rate of more than 10 per cent throughout 1950 the Americans believed that for social and political reasons such a programme was essential and had called for such a programme as early as May 1950, against the strongest possible opposition from Ludwig Erhard. In order to put pressure on the Germans so they would give up their resistance to the ABP ECA cut the scheduled aid by $35 million, roughly DM 150 million[68].

---

[62]Ibid., KfW HA Prot 10-1, Protokoll der 10. Sitzung, TOP 4.
[63]*Jb* 1950, p. 22.
[64]*Jb* 1950, p. 30.
[65]Pohl, *Wiederaufbau*, p. 82.
[66]KfW HA Prot 10-1, Ergänzende Niederschrift zur 17. Sitzung, TOP 1.
[67]Abelshauser, *Wirtschaftsgeschichte*, pp. 65 ff.; for the involvement of the KfW see *Jb* 1950, pp. 25 ff.
[68]Hardach, *Marshallplan*, p. 291.

The quarrel about a German contribution towards an investment programme went on all the summer and autumn of 1950. By November Abs announced that the ECA was officially prepared to release half of the scheduled tranche, DM 750 million, but only if there were German funds as well. Abs had more good news for his colleagues on the BoD. Only the lower ranks within the ECA, he stated, were still talking about the condition of release for the third tranche, while the higher ranks were prepared to drop any preconditions[69]. By this time West Germany had accumulated a massive trade deficit as a result of the Korean War, which threatened to destabilise European trade as a whole. That the Americans gave up their preconditions meant therefore a clear victory for the German politicians. The relative ease of the German negotiating success indicates the increased German bargaining power resulting from the Korean War, and not least from their worsened trade position. It shows also that the Americans regarded the economic crisis in Germany caused by a worldwide run on raw materials as so serious that they were prepared to give their aid without conditions just to stabilise the future ally.

In spite of this setback for the ECA, it could still claim to have scored two points. They managed to concentrate the investments of the third tranche in a few sectors, mainly in the basic industries, although the Germans at first had preferred a much broader utilisation of the funds. The altered economic situation made them change their minds and follow the US proposals[70]. Basic industries had become crucial to satisfy the increased economic demand the war in the Far East had created. Secondly, while the Germans had asked for the release of DM 1.35 billion and even hoped for 1.5 billion, the ECA gave only DM 1.02 billion, of which DM 135 million, nearly 20 per cent, had to go to Berlin to strengthen the city's economic and moral defence. Only by the end of 1951, in the face of severe economic problems, which had forced the Adenauer government directly to intervene in the economy did the Mutual Security Agency (MSA), the ECA's successor organisation increase the funds to the originally scheduled DM 1.5 billion[71].

The various programs and the utilisation for the different sectors of the economy up to the end of 1952 are shown in the table 4.1.2. Despite the political quarrels over programmes by the end of that year the Federal Republic of Germany had used DM 3703 million ECA counterpart funds for reconstruction, plus DM 625 million GARIOA funds with at least another DM 345 million for Berlin. The KfW itself handled DM 3307 million of those funds, including the first DM 310 million of money, which had arisen from interests and repayments[72]. These latter funds

---

[69]KfW HA Prot 10-1, Protokoll der 18. Sitzung, TOP 4.

[70]*Jb* 1950, p. 31.

[71]*Jb* 1951, p. 31; Hardach, *Marshallplan*, p. 316.

[72]*Jb* 1951, pp. 28 f., p. 31; *Jb* 1952, p. 37; Knapp, 'Deutschland', p. 50.

became the first proof that the system of revolving funds for strategic investment in the national economy was to become a major success.

Table 4.2.1
KfW Investment Finance with Counterpart Funds by the End of 1952
Program (in million DM)

Sector	ECA	GARIOA	ECA I	ECA II	ECA III[1]	ZT[2]	Total
Mining	50	135	150	116	130		581.0
Energy	58.5	110	220.7	134.3	356	87.5	967.0
Iron and Steel			37.9	54.8	75		167.7
Agriculture			121.5	111.2	140	22.3	395.0
Housing			81.5	115.3	280		476.8
Berlin			98.4	111.7	210		420.1
Transport and Publ. Util.	42.5	360	92.6	133.4	145	70.3	843.8
Other Industry		15	233.4	199.2		70.5	518.1
Others		5		190.1	83.7	60.2	339.0
Total	151	625	1036	1166.0	1419.7	310.8	4708.5
KfW share	94	265	937.6	1054.3	1209.7	310.8	4287.9[3]

[1] Programme still running by the end of 1952.
[2] ZT: Zins & Tilgung (Interest & Repayment).
[3] The total includes also money which was processed by the KfW without liability and funds, which were merely transferred to other financial institutions.

Source: *Jb* 1951, p. 34; *Jb* 1952, pp. 30-33; Knapp, 'Deutschland', p. 50.

The impact of the counterpart funds investments was considerable, at least in the early years, as Table 4.2.2 shows. But the counterpart funds were even more significant than these figures suggest. The funds were used in the framework of an overall reconstruction plan; that is they were used only for projects of particular importance for the whole economy, usually to help to increase and widen production in bottleneck sectors. This created a kind of multiplier effect which added to their special quality. Without investment in the bottleneck sectors other industries could not have expanded so quickly. Due to the way they were used the funds had an additional multiplier effect. Usually they only part-financed the projects, which necessitated companies to supply the rest of the money from other sources but it often helped to kick-start a project[73]. The existence of the counterpart

[73] Knapp, 'Deutschland', p. 49.

funds furthermore often had a psychological effect on the banks, too. The KfW reported some cases in which companies suddenly received previously refused loans from banks as soon as it became known that a project would be supported with ECA money[74].

Table 4.2.2
Share of ERP Loans in Gross Capital Investments in the Federal Republic 1949-1956[1]
(in per cent)

	1949	1950	1951	1952	1953	1954	1955	1956
Total	5.8	7.8	4.1	2.1	1.9	1.3	1.6	1.1
Commercial Enterprises	6.4	8.6	4.5	2.3	2.1	1.4	1.8	1.3
Industry[2]	7.1	13.3	4.6	2.3	2.0	1.9	2.1	0.6

[1] Without Berlin.
[2] Without building industry, electricity industry and small businesses.

Source: Baumgart, *Investitionen*, p. 50.

In spite of these impressive figures present research questions the economic necessity and thus the success of the Marshall Plan[75]. Its real significance in economic terms lay in its role of supplying dollar imports to Europe at times of severe dollar shortage and in initiating European economic co-operation. Its political importance, other than the psychological impact it had and the propaganda success it provided for the Americans was in the establishment of the OEEC, which provided the basics for the European integration, which was soon to come. The investment finance, which was carried out with the ERP counterpart funds could also have been made with central bank loans a fact experts already knew in 1949/50. The German administration, both that of the Bizone and later the Federal Government had political reasons for relying on the counterpart funds, as had the Americans. Using the ECA money meant a certain kind of independence from the BdL, which was after all, responsible for monetary stability. In this capacity the BdL could, and it occasionally did, block loans to the government. Secondly, loans from the counterpart funds were not regarded as public borrowing, which had a

[74] *Jb* 1949, p. 18.
[75] For the European context see Milward, *Reconstruction*, and for the German situation Abelshauser, *Westdeutschland.*

calming impact on the general population, which saw public debts traditionally as the seed of inflation[76].

The Marshall Plan and its counterpart funds allowed the Americans various rights of control and influence in the participating states. While the other European countries were eager and successful in protecting their sovereignty against this influence, occupied Germany had to allow much wider American interference[77]. In the Bizone, US controls and checks were in place at all stages, from the delivery of Marshall Plan goods and services on the establishment and the release of counterpart funds up to its utilisation with the final lender[78]. The procedure left the Germans only a right to make proposals for investments but it was certainly not a 'mutual agreement' as mentioned in articles IV and V of the Bilateral Agreement, despite some German successes in overriding American decisions[79].

Both BiCO and the ECA used their right of control and interference extensively, not least because there was still an wide-ranging list of banned or limited industries in place in Germany. Already during the 'at once' programme the Military Government cancelled the loan to the ball-bearing industry, to give just one example[80]. In the process of running ECA I and ECA II the Agency frequently interfered with the financing, in particular with export companies and housing construction where the Germans sometimes were only informed in retrospect about the introduction of tougher lending conditions.

During the course of the completion of ECA III new problems arose. On 6 March 1951 John McCloy, in his capacity as ECA Special Representative, wrote a letter to Chancellor Adenauer in which he demanded in an ultimatum a re-focusing of the German economy for defence purposes[81]. Certainly from there on did the Marshall Plan switch its focus from reconstruction to actively fighting the Cold War and preparing for a potential 'hot' war. In addition new restrictions and increased bureaucratisation had blocked the release of several hundred million DM. In particular German companies were barred from ERP loans when they came under suspicion of conducting business with Eastern Europe and the ECA even set up a 'black list' of companies for this purpose[82].

These direct controls were accompanied by other means of the Marshall Plan administration with stronger long-term effects. While the involvement of the ECA in the distribution of the funds originally was limited to 'first generation use', that is first time lending, this was soon to be changed[83]. ECA chief Hanes declared

---

[76]Abelshauser, *Wirtschaftsgeschichte*, pp. 58 f.
[77]Gabriel Kolko, Joyce Kolko, *The Limits of Power. The World and United States Foreign Policy*, New York 1972, p. 349.
[78]*Jb* 1950, p. 59.
[79]Becker, *ERP*, pp. 32 ff.
[80]KfW HA VS 65, BiCO/Memo(49)33. 30 March 1949.
[81]Reprinted in: Werner Abelshauser, 'Ansätze "korporativer Marktwirtschaft" in der Koreakrise der 50er Jahre', in: *VfZ* no. 30 (1982) pp. 715 ff.
[82]KfW HA Prot 10-1, Protokoll der 22. Sitzung, TOP 5.
[83]Becker, *ERP*, p. 30.

on 13 December 1949 in a letter to Minister Blücher that the repaid loans had to be used to set up '... a revolving source of capital...' within the framework of European recovery[84]. This meant that the German government, although the counterpart special accounts were kept in its name, had only restricted rights of disposal, even for the 'second generation' funds. In other words all new projects scheduled to be financed by repayments had to be agreed by the ECA as well (unless they were for the continuation of previous programmes) leaving only the small amount of interest payments for free German disposal[85]. In this way the Americans could determine what constituted an important investment and they retained a considerable influence on the development of the German economy.

As already mentioned, two amendments to the Economic Cooperation Act in 1952 (the Zablocky Amendment) and 1953, the US Congress extended American influence on the interests and repayments. Although they were only a formality from the mid-1950s onward, American control over the funds remained until 1960. This meant that the US had official control over the re-use of interest and repayments amounting to about DM 300 million per year. The *Zins und Tilgung*, or ZT programme (Interest and Repayment) was the KfW's main source of refinance until 1959 and provided more than half its funds every year[86].

The ZT programme and its operation caused a serious fall out between the Kreditanstalt für Wiederaufbau and Blücher's Ministry for the Marshall Plan. In October 1950 Blücher had asked the ECA to confirm that the banks had to immediately return all interest and repayments apart from their processing fees to the Special Accounts from where the money had to be disbursed again[87]. In doing so Blücher tried to increase his influence on the Special Assets not only vis-à-vis the banks, but also against his rival ministries of Economics and Finance. In spite of Blücher's claim the KfW was still authorised to extend repayments and even to allow their deferral[88]. In August 1952, in a further attempt to tighten his grip on the funds, Blücher issued a new credit authorisation, which limited the KfW's freedom of operation. From now on every deferment of repayments exceeding DM 500,000 had to be authorised by the ministry. One month later, Blücher went a step further. From now on there should be individual negotiations between his ministry and the KfW in each individual case which exceeded the limit. Worried about its independence (the Kreditanstalt recently had been burdened with a dubious loan to Yugoslavia without consultation) the KfW did not agree to this and threatened to stop all loans within the ZT programme. When Blücher did not give in to their

[84]KfW HA VS 7, letter ECA chief Hanes to Minister Blücher, 13 December 1949.
[85]Becker, *ERP*, p. 30.
[86]KfW HA Prot 10-1, Protokoll der 22. Sitzung, TOP 5; *Jb* 1951, p. 46; *Jb* various years (1953-1959), passim.
[87]KfW HA VS 118, subfile 'Wiedereinsatz von Zins und Tilgung', letter by Blücher to ECA Special Mission in Germany, 20 October 1950.
[88]KfW HA VS 178, note 'Übernahme der vollen Haftung der ERP-Mittel', 7 May 1956.

demands, the KfW indeed stopped the ZT programme. In doing so the Anstalt brought most of the centrally planned reconstruction to a halt. Since this was not their intention the Board of Managers tried to negotiate a solution to the situation. Two days later, in a letter to Ministerialrat Albrecht of the Bundesministerium für den Marshallplan (BMP), kept in a personal and friendly tone, Herbert Martini tried to defuse the situation and suggested negotiating a settlement. Albrecht's reply, an unusually long letter of seven pages was even more friendly in its tone but in its last paragraph it contained a clear threat that there was no legal regulation which made the KfW the sole lending institution. But the ministry's threat was double-edged. Withdrawing the KfW's status as *Hauptleihinstitut* would have meant setting up an institutional alternative which would have caused a severe and lasting disruption of the financing process at a crucial time of the reconstruction. To avoid this, the ministry started to negotiate with the Kreditanstalt. By March 1953 an agreement was reached which gave the KfW very much its own way. As before, it could decide on the deference of interests and repayments in its own right, it had only to stick to some formal criteria[89]. A lasting agreement finally came about with the signing of the ERP Special Assets Administration Act in August 1953. The law stated that the minister could authorise the main lending institutes to extend and defer the terms of repayments when they thought it necessary and appropriate. The affair demonstrated that the men in charge of the KfW, though usually loyal to ministerial requests, were powerful enough to defend their position and independence against any attempts to curb it. This power struggle was the only one of its kind during the period under investigation and drew the lines for the future.

The Mutual Security Agency and The Foreign Operations Administration

The attempts by the Americans to use economic aid for the purpose of military expansion in Europe finds its prime example in the Mutual Security Agency (MSA) and its successor organisation, the Foreign Operations Administration (FOA). Originally, the Marshall Plan was scheduled to run for four years until June 1952. The outbreak of the Korean War in June 1950 and in particular the intervention of Chinese troops in November that year predestined the premature end of the ECA[90]. The Americans did not stop all aid immediately as the example of ECA III has shown. It continued but on a smaller scale and therefore helped to make it clear to the Germans that there would be no ECA IV tranche as originally planned. The

[89]KfW HA VS 162, subfile 'BMBes, Vereinbarungen'; letter BMP, StSek. Goedecke to KfW, 15 September 1952; telex no. 977 to BMWi, 15 October 1952, containing a copy of the original telex to BMP, 13 October 1952; letter Martini to Albrecht, 15 October 1952; letter Albrecht to Martini, 21 October 1952; letter BMP to St.Sek. a.D. Binder, 5 March 1953. The criteria were not named.

[90]Michael Hogan, *The Marshall Plan. America, Britain and the Reconstruction of Western Europe 1947-1952,* Cambridge, New York 1987, p. 380.

change in American policy and its new direction became most evident in October 1951 when President Truman, under strong pressure from the public and Congress established the Mutual Security Agency and abolished the ECA in December that year. The MSA's task was to co-ordinate economic and military aid programmes with a clear shift towards the latter and to continue the work of the ECA. In reality, however, the established departments of the US administration took over the controls of the programmes, the State Department the economic aid and the War Department the military aid. The MSA, in consequence, lost the ECA's ministerial status and was reduced to a government 'agency' with its main task being to complete the European reconstruction programme, but now with a clear focus on defence and the Cold War[91].

While the MSA was only the visible sign of the militarisation of aid, pressure on the Germans 'to contribute towards western defence' had occurred before. The first climax of this pressure was the letter US High Commissioner John McCloy, in his capacity as ERP Special Representative to Germany, had written to Chancellor Adenauer on 6 March 1951. McCloy demanded immediate and direct action by the German government for control and direction of the economy towards a defence programme. He threatened to withhold further economic aid and, more importantly, any allocation of raw materials to West Germany in case of non-compliance and added a list of expected actions, such as control of currency, investment and state allocation of raw materials. All of these demands stood in complete opposition to West Germany's economic policy. It is of some significance that McCloy issued the demands as ECA representative and not as High Commissioner. The ambiguity of his jobs as High Commissioner which included representing German interests and as ECA Representative which was more concerned with overall American aims is obvious here once more. But the event and the language chosen made it clear that Washington expected a German defence contribution, at this stage even if it would carry the risk of jeopardising the reconstruction process. This was a total reversal of American policy since until then they had regarded West German reconstruction as the most vital part of their European policy. Now defence against a potential threat from the East had become the first priority. Adenauer replied that because of the negative psychological impact such measures would have on the population West Germany's defence contribution could best be achieved by improving the standard of living – or at least not letting it deteriorate – in order to create a moral and a psychological barrier against East German and Soviet Communism. Instead of state intervention he suggested a system of self-administration run by German industry[92].

Adenauer's reply was nothing but a weak attempt to escape American pressure. In reality German industry was already producing military equipment for

---

[91]Hardach, *Marshallplan*, pp. 130 ff.
[92]Abelshauser, 'Marktwirtschaft', pp. 737 ff.

the western countries, mainly in specialised sectors like optics and precision mechanics[93]. The *Bundesverband der Deutschen Industrie* (BDI, Federation of German Industry), certainly not without self-interest, suggested to some of its committees to support the industries of other western countries by taking on all kinds of orders for them, except for military hardware. In doing so the German industry would free some capacity for military production in those countries and, at the same time, expand the German export market. The self-imposed restriction regarding military production of which the BDI spoke was a hollow one. Engines, lorries, caterpillar tracks for armoured combat vehicles, optical equipment and even uniforms and individual pieces of military equipment (*militärische Einzelgeräte*) were not regarded as armaments by the Federation[94]. Still, contributions to western defence in terms of industrial production remained on a very small scale. Germany's real contribution was to bear the costs for Allied troops in Germany, which were some DM 7.4 billion in 1951-52, or about 6.6 per cent of the country's Gross Domestic Product (GDP)[95].

The general feeling of German business towards armaments in March 1952 remained reserved and is perhaps best described in the KfW's annual report:

> 'Im Gegensatz zu vielen anderen Staaten ist Westdeutschland – gleichviel aus welchen Gründen – bisher weitgehend davon verschont geblieben, die Arbeitskräfte seiner Bevölkerung, das verfügbare Kapital und die Rohstoffe in volkswirtschaftlich unproduktive Investitionen einzusetzen'[96].

With this kind of attitude from the Germans it was no surprise that the MSA in early 1952 argued that no further aid should be given to the Federal Republic unless the question of defence contributions had been solved[97]. However, the term 'defence contribution' was not clearly defined. It included more than just armaments production but anything and any kind of equipment, which was of use for armed forces, including, the Germans argued, their payment of the occupation costs. When the MSA finally released the first money to the KfW, new regulations were applied. The most important one, a result of changes to the 1952 MSA Act, stated that any aid given had to be classified in advance as a grant or a loan. The first MSA money was indeed a loan for the KfW by the Export Import Bank, amounting to $16.9 million, nearly DM 71 million[98]. All other funds were consequently given as grants. This money, known in the KfW as *MSA IV*

[93]PRO FO 371 93725 CE(W)1104/3; 1104/6; 1104/18; FO 371 93726 CE(W)1104/28.
[94]PRO FO 371 93272 CE(W) 1104/45/G, minutes of a BDI meeting, provided to the British by 'a delicate source'.
[95]Hardach, *Marshallplan*, p. 238.
[96]*Jb* 1951, p. 25. ' In contrast to many other states West Germany has been spared so far – for what ever reasons - from utilising the labour of its population, the available capital and raw materials for economically unproductive investments' (translation AG).
[97]Hardach, *Marshallplan*, p. 242.
[98]*Jb* 1952, p. 33.

Investitionsprogramm (*Anleihe*) (MSA IV Investment Programme (Loan)) remained the only loan by the MSA. For this particular reason the DM 71 million never became a part of the ERP Special Assets, although it was administered by it[99]. The funds were the basis for the KfW's 'DM 309 million programme', which went into sectors important for the defence purpose in its wider sense. It is another indication for the militarisation of the programme that for the first time some of this money could be used to rebuild previously dismantled plants (what the Germans called 'Remontage'). Until then this had been prohibited under ECA instructions because most of the plants had been regarded as capable of producing for armaments[100]. For the German economy this meant that some of the country's most famous plants, such as Krupp and Thyssen, did not have to scrape around for small credits but could rely for their rebuilding on counterpart funds for the first time.

The militarisation continued with the launch of two more credit programmes in 1953, the MSA Investment Programme IV and the MSA Productivity Programme, which both were intended by the Americans to strengthen the European Defence Community (EDC). MSA Investment IV had the size of DM 150 million and was announced by the MSA administration in a letter to Minister Blücher in March 1953. Loans were bound to certain conditions in order to strengthen the West German defence contribution. Companies eligible for funds either had to produce goods, which were needed by NATO or EDC countries, including parts or semi finished parts for such goods, or they had to be for firms which were suppliers for such companies in the first place. Under a third condition loans could be given to a company which bought new equipment or switched production if they were otherwise unable to fulfil defence contracts. The MSA conceded that because the conditions were so tough, half the money could go into basic industries to provide long-term support for future defence programmes. However, the MSA determined the size of the aid and the sectors which should benefit from it and the money had to be paid back into the Special Accounts in two instalments by 30 September 1954, allowing only short-term investments. To distinguish between both parts, the defence contribution was called MSA IV A and the loans to the basic industries MSA IV B[101].

In order to make any economic sense, that is to use the money for necessary medium and long-term investments, the KfW had to redeem the MSA IV B loans after a year with money originating from interests and repayments and due for loans in the ZT programme. The Foreign Operations Administration, which succeeded the MSA after its dissolution in July 1953 by President Eisenhower because of inefficiency, extended the MSA IV B programme for one more year, allowing the

[99]Carstens, *Bund*, p. 210.
[100]*Jb* 1952, p. 33.
[101]KfW HA BS 81, letter by Michael Harris (chief, MSA Special Mission) to the Minister for the Marshall Plan, 17 March 1953; Ibid., note 2 September 1954.

KfW to use the ZT money in the way it was originally scheduled. The extension became possible because the loans for defence developed so slowly that the immediate use of the 'B' money for direct rearmament would have been useless. Following the Federal Republic's accession to NATO the programmes were renamed MSA IV Defence Programme and comprised the full sum of DM 150 million[102].

It is certainly true that the defence programme was the KfW programme, which developed most slowly. German industry either had no more interest in armaments production following the experience of the past or was able to cover the necessary investments from other sources, most likely from profits. It has to be kept in mind that the cheap money from the Kreditanstalt für Wiederaufbau meant American controls and thus insight into company finance and therefore firms tried to avoid these loans whenever possible. In 1957 DM 25 million of the programme were used for housing constructions for refugees still living in old barracks which had to be used again to house West Germany's new army[103]. The MSA IV programme dragged on at least until 1967, but by then the Americans had given up their right of influence[104]. The administrative burden had become bigger than the political and economic benefit.

In contrast to the MSA Defence Programme, the Productivity Programme of DM 117 million did not suffer from slow progress but it could not commence until autumn 1953, due to extensive preparation works necessary to comply with all American demands[105]. Most of the money, DM 70 million was used to increase productivity of small and medium sized companies by introducing cost reduction and rationalisation schemes. The debtors had to apply for the loans at the Institute for the Promotion of Productivity in Frankfurt before the application went to the KfW, so the processing of applications took some time. Since no loan should exceed DM 100,000 there were a large number of requests, which increased the KfW's workload and prevented a more speedily processing so that by the end of the year only DM 7.2 million had been confirmed to the final debtors. Furthermore, the MSA demanded that all loans given via banks had to be topped up by them, which caused further delay. However, the fact that the KfW received nearly half the money by the end of 1953 and did not mention the programme in its 1954 annual report indicates that it had been wound up in that year[106].

---

[102]KfW HA BS 81, Vermerk für den Vorstand, 16 June 1954; ibid., note 2 September 1954; Hardach, *Marshallplan*, p. 134.

[103]KfW HA BS 82, letter Bundesministerium für wirtschaftliche Zusammenarbeit (BMwiZ) to KfW, 25 March 1957.

[104]Ibid., letter Bundesschatzministerium (BMSch) to KfW 8 August 1963, attached a letter from BMSch to BMWi, same date, which says that the USA in accordance with an agreement in 1960 would release the MSA IV funds for other purpose. By then DM 5.5 million had still been unused. See also KfW HA BS 81, table MSA IV Defence Programme, 31 December 1962.

[105]*Jb* 1953, pp. 40 f.

[106]*Jb* 1953, pp. 41 ff.

In the fiscal year 1953-54 American aid for West Germany under the ERP and its successor programmes terminated. The last transaction, a grant called FOA V, was once more a subsidy for the US farming industry. Agricultural products worth $15 million were given to the Federal Republic. The DM counterpart, 63 million was to be used exclusively for housing constructions for refugees from East Germany in West Berlin and in West Germany[107]. The high number of GDR refugees in 1953 had worsened an already tense housing situation especially in Berlin so the money provided another propaganda opportunity, demonstrating the strength of the Western economic system and the ability of its construction industry to provide the necessary housing. The FOA itself became International Cooperation Administration (ICA) as part of the State Department in 1955. In Germany it carried out its task from within the American Embassy but its main area of operation had moved to countries of the developing world[108].

After the Cold War had turned into a hot war in Korea American attitudes in Europe changed considerably. Aid was no longer a primary means of reconstruction; it had become a weapon of the Cold War and as such was applied in a wide variety of ways. Obviously, production of military equipment in the widest possible sense was one target. Perhaps more important, though, was the psychological impact the continuing aid had in West Germany and the propagandistic advantages which could be gained from such things as the housing scheme for GDR refugees. Thus it is no surprise that Germany's population by and large saw America and its aid as the country's salvation. By the end of the ECA/MSA programme West Germany was regaining its prosperity and had become a staunch bulwark against East German and Soviet Communism, a far cry from the deprived, starving and politically quite unreliable remnants of a country, which it must have been to American eyes in 1946-47. In this way the Marshall Plan and its successor programmes were a full success for the planners in the US State Department and the Pentagon.

---

[107] *Jb* 1953, p. 32; *Jb* 1954, p. 52.
[108] Hardach, *Marshallplan*, p. 134.

Chapter 5

German Money: Improvisation and Improvements

The history and the development of German funds for the Kreditanstalt für Wiederaufbau is to a very large extent a reflection of West Germany's situation as a whole in the first one and a half decades after World War II. The Cold War led to a change in US politics and brought, for example, an easing of American restrictions on prohibited industries and the release of German industrialists who had been held as war criminals. This certainly helped to smooth political relations between both countries and may have helped to get over the disappointment which unrealistic German expectations in the European Recovery Programme may have caused. Contrary to German expectations Marshall Plan funds were not nearly large enough to supply all the money necessary for reconstruction. In the period from July 1948 to June 1949 DM 15.8 billion were raised to finance the investment goods industry, a figure which rose to DM 188 billion (in 1950 prices) by 1956[1]. During the same time only DM 5.4 billion of counterpart funds from the Marshall Plan programme were available. In retrospect, this raises the question whether German expectations of the Marshall Plan were unrealistically high or their planning bad or whether Erhard had reconstruction priorities, which could indeed be covered with only an extended aid programme.

Furthermore, the Americans had different intentions of how to use ERP money. For them, the Marshall Plan should provide help for self-help[2]. On the financial side, the ERP should encourage the Germans to raise considerable amounts of German funds for the reconstruction process, while on the psychological and propaganda side, the Americans hoped to reap profit from the scheme as well. But the scarcity of German funds both private and public made reconstruction more difficult. Already during the reading of the KfW bill in the Economic Council in August 1948 strong doubts were voiced whether Bizonia could provide any funds and contribute significantly to the rebuilding of the country in the near future[3]. Following the currency reform Germany's capital market had virtually disappeared. While the reform had not touched material assets

---

[1]KfW HA VS 7, Memorandum on investment finance by Minister Blücher for Mr Hanes, dated 3 February 1950; Baumgart, *Investitionen*, p. 8.

[2]Werner Abelshauser, 'Hilfe und Selbsthilfe', in: Hans-Jürgen Schröder (ed.), *Marshall Plan und Westdeutscher Wiederaufstieg*, Stuttgart 1990, pp. 150 ff.

[3]*Wortprotokolle*, vol. 2, p. 773.

it had wiped out large parts of money assets. This particularly hit small savers who had already suffered in the 1923 hyperinflation. Since these people had now lost their savings twice in 25 years there was no reason and incentive for them to take their money to the banks or save in any other form of investment. Contrary to its later reputation, public confidence in the new currency was not very high, which is another reason why people did not save[4]. Instead money was used for consumption. Memories of the Great Depression, the Nazi armaments policy, the war, and the deprivation of the post-war years had caused a huge backlog of consumer demand which was partly released after the currency reform. During the second half of 1948, the man on the street was more interested in spending money on consumer goods than in savings, which of course had detrimental effects on the capital market. The situation changed slowly throughout the following decade and by 1959 *Bausparkassen* (building societies) had about DM 4 billion in assets as compared to DM 0.4 billion in 1950, while insurance companies had increased their funds from DM 0.6 billion to DM 3 billion over the same period[5].

Investment finance in the early 1950s, therefore, could not rely on the capital market and money had to be found from other sources. Tax reforms and price deregulation, which were enacted in 1948 in order to support the currency reform only favoured the consumer goods industry and produced very negative effects for the basic industries. With their prices freed and thanks to generous tax depreciation consumer goods industries could reinvest their profits, which gave them an advantage over basic industries the prices of which remained fixed. As a result, the traditional order for capital investment, capital market, state, self-finance, was turned on its head[6]. This had severe consequences for the whole national economy since self financing could not be controlled or directed into those industries which were essential for long-term economic reconstruction. In the views of both American and German experts this constituted a waste of financial resources, which posed a threat to reconstruction as a whole because the basic industries would lose out in the search for investment capital. The only way to counter this development was by channelling counterpart funds and German money through the KfW into those industries, which were most important for the recovery[7].

Until about mid-1949 there was another reason for the lack of German funds, namely the amateurism and sheer incompetence of the German authorities, in particular on the *Länder* level. This was paired with the egoistic self-interest of the *Länder*. It was only the American Military Government's threat to stop any further Marshall aid if there was not better German co-operation, which eventually

[4]The exchange rate of the DM against the Swiss Franc dropped from Sfr 45 in June 1948 to Sfr 18.5 in November 1948 at the Zürich stock exchange. See Dickhaus, *Bundesbank*, p. 66.

[5]Hankel, *Kapitalverteilung*, p. 37.

[6]Abelshauser, *Wirtschaftsgeschichte*, pp. 72 f.

[7]NA RG 260, OMGUS, Finance Adviser, box 111, folder 1, BiCO letter (BiCO/Memo (49)86) to ECA Germany, Supplementary Memorandum; *Jb* 1949, pp. 14 ff., esp. p. 16.

led to improvements[8]. Two years later at the height of the Korean War, during the negotiations for the release of the ECA III funds the Americans had to repeat such a threat, in order to achieve better German economic co-operation with their goals. By then the West German economy was in better shape than in 1949 so that it could contribute more easily although the Germans managed to avert the main American demand for a public investment programme. However, the fact that the Americans waited for two years to repeat their threat also shows that they recognised and took into account Germany's financial difficulties.

The situation on the financial markets finally returned to normal in 1953-54 in the aftermath of the signing of the London Debt Agreement in which West Germany recognised all pre- and post-war debts of the German Reich and the zones of occupation respectively[9]. After the settlement in London private foreign capital returned to the German financial market and helped to ease the shortage of investment capital. By that time the German economy was on its way to accumulate a huge capital surplus due to the export boom, which had been caused by an undervalued DM[10].

The following three subchapters will deal in detail with German and KfW attempts to raise investment capital and the problems they were faced with. They will look in detail at the years 1949-52, the most difficult years on the capital market, which saw a lot of 'improvisation' and deals with the Bank deutscher Länder, which were on the edge of the KfW's legal framework. Furthermore, the history of the KfW's bonds will be explored. It shows most clearly the improvements which took place in the 1950s German capital market but it also stresses once more the controversy between Ludwig Erhard and Fritz Schäffer on matters of economic and fiscal policy. Finally, a look will be taken at the *Investitionshilfe Gesetz*, which is of special importance to West German economic history. It signified a failure of large parts of Erhard's economic policy and brought a restoration of heavy industry's political power and marks, therefore, a turning point in the economic policy of the young republic.

5.1 BdL Money, 'Arbeitsbeschaffungsprogramm' and KfW Assets

When the Kreditanstalt für Wiederaufbau began its work on 2 January 1949 its biggest problem was funding. With a capital of only DM 1 million the Kreditanstalt was hardly able to fulfil American demands for a German

[8]KfW HA VS 38, note by von Ilberg, 14 June 1949 regarding a meeting in the VfW on 12 June 1949; Tröger, *Interregnum*, passim.

[9]For details and the importance of the Debt Agreement see: Abs, *Entscheidungen;* and Hans Peter Schwarz (ed.), *Die Wiederherstellung des deutschen Kredits. Das Londoner Schuldenabkommen*, Rhöndorfer Gespräche, vol. 4, Stuttgart 1982.

[10]See details in Hölscher, *Entwicklungsmodel.*

contribution to reconstruction finance. So one of the most urgent tasks for the Boards was to find sources to refinance the bank's business.

The idea of using the fixed assets of the currency reform, amounting to about DM 5 billion, was soon dropped for political and economic reasons[11]. Another alternative to refinance the KfW was attempted by the VfW in December 1948 when Herbert Martini negotiated with the German Mail in order to receive a long-term loan from mail saving accounts but by early January 1949 the KfW's hopes for DM 100 million were dashed because the German Mail insisted on giving the money only on a short-term basis. Instead DM 60 million could be borrowed from the unemployment insurance until the end of 1949, which was, however, only a fraction of the DM 400 million the KfW had expected from the insurance funds. But with the numbers of unemployed rising in 1949 it was not possible to receive more funds from this source. Although the situation on the labour market improved steadily from 1951 onward, the KfW was to receive only a total of DM 229 million from the *Bundesanstalt für Arbeitslosenversicherung und Arbeitsvermittlung* (BfAA) until 1958, a far cry from the sum expected in 1949[12].

With the first attempts to raise money a partial or even a total failure, the KfW was soon faced with its last option, borrowing from the Bank deutscher Länder. But according to the KfW law, borrowing from the central bank was allowed only in exceptional circumstances and on a short-term basis. This clause had been introduced in order to prevent unlimited credit expansion, which might have undermined the stability of the currency. If the rule had been applied strictly, the Kreditanstalt would have had serious trouble finding any money at all. Instead, the KfW was forced already during the 'at once' programme to ask for BdL money, as soon as it became clear that the GARIOA funds were not sufficient to cover the whole sum of DM 555 million scheduled under the programme. DM 273 million had to be pre-financed by the BdL, in anticipation of the expected release of ECA funds[13]. For political reasons, in order to satisfy American demands for German funds, but also to create confidence in the reconstruction process, the BdL loan was highly significant for the KfW's work at this stage. Since the money was given only until the release of the ECA I tranche, this transaction constituted only short-term lending which was within the framework of the law. The next scheme, the KfW's participation in the work creation programme and the way it was financed, crossed the border of what the law actually allowed.

By the end of 1949, due to record unemployment, the Adenauer government was under severe pressure both from the Allies and the Bundestag to produce a

---

[11]Pohl, *Wiederaufbau*, p. 37. Fixed assets were saving accounts or parts of saving accounts, which were not released after the currency reform. This was done with the intention to limit the money supply and thus to stabilise the value of the new money, but also to gain a critical manoeuvre mass of capital for emergencies.

[12]Pohl, *Wiederaufbau*, p. 48; KfW HS Prot 10-1, Protokoll der 2. Sitzung, TOP 3; *Jb* 1949, p. 33; KfW HA BS 45, Kreditfinanzierungs-Übersicht.

[13]*Jb* 1949, p. 22. The remaining DM 17 million was covered by bonds issued by electricity companies.

work creation scheme. The Americans were worried that the political system in the Federal Republic could be destabilised by two million unemployed. For them, the economic situation created two danger areas. For once, they feared that the Soviet Union or East Germany would use it for Communist propaganda thus drawing West Germany closer into their orbit. From the opposite side of the political spectrum they saw the danger of a resurgence of Nazism lurking. Although Economics Minister Erhard and the BdL were strongly opposed to the scheme it was prepared by an inter-ministerial working party on 2 February 1950 and passed by the Cabinet one week later[14]. The programme amounted to DM 3.4 billion but it was made up of various different programmes most of which had been developed some time before, so that only DM 0.6 billion was genuine new money[15]. As a gesture to convince the public of the government's real determination to fight unemployment, the Ministry of Labour instead of Erhard received overall control of the programme, although Erhard had claimed himself to be in charge of this kind of economic policy[16]. And indeed, only a fraction of the money went into real work creation, the largest part was used for investment finance and capital-intensive expansion of productivity[17].

The Kreditanstalt für Wiederaufbau was involved in the ABP in two ways. Some parts of the scheme were planned to be refinanced with expected ECA funds. For those, which were used for housing construction, the KfW again received short- term credits from the BdL. For the other part, worth DM 300 million it was necessary to 'strike special arrangements with the BdL'[18]. These 'special arrangements' meant that the KfW had to give the central bank some of their bonds in the face value of the loan. In addition, the BdL received a promise from the Federal Government to repay or take over these non-ECA loans after five years. In other words and contrary to the law the KfW received long-term loans from the Bank deutscher Länder. The BdL was quite reluctant to agree to the deal. Already during the planning stages of the ABP, Wilhelm Vocke, the BdL President, had written to Adenauer to remind him that the BdL had lent DM 500 million to the KfW and that the public believed that this was ECA money[19]. Vocke's letter indicates that the BdL knew that they were covering up transactions, which could spark inflationary tendencies and it was for the sake of avoiding inflation that the central bank was reluctant to refinance the Kreditanstalt. The BdL feared creating a precedent which in the future would allow credit expansion 'bis ins Blaue'[20].

[14]Volker Hentschel, *Ludwig Erhard. Ein Politikerleben*, München, Landsberg/L. 1996, p. 113; *Kabinettsprotokolle*, vol. 2, pp. 193 ff, esp. p. 194.
[15]*Jb* 1950. p. 25; Abelshauser, *Wirtschaftsgeschichte*, pp. 66 f., speaks of DM 5.4 billion.
[16]KfW HA VS 25, Abwicklung des Arbeitsbeschaffungsprogramms.
[17]KfW HA VS 10, Bericht über das Arbeitsbeschaffungsprogramm der Bundesregierung 1950.
[18]Ibid.; *Jb* 1950, pp. 26, 42.
[19]KfW HA VS 10, Bericht über das Arbeitsbeschaffungsprogramm der Bundesregierung 1950; DBB HA B 330/02011, letter Vocke to Adenauer, 2 February 1950.
[20]Pohl, *Wiederaufbau*, pp. 94 f.

Although the BdL was hesitant to lend the DM 300 million to the KfW, it received another DM 100 million, later extended to DM 116 million. The money was only used to improve the production capacity of export-oriented industries[21]. Again, this loan was scheduled to be redeemed by ECA III money, but when the ECA tranche was finalised, there was only half the sum listed for export industries and these were consequently used to pay for new projects instead of paying off the BdL. This move by the German authorities has to be understood as a reaction to American pressure to add further German money to support the ECA III programme and the ECA's cut of the third tranche when the Germans failed to do so. This was even stated in the KfW's 1950 annual report where it was called an additional credit creation programme[22]. In the following year the affair was closed with a succinct statement: 'Damit dürften die zur Finanzierung der Exportindustrie von der BdL gewährten Vorschüsse bis zur Rückzahlung der Darlehen den Charakter der Vorfinanzierung endgültig verloren haben und mithin als echte Kreditschöpfung gelten'[23]. But by then the economic situation had changed, as had the KfW's legal position in regard to central bank loans.

The work creation scheme in many respects was a test case. It proved that the KfW could act as a go-between for the BdL and the government in cases when credit expansion was politically asked for but economically unwise. It was not the government which received the loans but a highly respectable financial institution. The KfW passed its test as the government's economic emergency service. The Kreditanstalt proved that it would step in for the government when the latter was restricted by political and economic considerations. Consequently, it came as no surprise when the 1951 amendment to the KfW law allowed long-term borrowing from the Central Bank[24].

The work creation scheme itself which government officials, in an attempt of political 'spin', called 'Adenauer Programm' had to be regarded as a failure[25]. Nothing demonstrates this more clearly than the fact that nowadays it is no longer known as 'Adenauer Programm'. Because the people in charge, most notably Ludwig Erhard, never had a real intention actively to intervene into the labour market, the programme was doomed to failure right from the start. It has to be regarded as a propaganda exercise by the government in order to calm the public and to satisfy demands from the Americans. When the Korean War broke out, the

[21]*Jb* 1950, p. 28; 1951, pp. 35 f. In addition to this 'Investitionsprogramm exportintensive Industrie', there was another special programme to subsidise exports. This, too, was based on an extra BdL credit line and will be investigated in chapter 3.5.

[22]*Jb* 1950, pp. 31 f.; *Jb* 1951, p. 35.

[23]*Jb* 1951, p. 35 'The advanced payments made by the BdL in order to finance the export industry have therefore definitely lost their character as pre-financed funds until their repayment and thus have to be regarded as real credit creation' (translation AG).

[24]KfW Gesetz, 1951, Art. 4.

[25]KfW HA VS 25, Vertraulicher Vermerk by von Ilberg regarding meeting with the Finance Ministry, 13 April 1950.

little planning which had been done in the process was overtaken by events very quickly[26].

The actions of the Kreditanstalt and the Bank deutscher Länder were driven by the necessity to raise funds to keep investments for the reconstruction going. Although it was the KfW, which infringed the law by taking long-term money from the central bank, it was the BdL which bore the responsibility for striking the balance between a stable currency and supplying the money for the reconstruction process. That the BdL gave the loans in spite of the KfW law and its own reservation indicates that the money was indeed urgently needed and that the risk of inflation was not imminent, although the Korean War caused a temporary upsurge in prices.

The Kreditanstalt started operations with a humble DM 1 million, provided as the bank's company capital (*Grundkapital*) in equal share by both the *Länder* and the Bizonal administration[27]. The lack of sufficient funds meant that the KfW had no cash reserves for emergencies and this demanded urgent alteration. According to Pohl, Abs wrote to General Clay to ask for a special donation from counterpart funds in order to bring this change about and to increase the KfW's capital. And indeed the Kreditanstalt received a special contribution from the ECA in September 1949. However, it is unlikely Abs' letter was the reason for this donation[28]. First, General Clay had no authority over the ERP counterpart funds and the GARIOA funds were already drained. Second, Clay had retired as Military Governor in May 1949, four months before the KfW received the money. The real reason why the Americans gave the DM 94 million to the Anstalt was Berlin. Cut off from electrical power supplies following the Berlin Blockade, the western sectors of the city were not economically viable in the long-term. The need to build new power plants had been recognised by the British as early as 1946 when they started a first rehabilitation programme[29]. The crucial question was how to finance the project. Even before the blockade had ended, Abs had told members of the West Berlin administration that this question was so highly political that it was beyond BiCO's competence and that the decision was most likely to be taken in Washington itself. To the Americans he stated that the question was not 'if' but 'how' the project would be financed[30]. It appears that after the Allies approved the request of the Berliner Licht- und Elektrizitätswerke AG (BEWAG) for money the quickest way to channel the money to Berlin was via the Kreditanstalt. On 23 September 1949 the KfW received a letter from the Allied Banking Commission,

---

[26]Abelshauser, *Wirtschaftsgeschichte*, pp. 67 f.

[27]There is a difference between the German words 'Grundkapital' which means company capital in the sense of basic capital equipment and 'Eigenkapital' which has a wider meaning, including all the assets a company has acquired.

[28]Pohl, *Wiederaufbau*, p. 66.

[29]NA RG 260, OMGUS, Records of the High Commissioner for Germany, Records of the Allied Banking Commission, box 8, BiCO letter (BiCO/Memo(49)81) to Norman Collinson regarding the release of Counterpart Funds for Berlin, 1 August 1949.

[30]KfW HA VS 66, note 8 April 1949.

which announced the release of DM 94 million. Although the money was given as a gift several conditions were attached. DM 44 million, topped up by additional German funds had to go to the BEWAG's new power plant the rest was to be used in support of the mining industry[31].

With the gift the ECA killed several birds with one stone. Money for Berlin gave a very important political signal, while the German financial contribution to the deal fulfilled a further US demand. The loans to the coal mining industry were given at a crucial time, when the KfW was struggling to support the industry prior to the release of counterpart money. Finally, the positive effect for the KfW was a huge increase in its *Eigenkapital*, which in the long-run improved its ability to issue bonds. But it is safe to say that for the Americans this was only a positive side effect and contrary to the KfW's Annual Report the money was not given for this purpose in the first place[32].

Due to the steady influx of interest payments on the loans given from the DM 94 million, the 'ECA Special Allotment' (*ECA Sonderzuweisung*) grew considerably in size and reached DM 130 million in 1955 and DM 158 million in 1960. The Special Allotment was to play an important role in the redrafting of the KfW law in 1961 but by then it had already been surpassed in size by the legally required reserves (*Gesetzliche Rücklage*)[33]. This reserve was requested by the KfW law (article 10). The Kreditanstalt had to pay all net profits into the reserves until they reached 10 per cent of its liabilities. Any further profit should then be divided between the Bizonal administration and the federal government respectively and the *Länder*. However, due to increasing business, the 10 per cent mark was never reached although the profits rose as well[34]. The 1961 amendment to the law changed the system of the legal reserves totally. Before the amendment the reserves had reached DM 181 million in 1960 so that it constituted a considerable amount of capital for emergency finance. Although the KfW's *Eigenkapital* rose from DM 1 million in 1949 to about DM 340 million in 1960 it was only a second ranking source of German funds for the Anstalt. By this time the KfW's own bonds provided most money and their significance will consequently be investigated in the next chapter.

---

[31]PRO 371 76984 CE 3417; KfW HA Prot 10-1, Protokoll der 10. Sitzung, TOP 2; Pohl, *Wiederaufbau*, p. 66.

[32]*Jb* 1949, p.38.

[33]*Jb* 1955, 1959, 1960, Annual Balance Sheet.

[34]The net profits rose from DM 1.2 million in 1949 to 12.8 million in 1951 and to 22 million in 1960, see *Jb* 1951, 1960, Annual Balance Sheets.

5.2 The Bonds of the Kreditanstalt für Wiederaufbau

The issuing of bonds by the KfW is of special interest for various reasons. Although the amount of money raised by the sale of bonds between 1949 and 1961 never reached the volume of the counterpart funds, it was, for some years, the biggest single source of money for the Kreditanstalt. In a way, the changes and developments of the West German economy in the 1950s are best reflected in this part of the Anstalt's history. It highlights the political rows and infighting between the Economics Ministry and the Finance Ministry and it shows some of the KfW's financial manoeuvres. These aspects help to underline the economic and political significance the KfW held and the business it conducted.

Not everybody was glad that the Kreditanstalt für Wiederaufbau should be empowered to issue bonds. Already during the legislative process the *Länderrat's* Finance Committee voiced concerns. It was feared that the future reconstruction bank might sweep the German capital market, leaving no funds for the established banks[35]. The Bavarian deputy in the *Länderrat* even declined the whole KfW bill on the grounds that the new institution with its right of issue would threaten the old credit institutes[36]. This fear had been addressed during the reading of the bill in the Economic Council when it was repeatedly stressed that the new body should be no threat or competition to the existing banks[37]. In 1949 there was certainly no reason to fear that any KfW bonds would dominate the capital market, because the capital market was virtually non-existent. Hopes of up to DM 1 billion for reconstruction purposes from the capital market were dashed when only 30 per cent of the expected DM 100 million *Pfandbriefe*, or mortgage bonds, were signed[38].

In spite of this bleak outlook, the issuing of bonds was discussed within the KfW's supervisory board as early as 6 May 1949, not least because of strong American demand for German funds[39]. The Board of Directors discussed the issuing of two types of bonds. The first one, designed to support housing construction was to bear 3.5 per cent interest, the second one, for general purpose, 5.5 per cent interest. But even within the Board of Directors strong opposition was voiced against the project. Two members, representing the banking sector, voted against the 3.5 per cent bond. The result for the 5.5 per cent bond was even worse: when the vote was taken, it resulted in a tie. Since the KfW's statutes determined that in a tied vote the chairman's vote decided (and Schniewind had voted in

---

[35]BA Z 4/552, Protokoll über die Sitzung des Sonderausschusses Bankenaufsicht, 19 July 1948.

[36]BA Z 4/531, Wörtlicher Bericht über die 8. öffentliche Sitzung des Länderrats, 10 September 1948. The Bavarian action was not directed against a reconstruction bank as such. It was an attempt to protect the status and position of the big Bavarian banks, which had become West Germany's biggest banks following the Allied decartelisation ruling on Deutsche Bank, Dresdner Bank, and Commerzbank.

[37]*Wortprotokolle*, vol. 2, pp. 772 ff.

[38]*Die Neue Zeitung*, München, 10 March 1949.

[39]KfW HA Prot 10-1, Protokoll der 6. Sitzung, TOP 7.

favour of the bonds) the issue was accepted by the smallest possible margins[40]. The division the BoD showed on this occasion was all the more remarkable considering that its decisions were usually taken unanimously.

In order to make the bonds more attractive to potential buyers, the BoD received the Economic Council's permission to introduce two incentives. The 3.5 per cent housing bond received a status of tax exemption while the 5.5 per cent bond was tax reduced. In addition the interests for both papers were vouched for by the Bizonal administration, turning them into a kind of government bond[41].

For the Americans the issuing of the KfW bonds was seen as an indicator of the German capital market's real strength, which they thought the Germans downplayed consistently in order to gain more counterpart funds. They hoped to achieve a better overall result than forecast, which would vindicate their view. Therefore, the Military Government allowed the use of money from the blocked saving accounts to buy KfW bonds when they went on sale to the market on 15 September 1949[42]. This was a measure designed either further to increase the high result they hoped for or the Americans had second thoughts about the success of the bonds. Expectations ran high not at least because the Germans had predicted a high sale. Although the subscription for the 3.5 per cent housing bond ran only until the end of the year, Schniewind had hoped for a yield of up to DM 300 million[43]. However, the fact that the KfW most likely because of Abs' influence received a purchase guarantee from a banking consortium for DM 50 million for the 5.5 per cent bonds (which had no subscription deadline) indicates that not everybody was so optimistic about the result and suggests that the high forecasts were only made to soothe persistent American demands for German funds.

The subscription result in spite of all the concessions, which had been made was a major disappointment. The KfW did not even try to gloss it over but called it 'measly'. Until the end of 1949 only DM 8 million of the housing bonds could be placed. With DM 22 million sold on the open market the result of the 5.5 per cent bonds was only slightly better. But because of the banking consortium's guarantee, the KfW received from the banks the remaining DM 28 million, which had not been taken up by the market.

While the DM 8 million from the housing bonds was used in 1950 to support the reconstruction of the cities hardest hit by wartime bombing, the DM 50 million of the 5.5 per cent papers went into export industries (35 million), food processing industries (10 million) and to the French occupation zone (5 million)[44]. Despite the bad subscription result in 1949 the papers were introduced to the stock exchange in 1950 to gain the status of *Lombardfähigkeit* that is they could be used

---

[40]Pohl, *Wiederaufbau*, pp 67 f.
[41]Ibid.
[42]NA RG 260, OMGUS, Finance Adviser, box 111, folder 1, Supplementary Memorandum to BiCO/Memo (49)25; *Der Volkswirt*, No. 37, 16 September 1949; *Jb* 1949, p. 33.
[43]BA Z 13/1174, Protokoll der 65. Direktorialsitzung.
[44]*Jb* 1949, pp. 34 f.

as securities for loans[45]. When the Korean War broke out in June that year, the situation on the capital market deteriorated and the Kreditanstalt had to spend several million to keep the rate of its bonds at par value[46]. Faced with the aftermath of the damage caused by the Second World War and the task of rebuilding the country when there was hardly any capital available, the support with millions of marks of the par value of some bonds seems like an eccentric luxury. But it was a decision, which paid off well in the long run. The support of the bonds during these difficult times made sure that the papers of the Kreditanstalt received high customer credentials continuously from the 1950s to the present day and this explains why KfW bonds became a success story from the late 1950s onward.

Back in the early 1950s, with the capital market still not functioning properly the relatively small amount of money the KfW raised from the sale of its bonds had only a small impact on the Anstalt's business. Much more important was the utilisation of the bonds to secure KfW lending and the redemption of letters of commitment given by the Kreditanstalt. The first money gained in this way were the DM 60 million from the unemployment insurance. In 1954 the KfW redeemed these bonds with a letter of commitment. The returned bonds were immediately placed again on the capital market, thus raising another DM 60 million[47]. The same kind of money creation, just the other way round, occurred when the KfW redeemed the letters of commitment it had given for the DM 265 million GARIOA money with bonds. When the Federal Republic took over the GARIOA accounts, it also acquired these KfW bonds, which were deposited with the BdL as a security for the loan. But because it proved impractical that the Kreditanstalt was bound to the fixed repayment dates for the bonds, it was decided in 1952 to substitute the bonds once more for letters of commitment. The third transaction in which KfW bonds were given as securities took place during the work creation scheme, when the Kreditanstalt gave its 5.5 per cent papers to the BdL in order to receive the loans. While it was hardly able to sell bonds on the market the KfW could in this way, and with the co-operation of other public bodies, create an additional DM 325 million[48]. Hence public bodies like the BdL, the ministries, and the Unemployment Insurance Agency were heavily involved in the economic process when they acted to replace the capital market. As the system ran silently this state intervention was not realised by the general public so that fears of inflation did not arise.

The mid-1950s saw no further bonds issued by the Kreditanstalt, instead there was a continuous political row between ministers Erhard and Schäffer on

---

[45]Pohl, *Wiederaufbau*, pp. 69 f.

[46]*Jb* 1950, p. 41.

[47]*Jb* 1954, p. 41.

[48]*Jb* 1952, pp. 41, 43 and Annual Balance Sheet; slightly different figures can be found in a letter by the KfW to Minister Erhard, which gives the amount of the 5.5 per cent bonds with DM 375 million of which only DM 32 million had been placed on the capital market, see BA B 102/4898, BoM letter to Erhard, 28 July 1953.

matters of supervision of the KfW and on matters of general fiscal and monetary policy, in particular the issue of new bonds by the Anstalt. In the first version of the KfW law, supervision of the bank lay with the Executive Council[49]. Immediately after the 1951 amendment, which allowed the supervision to be carried out by a ministry a row erupted between Schäffer and Erhard over who would be in control of the Kreditanstalt. Because of Schäffer's ideas to incorporate the ERP Special Assets into the normal federal budget, Minister Blücher, who feared for his influence, perhaps even for his ministry, sided with Erhard, supporting the Economics Minister's claim[50]. Chancellor Adenauer, in his usual manner postponed a decision for the time being in order to consult with Abs. Only in February 1954 was the matter eventually settled when the Cabinet agreed to delegate the supervision to Erhard[51]. This outcome, which also demonstrates Erhard's increased influence as 'creator of the economic miracle' obviously enhanced his influence over the Kreditanstalt für Wiederaufbau. The bank certainly welcomed the decision since they were closer to Erhard and his policy than to that of the orthodox and very economical Schäffer. Perhaps the best example of the different approaches was the planned issue of new 5.5 per cent tax reduced bonds by the KfW, which had been scheduled to take place in 1953/54. At the latest since spring 1953 the KfW had planned the issue of these new bonds worth DM 200 million. Due to increased demand the sum was later raised to DM 250 million. The money to be raised was intended for loans to the export industry and to the iron and steel industry. However, over a period of three weeks the KfW changed the beneficiaries of these loans at least three times[52]. This indicates either dire need for money and a lack of planning or, more likely, that the Kreditanstalt was looking for the best way to sell their wish for new bonds to the ministry in order to get permission for the new issue. Furthermore, the first letter to request permission for the new bonds was sent by the KfW to the Economics Ministry instead of the Ministry for Finance, which was in charge of monetary and credit affairs[53]. This 'mistake' was certainly intentional, since the Finance Ministry was not in favour of new KfW bonds and it would have been logical for the Kreditanstalt to seek Erhard's support on the matter. The KfW complained to the Economics Ministry that Schäffer was opposed to the new issue because he regarded the Anstalt's operations as too independent and feared that the issuing of new bonds would extend this independence. And, of course, Schäffer was opposed to it because of the ongoing row on the question of supervision[54]. Minister Schäffer argued that the new KfW bonds would absorb any funds from the still tight capital market and thus

---

[49]KfW Gesetz 1948, 1949, 1951, § 12.
[50]BA B 102/17998A, passim.
[51]*Kabinettsprotokolle*, vcl. 5, pp. 157 f.; vol. 7, pp. 71 f.
[52]BA B 102/4898, KfW letters to the Economics Ministry, 6 and 13 August 1953; KfW HA VS 192, KfW letters to the Economics Ministry, 28 July 1953, 6 and 13 August 1953.
[53]BA B 102/27993, note from Economics Ministry (BMWi), Abt. VI to StSek. Westrick, 24 October 1953; KfW HA VS 192, KfW letter to Economics Ministry, 28 July 1953.
[54]KfW HA VS 192, letter Neubaur to StSek. Westrick, 7 December 1953.

prevent the successful placement of a new DM 200 million government bond[55]. When the Cabinet finally opted in favour of the KfW bonds in March 1954, Schäffer repeated his concerns and, in addition, challenged the legality of the Cabinet's decision. Faced with such a strong opposition, Adenauer wanted to avoid bad publicity and the Cabinet finally backed down and stopped the Kreditanstalt's plans[56]. After this defeat no further attempt to launch new security papers was made by the KfW during Schäffer's time as Finance Minister.

Fritz Schäffer had created a lot of enemies for himself in the government and in industry due to his tight budget policy, in particular before the 1957 general elections (although the 'election gifts' were still considerable). Because of the antagonism Schäffer had created for himself amongst important people Adenauer replaced him as Finance Minister after the elections. It was only then that the KfW reconsidered the issue of new bonds. By now, the economic situation had improved enormously. The money and capital markets were in much better shape in 1957-58 and for the first time the KfW was publicly satisfied with the development. Although the 1957 change in the pension system caused a considerable loss for the capital markets, they were booming as never before, so that even the first large scale private German capital exports of about DM 780 million took place[57]. Although the capital markets and the economy as a whole had improved, the KfW's task did not get smaller, on the contrary, new work arose causing greater need for funds. While big companies now covered most of their investment on the capital markets, more funds from the ERP Special Assets became available for *Mittelstand,* Germany's small-scale businesses in trade and crafts (*Handel und Handwerk*). This left a funding gap with the medium sized companies (*Mittlere Industrie*), which could apply for loans between DM 100,000 and DM 3 million. In order to provide money for them the KfW planned the issue of long-term bonds to the face value of DM 100 million[58]. In the previous meeting only DM 75 million had been discussed for this purpose, since the hope was voiced that the early repayment of big loans would provide a source of money, which could help to finance the *Mittelstandsprogramm*. The big loans to large industries were indeed repaid before they were due[59]. Both the economic need for a *Mittelstandsprogramm* and its political importance is demonstrated by the fact that, although the money of the early repayments was available, the scheme was increased. After all, middle class entrepreneurs were not only important supporters of Adenauer's Christian Democratic Party but one of the backbones of the German economy.

The second major new area of activity for the KfW became overseas loans. So far, the Kreditanstalt had been involved in export financing by granting loans to

---

[55]BA NL 168/34 letter by Schäffer to Staatssekretär Hartmann regarding Cabinet meeting, 19 February 1954.

[56]*Kabinettsprotokolle*, vol. 7, pp. 96 f., 131 f., 153.

[57]*Jb* 1957, p. 35; *Jb* 1958, pp. 32 ff.

[58]KfW HA Prot 10-3, Protokoll der 36. Sitzung, TOP 1.

[59]KfW HA Prot 10-3, Protokoll der 35. Sitzung, TOP 3; *Jb* 1958, p. 39.

suppliers (*Lieferantenkredit*). It now started to give credits to buyers or helped to change the terms of debts. The first and most prominent example of this kind of transaction was the case of India. Strong foreign policy and Cold War implications the details of which will be discussed later played an important role for the KfW's involvement in this transaction. To raise the money for the Indian debt resettlement, the KfW pioneered the German capital market by introducing a new type of bond, the so-called *Kassenobligation*. This bond offered the advantages of both the short-term money market and the long-term capital market, providing the flexibility of a short-term security and the profits of a long-term bond. It became hugely successful not least because it was an interesting security for small investors[60].

The difference between the first issue of KfW bonds in 1949 and the situation in 1959-60 is striking. While only about 10 per cent of the first issue of DM 375 million could be placed on the open market and the rest had to be taken on by public bodies, the KfW issued securities to the value of DM 730 million between 1958-60 and planned further large scale issues for the years ahead. Different periods of validity as well as a variation in interest rates, conformed to the market situation, made the bonds very popular with investors[61]. The care the Kreditanstalt had given to the rate of its bonds, even during difficult times, now paid off and KfW securities were soon regarded as premium bonds.

5.3 The Auxiliary Investment Law

The *Investitionshilfe Gesetz* or Auxiliary Investment Law is of special significance for the history of West German reconstruction. It was a clear sign that Erhard's economic policy had failed in at least two decisive areas. First it showed that the Minister's ideas of how the reconstruction should proceed, that is by the growth of the light and consumer goods industry, was not sustainable without investment into basic industries. Second, the law meant a return of the political influence and powers of the industrial associations (*Spitzenverbände*), namely the *Bundesverband der Deutschen Industrie,* the *Bundesverband deutscher Arbeitgeberverbände*, (BDA, Federation of German Employer Associations) and the *Deutscher Industrie und Handelstag* (DIHT, German Industry and Trade Diet, the association of small and medium sized companies). Contrary to Erhard's ideas of market policy the associations, especially the BDI which represented heavy industry, regained much although not all of their previous political weight but for the first time since the end of the war they would once more be a serious player on the stage of political lobbying and influence.

---

[60] *Jb* 1958, p. 39.

[61] *Jb* 1960, pp. 47 f.; Annual Balance Sheet; KfW HA Prot 10-3, Protokoll der 43. Sitzung, TOP 3.

Paradoxically, this failure of Erhard developed out of his very own economic policy. By 1946 the British and American Military Governments had both realised that the reconstruction of the German economy even just to a level of mere self- sustainability could only be achieved if all resources were concentrated in the basic industries. This policy, which had to put special emphasis on coal production paid off during 1947 when production in the economy as a whole picked up again[62]. The currency reform of 20 June 1948 and the *Leitsätzegesetz* (law concerning price levels) the following day changed the situation. Erhard had lifted the price fixing for all goods and services with the exception of fuels, electricity, iron and steel, rents and basic foodstuffs. The light and consumer goods industry were now able to invest their new profits to expand production while at the same time they could receive short-term bank loans as well[63]. The basic industries on the other hand lacked the possibility of large scale self finance through profits or tax depreciation because their prices remained fixed. Since Erhard had the idea of economic growth based on consumption he preferred the consumer goods industries to such an extent that he was even prepared to delay overall reconstruction. As early as February 1948 he stated in defence of his policy: 'Wenn Sie mir sagen: Dann dauert der deutsche Wiederaufbau 5 oder 10 Jahre länger: dann antworte ich: in Gottes Namen, soll er 5 oder 10 Jahre länger dauern'.[64] While the basic industries were starved of investment capital as a result of Erhard's policy, the self-financing of the consumer goods industry meant a huge loss or at least a waste of funds to the reconstruction of the national economy, since much of the funds for self-financing were utilised for projects not essential to the national economy. Erhard's lack of a strategy for capital formation was going to have severe consequences.

Erhard's political decision as Director of Economics and Minister for Economics respectively, to build the recovery on consumer goods industry had already had serious consequences after the currency reform and even more after the founding of the Federal Republic. Although investments made up to 20 per cent and more of GDP in 1949-51 this impressive figure tells only half the story. Self-financing at one point made up 77 per cent of all investments with another high share coming from public expenditure. However due to Erhard's preferences hardly any of this money was used in the basic industries. It was only with the utilisation of the counterpart funds that the growing gap in investments in these sectors could be bridged and covered to some extent[65]. At the same time when the crucial growth rate of coal output began to decline the rest of the economy also

[62]Heiner R. Adamsen, *Investitionshilfe für die Ruhr. Wiederaufbau, Verbände und Soziale Markwirtschaft 1948-1952,* Wuppertal 1981, pp. 33 ff.

[63]Abelshauser, *Wirtschaftsgeschichte*, p. 53.

[64]Sitzung der Sonderstelle Geld und Kredit on 25 February 1948, quoted in Adamsen, *Investitionshilfe*, p. 41. 'If you tell me: this way the German reconstruction will take five or ten years more: then I will reply: in God's name, let it take five or ten more years' (translation AG).

[65]*Jb* 1949, p. 16; Adamsen, *Investitionshilfe*, pp. 45ff., 48 ff., esp. p. 51.

slipped into 'relative stagnation' with high unemployment and inflation turned in deflation[66].

The approach taken by the German administration was not well received by the Americans. Their interest in and concerns about the recovery of Germany's basic industries was based on their recognition of the importance of the sector also in terms of European reconstruction as a whole. Lack of coal and steel from the Ruhr did not only affect Germany but also its European neighbours and their reconstruction process. The German effort they saw was deemed as quite inadequate. When the Germans published their first plan for investment finance for the years 1950-52, jointly drafted by the Economics and Marshall Plan Ministries in autumn 1949, it was strongly criticised by the Americans. Both the ECA and the Allied High Commission called the German plan inadequate, pessimistic, and contradictory. The American reaction sparked off an intensive US-German exchange which became known as the *Memorandenkrieg* or war of memoranda[67]. That the American demand for a proper long-term investment strategy in particular for the basic industries was long overdue became obvious soon after the outbreak of the Korean War. The hostilities in the Far East brought about not only a general price increase but also a rise of production figures. Both consumer goods and strategic materials became scarce commodities in the western world and it was only the West German economy, which still had free production capacities in mid-1950. For example the iron and steel industry by summer 1950 had not even reached the production limit of 11.1 million tons annually, which the Allies had imposed in the late 1940s and there were still spare capacities. The limit was eventually reached and surpassed by the end of the year but only because of an increased demand from abroad, which had developed as a result of the Korean War[68]. However, owing to the increased production of goods in nearly all sectors of industry the failure to improve basic industries showed its effects. Iron and steel became short supply commodities and electricity had to be rationed again for a short time during the winter of 1950-51[69]. But it was the shortage of coal caused by the rapid expansion of demand following the outbreak of the war in Korea, which lay at the heart of the problems. Since the currency reform coal output had grown at a much slower rate than the rest of the economy and now serious repercussions for all other industrial sectors emerged. Coal became the overriding problem in Germany throughout 1951 and it was on the Cabinet agenda for the rest of the year[70]. Although iron and steel, electricity and other sectors developed into secondary bottlenecks which could not satisfy the demand or even fell back in their

---

[66]Growth rate of output 1947: 32 per cent, 1950: 7.7 per cent, from November 1950 onwards stagnating for two years, see Abelshauser, *Wirtschaftsgeschichte*, pp. 69, 56.
[67]Adamsen, *Investitionshilfe*, pp. 67 ff.
[68]Adamsen, *Investitionshilfe*, p. 93.
[69]Knut Borchard, Christoph Buchheim, 'Die Wirkung der Marshallplan-Hilfe in Schlüsselbereichen der deutschen Wirtschaft', in: *VfZ*, No. 35 (1987), p. 331.
[70]Adamsen, *Investitionshilfe*, p. 84; *Kabinettsprotokolle*, vol. 4, passim.

output due to the lack of coal, the general situation in production that winter made it clear that these sectors needed a huge amount of money as well to meet with the increased demand which resulted from the Korean War.

Indirectly the Americans had a very strong influence on the AIL. Already in 1950 they had made the release of ECA III conditional on the creation of a German investment plan of DM 1 billion under ECA control, a demand the Germans were able to avert[71]. German attitudes changed when it became clear that there would be no ECA IV tranche, which could be used for investments in basic industries. In its November 1950 report the *Wissenschaftlicher Beirat beim Bundeswirtschaftsministerium* (Advisory Council with the Federal Ministry of Economics) demanded a redistribution of investments. At its December meeting at which Abs and experts from the ministry were also present, various solutions to the investment problem were discussed. However, Pohl's claim that Abs was the spiritual father of the AIL cannot be sustained, for by that time he made his proposal, it was one of many suggestions, although in the end his proposal came close to the law[72]. Surprisingly, the KfW's BoD only discussed ways of raising money to fill the gap the cancelled ECA IV tranche had created on 31 March 1951. Abs voiced strong criticism of the policy of the absent Economics Minister Erhard for the lack of a long-term strategy[73]. While possible solutions to the problem were discussed during the meeting, no decision was taken.

In the meantime the German economy had to cling to two desperate short-term measures. First, massive amounts of coal of up to ten million tons had to be imported from the USA in 1951 in order to keep the industry going, although US coal was more expensive than Ruhr coal[74]. The price difference, but most of all the sheer size of imports, contributed to the draining of Germany's dollar reserves, which brought the country nearly to its knees. Despite this damaging effect the German administration sanctioned, perhaps even encouraged, the imports because they saw them as a means to convince the Allies to reduce the size of the forced German coal exports which were still going on as part of the occupation policy. These forced exports were quite considerable, amounting to about 20 per cent of the whole coal output[75]. When the Allies did not take up these requests, the Germans were left with the only other feasible short-term solution: (re)-introduction of economic controls (*Wirtschaftslenkung*) on a wider scale. As the American demand to reduce the output of consumer goods was not acceptable to Erhard, controls were the only option left. Since controls were also incompatible with Erhard's idea of economic policy as long as governmental authorities carried

[71]Adamsen, *Investitionshilfe*, p. 84.

[72]Pohl, *Wiederaufbau*, pp. 103 f; Abs repeated his claim in Schwarz, *Wiederherstellung*, p. 78 where he claims to be the 'only legitimate father of the law'. See also Adamsen, Investitionshilfe, pp. 111 f.

[73]KfW HA Prot 10-1, Protokoll der 20 Sitzung, TOP 3.

[74]*Jb* 1951, p. 19.

[75]*Jb* 1950, p. 16.

them out he had to rely on business and industrial associations to get them in place. Under the motto of 'mobilising industry's own responsibility', the BDI offered their 'good service' to Adenauer which allowed the Economics Minister to save face and avoid direct state intervention[76]. The introduction of *Wirtschaftslenkung* based on the co-operation of the associations obviously opened the doors even further to their returning influence on politics and public life.

Because of the growing political pressure from the German public, Parliament and the Americans, about a dozen serious plans to end the misery of investment finance had been developed by the end of 1950. The plans can roughly be divided into two groups, those which favoured a purely market orientated solution and those which supported direct state intervention. Plans of the first group were, apart from the *Beirat's* report, the *Wuppertaler Plan*, the proposals of the *Niederbreisiger Arbeitskreis*, Erhard's *Sparmarkenplan* and a memorandum by the BDI. The *Wuppertaler Plan* was drafted by a group of entrepreneurs who represented medium-sized businesses and who had the backing of parts of Blücher's Liberal party. The main aim, apart from financing the bottleneck sectors was the idea to give the workforce a share in company assets in an attempt to prevent a spread of co-determination from the coal and steel industry to other sectors[77].

The proposals of the *Niederbreisiger Arbeitskreis*, a group made up of Christian Democrats, the FDP and the Deutsche Partei, was the most radical plan. It demanded a redistribution of purchasing power, similar to Erhard's plan, and the abolition of all price controls. But since they were prepared to accept a general price increase of 10 per cent which would have particularly hit the lower income groups of the working class the proposal was unacceptable to Adenauer who by then depended on trade union support for his European policy.

That even the prophet of the market economy, Ludwig Erhard, had to come up with a plan showed the seriousness of the situation. But he had to be particularly careful with his proposals and make them as *marktkonform* as possible, in order not to stir up more scorn from his political opponents. His *Sparmarkenplan* (literally 'saving token' plan) worked similar to trading tokens. Retailers should put a surcharge on all commodities. The buyers would receive trading tokens to the value of the surcharge, which would be exchanged for bonds when a certain amount was reached. Erhard advocated his plan by stressing the psychological effects. His plan might have constituted an enforced savings for the public but this was still preferred, for example, over any new tax to help the industries since the public would have regarded those as a 'rearmament tax'[78].

Surprisingly, neither the SPD nor the trade unions came forward with proper proposals of their own. The SPD's weak action was due to Kurt Schumacher's domination of the party and his preoccupation with the question of

[76]Abelshauser, *Wirtschaftsgeschichte*, pp. 78 ff.
[77]Adamsen, *Investitionshilfe*, pp. 106 ff., 124 ff.
[78]Adamsen, *Investitionshilfe*, pp. 113 ff., 120 ff.

co-determination at that time thus missing a big opportunity to influence events[79]. Instead, the most prominent plans on the interventionist side came from Minister Schäffer and from Abs. Abs' idea was based on utilising the (already generous) tax depreciation. Twenty-five per cent of all values written off by business should be used to sign bonds, which should in turn be used for investment finance in the basic industries. Quite correctly, Abs called his plan 'a sacrifice for the basic industries'. The Schäffer plan finally consisted of two parts one of which was an attempt to capitalise on the current crisis. Schäffer had planned to introduce a special tax similar to the British Purchase Tax. However, this tax revenue was not intended for investments but as a method to balance the budget and to absorb surplus purchase power, after all, the Korea boom had caused strong inflationary pressure[80]. To raise money for investment, Schäffer simply preferred the Abs Plan, which would have been the second part of his proposal.

The industrial associations saw most of these plans as negative because they entailed direct state intervention. But following the near collapse of the West German economy in January/February 1951 and growing US pressure on Adenauer to intervene in the economy all indicators pointed in the direction of such an intervention[81]. To prepare for a solution Adenauer invited trade unionists and members of the leading business associations to a meeting in the Chancellery to discuss the matter with the government on 9 April 1951. The managers' intention was to avoid intervention at all costs and so they met with Erhard, their strongest ally, a day before the talks with the Chancellor. It was not difficult to convince the Economics Minister that the best solution for an investment programme had to come from industry since this would have allowed him to stick to the principle of the market economy and save face at the same time. The associations suggested raising investment money themselves from amongst their members. On 10 April, just one day after the meeting in the Chancellery the associations' proposal was discussed in Cabinet. However, while the BDI's memorandum of 28 March spoke of action, which should be completely voluntary, the position now was different. The risk that some, or many, entrepreneurs would not follow their association's proposal to raise DM 1 billion for the basic industries posed too great a risk, not only of embarrassment for the organisations but also of state intervention in case the plan was unsuccessful. Therefore, the whole idea had to be embedded into a legal framework[82]. But the utilisation of the legislative structures by private associations caused strong criticism from all sides and in itself was enough to show

[79]Lewis J. Edinger, *Kurt Schumacher. A Study in Personality and Political Behaviour*, Stanford/Cal., London 1965, Appendix A, meetings with political advisers.

[80]Adamsen, *Investitionshilfe*, pp. 133 ff.; The Purchase Tax was a surcharge levied on the purchase of all non-essential goods.

[81]The climax of this development was McCloy's letter to Adenauer on 6 March, in which McCloy threatened to stop all economic aid and all deliveries of raw materials to Germany if German attitudes would not change. See Abelshauser, '"Korporativer" Marktwirtschaft', in *VfZ* No. 30 (1982).

[82]*Kabinettsprotokolle*, vol. 4, pp. 290 ff.; Adamsen, *Investitionshilfe*, pp. 154, 161, 194.

the changes within the government's economic policy. The associations, previously shunned by Erhard because of their potential influence on economic policy, were promoted into exactly this position when they were allowed to draft proposals on how to raise investment funds[83]. It has to be understood, though, that participating businesses were not supposed to donate funds without any compensation. For the money companies contributed towards the scheme they were to receive interest-bearing special bonds which they were allowed to redeem after a certain period of time.

Before the legislative process in parliament began there were three months of preliminary talks. One of the most controversial questions to be dealt with was which bank should handle the funds. Both the Economics and Finance Ministries were in favour of the Kreditanstalt für Wiederaufbau doing the job while the industry wanted 'their' Industriekreditbank to be in charge[84]. While the ministries, certainly the Economics Ministry, did not want any state intervention, they were keen on retaining control of the funds. The KfW's Board of Managers seemed to have been divided on the issue with Neubaur in particular opposed to the KfW's involvement. Abs on the other hand was in favour of the Kreditanstalt's involvement especially after Adenauer had accepted a proposal to streamline the administration of the expected funds[85]. But when by the end of May a first draft of the bill was presented, the KfW declared itself unable to carry out the task. The reason given was that it was impossible for the KfW to deal with the expected three million banking transactions in 18 months. There was another reason as well, perhaps even more important to the KfW than the unsolved personnel question: the bill suggested a legally independent *Sondervermögen* to which the KfW should be fully liable. Even more unacceptable for the Board of Managers was the clause, which stated that it should be subordinated to the proposed administrative body of the Special Assets, the AIL-Kuratorium. On 1 June Martini sent a telex to Neubaur, which held the solution to the problem. Martini asked '... ist es nicht für uns am besten, daß wir der IKB die ganze Arbeit und die Ehre überlassen, wir selbst nehmen aber dafür einen großen Anteil des Geldes?'[86] His idea not only made the KfW's involvement possible, it was also a very important political compromise. In accordance with the associations' demands there was eventually an *Investitions-hilfe-Sondervermögen* established at the IKB, nevertheless most of the money would go via the KfW. This was achieved by a clause, which stated that all projects, which were to benefit from AIL funds but had previously been supported

---

[83]Abelshauser, *Wirtschaftsgeschichte*, pp. 82 ff.

[84]Adamsen, *Investitionshilfe*, p. 174.

[85]KfW HA VS 187 (Handakte Neubaur), note 5 May 1951 regarding the collection of the [IHG] money, point 4: '... die Finanzämter überweisen [der KfW] ...die Einzahlungsbeträge, with a handwritten remark 'lieber die IKB als wir.'; note on a meeting of the Bundeskanzler-Ausschuß für Investitionen, 18 May 1951.

[86]KfW HA VS 187, note 30 May 1951; telex from Martini to Neubaur, 1 June 1951. 'Would it not be best for us to leave all the work and honour to the IKB while we take a big share of the money for ourselves?' (translation AG).

with KfW loans had to be dealt with by the Kreditanstalt. The same applied to any loan to companies under Allied Law 27. In this way the associations' influence on loans could be limited, at least in the eyes of the public. Finally, Abs expressed his hope that it would be the Economics Ministry instead of the *Kuratorium*, which would have the final decision on any AIL loans thus preventing group interests becoming dominant[87].

After the BDI had revised the bill, it eventually went to the Bundestag on 9 July. With the Americans still on his back and the need for money growing, Adenauer hoped to get the bill through the legislative process within one week, just before the parliamentary holidays. The timing was chosen not least to avoid unpleasant questions and objections to the bill in parliament, but his well calculated attempt failed following heavy resistance from all parties, including his own. Under the normal parliamentary procedure it took the bill until January 1952 to be enacted and finally published[88].

It was during the legislative process when the government suffered another embarrassing blow. In order to start the investment process in summer 1951 the government asked the Bank deutscher Länder for a loan of DM 120 million. In its meeting on 18 July the Central Bank Council declined this request on the grounds that a proposed bill which was not even in the legislative process was not sufficient as security. Once more, the BdL prevented credit expansion 'into the blue'. However, the Central Bank Council agreed to grant the loan on the basis of accepting expected interest payments of ERP loans as securities combined with tough conditions for the government on the redemption of these loans[89].

The money was distributed according to the decision taken by the *Vorkuratorium*, a provisional body, which prepared the work of the real *Kuratorium* prior to the latter's establishment. The *Kuratorium* consisted of 20 members, but only nine of those had voting rights, the other 11 had merely an advisory role. Three trade union representatives faced five deputies from industry and the *Kuratorium's* president who was appointed by the government on the suggestion of the industry[90]. The trade union participation was therefore only a token gesture to keep the unions aboard during a politically difficult time, an equal say in the matter was never intended for them.

The law itself contained several articles, which were purely politically motivated. All commercial businesses (*Gewerbebetriebe*) had to contribute towards the AIL Special Assets, except those sectors or institutions which were named for exemption. That even public radio stations were explicitly named as commercial businesses was a direct attack on the Nord-West Deutscher Rundfunk (NWDR), nicknamed 'Nord-West Deutscher Rotfunk' (Red Radio Station), a quite

[87]KfW HA Prot 10-2, Protokoll der 21. Sitzung (Sondersitzung), TOP 1.
[88]Adamsen, *Investitionshilfe*, pp. 181 ff.; *BGBl* 1952 (I), No. 1, henceforth quoted as IHG.
[89]KfW HA VS 186, Zentralbankratsbeschluß zur Vorfinanzierung der Investitionshilfe vom 18 Juli 1951, undated note; Pohl, *Wiederaufbau*, pp. 112 f.
[90]*IHG* Art. 26.

influential station on an anti-Adenauer line[91]. While articles 1 to 35 of the law defined the task and the operation of the *Investitionshilfe*, articles 36 and 37 contained the politically really important clauses. Article 36 allowed special tax depreciation for the basic industries of up to 50 per cent in one year. It was a kind of compensation for them since the other industries had already benefited from all kind of depreciation and self-finance in the aftermath of the currency reform. With some justification Adamsen calls the tax depreciation a delayed gift to the basic industries not least for political reasons. At the same time Adenauer was negotiating with the Allies about the lifting of all remaining industrial control. With the Schuman Plan negotiations also going on, Adenauer could kill two birds with one stone. The private industries would receive state support to widen bottlenecks while at the same time the companies could improve their competitiveness within the European Coal and Steel Community (ECSC)[92]. In the end, the special tax depreciation amounted to a total of DM 3.2 billion, three times the sum of the investment aid itself. Since it meant a tax loss for the budget it has to be called a (hidden) subsidy for the industries.

The restoration of proper price levels as outlined in article 37 finally allowed Erhard to raise fixed prices to the real market level without the consent of the Bundestag. Although this was a very powerful tool in theory, in reality it was more of a token gesture to please industry. Particularly in the most important field of coal prices Erhard used it rarely and only very carefully since he knew that his economic policy depended heavily on low fuel and energy prices.

When the AIL had been proposed by the BDI much emphasis had been laid on the necessary funds for the major bottleneck, the coal mining industry of the Ruhr. However, this emphasis changed during the programme. Already the first distribution proposal of the *Kuratorium* showed an equal share for coal, electricity and iron and steel of DM 300 million each and DM 100 million for other bottleneck sectors and industrial water supply instead of a preference for coal. Table 5.3.1 shows the development and final distribution of the aid, which signified a constant deterioration of the position of coalmining compared to the other beneficiaries.

Erhard's decision of 24 September on how to distribute the funds was a compromise. He had to react to previous proposals by the Investment Department of his ministry and the proposals made by industry's *Fachreferate*. Following the release of the ECA III reserve a new allocation had to be drawn up before the minister decided on the final distribution. But Erhard lacked an overall structural concept and depended much more than usual on information from the industrial associations since his ministerial apparatus in this sector was not worth mentioning. Thus the *Kuratorium's* power and influence increased steadily and the associations gained more and more influence on the decision making process. 'Das Kuratorium [wurde] somit ein relativ eigenständiges strukturpolitisches

[91] *IHG* Art. 3, Art. 2 (2); Adamsen, *Investitionshilfe*, p. 17.
[92] Adamsen, *Investitionshilfe*, p. 22 ff.

Entscheidungsgremium; die Wirtschaftsverbände selbst, unter Einschluß der Gewerkschaften, führten die eigentliche Investitionslenkung durch'[93]. What was left for the government was the right to veto individual decisions. The loser in the decision making process was the coal mining industry, whose share of investment money declined steadily. This was in sharp contrast to the announced intention under which the AIL had been initiated and consequently, the lack of investment funds in the sector continued. The power industry, favoured by Erhard, could just about keep its share, while the iron and steel industry, which appeared as the winner in the process, receiving the biggest share of the direct investment aid thanks to the influence of the *Kuratorium*, which proved to work and processed the funds very quickly. By May 1952 more than DM 900 million were confirmed for the various projects and by mid-1953 nearly DM 800 million had been paid out[94].

Table 5.3.1
Proposed and Final Distribution of Loans under the Auxiliary Investment Law
(in million DM)

	Original *Kuratorium* proposal	Erhard's proposal on 24.9.51	Decision by BMWi	Means agreed by the *Kuratorium*
Coal mining	300	260	234	228.2
Electrical Power	300	380[1]	252	241.8
Gas Supply	-	-	126	106.1
Iron and Steel	300	260	278	296.5
Rail freight cars	-	50	50	50
Water Supply	100[2]	10	60	77.4
Others	-	40	-	-
Total	1000	1000	1000	1000

[1] Including funds for gas supply.
[2] Including money for Others.

Source: Adamsen, p. 264.

About 70 per cent of the DM 1 billion investment aid was channelled through the Kreditanstalt für Wiederaufbau although the AIL Special Assets were established

[93]Adamsen, *Investitionshilfe*, p. 200 f. 'Thus the *Kuratorium* became a relatively independent body taking decisions on structural policy; the economic associations, including the trade unions, carried out the real guiding of investments' (translation AG).
[94]Adamsen, *Investitionshilfe*, pp. 200 f., 212.

at the Industriekreditbank. The clause, which had asked for the continuing financing of projects begun with counterpart funds should have been a compromise to settle the question of which bank should be in charge of the Special Assets. But since it was the *Kuratorium* which made the final decision on which company should receive a loan the Kreditanstalt had become a mere executive organ with only limited influence. The only gain the KfW could claim were the usual interest rate profits and the fact that it maintained business contacts with former clients. Nevertheless, in the Annual Report the KfW stressed the importance of the AIL, in particular article 36, but it complained about the difficult and long running processing of AIL loans which was partly due to the way the loans were redeemed with bonds[95]. The activities of the Kreditanstalt up to the end of 1953 are summarised in Table 5.3.2.

Table 5.3.2
KfW Loans under the Auxiliary Investment Law until 1953
(in million DM)

Sector	Scheduled by the *Kuratorium*	Money via the KfW	Money paid out to KfW	Money confirmed by KfW	Money paid out by KfW
Coal Mining	229.2	211	200	195.5	186.8
Electricity	241.7	165.05	162.05	159.05	158.95
Iron and Steel	296.5	284.55	258.05	243.05	235.05
Gas Supply	107.1	35.27	35.27	35.27	34.71
Water Supply	72.5	9.8	9.55	9.3	9.3
Rail Freight Cars	50				
Total	997	705.67	664.92	642.17	624.81

Source: *Jb* 1953, p. 49.

The table shows the sectors in which the KfW had been involved previously with ERP funds and where new projects were financed. The main beneficiaries apart from rail freight cars, which had been supported with GARIOA money before were water supply and gas. Industrial water supply in particular meant the improvement of industrial infrastructure for the iron and coal sector in the Ruhr. The difference in the amount of money scheduled by the *Kuratorium* for the electricity industry and the sums eventually provided for the KfW indicates that there were both large

[95] *Jb* 1952, p. 44.

new projects and old ones which had to be completed or even expanded, while the iron and coal industries received their money mainly to go on with previous ERP investments or because they were still under Law 27. In 1954 the KfW's involvement in the AIL was in its final stage and the last money, less than DM 60 million, was given to industry. In the Annual Reports the whole matter of the AIL was mentioned only in a very short paragraph and it seems that the Kreditanstalt was happy to bring it to a close[96].

The economic and even more so the political effects of the Auxiliary Investment Law were considerable. In the economic field it was not so much the raising of DM 1 billion by industry, which was celebrated in a good propaganda stunt as 'a sacrifice'. It was certainly not a sacrifice since all businesses, which had to give money were refunded and most of them even made a profit due to the high interest rates of the bonds. The KfW went a step further and called the investment aid insufficient. Adamsen estimates the total value of investments which were initiated by the AIL to be DM 5.7 billion reducing industry's 'sacrifice' to a mere 20 per cent. The really important part of the law in terms of investment finance was the depreciation allowance under article 36 which ran to some DM 3.2 billion in total. The rest, about DM 1.4 billion, came from normal depreciations, other means and special tax allowances. In the words of the KfW's Annual Report, 'the depreciation might bring about a level of compensation for the insufficient money aid.'[97]

Nevertheless, although the law helped to alleviate a severe investment crisis at a difficult moment for West Germany's economy, its real impact was one of far reaching political consequences. East German scholars saw the AIL as the attempt of heavy industry to rehabilitate itself from its involvement in the Nazi regime which had left it in disgrace. Now it could regain and re-establish its economic, political and military power once more. Adamsen does not see an increase in political power for industry, in particular heavy industry but he agrees in part to the rearmament theory, based on the wider developments in the early 1950s in terms of the European Defence Community and the question of a German defence contribution and re-militarisation[98]. However, in the light of what the associations had achieved – a solution not based on state intervention, the limited period of the AIL was running, the additional tax depreciations, and the expected end to all price fixing – it is very difficult not to speak of an increase in political power. For Abelshauser, the AIL symbolises a return in full to a corporative style of economy which had a long tradition in Germany. His argument implies a rise in political power for industry, which fundamentally transformed the market economy[99]. Finally, Jáckli emphasises how this development occurred. In his opinion the associations, representing big industry, regained power. The losers

---

[96] *Jb* 1954, p. 40.
[97] *Jb* 1951, p. 37; Adamsen, *Investitionshilfe*, pp. 23 f.
[98] Adamsen, *Investitionshilfe*, pp. 103 ff.
[99] Abelshauser, *Wirtschaftsgeschichte*, pp. 76 ff, esp. pp. 82 ff.

therefore were the medium sized businesses and the trade unions, which saw a real loss of political influence against big industry[100]. Seen in connection with the failure to introduce co-determination into the whole of German industry, well beyond the coal and steel sectors, the 'anti-socialist' and 'market conform' solution, which was found to be the problem of the German investment crisis, likewise must have pleased the Americans and conservative circles in Germany. It meant another step away from any form of socialist experiment.

[100] Jáckli, *Kohlepfennig*, p.74.

Part III
'Guiding' the Economic Reconstruction

Chapter 6

Agriculture

State intervention in support of agriculture, either directly through tariffs and price guarantees or indirectly through subsidised credits as offered from the Kreditanstalt was a development which had occurred long before 1945. Since the late 19th century agriculture in the whole of western continental Europe had been more strongly affected by state regulation and intervention than any other economic sector and consequently agriculture had become more and more exempt from the market economy. This trend accelerated with the onset of the agricultural crisis of the late 1920s which increased protectionism so that post-war developments were to some extend already pre-determined[1]. What changed in the post-war period was the reason for state intervention in a sector which altered its structure considerably and at the same time lost its economic significance. State intervention in Germany in the late 1940s was given in a desperate effort to increase food production as the country faced starvation. From 1955 onward, subsidising agriculture became a means to prevent large parts of the population – in 1955 20 per cent of the workforce was still employed in agriculture – from falling into poverty. Whether this was done as part of the public self-portrayal and self-definition of the young Federal Republic, as Thiemeyer claims, or as part of the politically motivated support for an anti-modernist image of the family based small-scale farming is open to debate[2]. What is certain is the fact, that state aid and loans from the Kreditanstalt paid for and helped to cushion the social impact of the structural change which appeared in West German agriculture during the 1950s.

The changes which took place in German agriculture between 1945 and 1955 were considerable and they even accelerated during the second half of the 1950s. Nazi economic policy and its ruthless exploitation of the occupied territories had ensured a fairly stable food supply in Germany up until the very last months of the war[3]. Then the food supply especially of the western zones of occupation dropped below a critical level and remained there for several reasons. The division of the former Reich meant that the western areas lost access to the agricultural surplus areas in the east which had made up 25 per cent of the arable land of the

[1]Guido Thiemeyer, *Vom 'Pool Vert' zur Europäischen Wirtschaftsgemeinschaft. Europäische Integration, Kalter Krieg und die Anfänge der Gemeinsamen Europäischen Agrarpolitik 1950-1957*, München 1999, pp. 14, 17.

[2] Thiemeyer, '*Pool Vert*', pp. 27, 30.

[3]Alan Milward, *Der Zweite Weltkrieg*, in: Wolfram Fischer (ed.) *Geschichte der Weltwirtschaft im 20. Jahrhundert*, 6 vols., vol. 5, München 1977, pp. 270 ff.

Reich before the war. At the same time there were more people to feed since the population in the American and British zones had increased by nearly 20 per cent due to the influx of refugees and expellees[4]. In particular North Rhine Westphalia with the all-important Ruhr area and little agriculture was unable to provide enough food for its population. The situation was worsened by a lack of fertilizers, horses, and manpower. The 1945 potato harvest for example was less than 30 per cent of the average of the 1935-1939 period. The lack of chemical fertilizers, high quality seeds and work animals, men and machines was accompanied by a structural problem. About one-third of the two million farms in West Germany had less than two hectares of land for cultivation which did not allow a sufficiently high rate of productivity[5]. Even with large-scale but uncoordinated imports of American foodstuffs in 1945 and 1946 the level of official rations could not be sustained which in turn had a detrimental impact on labour productivity[6].

When during the severe winter of 1946-47 people died of starvation the Allied realised that aid on a large scale had to be organised. The harsh winter was followed by an extremely dry summer which reduced the already meagre harvest by another 20 per cent. Despite German criticism about the bad quality of the supplies it was the first food relief programme organised by US authorities in 1947, GARIOA, which prevented mass starvation in Germany that year. Before the GARIOA programme had begun food supply in the Ruhr had reached crisis point and was close to collapsing. The situation changed with the harvest of 1948 which turned out to be a record one thanks to perfect weather conditions and not least because of the increased use of fertilizers which had also been imported under GARIOA[7].

Although it has been argued that from 1948 onwards the food situation in West Germany was no longer characterised by hunger food supply remained a serious problem. Not even the Nazis in their drive for autarky had managed to become self-sufficient in foodstuffs and by 1950 they accounted for 44 per cent of West Germany's imports[8]. Although some of these imports may have been paid for

---

[4]Ulrich Kluge, 'West German Agriculture and the European Recovery Program 1948-1952', in: Jeffery Diefendorf, Axel Frohn, Herman-Josef Rupieper (eds) *American Policy and the Reconstruction of West Germany 1945-1955*, Cambridge/Mass., 1993, p. 157; Clay, *Decision*, p. 314.

[5]Milward, *Weltkrieg*, p. 282. Although Milward refers to the French example, the situation in Germany was likely to be worse since the impact of the war was more severe; Kluge, 'West German Agriculture', p. 157.

[6]Clay, *Decision*, pp. 263 ff.

[7]Mark Roseman, *Recasting the Ruhr, 1945-1958: Manpower, Economic Recovery and Labour Relations*, Oxford, New York 1992, pp. 59 ff.; Clay, *Decision*, p. 270; the most notorious criticism was the 'Hühnerfutter Rede' by Erhard's predecessor as Director of Economics, Johannes Semmler.

[8]Friedrich Wilhelm Henning, 'Soziale Marktwirtschaft und Landwirtschaft 1948/49-1955', in: Dietmar Petzina (ed.), *Ordnungspolitische Weichenstellung nach dem Zweiten Weltkrieg*, Berlin 1991, pp. 101, 114 f.

with Marshall Plan or GARIOA money, it still meant a massive drain of the Federal Republic's dollar reserves. The dangerous drain of dollars for food imports had been reason enough for the Bizonal administration to appoint in addition to the Directors of Economics and of Finance the Director for Food, Agriculture, and Forestry to the Kreditanstalt's Board of Directors, as well as another representative for agriculture[9]. Up to 1953 there was a third agricultural lobbyist on the board, Andreas Hermes, Minister for Agriculture during the Weimar Republic and now head of the *Landwirtschaftliche Genossenschaftsbanken* (Agricultural Cooperative Banks). A further indication of the seriousness of agricultural finance problems is the establishment of the *Agrarkreditausschuß* (agricultural credit committee) as one of the Board's subcommittees[10].

Despite this presence of people representing agricultural interests and the importance of domestic foodstuffs, the KfW in its first draft of the 'at once' programme scheduled only DM 5 million to agriculture but the amount was subsequently raised to DM 53 million[11]. The Deputy Director of the VELF, Wilhelm Niklas, who would become Minister for Agriculture later that year, wrote an angry letter to the KfW in which he demanded at least 15 per cent of all the Kreditanstalt's funds for agriculture[12]. In a letter to BiCO, the VfW supported the VELF by describing German agriculture as antiquated in its methods and production. Because of this the food deficit would run up to $1.25 billion by 1949-50, even if the calorie intake were reduced by 10 per cent compared to pre-war standards, which was politically not acceptable. To improve the situation the VfW suggested large-scale schooling and training of farmers and investments in soil improvements like re-parcelling (*Flurbereinigung*), land drainage, land reclamation, resettlement of refugees, and the improvement of pastureland and meadows. The costs of these measures which did not promise any direct return were estimated by the VfW at up to DM 500 million a year. Erhard's administration justified the costs with the long-term benefits for the national economy as a whole. Half the money should be provided by German sources, the other half from counterpart funds with an initial DM 50 million as part of an emergency programme[13].

Due to lack of funds agriculture received only DM 48 million under the 'at once' programme, less than a fifth of the amount the VELF had asked for, but still ten times the amount originally scheduled. The money had to be pre-financed once

---

[9]During the years under investigation, the representation was always given to a member of the *Landwirtschaftliche Rentenbank* (Agricultural Mortgage Bank). Only in later years a representative of the *Bauernverband* (Farmers' Association) was to take its place.
[10]KfW HA-Prot 10-1, Protokoll der 1. Sitzung TOP 9. Only four minutes of meetings could be found and the committee itself was dissolved in 1969, see KfW HA-VS 202.
[11]KfW HA-VS 65, letter, presumably by the BoM, to the Kreditausschuß, 20 January 1949; Pohl, *Wiederaufbau*, p. 53.
[12]KfW HA-BA Sch 4, letter VELF, Dr Niklas to KfW, 15 February 1949.
[13]Ibid., VfW letter to BiCO, 26 May 1949.

more in anticipation of ERP money and was given for various short- and long-term projects. These included loans to rebuild war damaged farm buildings (DM 10 million), soil improvement (DM 15 million), the food processing industry (DM 3 million) and medium term loans to restock equipment (*Inventarkredite*, DM 20 million). Since BiCO insisted on an equal basic rate of interest of 5.5 per cent for all borrowers the programme proceeded only very slowly as it meant 7.5 per cent interest rates for the farmers. This was an exceptionally high rate in the agricultural sector, particularly in comparison to the favourable terms farmers had received during the Nazi years. Therefore, only the medium term re-equipment loans were taken quickly. Apart from credits to the food processing industries the money was given as 'global loans' to the agricultural special banks which in turn handed it to regional branches or directly to the final borrower. This method was necessary to avoid the Kreditanstalt being overloaded with thousands of applications for small credits. Late in 1949, in an attempt to improve the daily diet, in particular the milk supply for children, the KfW provided additional DM 10 million from its bond sales for the construction of fishing trawlers and for dairy factories[14].

Support to agriculture was given in indirect ways, too. As part of the 'at once' programme's section 'other industries' the KfW had suggested to BiCO the release of funds to the potash industry and for a programme to build agricultural tractors. BiCO demanded further information from the Anstalt for both projects in particular because potash fell under the sector of Prohibited and Limited Industries (PLI)[15]. But since potash, an essential ingredient for the production of fertilizers was in short supply in the whole of Europe and some of the production was intended for export, BiCO apparently had no further reservations against either of the programmes, not least because 15,000 tractors out of a total production target of 40,000 were scheduled for export[16]. Both schemes would create hard currency revenue and, if the products were exported to other European countries, would help to improve the situation in agriculture on the Continent.

With the tractor programme the Kreditanstalt für Wiederaufbau helped to initiate a development which was unique in its size and success. In 1948-49 there were only 67,000 tractors in use in the whole of the Bizone whereas five times as many were needed. By 1953 the number of tractors in use had trebled and by 1960 it had increased more than twelve-fold to 824,000[17]. These figures show both the relative backwardness of West German agriculture in the late 1940s and the huge structural changes which took place during the 1950s.

By the end of 1952 the KfW had given loans to support agriculture and the food processing industries amounting to DM 450 million[18]. The sources of the

[14]*Jb* 1949, pp. 28 f; *Jb* 1950, p. 51; Pohl, *Wiederaufbau*, p. 63.
[15]KfW HA-VS 65, BiCO letter (BiCO/Memo (49)33) to KfW Chairman, 30 March 1949.
[16]Pohl, *Wiederaufbau*, p. 60.
[17]Kluge, 'West German Agriculture', p. 160; Arnd Bauerkämper, 'Landwirtschaft und ländliche Gesellschaft in den 50er Jahren', in: Axel Schildt, Arno Sywottek (eds), *Modernisierung im Wiederaufbau*, Bonn 1993, p. 193.
[18]*Jb* 1952, p. 51.

money are shown in Table 6.1. These loans, in some cases the money was even given as grants, made up about 10 per cent of all counterpart aid given. In the early years this singled out agriculture as the most subsidised of all commercial sectors, second only to housing construction and one which stood well outside the market economy[19].

Table 6.1
Source and Utilisation of KfW Loans to Agriculture 1949-1952
(in million DM)

	ECA I	ECA II	ECA III	ABP	others	Total
Bldng. reconstr.	22	25.8		1.1		48.9
Soil improvement	30.9	33.1		10.4		74.4
Resettlements	8.6	9.1	20[1]	44.5		82.2
Med. term invest. loans	44.9	30.8	79		1	155.7
Dairy and food Industry	15	10.9	29.3	3.3	15.8	74.3
Others		1.4	11.9		1	14.3
Total	121.4	111.1[2]	140.2[3]	59.3	17.8	449.8

[1] Only handed over to Lastenausgleichsbank.
[2] Without grants of DM 73.6 million.
[3] Without grants of DM 40 million.

Source: *Jb* 1952, p. 51.

As the table shows, the biggest share of loans went to medium-term investment credits. The term includes investments in all kinds of machinery and labour saving devices. While these loans were available to small, medium-sized and large farmers, they were essential for the medium-sized farmers (12-24 ha) because their costs for replacing labour with machinery was about five times as high as those for small or large farms[20]. The second biggest share of the funds given until 1952,

[19]From a total of DM 262 million in grants given from the ERP Special assets until 1956, DM 157 million went to agriculture, see Baumgart, *Investitionen*, pp. 30, 96 f.; *Jb 1952*, p. 46. One has to deduct BdL money, AIL funds, and other sources from the total of DM 5.3 billion which had been processed by the Kreditanstalt until the end of 1952.

[20] Bauerkämper, 'Landwirtschaft', p. 193, gives the replacement costs of labour for small and large farms (less than six or more than 60 ha) with DM 6-12,000 as compared to DM 30-60,000 for medium-sized farms.

figure is impressive. Nevertheless, only a relatively small number of projects could be financed since usually a whole new farm had to be set up and equipped with all the machinery and livestock. The major problem the KfW was faced with was once more the question of securities which could hardly be expected from refugees. In March 1950 the Kreditanstalt raised the matter in a letter to the BMP. They suggested exempting the banks involved in loans for refugee resettlement from any liabilities for these credits in order to speed up the processing of loans by reducing the banks' risk. In April the KfW repeated their plea twice and reminded the BMP of the growing tensions and dissatisfaction amongst refugees. The ministry finally responded and agreed to postpone any claims for securities until a new settlement was entered into the land registry[21]. Despite some efforts, the integration of refugees who were previously independent farmers into West German agriculture failed for various reasons as previous research has shown. Three-hundred thousand refugees had been registered as independent farmers in 1939. By 1949 they ran less than 1,000 farms. When in 1960 this figure climbed to 60,000 it was only because more than half of these farms had a size of 5 hectares or less so that they could only be used for secondary occupation (*Nebenerwerbsstellen*)[22]. These small-scale farms were seen as a less than ideal solution to the problem of integrating the refugees since they held not the same social status as full-scale farms and caused other structural problems such as the question of long-term viability[23]. But since the western Allies had not carried out a land reform there was a lack of available land. However, the impact of the emerging structural change which made former farmers find employment in other sectors helped to avoid possible social tension and political dissatisfaction which could have arisen from the comparatively small number of resettled refugees.

Soil improvement and the dairy and food processing industries received nearly the same amount of money from the Kreditanstalt. The first included everything from reforestation and small plot re-parcelling to productivity improvements, the encouragement of mechanisation even for small farmers, draining fields, and the *Emsland Projekt*. Under that name half a million hectares of new land for cultivation was claimed[24]. This land in turn could be used to help resettle some of the refugee farmers also easing some of the political and social tensions within this group. Soil improvement was certainly one of the most important tasks the KfW supported although it was usually an endeavour which yielded little direct financial benefit. This was different to loans to the dairy and food processing industries. Credits to the dairy sector were mainly used to improve the milk supply and were aimed at promoting better public health, especially

---

[21]KfW HA-BA Sch 27, KfW letters to the BMP, 16 March 1950, 11 April and 26 April 1950, BMF letter to BMP, 13 May 1950.

[22]Bauerkämper, 'Landwirtschaft', p. 189.

[23]Herbert Kötter, 'Die Landwirtschaft', in: Rainer M. Lepsius, Werner Conze (eds), *Sozialgeschichte der Bundesrepublik. Beiträge zum Kontinuitätsproblem*, Stuttgart 1983, p. 128.

[24]Kluge, 'West German Agriculture', p. 166.

amongst children. The main beneficiaries in the food processing industries were the sugar refineries[25]. Since sugar could be sold quite easily on the export markets, it not only improved and satisfied the domestic market but also helped to further the West German currency situation, for the raw material, sugar beet, was traditionally grown in Germany. The overall success of these investments is impressive. Although the size of arable land had increased by about only 1 per cent, the harvest of bread wheat was about one-third higher in the early 1960s than it had been in 1950, the yield of sugar beet had increased by 40 per cent. At the same time average milk production per cow had risen from 2,400 litres per year to 3,400[26].

Nearly DM 50 million were given to the reconstruction of war damaged farm buildings since farm destruction had occurred on a large-scale. Some estimates spoke of the destruction of up to 64,000 farms by the end of the war. The destruction was concentrated along Germany's western borders in the so-called 'red zones', the ministerial term for areas which had experienced heavy ground fighting in 1944-45. By the end of 1950 the KfW had given more than 3,000 global loans for the purpose of reconstruction in those areas and they had a wider impact, too[27]. Since many of the destroyed farms lay in areas such as the Eifel, with relatively harsh weather conditions and soil unfavourable to farming, the loans also helped to ease the strain on the farmers. New sheds and stables, for example, allowed animal breeding and the eradicating of tuberculosis in cattle which helped to improve farmers' income and general food supplies at the same time.

When the Americans released the money for the 'at once' programme in 1949, the farmers responded slowly. This was not only because they were confronted with a new system of financial aid at the beginning of the harvest season. The real reason was the handicap of interest rates which on the American's insistence were 5.5 per cent for the KfW and consequently 7.5 per cent for the farmers[28]. This rate was too high for long-term farm investments and appropriate only for the food-processing industry and medium term loans to buy machinery. As soon as the counterpart funds came under German administration the Kreditanstalt tried to lower the rates. At a meeting at the Landwirtschaftliche Rentenbank on 22 December 1949 during which the first ERP loans by the KfW for the French zone were also discussed, new rates were set[29]. The KfW on this occasion stressed that it was a matter for the banks and not the *Land* governments to decide on the granting

---

[25]*Jb* 1952, p. 50.
[26]Bauerkämper, 'Landwirtschaft', pp. 191 f.
[27]KfW HA-BA Sch 47, map 'Notstandsgebiete in der Bundesrepublik'; *Jb* 1950, p. 53; Kluge, 'West German Agriculture', p. 157.
[28]*Jb* 1949, pp. 28 f.
[29]Due to the earlier French policy of economic exploitation of their zone of occupation, the 'at once' programme had been limited to the American and British zones, see Abelshauser, *Wirtschaftsgeschichte*, pp. 37, 39.

of loans thus strengthening the banks' authority against political influence[30]. In the end the Kreditanstalt won the argument and from then on loans from ERP funds were given according to the conditions shown in Table 6.2.

For political reasons the BdL was not prepared to grant loans under the work creation scheme's *Schwerpunktprogramm* to the KfW on similarly favourable low interest terms. Instead the BdL insisted on a 4 per cent base rate for the Kreditanstalt. To grant loans to the farmers on reasonable interest rates and to make the *Schwerpuktprogramm* work for farming the *Land* governments of Bavaria, Lower Saxony, and Schleswig Holstein (which were the only ones to benefit from the scheme due to their large numbers of refugees) agreed to cover 2 per cent of the final borrowers' 4.5 per cent interest rate. It was a difficult decision for these relatively poor *Länder* and indeed, by 1954 they were so indebted that they could no longer afford to pay for the scheme[31]. Nevertheless, the extra cheap and long running loans to agriculture, in particular money for the re-parcelling of small plots and land cultivation which then allowed increased mechanisation and new machinery, paid off as production increased on a huge scale.

Table 6.2
Interest Rates and Validity of Loans from ERP Funds to Agriculture
(in per cent and years)

	KfW rate	Final rate	Validity yrs.	Repayment free yrs.
Land cultivation	1.25	2.5	37	3
Refugee settlement	1.25-1.75	2.5	44	3
Farm rebuilding	3	4	42	3
Food industry	5.5	7.5	10	1-3
Med. term invest. Loans (ECA I&II)	3.5	5	10	-

Source: KfW HA-BA Sch 5, Vermerk Schölzel, 26.1. 1954.

The growth in agricultural production and the developing oversupply brought about a decisive change in agricultural policy in 1951. The pricing method was changed from a system of maximum prices to one of minimum prices, in other words

[30]KfW HA-BA Sch 27, minutes of a meeting at the Landwirtschaftliche Rentenbank on 22 December 1949.

[31]KfW HA-BA Sch 37, note 17 February 1954 regarding a meeting at the BMELF on 10 February 1954. The matter could only be settled in 1957 since none of the involved federal ministers were prepared to take on the costs of DM 43 million.

protectionism for the farmers[32]. The change also symbolised an end to attempts to integrate agriculture as a whole in the market economy and the beginning of even more subsidies. The political lobby for agriculture prevailed into the Federal Republic although the large landowners east of the river Elbe had lost most of the influence in politics they had enjoyed during the Kaiserreich and the Weimar Republic. The *Grüne Front* secured their influence in the first Bundestag (1949-1953) with their presence in all parties except the KPD[33]. The battle over whether or not agriculture should become more market oriented had already being fought during the Bizonal period. Here the VELF Director, Hans Schlange-Schöningen, was regarded as consumer friendly and therefore pro market. He came under severe pressure from the farmers' associations, in particular from Bavarian members. Adenauer in the end bowed to their pressure and did not nominate him as Minister for Agriculture[34]. The job was given instead to his deputy in the VELF, Niklas, who was regarded as a mild protectionist of agricultural interests. But with his Staatssekretär, Sonnemann, a wholehearted protectionist became the second man in the ministry, which left little doubt about the course of the new government. Schlange-Schöningen's previous attempts to introduce the market economy to agriculture were abandoned for the sake of the farmers' political support[35].

Other than the farming vote, which went mainly to the conservative parties of the government coalition it was foreign policy, namely the Cold War and the emerging European integration which provided further reasons for the West German administration to support farmers. For one, there were growing numbers of agriculturists fleeing the GDR in the hope of a better living in the West. In 1951, 4,343 went to the West, in 1952 the figure had risen to 14,141 before it peaked at 37,396 in 1953, and these figures do not include family members. As a result 13 per cent of all cultivated land in the GDR was abandoned[36]. Although there was never enough land in West Germany to resettle all of these farmers and most had to look for other jobs so the number of resettlements steadily declined during the 1950s Cold War politics might have played a role in the continuing support for farming as well[37]. The decline in resettlement figures was also the result of the

---

[32]Henning, 'Soziale Marktwirtschaft', p. 105.

[33]Kötter, 'Landwirtschaft', pp. 117 f.; Henning, 'Soziale Marktwirtschaft', p. 114. The term *Grüne Front* was first used in 1929 to describe a loose alliance of various German agricultural interest groups. See also Hans-Peter Ullmann, *Interessenverbände in Deutschland*, Frankfurt/M. 1988, pp. 144 ff., 247 ff.

[34]Henning, 'Soziale Marktwirtschaft', p. 108; Pünder, *Interregnum*, p. 284; see also Günter Trittel, 'Hans Schlange-Schöningen. Ein vergessener Politiker der "ersten Stunde"', in: *VfZ* No. 35 (1987), pp. 25 ff.

[35]Henning, 'Soziale Marktwirtschaft', pp. 109, 113.

[36]Steininger, *Deutsche Geschichte*, p. 454.

[37]Franz Josepf Bauer, 'Der Bayerische Bauernverband, die Bodenreform und das Flüchtlingsproblem 1945-1951', in: *VfZ* No. 31 (1983), pp. 476 ff; Hans Heinrich Herlemann, 'Vertriebene Bauern im Strukturwandel der Landwirtschaft', in: Eugen Lemberg, Friedrich

biggest structural change in the history of modern Germany. Between 1950 and 1956 more than 800,000 fully employed workers left agriculture to find employment in other sectors. The share of the sector's workforce fell from 25 per cent in 1950 to 18 per cent in 1956 and continued to fall thereafter[38]. While agriculture 'slimmed down' (*gesundschrumpfen)* it provided, at the same time, new workers for the ever more booming secondary and tertiary sectors.

In the face of the accelerating food production in Europe and with agricultural integration looming in the wake of the Coal and Steel Community, further subsidies for German agriculture were necessary to enable farmers to keep up with their European competitors. Although this development was based on fairly old-fashioned, if not totally out-dated ideas of the 19th century nation state, it set a trend which would haunt Europe for the rest of the century.

The year 1955 saw a new high point in the development of agricultural subsidies, taking agriculture conclusively out of Erhard's market economy. In spite of the declining number of farms and the growing size of the harvests which began to produce mountains of surplus, the Adenauer government passed the *Landwirtschaftsgesetz* (agricultural law), better known as the *Grüne Plan*. The scheme was heavily motivated by politics that is to slow down the migration from the land. Traditionally, farmers held a more conservative view on political matters which made them natural voters for Adenauer's CDU. The subsidies enabled in particular small and medium-sized farmers to stay in business by improving their productivity without which they were unable to run a profitable farm and to sustain competitiveness. Therefore, money was given to a certain 'middle class' of farmers who were supposed to be 'rooted to the soil' (*bodenständig*) and determined to hold on to traditional political views and to old ways of life in spite of the modernisation which went on all around them[39]. The *Grüne Plan*'s economic aim therefore was to increase agricultural productivity and improve the income situation of farmers which lagged far behind the development of wages and income, in particular in industry, in order to make them stay on their farms[40]. The social aspect of the plan then was so stabilise the deteriorating income situation in rural areas and help to prevent 20 per cent of the rural population from sliding into poverty. At the same time this was supposed to stabilise the *gesellschaftspolitische* structure of the young republic by sustaining the myth and image of the small-scale family run farming business[41].

Although the *Grüne Plan* was propagated with those structural policies in mind there is one more aspect to it. West Germany's backward agricultural sector had to be made fit for the emerging European Economic Community, the EEC.

Edding (eds), *Die Vertriebenen in Westdeutschland - Ihre Eingliederung und ihr Einfluß in Gesellschaft, Wirtschaft, Politik und Geistesleben,* 3 vols., Kiel 1959, vol. 2, p. 76.

[38]Baumgart, *Investitionen*, pp. 102 f.

[39]Baumgart, *Investitionen*, p. 100.

[40]Bauerkämper, 'Landwirtschaft', pp. 194 f.

[41]Thiemeyer, *Pool Vert*, pp. 30, 262.

Ludwig Erhard's and Franz Blücher's attempt in the Cabinet to integrate agriculture into the market economy had failed due to Adenauer's veto and his idea to subordinate agricultural policy under the foreign policy. Thereafter there was no way to prevent the establishment of the EEC as an organisation which would provide supra-national protection against outside market forces. The new body was seen by all European governments which participated in the community as a perfect instrument to keep European farming outside any trade liberalisation and competitive markets[42]. But at least inside the common market German farming had to face and withstand a competitive market.

A key component of the *Grüne Plan* was the increased re-parcelling of scattered plots which was now often accompanied by the wholesale relocation of farms out of the often cramped villages and towns. Over 14,000 farms were relocated under the scheme while 10 per cent of all agricultural land was affected by re-parcelling[43].

Baumgart calculated the share of ERP funds to agriculture between 1949 and 1956 to be 7.4 per cent of all ERP loans which indicates a decline in agriculture's share since 1952. Up to 1955 the KfW had lent DM 571 million to farming, DM 480 million of which came from ERP funds. The *Grüne Plan*, though, had a different dimension. In 1955 alone, money from the federal budget amounting to DM 1 billion was scheduled and it was to be increased to DM 2.2 billion in 1956. These figures did not include money provided by the Länder governments and local authorities[44].

With the 1955 *Landwirtschaftsgesetz*, new lending patterns for the KfW emerged. Until then funds for agriculture had been determined by the so-called 'coloured zones'. The 'red zone' was defined as having suffered from heavy fighting and was mainly in the west of the country. The 'blue zone' defined areas impoverished due to a high rate of unemployment and a high influx of refugees. Schleswig-Holstein, the Emsland in the north-west corner of the Republic, north-east Hesse, parts of northern Bavaria, and the Rhineland were the areas most affected. The 'green zone' finally was defined as regions of structural agricultural weakness and comprised eastern and parts of northern Bavaria, several districts of Rhineland-Palatinate and Hesse and stretches of Lower Saxony. Now the Kreditanstalt für Wiederaufbau was asked to give up these criteria and instead disburse any funds throughout the whole of the country to places and projects which were most in need of money[45]. Table 6.3 shows loans to agriculture given by

---

[42]Thiemeyer, *Pool Vert*, p. 115; Henning, 'Soziale Marktwirtschaft', p. 115; Alan Milward, 'Entscheidungsphasen der Westintegration', in: Ludolf Herbst (ed.), *Westdeutschland 1945-1955*, p. 245.

[43]The test case and some of the difficulties it experienced are described in: *Der Spiegel*, No. 12, 1955, pp. 18 ff.; Bauerkämper, 'Landwirtschaft', p. 194.

[44]Baumgart, *Investitionen*, pp. 98 f; *Jb* 1954, p. 45.

[45]KfW HA-BA Sch 47, map 'Notstandsgebiete'; letter BMELF to KfW, 15 November 1954.

the KfW in 1956-1960 and a comparison with Table 6.1 shows that now the emphasis had shifted to the improvement of infrastructure in general.

Most of the money came from the ERP Special Assets that is from interests or repayments of previous ERP loans. Of course, since the federal government was contributing at least DM 1 billion to agriculture every year, the importance of KfW loans declined. Money for the position 'general agriculture' included loans for further mechanisation and rationalisation as well as credits for the establishment of *Aussiedlerhöfe* (relocation outside the village or town) and the repair or extension of existing farm buildings. Loans for the re-parcelling of small plots were supplemented with money designated for the construction of *Wirtschaftswege* (small roads for agricultural use) to improve farmers' access to their fields and transportation facilities for harvests. The electricity supply to rural regions previously without connection to the national grid allowed farmers in more remote and backward areas to use all kinds of electrically powered machinery like milking machines and cutters. In some parts along the border with the GDR it meant the return of electricity supply which had been interrupted due to the partition of the country[46].

Table 6.3
Confirmed KfW Credits to Agriculture 1956-1960*
(in million DM)

	1956	1957	1958	1959	1960	Total
Agricult., general	10.3	24.2	71.1	53.9	34.3	193.8
Rural electricity	14.4	0.6	18.8	5.6	6.3	45.7
Rural water supply	19.7	46.8	41.6	45.4	42.0	195.5
Agric. road constr.		10.0			11.7	21.7
Food industry	0.2	4.3	28.5	23.6	27.0	83.6
Fishing vessels	0.7		6.0	5.6	6.1	18.4
Total	45.3	85.9	166.0	134.1	127.4	558.7

* Due to changes in the presentation of the annual reports and because of ongoing changes in the planning, these figures are only approximations.

Source: *Jb* 1957-1960, passim.

The biggest single slice of KfW money went into the rural water supply which in many areas was in an appalling state. Provisions under the term *Wasserversorgung*

[46] *Jb* 1957-1960, passim.

did not only mean the connection to a modern supply of fresh water in remote areas, it also took care of sewage, farm cesspits and regional sewage plants which all helped to improve public health[47]. The Kreditanstalt had already received a letter from the Bayerische Gemeindebank-Girozentrale in 1949 which desperately asked for money to improve the water supply for nine Bavarian districts. Single cases of typhoid fever had already been reported and the outbreak of an epidemic was feared if the water supply could not be improved[48]. Due to the shortage of funds in 1949 no money could be given for such projects but they were tackled with much greater urgency after 1955 when the means had become available.

Without help, West German farming would have been unable to recover let alone surpass its pre-war production within such a short time. At first American fertilizers and later Bizonal and West German administrative involvement were essential for the recovery. Projects such as the re-parcelling of small plots were only possible with large-scale financial support provided by the counterpart funds. Consequently, the KfW as the central institution for the distribution of the ERP funds took a leading role in farm subsidies. The farmers, who had initially demanded an end to price controls in 1948 so that they could participate in the post currency profit rush, changed their view in 1951 when the price rise of the Korea crisis was over. Adenauer met their new demands for protection because of political and ideological reasons, despite protests from Erhard and Blücher. It was once more the Kreditanstalt für Wiederaufbau which helped finance the important but less profitable long-term investments in the country's agricultural infrastructure. Although the KfW itself warned against the growing agricultural surplus production encouraged by these subsidies it stuck to the course given by the politicians[49].

---

[47]*Jb* 1956-1960, passim.
[48]BA Z 45 F-Fin 9/4, I. Fiche, letter Bayerische Gemeindebank (Girozentrale) to the KfW's Board of Managers, 11 May 1949.
[49]*Jb* 1958, p. 23.

Chapter 7

Basic Industries

Basic industries, in this context defined as the Ruhr coal industry, the steel and the electrical power industries were of particular importance during the reconstruction process. Well beyond their economic significance which was central to German and European recovery, they were a political battleground as well. In the coal industry for example the Americans, prior to the Schuman Plan and the establishment of the European Coal and Steel Community (ECSC) had to try to accommodate French demands for Ruhr coal and security against Germany whilst they were faced with German resistance to Allied influence in the industry. Furthermore, in terms of economic policy and ideology the Ruhr mines were for years at the centre of a row about whether or not the industry should be nationalised. The same political conflicts were present in the iron and steel industry but there was a remarkable economic difference between the two. The share of iron and steel's investment from counterpart funds was much smaller compared to coal. The reasons for this will be given in section 7.2. The electrical power industry, finally, was much less influenced by international policy but it nevertheless took a special role in the reconstruction process, not least because of its ownership. Although it appears that the sector needed least counterpart finance it actually received the biggest share within the early years of reconstruction. It was also in the electricity industry that the Kreditanstalt first got involved in structural policy.

7.1 Ruhr Coal Industry

Although there was little damage to the pits themselves in 1945, of all the economic sectors described here Ruhr coal mining was the one most affected by Nazi rule and the impact of war. The reason for this paradox lay in Nazi economic policy which had neglected investments in the capital extensive mining industry. Since 1936 no major investment in maintenance or machinery had taken place and no new shafts had been sunk. Instead, the existing pits had been ruthlessly exploited without any long-term considerations. During the war, forced labour from deported foreigners and prisoners of war was used to keep output figures high. By the end of the war slave labour at the coalface made up nearly half the workforce. Consequently, with the liberation of the deportees and POWs the underground workforce shrunk to some 127,500 men, just half its 1938 size. Due to the structural changes which had taken place in mining in the 1920s and 1930s, many of these men were near retirment age[1]. After Germany's defeat the food supplies to the Ruhr had collapsed and caused malnourishment among the population. This, together with the lack of decent housing resulting from Allied air raids on the Ruhr led to a severe decline in coal production. By the end of 1945 coal output was less than 40 per cent of the 1938 output[2]. Worse from a German perspective, Ruhr coal was also exported to the neighbouring countries as hidden reparations on a large scale and to enable the reconstruction of those countries. In particular France received large quantities during the late 1940s to carry out its ambitious Monnet Plan. The scheme had been set up to modernise French industry and to expand its capacity with the aim of replacing Germany as the economic centre of Europe, thus preventing Germany from starting another war in the future[3]. In their attempt to prevent future German aggression the British followed a different path which was in line with the Labour Party's desire for public ownership. In December 1945 the British Military Government expropriated the pits and in October 1946 they announced their intention to nationalise them[4].

Throughout 1945 and 1946 the coal supply situation remained critical despite strong Anglo-American efforts to raise output. Production figures did not even reach 50 per cent of pre-war levels and the French still demanded a large share of it. The cold winter of 1946-47 with its 'stagnation crisis' terminated what had already been achieved in German reconstruction and worsened the European coal situation altogether[5]. British coal supplies to France and Belgium which amounted to 38,000 tons and 4,500 tons respectively in September 1946 dropped to 1,500 tons for France and to zero for Belgium in February 1947. This collapse was not only a result of the cold winter since no coal was sent to France or Belgium in May and June 1947 either, but it was a sign of the collapse of British coal mining altogether[6].

As a result of the emerging Cold War the tide began to turn for Ruhr coal mining. US Secretary of State Byrnes' speech at Stuttgart in September 1946 was the first sign that the Americans were to help with Germany's reconstruction. Mid-term elections in the USA in November 1946 returned a Republican majority to Congress which had many reservations or was even openly hostile to the Soviet Union. Congressmen began to demand an end to Americas 'Morgenthau policy' in Germany and the country's integration into the western camp[7]. Marshall's Harvard

---

[1]Abelshauser, *Ruhrkohle*, pp. 16 ff; Roseman, *Ruhr*, p. 24.
[2]Mark Roseman, 'The Uncontrolled Economy: Ruhr Coal Production 1945-48', in: Ian Turner (ed.), *Reconstruction in Post-War Germany*, Oxford, New York 1989, p. 95.
[3]Hogan, *Marshall Plan*, p. 32.
[4]Abelshauser, *Ruhrkohle*, pp. 15, 24 f.
[5]Roseman, 'Economy', p.107; Clay, *Decision*, pp. 193 f.; Abelshauser, *Westdeutschland*, pp. 36, 39f., 43, 47.
[6]PRO FO 371 62497; John Gillingham, *Coal, Steel, and the Rebirth of Europe 1945-1955*, Cambridge 1991, pp. 48, 84 f.
[7]Gillingham, *Coal*, pp. 112 ff.

speech in June 1947 marked the official change in US policy in Europe and in Germany in particular. The next step to rehabilitate Ruhr coal was a NBC radio broadcast by General Draper, US Deputy Military Governor in Germany, and Assistant Secretary of State, Thorp, on 16 August 1947 with the title 'Germany's Coal: Key to the Marshall Plan'[8]. Both the Harvard Speech and the broadcast were attempts by the Truman administration to sell the new US policy to the American public, which partly still hung on to Morgenthau's idea of de-industrialising Germany. The US government had realised that if they rebuilt German basic industries they would also support the European reconstruction. Economic improvements in Europe, especially in France, were seen as the best way to alleviate French fears of a German revival and at the same time a means to prevent the spread of Communism on the old continent.

On the ground, the British meanwhile had tried to increase the workforce at the coalface in order to boost output. All attempts, both on a voluntary and on a cohesive basis showed little success and the number of miners rose only very slowly. Only when the Joint Economic Area, the Bizone, was established on 1 January 1947, the previous *Gießkannenprinzip* ('watering can principle') of scattering funds and materials was abandoned and more resources were poured into mining as the new key sector of reconstruction[9]. In particular increased food rations for miners became a reason for men to enter the pits and with an increasing number of men at the coalface, output increased as well.

However, the system under which these additional rations were provided and which had been introduced to give an additional incentive for higher output drained so many resources from other sectors and redirected scarce food supplies from the rest of the population that it could not be maintained[10]. Nevertheless, Gillingham's judgement that British coal policy was a total failure and that the Americans had to correct every British mistake is not balanced enough. It neglects not least the economic strain under which Great Britain suffered and it does not take into account the special situation and deficiencies of the Ruhr in 1945-1950.

In August 1947, during the Washington Coal Conference, the Americans scored important political points when they convinced the British to suspend the nationalisation of the Ruhr coal industry for five years[11]. The American argument that such an important decision should be avoided in order not to predetermine any possible German settlement of the matter in the future is a hollow one since the postponement in itself constituted a predetermination. The American stand against nationalisation derived much more from a principal dislike of any socialist ideas, which had already become obvious in 1946 when General Clay had vetoed nationalisation of industry in Hesse. He told his deputy that time was working for the Americans and against socialisation. If they could revitalise the German

---

[8]PRO FO 371 65344.
[9]Gillingham, *Coal*, pp. 121 ff.; Abelshauser, *Wirtschaftsgeschichte*, pp. 41 f.
[10]Roseman, 'Economy', p. 115.
[11]Roseman, *Ruhr*, p. 85.

economy the question would not arise again[12]. Another reason for OMGUS's opposition to nationalisation was that about two-thirds of top grade pits in the Ruhr belonged to a Maryland holding company via the US registered Hugo Stinnes Corporation[13]. This company would have suffered a financial loss in the case of socialisation as well as a loss of long-term influence on an important part of German industry.

Instead of socialisation the Washington Coal Conference suggested the strengthening of the German coal management. Consequently, in November 1947 the *Deutsche Kohlenbergbau Leitung* (DKBL) was set up to act as trustee for the expropriated pits. To control the DKBL's activities, the Allies in turn set up the UK/US Coal Control Group (UK/US CCG) as a branch of BiCO. With the threat of nationalisation averted and their position within the framework of the DKBL strengthened, German management regained some of its old confidence and influence over the workforce which also helped to improve output figures. Despite the improvements in the second half of 1947 many problems remained. The DKBL had to invest RM 2 to 2.5 per metric ton of coal produced while it received only RM 1.5 per ton for its sales[14]. The lack of long-term investment capital which resulted from the collapse of the German capital market was a severe handicap. On the rare occasions that a bank had enough funds, it was not prepared to lend them to pits which were under Allied control. Investments in the mines financed by profits were not possible either. The Allies had fixed the price for Ruhr coal exports at $10.5 per ton while the world market price was $25 to $30, thus the mines lost $200 million before the end of 1947 because of forced coal exports[15]. The forced exports to neighbouring countries in particular to France, was a reason for the DKBL not to push harder for an increase in output. Instead of trying to maximise production and increase the arithmetical deficit, the DKBL secretly devoted its best trained miners to extend the mines' future capacity instead of increasing the output. In the eyes of the coal administration this was a legitimate compensation for the lack of investments since 1936 while they hoped at the same time for higher profits in the future when coal price controls were lifted. From the German authorities the DKBL received sympathy if not hidden support for its actions because it was ultimately the Bizonal administration which had to cover the pits' losses[16].

In 1948 there were more setbacks for the mining industry, despite previous improvements. The first big blow was of a political nature and came in the form of the appointment of Ludwig Erhard as the Director of the *Verwaltung für Wirtschaft*

---

[12]Abelshauser, *Ruhrkohle*, p. 29.
[13]Kolko, *Limits*, p. 140.
[14]Roseman, *Ruhr*, pp. 85 ff.
[15]Abelshauser, *Ruhrkohle*, p. 36.
[16]NA, RG 260, OMGUS, BiCO, box 48, Joint Chairmen meeting with Bizonal officials, BiCO letter BICO/Memo (48)105 to President, Bizonal Economic Council, 21 December 1948; Roseman, *Ruhr*, p. 91.

(VfW) on 2 March 1948[17]. The currency reform and his economic policy thereafter made it clear that the basic industries and in particular coal mining were not on Erhard's list of priorities. The only positive effect the reform had for the mines was that money and therefore wages had regained their importance so that absenteeism in the pits fell and output rose. But this advantage was easily outweighed by the problems the reform brought for the industry. The fact that the new DM now was a 'hard' currency and the fact that its introduction brought a severe cut in money supply caused a crisis of liquidity for the collieries[18]. Now even more than before the currency reform, banks were reluctant to give loans to the expropriated pits. The cash shortage was made worse when prices for consumer goods and non-basic foodstuffs were freed but those for basic goods including coal remained fixed[19]. The basic industries were now not only prevented from reinvesting any profits but also lost their last connection to banks, which would widen the investment gap between them and the consumer goods industries. The price for one metric ton of coal, fixed by the Nazis at RM 10.5, had risen to RM 25 by the time of the currency reform. Although it was raised further by Erhard on 1 August 1948 to DM 32.5 it was not enough to cover the necessary investments in mining which in 1948-49 were estimated at DM 1.5 billion for the next three years. The situation was worsened by the fact that a third of production which had to be exported was still sold at the old price on the orders of the Allies. The demand for Ruhr coal in western Europe was so high that the Allies had to insist on keeping even unproductive pits in operation. The resulting deficit was first covered by the budget of the British zone of occupation and later by the Bizone[20].

Erhard had certainly no intention of using his spare resources for subsidising the mines but at the same time he could not free prices which would have allowed more self-finance for the pits. His own plan for economic reconstruction depended on cheap coal to produce cheap energy to create a competitive advantage for the consumer goods industries and German exporters. How much he relied on cheap coal became clear one year later when he stated that a price increase for coal could trigger a general price rise of 25 per cent[21]. The paramount problems of Ruhr coal mining, insufficient output, forced exports, fixed prices and a lack of funds would continue until the early 1950s with both German and Allied administrations trying to gain political or economic capital from the insufficient capital supply and output figures. The Germans were more successful as they achieved eventually the abolition of Allied controls and the scrapping of additional German investment programmes demanded by the Americans.

---

[17]PRO FO 371 70582 C 1842. For Erhard's ideas see: Ludolf Herbst, 'Krisenüberwindung und Wirtschaftsneuordnung. Ludwig Erhards Beteiligung an der Nachkriegsplanung am Ende des 2. Weltkrieges', in: *VfZ* No. 25 (1977), pp. 305 ff.

[18]Roseman, *Ruhr*, p. 127; Gillingham, *Coal*, p. 185.

[19]Benz, *Gründung*, p. 90; Roseman, *Ruhr*, pp. 124 f.

[20]Abelshauser, *Ruhrkohle*, p. 65; Roseman, *Ruhr*, pp. 125 ff.; Clay, *Decision*, pp. 195 f; Roseman, 'Economy', p. 122.

[21]*Kabinettsprotokolle*, vol. 1, p. 92.

The second major setback for the collieries in 1948 was the publication of Military Government Law No. 75 on 10 November. It outlined in detail the deconcentration and breaking up of the German coal and steel combines[22]. Although the law left the nationalisation issue to a future German government it dashed hopes for a quick return to private ownership. In spite of the law being a compromise between the Allies' ban on cartels and economic conglomerates of February 1947 and the necessity to retain a certain size for the companies' economic viability Law 75 was regarded as a severe blow to the economic situation of the coal mines and showed once more the ambivalence of Allied policy[23]. The law also meant a shift in Allied priorities; increasing coal output now came second to dismantling the integrated structure of the Ruhr industries. Abelshauser concluded that in face of the coal shortage Allied decartellisation policy also served their material interests since the shortfall in Europe had to be made up with imports from Britain and the USA[24].

For the British it meant limiting German competition on the north-west European coal market, the Americans for their part could fill the European coal gap with their own supplies. Nevertheless American coal policy remained ambivalent which showed itself once more when they intervened in Erhard's policy during the consultations for the 'at once' programme. BiCO increased the share of money designed for coal mining from DM 75 to DM 135 million in an attempt to refocus reconstruction efforts back to the basic industries and coal in particular, partly to balance the negative effects of their decartelisation policy[25].

The 'at once' programme became the first in a long line of projects with which the Kreditanstalt für Wiederaufbau supported the coal mining industry. The money was scheduled for three special areas. DM 35 million had to be used to redeem intermediate finance (*Zwischenfinanzierung*) or to pay overdue bills. DM 90 million went to 60 different pits for all kinds of investment. By the time the plan had been drawn up it was not quite clear whether this included miners' housing construction as well. In the end, some DM 23 million went into such projects, while the remaining DM 10 million were used to pay for new ERP imports[26]. The latter case demonstrates that counterpart loans had to be used to pay for new ERP imports simply because it was the cheapest and often the only money available to pay for them. In the end five collieries dropped out of the programme and the money went to 55 mines where it was spent within three months[27].

---

[22]Abelshauser, *Ruhrkohle*, p. 51. The law reprinted in: Ruhm von Oppen, *Documents*, pp. 335 ff.

[23]Peter Hüttenberger, 'Wirtschaftsordnung und Interessenpolitik in der Kartellgesetzgebung der Bundesrepublik 1949-1957', in: *VfZ* No. 24 (1976), p. 290.

[24]Abelshauser, *Ruhrkohle*, p. 56, see also p. 50.

[25]Pohl, *Wiederaufbau*, p. 53; *Jb* 1949, p. 21. The KfW's language states the facts a bit more diplomatically.

[26]KfW HA-Prot 10-1, Protokoll der 5. Sitzung, TOP 5.

[27]*Jb* 1949, p. 21.

After the 'at once' programme money had been spent the KfW was faced with the task of raising another DM 100 million for the third quarter to keep investments going until the expected release of the first ERP counterpart funds[28]. Half of the DM 100 million came from the special ERP allotment, the other DM 50 million were short-term borrowings which had to be offset against the first anticipated ECA tranche. DM 32 million of these came from bills of exchange written out by the collieries themselves[29]. This was actually a money-creating scheme similar to the Nazis' MEFO system, only on a scale of millions instead of billions. The mines issued bills of exchange which were accepted by the Kreditanstalt so that they could be drawn at the Bank deutscher Länder on the account of the KfW. The bills accepted by the Anstalt were then offered to the banks but without their responsibility to prolong them. Thus the whole risk remained with the Kreditanstalt. The only 'security' the KfW received was the confirmation by the Allies that it would be the first to claim a mortgage on the pits when these were released from Law No. 75. Even some senior German officials were extremely critical of this kind of financing which they called 'unhealthy' but it went on regardless[30]. By the end of August 1949, BiCO applied to the ECA for the release of counterpart funds. When the ERP administration released the first tranche in early 1950, a third of the DM 150 million scheduled for mining under the ECA I programme had to be used to redeem the bills of exchange and the loan from the unemployment insurance leaving just DM 100 million for the urgently needed new investments[31].

Two events in 1950 changed the whole political framework of the Ruhr mining industry but they did not change the economic situation, on the contrary they caused an even higher demand for money in the short-run. The first event was an announcement by the French Foreign Minister Robert Schuman on 9 May 1950 that proposed the establishment of a joint European coal and steel industry under a common administration. The Schuman Plan, the name under which the proposal became famous, was the French reaction to the political disappointments France had suffered since 1947 on the question of how to treat the defeated Germany. By 1948 it had become obvious that the ambitious Monnet Plan could not be achieved while at the same time American attempts to rebuild Germany seemed to threaten French security interests. By early 1949 France was forced to recognize that its policy of keeping Germany's industry at a low level and replacing German goods with its own products had failed. In face of the American approach to rebuilding Germany the Schuman Plan was the only feasible way to rescue at least some of the

---

28 Pohl, *Wiederaufbau*, pp. 57 f.

29 *Jb* 1949, p. 24; *Jb* 1951, p. 34; *Jb* 1949, p. 24; Pohl, *Wiederaufbau*, pp. 56 ff., the remaining DM 18 million were a loan from the social security funds.

30 BA B109/269, note on meeting with Combined Steel Group, 3 August 1949. Here, the critical voice was Heinrich Dinkelbach, a former steel manager and now charged by the British with running the 'Stahltreuhandvereinigung'; Pohl, *Wiederaufbau*, pp. 57 ff.

31 NA RG 260, OMGUS, Finance Adviser, box 111, folder 1, BISEC/Memo(49)25 (BICO/Memo(49)86), 26 August 1949; *Jb* 1949, p. 24; *Jb* 1950, pp. 21 f.

security policy[32]. Furthermore, the Americans would support the plan since it was regarded as a first step towards European integration. For the German Government the Schuman Plan and the establishment of the European Coal and Steel Community (ECSC) on which the negotiations began within four weeks after Schuman's announcement were a good bargain[33]. It improved West Germany's international reputation and proved Adenauer's willingness to commit himself to *Westintegration* and reconciliation with France. While he could only win politically, he had little to lose in economic terms. The matter of the price of Ruhr coal remained in Allied hands despite an extension of German self-administration. It was intended that price controls should be handed over to the ECSC's High Authority (HA) as soon as it was established. The HA should then set the prices in agreement with the German government, the mining companies, the DKBL and the *Deutscher Kohlenverkauf* (DKV), the Ruhr's distributing agency[34]. Only dual pricing for German coal, export prices had risen to about 15 per cent above domestic ones, had to be abolished by February 1953, which was done by increasing internal prices. Regardless of this price increase, German coal still remained the cheapest within the community[35]. Thanks to foreign demand for cheap German coal the federal government could be sure that prices stayed low, which was Erhard's main policy in keeping German production costs low, in particular in the steel industry. While Adenauer was the political beneficiary of the negotiations the coal mining industry feared it had to pay the economic price for his success with the abolition of the quasi-cartelised DKV. But the industry's concerns were unfounded. It had already become evident that the decartelisation in coal and steel had failed and re-cartelisation was on its way, a fact even the French had realised and accepted by then[36].

The ECA's announcement of the release of the second tranche of money almost coincided with the second event, the outbreak of the Korean War which had a number of negative economic effects on the German economy. Panic buying, both in the private and industrial sector led to a sharp rise in inflation. From August 1950 to February 1951 alone, the cost of living rose by 11 per cent while there were price increases of up to 25 per cent in some sectors of industry due to an international run on raw materials[37]. Again, the coal industry could not profit from the price increase since its prices remained principally fixed. Then, from autumn 1950 onward, the German economy experienced a phenomenon which became

[32]Milward, *Reconstruction*, pp. 156 f., 162 f.

[33]Gillingham, *Coal*, pp. 228 ff, also with details on the negotiations.

[34]Gillingham, *Coal*, p. 321; Roseman, *Ruhr*, p. 151. The DKV had been set up by the British Military Government in February 1948 as the successor of the North German Coal Distribution Office in order to keep the distribution of coal going smoothly. See Isabel Warner, 'Allied-German Negotiations on the Decartellisation of West German Steel Industry', in: Turner, *Reconstruction in Post-War Germany*, p. 171.

[35]Gillingham, *Coal*, p. 322; Roseman, *Ruhr*, p. 151.

[36]Gillingham, *Coal*, pp. 266, 312.

[37]*Jb* 1950, p. 22; Adamsen, *Investitionshilfe*, p. 106.

known as the 'Korean Boom'. Productivity and output rose even faster than prices[38]. But with the boom the structural weakness of Erhard's economic policy appeared. The political preferences for the consumer goods industry and fixed prices made the small German capital market invest only in consumer goods, for they promised higher and quicker returns, thus leaving the coalmines without the necessary funds for rationalisation and expansion. While the average growth of the economy, which had already surpassed pre-war levels, was 32 per cent from April 1950 to April 1951, with peaks in investment goods of 52 per cent, coal output which had not reached pre-war figures was nearly stagnating at 11 per cent. The second ECA tranche was in no way big enough to provide the necessary investments in coal mining to reverse this development. The money dedicated to coal, DM 116 million, was not even enough for the sinking of a new mine shaft which cost DM 200 million and only brought a return of investment after ten to 15 years[39].

One important reason for the insufficient coal supply was the age structure of the Ruhr pits. As Table 7.1.1 shows, only 3 per cent of all output came from new mine shafts. Most of the production came from the older mines, where production was more expensive and rationalisation and mechanisation more difficult to introduce, since the shafts ran deeper into the ground. With industrial output rising as a result of additional demand from abroad generated by the Korean War, coal output by the end of 1950 was no longer sufficient to cover the urgent requests from the electrical power plants and the iron and steel industry. Two days before Christmas 1950, the government was forced to introduce a two hour electricity cut for private households in the evening hours and on 15 January 1951, industrial power supplies were cut as much as 25 per cent[40].

Table 7.1.1
Hard Coal Output and Pits' Age Structure in 1952

Pit age (years)	0-25	25-75	75-100	More than 100
Share of output (%)	3	37	45	15

Source: Werner Abelshauser, 'Korea, die Ruhr und Erhards Marktwirtschaft', in: *Rheinische Vierteljahresblätter*, 45. Jg. (1981), p. 300.

The measures, planned to last until the end of March, could be lifted again in mid February, but they served the German government well. Adenauer could threaten the Allied High Commission (AHC) that West Germany would have to go to a five,

[38]Abelshauser, *Wirtschaftsgeschichte*, pp. 64, 68.
[39]*Jb* 1950, p. 24; Adamsen, *Investitionshilfe*, p. 70; Abelshauser, *Ruhrkohle*, p. 68.
[40]Werner Abelshauser, ' Korea, die Ruhr und Erhards Marktwirtschaft', in: *Rheinische Vierteljahresblätter*, 45 Jg. (1981), p. 288.

or perhaps even a four-day working week if there were no considerable reductions of the mandatory coal exports[41]. Adenauer's statement, of course, exaggerated the situation in order to gain political concessions. Nevertheless, the economy could prevent serious production cuts only by falling back on a black market for coal. An embarrassed Ludwig Erhard was forced to admit to the public that this black market was estimated to be worth up to one million tons per month[42]. In any case, a reduction of Ruhr coal exports to the other Western European countries was out of the question since Great Britain had reduced its exports to the continent from 12 million tons to four million tons in late 1950 and, according to Abelshauser, to one million tons in 1951[43]. The ECA administration in Paris requested Britain to increase their exports again. Before the war, they had amounted to 25 to 30 million tons annually and now the ECA blamed British policy of nationalisation for the drop. Furthermore, the ECA suspected that the Europeans and in particular the Germans, were not really willing to increase their coal output. The need for Ruhr coal everywhere in Western Europe for use in armaments and other defence purposes made it a formidable weapon in Adenauer's fight to regain full control over affairs in the Ruhr area. By promising the German public not to cut household supplies of coal, he made it a domestic political issue and put pressure on the Allies not to increase German coal exports against their will[44].

The Americans reacted with pressure of their own. While DM 100 million of the ECA II tranche were used to continue financing programmes begun with ECA I money and DM 16 million went into the open cast brown coal fields at Aachen where mining was cheaper and the output could be used to fire local power plants, the Americans withheld the third tranche. This was to force the Germans to come up with an investment programme of their own. ECA delayed the release of ECA III for six months until the end of March 1951 and reduced the first instalment to half the sum the Germans had expected, only to increase it later to about 80 per cent of the original sum[45]. A surprisingly small amount of ECA III money, DM 80 million, was scheduled for mining. It was only in 1952 that the MSA released another DM 50 million from the ECA III reserves, bringing the total amount to DM 130 million. The reserve money was given only on the condition that the Germans themselves raised another DM 100 million medium term credits for the mining industry. Once more it was only due to the influence of Abs and the Kreditanstalt's

---

[41]Abelshauser, 'Korea', p. 289.
[42]Abelshauser, *Ruhrkohle*, p.70.
[43]NA RG 59, General Records of the Department of State 1945-1957, lot 70 D 467, box 4, Current Economic Developments, 10 September 1951; Abelshauser, 'Korea', p. 293.
[44]NA RG 469, Records of the US Foreign Assistance Agencies 1948-1961, Office of European Operations, German Division, Subject Files, box 3, folder Germany, commodities, coal 1951, ECA cablegram from Chief, ECA Mission Paris to ECA Administrator Foster, 18 August 1951; Cablegram from ECA Frankfurt to ECA Administrator, 28 June 1951.
[45]*Jb* 1950, pp. 22, 30 ff. Originally the Germans had expected DM 1.8 billion.

promise to provide a 90 per cent guarantee for the sum that a banking consortium did in the end lend the money for five years[46].

The output figures for the industries as given in Table 7.1.2 show the problem the German economy faced. While the growth rate of the economy as a whole increased, the growth rate of mining actually declined. Though the net output increased every year, it did not grow fast enough to supply a faster growing industry's demand for coal.

Table 7.1.2
Production Output of Industry and Coal Mining 1946-1951
(1936 = 100)

	1946	1947	1948	1949	1950	1951
All industry	34	44	63	90	130	141
Coal mining	51	65	81	96	109	116

Source: Abelshauser, Korea, p. 297; *Jb* 1950, p. 16; *Jb* 1951, p. 19.

The only way for German industry to satisfy its demands for coal without cutting production was to buy coal from the USA. Although a ton of American coal was $3 to $13 more expensive than Ruhr coal German companies bought as much as they could. While in 1950 4.3 million tons were imported to Germany, the figure rose to about ten million tons in 1951 and to 12 million tons in 1952. As a result, German dollar reserves dwindled. In the last three months of 1951, three-quarters of all German export profits from trade with the dollar area went into coal purchase[47]. The government in Bonn had no intention of following American demands to channel coal first and foremost into industries producing strategic materials but instead stressed the danger of job losses in case the consumer goods industries were to be restricted. The Cabinet regarded the economic situation as critical, but only in terms of a threat from the trade union. They feared that the price of coal could rise as a result of higher wage claims by the miners. The government believed that 30 per cent of miners' union members were communists who pushed for higher wages in order to destabilise the West German economy but this perception was very much based on 'selective memory' of events in the Weimar Republic[48]. The fact that the Adenauer administration did not seriously intervene against coal imports and the dollar drain is another sign that they used it as a means of exerting political pressure to rid the Ruhr of Allied control.

[46]*Jb* 1952, pp. 31, 52.

[47]*Jb* 1951, p. 19; *Jb* 1952, p. 19; Abelshauser, 'Korea', pp. 293, 295.

[48]*Kabinettsprotokolle*, vol. 4, pp. 440 f.; Christoph Nonn, *Die Ruhrbergbaukrise. Entindustrialisierung und Politik 1958-1969*, Göttingen 2001.

With large-scale coal imports happening, the German government could argue that it had the choice between the dollar drain with its negative impact on the balance of payments or mass unemployment in the consumer goods industries, which was unacceptable for domestic political reasons, even in the eyes of the Americans. From this position the Germans could press for an end to mandatory coal exports. These were still regarded as hidden reparation payments since the International Authority of the Ruhr (IAR) had fixed the price of German export coal at $11 per ton and demanded 6.2 million tons delivered in the third quarter of 1951, while the Germans had to pay $20 per ton for their US imports[49]. However, the USA knew that the other western European countries depended on German coal exports and that these exports represented '... Germany's most important contribution to the stability of the European economy as a whole ...' so they could not be lifted[50]. A higher import of US coal into Europe to relieve German exports was not possible due to a lack of loading facilities and shipping which was tied up because of the Korean War. In the end the German dollar drain only stopped when, with the end of the war in Korea in 1953, US coal exports to Germany declined[51].

Long before that, in 1951 the Americans increased the pressure on Adenauer. It was only after McCloy's letter to the Chancellor on 6 March 1951 in which he threatened to withhold raw materials from Germany that the German government realised that some kind of action was necessary to prevent direct US intervention in the German economy[52]. During a special Cabinet meeting on 6 March 1951 Erhard proposed a price increase for coal to solve the problem. His approach was to attempt a market liberalisation for the coal industry but with the proviso that other sectors did not suffer from the price increases[53]. Strong objections were voiced during the meeting, in particular from H.J. Abs. Abs' resistance to price increase is somehow surprising given that he was a member of a six strong DKBL committee, whose purpose was to plan for the restructuring of the Ruhr and in this capacity he should have had an interest in increasing the profits of the pits[54]. The most likely reason why he opposed the price increase was fear of another inflationary increase at a time when the economy was still struggling with the effects of the price increases which had been caused by the outbreak of the

---

[49]*Kabinettsprotokolle*, vol. 4, pp. 414 f, footnotes 4, 8.

[50]NA RG 469, Records of the US Foreign Assistance Agencies 1948-1961, Office of European Operations, German Division, Subject files, box 3, folder Germany Commodities Coal 1951, ECA cablegram to Frankfurt, 6 July 1951; the quote in: NA RG 466 Records of the US High Commissioner in Germany, Classified General Records 1949-1952, box 33, folder Briefs on Germany, Summary 19 November 1951.

[51]NA RG 59, General Records of the Department of State, 1945-1957, box 4, Current Economic Developments, 26 February 1951, 10 September 1951; *Jb* 1953, p. 22.

[52]See Abelshauser, 'Marktwirtschaft'.

[53] Nonn, *Ruhrbergbaukrise*, p. 25 and passim. Nonn sees a contrast between Erhard's market approach and Adenauer who favoured the 'corporate' model which increased their personal dispute.

[54]*Kabinettsprotokolle*, vol. 4, p. 207; Abelshauser, *Ruhrkohle*, p. 53.

Korean War. Instead of taking such a risk it was safer to wait for the money provided under the Auxiliary Investment Law, which was already in its planning stages. Therefore, the only measure introduced was a law in October 1951 which allowed a special levy of DM 2 per ton of coal sold. The money raised was destined exclusively to subsidise miners' housing construction[55].

Although the AIL was set up in the first place to support the coal mining industry, only DM 228 million, or 23 per cent of the direct financial aid, went to the collieries[56]. The *Kuratorium* did not allocate more money to the pits because there was no hope of getting the price fixing for coal lifted and because of the influence of a very powerful steel lobby, the *Walzstahlgruppe* (Rolled Steel Group) which was able to divert funds for its own clientele. With a boom in the steel market at hand the group successfully lobbied for the abolition of price fixing for steel[57]. With a growth in both the domestic and the export markets, and with freed prices, the steel market was more profitable than coal, especially whilst coal prices remained fixed at a relatively low level. It has to be kept in mind that contrary to the USA and to a much larger extent than in France, coal and steel industries in Germany until 1945 were *verflochten* (vertically interconnected) and managers, even those on the *Kuratorium* held to this tradition. Therefore, coal managers would make a 'sacrifice' for the sake of the steel industry's profits. And another special tax depreciation of DM 850 million under the law had a much bigger effect on the pits than the direct aid granted[58].

The Kreditanstalt's involvement in financing the coalmining industry up to the end of 1952, when the negative effects of the Korean War were under control is shown in Table 7.1.3. After the initial high investments in 1949, the loans became smaller until 1952, when AIL money first became available on a large scale. The table once more indicates the low priority loans to the mining industry received from Erhard, a trend which was to continue for the rest of the decade. Until 1952 the loans were given to 46 companies mining hard coal, eight companies mining brown coal and six other mining companies. 76.7 per cent of the money went into hard coal mining, 20.4 per cent into brown coal mining and 2.9 per cent to the six other companies. In the most important sector of hard coal mining, the money was used to extend mechanisation at the coalface, for the sinking of new shafts, the deepening of existing ones or for the opening of new coalfaces. Above ground, the pits' power stations were improved and expanded and coal processing plants and coke plants were built or repaired[59]. Money for brown coal was not only given

[55]Roseman, *Ruhr*, p. 140.
[56]Abelshauser, *Ruhrkohle*, p.70.
[57]Gillingham, *Coal*, pp. 307 f.
[58]Adamsen points out that the clause in the AIL which denied any close connections of *Kuratoriums'* members to any of the favoured industries was not observed. Even supervisory board membership in affected industries did not matter, Adamsen, *Investitionshilfe*, p. 210; Abelshauser, 'Korea', p. 306.
[59]*Jb* 1950, p. 43; *Jb* 1952, p. 52. In 1952 the supported number of soft coal companies had risen to nine.

because it was easier to mine in open-cast mines but because the fields of Aachen supplied Germany's biggest single power company, the Rheinisch-Westfälische Elektrizitätswerke (RWE) with the necessary fuel for its electrical power plants. In addition to the money given directly to increase coal output by the end of 1950 DM 23 million had been designated for a miners' housing programme in colliery owned houses[60].

Table 7.1.3
KfW Loans to the Coal Mining Industry 1949-1952
(in million DM)

Source	Amount	Money confirmed in 1949	1950	1951	1952	Money paid out by 1952
GARIOA	135	135				135
ECA SA	50	50				50
ECA I	150	50	100			150
ECA II	116		89.7	25.8		115.5
ECA III	130			67.5	62	109.6
AIL	202*			6.5	134.8	106.3
Others	5.9				4.5	3.5
Total	788.9	235	189.7	99.8	201.3	669.9

*Balance at the end of 1952, later increased to DM 228 million.

Source: *Jb* 1951, pp. 28 f.; *Jb* 1952, p. 52.

These DM 23 million constituted about 10 per cent of the total money spent for miners' housing construction and thus has to be seen as an important contribution to improve the manpower situation which was critical not at least because of the lack of housing.

For a sector in such desperate need of investment finance loans of less than DM 770 million seem small but credits from the Kreditanstalt für Wiederaufbau had a significant impact on the Gross Capital Investment (GCI) in the coal mining industry. It was in fact here that the counterpart funds had their biggest share in the reconstruction process of any economic sector as can be seen in Table 7.1.4.

The high proportion of ERP funds in 1949 resulted from the pre-financing of the expected ECA I tranche in the aftermath of the 'at once' programme at a time when ECA I had not been released. They are also a sign of the strong American influence on German reconstruction and the desperate need for money at this time.

[60] *Jb* 1950, p. 43. See also Chapter 8.

The decline of the corresponding proportion of GCI which came out of ERP funds in 1951 and 1952 was due to the pre-financing of projects in 1950 in anticipation of ECA III money so that these funds were simply no longer available in those years. A further reason for the decline was the AIL and its massive investment-by-tax-depreciation scheme which began to make an impact on investments in 1951.

Table 7.1.4
Total Share of ERP Funds for Coal Mining and Share of ERP Financed Gross Capital Investment in Coal Mining 1949-1952
(in per cent)

Year	1949	1950	1951	1952
ERP share for coal mining	25.4	13.2	8.5	9.2
Share of GCI	47	40	13	4.9

Source: Baumgart, pp. 122 f.

Since the Kreditanstalt also handled the AIL funds its share in the GCI of coal-mining would have been bigger in 1951 than the figures indicated in the table. The same is true for 1952, although the special tax depreciations allowed the pits a higher rate of self-finance so that outside sources may have lost some of their significance. The most revealing and interesting figures are those of the share of ERP money in gross capital investment in 1949 and 1950. They clearly indicate that insufficient sources of long-term capital were available. It is astonishing that DM 235 million could provide for nearly half of the mines' long-term investments and it shows how reluctant banks were to give long-term money to the pits. This was because of the relatively low return they could expect and because the collieries could not provide any security, for they were still under Allied laws No. 75 and 27 respectively[61]. The existing situation was somewhat paradoxical. Although the value of the collieries and their equipment was estimated to be about DM 2 billion they could not provide sufficient securities for the banks and the KfW had to give the credits to the mines as *Direktkredite* (direct loans). This was in conflict with the KfW law which clearly stated that direct loans should only be

[61]Law No. 27 of the Allied High Commission replaced Law No 75. of the Allied Military Government in May 1950, giving details on the restructuring of the Ruhr conglomerates, see Steininger, *Deutsche Geschichte*, vol. 2, p. 331; Abelshauser, *Ruhrkohle*, p. 54.

given in very exceptional circumstances[62]. However, Table 7.1.5 shows that by the end of 1951 these exceptional circumstances had become the rule.

Table 7.1.5
Secured and Unsecured Loans to the Coal Mining Industry by 1951
(in million DM)

Secured loans given via banks		27.8
Secured direct loans		10.7
Unsecured loans (companies requested to secure after release out of Allied control)		180.0
Loans unsecurable due to Law 27		351.8
	Total	570.3

Source: *Jb* 1951, p. 53.

Less than 5 per cent of the loans were given through banks and less than 10 per cent were secured at all. For the rest, the Kreditanstalt could only rely on a pledge from the Combined Coal Control Group (CCCG) from March 1949 that the KfW would be the first to receive any mortgage securities as soon as the companies' integrated structures were broken up (*entflochten*) and set up again under the guidelines of Law No. 75. What the KfW was uncertain about was whether or not the Allied commitment was legally binding as time went on[63]. Despite this risk the KfW had to give the loans because of the desperate need for coal and longer-term political planning and thinking of the Adenauer government. Economic reconstruction and growth were Germany's only way back into the world economy and the international community and the KfW helped to go down this path by providing the necessary funds[64]. Both the CCCG's pledge and its continuous consent to those loans (all investments above a certain amount had to be authorised by the Group) indicate that the Allies perceived the situation in a similar way although they may have looked much more to the impact German coal or the lack of it had on European reconstruction in general. The logical conclusion from this situation was that the Allies would return the confiscated plants and assets to the Germans sooner or later.

Despite all efforts, output per man in 1952 remained 30 per cent below the 1938 level. This was in part because of an over-aged workforce and a high

[62]Abelshauser, *Ruhrkohle*, p. 22; KfW Gesetz Art. 3, see also Chapters 2 and 3.
[63]KfW HA-Prot 10-2, Protokoll der 22. Sitzung, TOP 5.
[64]Werner Bührer, Hans Jürgen Schröder, 'Germany's Economic Revival in the 1950s. The Foreign Policy Perspective', in: Ennio Di Nolfo (ed.), *Power in Europe? II*, Berlin, New York 1992, p. 174.

fluctuation of workers as result of the continuing lack of housing. Regardless of the deficit in that year, the OEEC planned to achieve a coal production of 150 million tons in 1956. The KfW estimated the total investments necessary to accomplish this output to be DM 4 billion. If this plan had succeeded, pre-war output would have been surpassed by 10 million tons. The OEEC figures however, were to a large extent politically motivated wishful thinking and in 1954 a more realistic target was set with an annual output of 140 million tons in 1961[65]. Even these reduced levels had political reasons which became evident when the ECSC adopted the plan in order to cover French demands for coal and coke. Despite Ludwig Erhard's attempts to bring the coal industry into the realm of the market economy, it was once more made a pawn of national policy and sacrificed to accommodate foreign policy interests, a policy which had been in place since the 1930s[66].

As if to negate all this planning, 1953 proved to be the year which saw the rise of large stockpiles of coke and coal which were caused by the reduced demand following the end of the Korean War rather than by a sudden rise in output. Nevertheless, when the Kreditanstalt tried to justify further investment in Ruhr coal mining it was done on the basis of highly questionable statistical evidence. The KfW claimed that France had invested four times as much money as Germany in coal mining between 1948 and 1952 but they did not mention the fact that the French started from a much lower level of GCI[67]. Furthermore, the French investments were made for political reasons under the planned economy of the Monnet Plan and these efforts had only been partly successful. Although the French pre-war output was surpassed due to higher mechanisation, the output per man-shift in the Ruhr remained still higher in 1953 than in any other European country despite trailing well behind pre-war levels of output[68]. The geological advantage of the Ruhr mines guaranteed the German pits a competitive lead over its European neighbours despite a lower productivity and output than before the war.

From about 1954-55 onward, in the wake of the liberalising of the German energy market, Erhard renewed and increased his efforts to bring coal mining into the market economy. There, the main problem remained one of manpower and in particular the high fluctuation of miners. To encourage them to stay in the pits two strategies were pursued. The provision of cheap housing for miners became a key element and was supported by the ECSC, in particular after an increased number of miners left the pits in 1955-57[69]. Table 7.1.6 shows the size of the High Authority's financial contribution to the Ruhr coal industry. The Kreditanstalt, to its own disappointment had become the Coal and Steel Community's 'agent' in Germany in 1954 with the task of distributing the European funds according to national law. As

[65]*Jb* 1952, p. 19, *Jb* 1954, p. 21; *Statistisches Handbuch von Deutschland 1928-1944*, Hg. vom Länderrat des Amerikanischen Besatzungsgebietes, München 1949, p. 279.
[66]Milward, *Reconstruction*, pp. 131 ff.; Nonn, *Ruhrbergbaukrise*, p. 25.
[67]*Jb* 1953, pp. 22 f.
[68]KfW HA-Prot 10-2, Protokoll der 25. Sitzung, Anlage 1, Vortrag Neubaur.
[69]Nonn, *Ruhrbergbaukrise*, pp. 34 ff.; Roseman, *Ruhr*, passim, in particular his detailed tables pp. 153, 277, 296; *Jb* 1955, pp. 22 f.

a mere 'agent' the KfW could not distribute the loans under its own obligation and liability as it did with the ERP Special Asset funds, which reduced the Anstalt's influence[70].

Money from the ECSC until 1955 was usually given for rationalisation and on the condition that the sum had to be doubled or even tripled using German funds, either from the capital market or by the pits' self financing schemes. In an attempt to supply enough cheap dwellings to make the miners stay with their collieries the loans given thereafter went into the construction of miners' housing. However, due to the peculiar way the Annual Reports state the figures it is very likely that larger sums were involved than those shown in Table 7.1.6. Gillingham speaks of $ 65 million for miners' housing in the whole of the ECSC until 1958, which helped to build 36,000 dwellings, two-thirds of them in Germany[71]. With further financial aid from the federal and the North Rhine Westphalian government, as well as from the pits, housing provided for miners was certainly one of the best and most modern in the whole of Germany, yet rents were still very cheap.

Table 7.1.6
Confirmed KfW Loans to Coal Mining 1953-1960
(in million DM)

Source/year	1953	1954	1955	1956	1957	1958	1959	1960	Total
ERP/MSA	31.5[1]	4.1	40[3]		75[6]	78	49.6	30	308.2
StEG	1.4	1.6							3.0
AIL	24.2	13.4							37.6
ECSC*		131[2]	49.7[4]		18[7]	10[7]	7.4	(55.9[8])	216.1
Others	6.5	1	225.2[5]	18	70	2	104.3	55.7	482.7
Total	63.6	151.1	314.9	18	163	90	161.3	85.7	1047.6

* The Annual Reports are anything but clear about these loans so the figures are a very careful and conservative estimate.
1) Plus DM 50 million '*Aufstockungskredit*' with KfW guarantee.
2) $31.2 million loan, 25 per cent of an ECSC package with 50 per cent own funds and 25 per cent other German funds.
3) DM 15 million for brown coal.
4) $ loan.
5) Including DM 110 of 2).
6) First instalment of a 3 year DM 225 million programme.
7) Miners' housing.
8) Medium term funds to be redeemed by KfW funds and money under trusteeship.

Source: *Jb* 1953-1960, passim.

70 Harries, *Wiederaufbau*, pp. 53 f. The Annual Reports are not very clear about these loans and it appears that the figures were given rather casually.
71 *Jb* 1954, pp. 46 f.; *Jb* 1955, p. 49; Gillingham, *Coal*, p. 343.

Another means to encourage miners to stay was of course pay incentives. When the Nazis had stopped wage increases in 1936 a miner's average gross pay per hour was RM 1. By 1948 it had increased to DM 1.21 and to DM 2.07 in 1952 and eventually to DM 2.20 in 1954[72]. Miners' wages were traditionally amongst the highest labour wages in Germany but with the iron and steel sector booming and short of labour, the steel plants could and did offer similarly high wages. Consequently, by 1955 the miners left the pits in increasing numbers to earn the same money for less dangerous and less hard work and most certainly under working conditions which were more favourable than those under-ground[73].

The loss of trained labour naturally meant a reduction in productivity and output for the collieries. But with the coal price still fixed, the *Unternehmensverband Ruhrbergbau* (UVR), the mines' employers association, was hardly able to grant the 12 per cent pay rise demanded by the miners' union in 1955. Despite this, the wage claim was not criticised by the UVR: it was perhaps even secretly welcomed since it gave the pit managers a chance to call for another increase in the coal price. The pay rise would have increased miners' average hourly pay to DM 2.60. The resulting increased costs plus some extra, the managers hoped, would be covered by a rise of the coal price. Both the miners' union and the UVR passed the problem to the politicians. Erhard knew that the miners' wages had to rise to keep them in the pits but he also knew that the average price for coal would rise from DM 62.40 in 1954 to DM 68.60 per ton, increasing first electricity prices and then reduce the margins of the iron and steel industry before it would affect the rest of the economy. In addition, a pay rise for the miners would trigger demands for wage rises in other sectors[74]. As a response to this wage crisis and to avoid the negative effects of a direct pay rise, the federal government and the government of North Rhine Westphalia started to directly subsidise miners' wages in October 1956. The so-called *Bergmannslohn* (miner's wage) added up to DM 2.50 to a miner's daily pay at the expense of DM 200 million a year for the tax payer and put the miners back at the top of the wage scale. In addition to this the collieries were allowed a special depreciation for underground machinery and a 6.5 per cent reduction of the *Knappschaftsbeiträge*, the special miners' pension funds, again at the taxpayers' expense. It is doubtful whether the *Knappschaften* at this stage really needed this subsidy for in November that year they lent the KfW DM 3 million for 15 years[75]. It was in actual fact nothing but a substitute to reduce wage costs (*Lohnersatz*).

---

[72]*Der Spiegel*, No. 12, 1955, p. 12.
[73]*Jb* 1955, pp. 22f.; *Jb* 1956, p. 21.
[74]*Der Spiegel*, No. 12, 1955, pp. 12 ff. The average price per ton had risen from DM 38.80 in 1948 to DM 42.90 in 1950 and to DM 52.70 in 1952.
[75]*Jb* 1956, p. 27; Abelshauser, *Ruhrkohle*, p. 85; Roseman, *Ruhr*, p. 104; Nonn, *Ruhrbergbaukrise*, pp 44 f. A miner's average weekly pay in February 1956 was DM 116.60, DM 119.80 in August and DM 126.23 in November so that the subsidies made up more than 10 per cent of the wages, see *Statistisches Jahrbuch* 1957, p. 522; Werner Abelshauser, 'Kohle und Marktwirtschaft. Ludwig Erhards Konflikt mit dem

In 1956 Erhard and the UVR eventually reached their main objective, the abolition of the price fixing by the High Authority and the German government. However, it was not without reason that the KfW's Annual Report spoke only of '... the abandoning of price controls in principle ...'[76]. Erhard was as much in favour of price liberalisation as he feared a new surge in prices. He had reached a gentleman's agreement with the Ruhr managers and at the same time was preparing for the liberalisation of coal imports. His hope was that in the long-term US coal would keep a limit to price rises for Ruhr coal[77]. In return for all the assistance they had received, including another price increase of DM 2.34 per ton, the pits would keep 'price discipline' that is to say not to raise prices excessively[78]. In doing so Erhard once more walked a tightrope between his desire for *Marktwirtschaft* and the need for price stability. With general elections looming the following year he was forced to make this political compromise.

Despite all investments and subsidies the Ruhr coal industry was not able to significantly increase its output and to meet the demand for coal, not even the reduced ECSC target of 140 million tons in 1961. Table 7.1.7 shows the development of coal production and the coal imports and exports from and to Germany from 1950 to 1960.

Coal imports soared to 16 million tons in 1955 to cover the demand of the post-Korean War economic boom, the *Wirtschaftswunder*. They rose even further when the re-established US German Treaty of Friendship and Navigation, signed by Adenauer in October 1954 during a visit to Washington, came into force in 1956 and when international sea freight rates dropped further in 1957 in the aftermath of the Suez Crisis. Attempts by individuals to profit from the coal surplus in the US where most mines were on a four-day working week by cutting transatlantic freight costs from DM 46 to DM 29 per ton of coal certainly had an additional stimulating effect on coal imports into Germany[79]. The rise continued in 1957 surpassing the 21 million ton mark with an expectation to exceed the 25 million mark and even getting close to 30 million tons or more than 20 per cent of German production in 1958. In a political u-turn, the German government re-introduced a special import tax of DM 20 on every ton of coal from outside the ECSC area if they exceeded a five million ton limit to protect the Ruhr from this mainly American competition. The KfW in its Annual Report mildly criticised the measure and paid lip service to

---

Unternehmensverband Ruhrbergbau am Vorabend der Kohlekrise' in: *VfZ* No. 33 (1985), pp. 494 ff.; KfW HA-BA 5, Vertrag zwischen der KfW und den Ruhrknappschaften, signed 20 October 1956.

[76]*Jb* 1956, p.27

[77]Nonn, *Ruhrbergbaukrise*, pp. 37, 43 ff.

[78]Abelshauser,'Kohle', p. 495.

[79]*Foreign Relations of the United States*, 1952-54, vol. VII, part 1, p. 592, henceforth quoted as *FRUS* with year and volume; Werner Bührer, 'Der Bund deutscher Industrieller und die Außenpolitik der BRD in den 50er Jahren', in: *VfZ* No. 40 (1992), p. 252; Nonn, *Ruhrbergbaukrise*, p. 28; *Der Spiegel*, No. 39, 1956, pp. 20 ff.

the concepts of liberal trade policy[80]. Again, the principles of the market economy were sacrificed for group interests. The Americans protested publicly against the introduction of the coal tax. They feared that other European countries could follow the German example and introduce coal duties as well. The US government considered serious counter measures against the Germans and any other country if a further case emerged but had also secretly some sympathy for the German government which fielded once more the argument of a communist revival in the Ruhr[81].

Table 7.1.7
German Hard Coal Output and Coke and Coal Exports and Imports 1950-1960
(in thousand tons)

Year	1950	1951	1952	1953	1955
Coal production	110.755	118.925	123.278	124.472	130.728
Coal imports	4.066	9.650	11.792	9.459	16.000
Coal exports	15.988	13.665	12.700	14.168	13.185
Coke exports	8.147	9.890	10.641	9.103	11.266

Year	1956	1957	1958	1959	1960
Coal production	134.407	133.156	132.582	125.586	126.053
Coal imports	18.730	21.592	16.241	8.514	6.906
Coal exports	12.844	13.573	11.645	14.985	17.914
Coke exports	10.963	10.048	9.375	8.981	10.885

Source: *Statistisches Jahrbuch 1952-1961*, passim.

The 1956-57 supply crisis, arisen out of the Ruhr's inability to supply the demand for coal which was forecast to surpass 160 million tons by the mid-1960s, turned into a political crisis. In 1956 the index of coal production stood at only 123 (1936: 100) while the index for industrial output had more than doubled to above 200[82]. The political crisis unfolded after the 1957 general election which the Adenauer government had run under the slogans *Stabilität* and *Keine Experimente* ('stability' and 'no experiments'). The election brought an absolute majority for the CDU in

[80] *Jb* 1958, p. 24.
[81] *FRUS* 1958-60, vol.VII, part 1, pp. 96, 100 ff; Nonn, *Ruhrbergbaukrise*, pp. 104 ff.
[82] *Jb* 1956, p. 27.

Parliament, the first and only one in West German post-war history. The day after the vote the UVR announced publicly a price increase of DM 4.70 per ton of coal and of DM 6.25 for coke, coming into force on 1 October, just two weeks after the elections[83]. Although they had informed Erhard months before the elections about such a move the timing was a major embarrassment for the government and for Erhard in particular. It caused strong criticism from all sides and publicly the Economics Minister tried to pass the buck and distance himself from the price rise although in private he was in favour of the development. Erhard bowed to Cabinet discipline and at the same time he tried to save face by agitating against the rise[84].

The estimates and hopes of the UVR for higher profits proved to be a miscalculation. Within six months, coal stockpiles mushroomed and grew to 10 per cent of annual output. Since there were literally no unsold coal stocks in 1957, the development must have come as a shock to most people. While since 1955 the Economics Ministry had developed scenarios under which coal demand would shrink drastically, only the trade unions had raised a warning voice on the eve of the crisis but they had been ridiculed. Although there were several causes for the development, one was the arrogance of the UVR managers which did not read the signs. It was their opinion that '... Ruhrkohle wird nicht verkauft, sondern von Versandabteilungen des Ruhrbergbaus an den Verbraucher verteilt'[85].

There were also major technological developments which reduced the need for coal. While, for example, in 1952 one ton of coke was needed for the production of one ton of steel, the demand had dropped nearly 20 per cent by 1960 and there were similar savings in electricity production. There was a wider economic reason for the stockpiles, too. 1958 saw for the first time a decline in growth rates which signalled and would eventually bring about the end of the 'Economic Miracle'. It was not the tariff on American coal which reduced imports from 1958 onward but the economic slow-down which reduced steel demand by 7 per cent. In some respects the reduction of imports even had a detrimental impact on the UVR since they had controlled nearly 70 per cent of the transactions[86].

Most importantly, coal was increasingly replaced by oil and gas which became less and less expensive. From 1957 to 1960 the price for heavy crude oil fell from DM 142 per ton to DM 60 and for light crude oil, from DM 242 per ton to DM 125. This reduction was despite the fact that a special tax was imposed on them. The coal price on the other hand had increased 7 to 8 per cent annually over this period, which was about three to four times the inflation rate[87]. Oil and gas had

---

[83]Abelshauser, 'Kohle', p. 489 f.

[84]Abelshauser, *Ruhrkole*, p. 88; Nonn, *Ruhrbergbaukrise*, p. 52. The minutes of Erhard's meeting with the UVR on 1 October 1957, reprinted in Abelshauser, 'Kohle', pp. 503 ff.

[85]Nonn, *Ruhrbergbaukrise*, p. 26; the quote in: Abelshauser, *Ruhrkohle*, p. 88. '... Ruhr coal is not sold but is distributed to the consumer by the Ruhr mines' dispatch departments.' (Translation AG).

[86]Nonn, Ruhrbergbaukrise, pp. 31, 75 f.

[87]Abelshauser, *Ruhrkohle*, p. 89; Deutsche Bundesbank (ed.), *40 Jahre Deutsche Mark*, Frankfurt/M., 1988, p. 7.

also the psychological advantage on their side of being the 'modern' forms of energy and being less messy than coal convinced households to switch to them as well.

As a reaction to the surplus crisis, the workforce of all German mines was cut by 20,000 men to 523,000 in 1958 and down to 472,000 in 1959. In the Ruhr itself, the size of the underground workforce dropped from 312,000 at its peak on 1 January 1958 to 238,000 in 1960. The UVR hoped for a total reduction of 150,000 miners in the Ruhr over a period of the next four years to avoid social tensions. Pit closures were to accompany the redundancies although with the economy still booming all but the oldest miners would have found new jobs very quickly[88]. Large amounts of money had to be spent by the collieries in order to redeem big customers' coal contracts with foreign suppliers so that the Ruhr coal could be sold to them again. Stockpiling, too, had to be financed. In summer 1959, before the coal glut had reached its peak already DM 1 billion was tied up in stockpiles[89]. The money provided by the Kreditanstalt was used according to its long-term nature for further rationalisation and the deepening of shafts. The share of money the pits spent on rationalisation rose from 66 per cent in 1958 to 87 per cent in 1961 and was mainly used to introduce machines to cut the coal and to replace the previously used pneumatic drill-hammer. In contrast, the money to finance stockpiles came now from the ECSC and was given in the usual way, either as sureties or as loans via the KfW[90].

Coal mining as a central part for German and European reconstruction was used more than any other sector of the economy as a pawn both in occupation policy and economic policy. Due to past developments and because of the industry's structure but also because of its current political role the industry had to be supported financially by the Kreditanstalt für Wiederaufbau. The reason for the support changed over a decade dramatically from providing long-term investment to get coal production going again to sustain the industry as a supposedly vital part of the national economy in the late 1950s and thereafter. In both cases the KfW's operations and funds were crucial for the task.

---

[88]*Jb* 1958, p. 23; *Jb* 1959, p. 30; Roseman, *Ruhr*, p. 277; KfW HA-BA 5, note on a visit of UVR representatives at the KfW, 15 July 1959.

[89]KfW HA-BA 5, note on a visit of UVR representatives at the KfW, 15 July 1959. By the end of 1959 11 million tons of hard coal and 6.8 million tons of coke had to be stockpiled, see KfW HA-BA 6, paper 'Zur Lage im deutschen Steinkohlenbergbau' 5 April 1961.

[90]Ibid., note 'Gesichtspunkte für die Beantragung weiterer ERP-Kredite für den Ruhrkohlenbergbau im ERP-Haushaltsjahr 1962', Essen, 15 September 1961; *Jb*, various years, passim. KfW HA-BA 4, KfW draft for a loan contract, 26 January 1959; KfW letter to the ECSC's High Authority, 11 February 1959; *Jb* 1960, p. 51. None of the loans or guarantees for stockpiling is shown in Table 7.1.6.

7.2 The Steel Industry

One of the western Allies' major war aims was the break up of the German cartels in the coal and heavy industries which were seen in particular by the Americans as one of the causes of the Nazi rise to power and the outbreak of the Second World War. US Secretary of the Treasury Morgenthau's notorious plan and JCS 1067 became the most visible and extreme sign of this policy. In the aftermath of the war and throughout the early reconstruction period the iron and steel industry became the battleground of different and, particularly in the case of the USA, changing policies. As a result of the armaments and war production the German iron and steel industry had experienced an investment boom while at the same time the Allied strategic bombing campaign had had only a very limited effect. Consequently, the Americans and even more the French saw the industry as being at the core to a potential future risk to European peace and they wanted to get rid of it.[91].

The British on the other hand, in whose zone of occupation the main industrial area of the Ruhr was located, were aware of Germany's economic capacity for the reconstruction of Europe. To enable the utilisation of the Ruhr's heavy industry for this purpose they allowed German steel companies to establish the *Wirtschaftsverband der Eisen- und Stahl Industrie* (WVESI) in late 1945[92]. In March 1946 the Allied Control Council agreed to limit German iron and steel production to 5.8 million tons per year in accordance with the Potsdam Agreements. The figure was a compromise between the Soviet and French demands for only 4.9 million tons and the British claim for nine million tons annually. In August 1946 the British Military Government expropriated all steel plants and associated coalmines and put them under military administration[93]. As already stated, the Congressional elections in autumn 1946 brought about a change to both US domestic politics and to US occupation policy in Germany, although at first it only increased contradictions in the latter[94]. In a joint US-British study group in May 1947, the Americans proposed to raise the level of Bizonal capacity for steel production to 14 million tons. Less than six months before, in December 1946, during a meeting of the two Military Governors with their Foreign Ministers, General Clay had objected to a capacity of 11 million tons as 'dangerous war

---

[91]Industry's gross fixed capital rose by 75 per cent between 1935 and 1945 while a depreciation of about 37 per cent of the basic value took place at the same time; Allied bombing concentrated on housing areas and traffic infrastructure. Seven times more bombs were dropped on each than on industrial plants, see: Werner Abelshauser, 'Probleme des Wiederaufbaus der westdeutschen Wirtschaft', in: Heinrich-August Winkler (ed.), *Politische Weichenstellung im Nachkriegsdeutschland 1945-1953*, Göttingen 1979, pp. 215 f; *US Strategic Bombing Survey (Report # 3)*, pp. 44 f.

[92]Gillingham, *Coal*, p. 193.

[93]Krieger, *Clay*, p. 13; Warner, 'Negotiations', p. 157.

[94]Gillingham, *Coal*, pp. 112 ff.

potential'[95]. This change in opinion was not so much the result of the change in US domestic policy but due to the failure of the Moscow Conference of Foreign Ministers one month earlier. Nevertheless, the Americans could not just impose their ideas they had to take strong political considerations in regard to their allies. France once more saw its security threatened by the revival of the Ruhr while at the same time it was not able to fulfil its own far-reaching modernisation plans. France was very important to American foreign and European policy, but the Americans had to tread very carefully, not least because of a strong French Communist Party. For any expansion of Ruhr steel capacity the USA had to come up with a conciliation for both the French government and public. The Americans in the end had to agree on a limit of 10.7 million tons per year which was close to the figure originally suggested by the British[96]. The French gained another concession, the establishment of the International Authority of the Ruhr. But while the French had hoped to control the Ruhr's steel production and coal exports which were even more important for their Monnet Plan, the Americans managed to equip the IAR only with very limited power on the important issues of the Ruhr. Instead, the real authority remained with the Military Governors[97].

The trouble for the iron and steel industry was not over in spite of the capacity increase. By the end of 1947 the British Military government began with the dismantling of plants[98]. Although only armament plants and so-called 'surplus capacity', that in excess of a normal peacetime production, were targeted dismantling caused uproar among the German population. Contemporary German estimates of the value of the dismantling were much exaggerated[99]. Compared to 1936 steel production in the area of West Germany more than doubled during the war to about 35 million tons due to huge state investments. Highly politically motivated estimates of a production capacity in 1947-48 grossly exaggerated the bomb damage and even more the losses due to dismantling, estimating a remaining capacity of about 14 million tons. Only during the 1960s and 1970s much more accurate and objective estimates were produced by Abelshauser and Krengel[100].

In addition to dismantling, British and even more so American military authorities stuck to the idea of decartelisation. The primary aim of dismantling was to end the near monopolistic position of six steel concerns which controlled nearly 80 per cent of German crude steel production; the secondary aim was to end

[95]Alan Kramer, 'British Dismantling Policy 1945-1949', in: Turner, *Reconstruction*, pp. 139, 141.
[96]Kramer, 'Dismantling', p. 141.
[97]Milward, *Reconstruction*, pp. 74, 156 f.
[98] Gillingham, *Coal*, p. 189.
[99]Perhaps the most famous and influential work was Gustav Harmsen, *Am Abend der Demontage*, Bremen 1951.
[100]Karl Roskamp, *Capital Formation in West Germany*, Detroit 1965, p. 171; Christoph Buchheim, 'The Nazi Boom An Economic Cul-de-Sac', paper given at St. Anthony's College, Oxford 21.2.1997; Harmsen, *Demontage*, p. 26; Abelshauser, *Westdeutschland*; Krengel, *Anlagevermögen*.

Verbundwirtschaft, the ownership and operational integration of coalmines, steel plants and processing factories, which was the common form of organisation in the Ruhr area[101]. To prepare for this reorganisation the two Military Governors issued Military Government Law No. 75 which had an important effect on the Kreditanstalt's work. On the one hand the law spoke out strongly against excessive concentration of economic power and ordered the liquidation and the splitting up of 26 leading steel and coal companies. Furthermore, it stated that former owners or major shareholders who were strongly affiliated with the Nazis were banned from further ownership or participation in the running of the new companies. On the other hand it allowed the establishment of a trusteeship under German management and left the question of the industry's socialisation to a German national government. In this way, the Americans hoped to bury for good the British idea of nationalisation. On the German side the law provoked unanimous rejection. All the main political parties, the industrialists and the trade unions as well as the general public were strongly opposed to the law and tried to sabotage or slow down its implementation. With former managers acting as trustees for the companies, under the impact of the increasing Cold War as well as the Korean War they were sure to succeed.

When the Kreditanstalt für Wiederaufbau took up its operations in January 1949 and began to develop its 'at once' programme the steel industry was not a priority. Indeed, as Tables 7.2.1 and 7.2.2 show, the iron and steel industry was the one basic industry which profited least from counterpart funds. Only with the introduction of the AIL was more outside money directed into the industry. There were various reasons for this. Most important was the production limit imposed on steel output. Although it had been raised to 11.1 million after the French zone of occupation had joined the British and Americans to form the Combined Steel Control Group (CSCG) in April 1949 there was a much higher output potential. The Ruhr had produced nearly 15 million tons of steel in 1939[102]. There were in addition the huge plants of the former 'Reichswerke Hermann Göring' at Salzgitter and some smaller plants in northern Bavaria which had contributed to German steel production[103]. The war damage was relatively small: only one rolling mill had been totally destroyed by bombing[104]. The dismantling and reparations so highly condemned by the Germans at that time was not of the scale people such as

[101]Warner, 'Negotiations', p. 157. The companies were Vereinigte Stahlwerke, Krupp, Hoesch Werke, Klöckner Werke, Gutehoffnungshütte and Mannesman. For a detailed study on the topic see: Isabel Warner, *Steel and Sovereignty. The Deconcentration of the West-German Steel Industry 1949-1954*, Mainz 1996.

[102]Adamsen, *Investitionshilfe*, p. 93; Heinrich Deist, 'Organisationsprobleme der Eisen- und Stahlindustrie', paper given on 28.10.1948 to the *Arbeitsdirektoren* of the iron and steel industry, reprinted in: Viktor Agartz, Heinrich Deist (eds), *Gesetz 75 und Ruhrstatut*, Köln 1949, pp. 15 ff.

[103]The Silesian steel plants had been handed over to Poland while those in the Saar were operated as part of French industry until 1956. For the Saar industry see below.

[104]Abelshauser, 'Probleme', p. 216.

Harmsen claimed it was. The German government calculated in the 1950s the loss due to reparations in all sectors of the economy to RM 2 billion in 1938 prices or to RM 2.96 billion in replacement costs. Dismantling losses amounted to 3.5 per cent of West German gross fixed capital in 1948. Although the Adenauer government was committed to pay compensation to the affected companies they were obviously not allowed to utilise counterpart funds for the purpose. Nevertheless new industrial investments of DM 10.2 billion took place between 1948 and 1950[105].

Table 7.2.1
Confirmed KfW Money for the Iron and Steel Industry 1949-1953
(in million DM)

Source	1950	1951	1952	1953	Total
ECA I	37.9				39.4*
ECA II	39.1	15.2	0.3		54.6
ECA III		72.8	2.2		75
MSA			8.9	12.5	21.4
AIL		25.5	222.3	36.7	284.5
Others	14.1	3.0	3.4	29.4	49.9
Total	91.1	116.5	237.1	78.6	523.3/524.8*

* Due to ongoing changes in the programmes the figures vary, depending on whether they are from the Annual Reports or from the later survey. Due to the ongoing alterations all Annual Reports between 1950-53 show different figures for this sector.

Source: KfW HA-BA 6, 'Übersicht über die der KfW zur Verfügung gestellten Mittel', 8.2. 1954, *Jb* 1950-1953, passim.

Furthermore, while there existed a steel capacity in excess of the production limit the Americans still had to take French reactions into consideration which might explain why the ECA committed so little money to the German steel industry. And there were, finally, the questions of German competition with British and French attempts to replace Germany as the main producer of steel in central Europe which also prevented the flow of more counterpart funds. When Germany re-entered the European steel market in 1949, its steel exports amounted to about a quarter of British exports. Only two years later, German exports exceeded those of Britain[106]. Although the Korean War might have distorted the real picture in that Britain had to use its own steel for the war and armaments effort, it remains a fact that German iron and steel production capacity had increased.

[105]Kramer, 'Dismantling', p. 151; Gillingham, *Coal*, p. 206.
[106]Milward, *Reconstruction*, p. 368.

Table 7.2.2
Gross Capital Investment in the Iron and Steel Industry 1949-1951 and the ERP's Share in it
(in million DM and per cent)

	1949	1950	1951
Gross Capital Investment	280	380	600
ERP loans at the end of the year		68	84
ERP share in GCI (%)		18	14

Source: Adamsen, p. 262.

When BiCO requested the release of counterpart funds in August 1949 the iron and steel industry was not listed as an independent section but was part of 'other industries' with the added remarks that to reduce existing bottlenecks only a little money was needed[107].

As in the case of the coal mining industry most of the ECA money was given as direct loans since the expropriated companies could not offer enough securities for the banks[108]. Despite this the payout was slow because of CSCG's close involvement in the planning process. The Group had to agree on all projects even before they could be considered by the ECA. The KfW's Annual Report states that most of the ECA I money was used to clear up war damage while only the second tranche could be used to actually remove bottlenecks[109]. It seems as if the KfW was playing with words here since any bottleneck would have resulted from war damage. But in choosing these words the Kreditanstalt could demonstrate its active involvement in the reconstruction process.

Before the second ECA tranche was released and while the first one was still being processed a major political event, Robert Schuman's proposal of a European coal and steel community changed the situation. Adapting an old English phrase, the plan can be described as 'if you cannot beat them, make them join you'. French policy towards Germany since the end of the Second World War was based on an extreme feeling for security against Germany regaining its old strength. Consequently, France had obstructed any policy in the Allied Control Council which tried to establish any kind of German central administration. The evident failure of the Monnet Plan to replace Germany as Europe's industrial workshop by taking over its role as the major iron and steel producer on the Continent coincided

---

[107]NA RG 260, OMGUS, Finance Adviser, box 111, folder 1, BISEC/Memo (49)25 (BICO/Memo(49)86).
[108]*Jb* 1950, Anlage 3. By the end of 1950 DM 71.7 million out of a total of 92 million were given as direct loans.
[109]*Jb* 1950, pp. 42, 46.

with the emerging Cold War. The latter made the Americans change their policy in 1946-47 in regard to German reconstruction, which undermined the French policy completely. The London Ruhr Conference in February 1948 gave a final blow to French security policy and French ambitions. The IAR received only limited powers, the nationalisation of the Ruhr industries, which would have meant the permanent expropriation of the old 'Chimney Barons' was left to a future German government and finally it had become clear that the production limit on German steel would be abolished some time in the future. Therefore, France had to find a new way to defend its security interests and the ultimate solution became the Schuman Plan with its idea of a supra-national authority in control of Western Europe's coal, iron, and steel industries[110].

While German industrialists appeared somewhat sceptical towards the plan, Adenauer realised its potential for Germany's political rehabilitation and Franco-German reconciliation. The negotiations which began in June 1950 ended with a compromise treaty which was signed in April 1951[111]. The treaty on the ECSC came into effect in August 1952 and when its High Authority was established, the IAR, loathed by the German Ruhr managers, was abolished.

Only 10 months after its outbreak the Korean War had altered the situation of the iron and steel industry significantly. When Foreign Minister Schuman on the occasion of the signing of the ECSC treaty wrote to Adenauer saying that the time had come to abolish the IAR, to lift the production limits imposed on all German industries and to return West Germany's economic sovereignty, it was not a gesture of goodwill but the acceptance of circumstances[112]. The war had created a situation in which the West depended on West German production capacity and throughout its duration it had a stimulating effect on German iron and steel making.

Faced with the war in East Asia and with a worldwide shortage of steel as a result, the Americans put political considerations on French security interests in second place. In any case the security issue had lost much of its sensitive nature after Schuman's announcement. With DM 75 million released for the iron and steel industry in the third ECA tranche, the Marshall Plan Administration took the Korean War into account and for the first time iron and steel received nearly as much money as the other sectors of the economy. However, it had taken the Americans quite a long time to 'convince' the Germans to put most of ECA III into the basic industries[113]. The Ruhr with its surplus capacity for steel was to be utilised for 'western defence'. A study by the Military Security Board (MSB) on 'The Possibility of Germany's Contribution to the Western Defence Effort' in December 1951 named eight Ruhr steel plants which were still able to produce armour plate. The MSB study stressed that the plants' monthly output of medium and heavy

---

[110]Milward, *Reconstruction*, pp. 145, 162 f.

[111]Ludof Herbst, *Option für den Westen. Vom Marshall Plan bis zum deutsch-französischen Vertrag*, München 1989, p. 77.

[112]Werner Abelshauser, *Die langen Fünfziger Jahre*, Düsseldorf, 1987, pp. 102 f.

[113]*Jb* 1950, pp. 31 f.

armour plates had risen from an average of 3,000 tons and 12,000 tons in the first quarter of 1951 to 19,000 tons and 100,000 tons respectively in the fourth quarter[114]. This increase could not be achieved by just utilising the surplus capacity but needed additional financial means. Surprisingly, there is not much evidence that these plants received special treatment or extra money from ECA II. Only the Hüttenwerk Hörde had a significantly higher share than all the other companies[115]. The question is therefore where did the money come from? The steel plants must have had either enough reserves or other sources of funding like short-term bank credits, self-finance via tax depreciations or returned profits. With a stream of orders coming in from abroad after the outbreak of hostilities in Korea, the significant rise in profits can easily be explained. These orders were not only of economic importance, they also had a political impact. The German steel manufacturers took on so many orders that they could not supply both the domestic market and the foreign customers. The delays resulting from this, mainly for the foreign customers, were deliberate. By stressing that they were not allowed to produce more than 11.1 million tons a year they put pressure on the Allies to lift the production limit. Blowing the same trumpet, the KfW argued that the best contribution Germany could offer to western defence was an extended production in the basic industries, in particular in iron and steel for which Allied control should be lifted[116]. In September 1950 the Allies permitted a higher steel quota by allowing the Germans to deduct the share of the export and defence production, before in August 1951 the limits were lifted completely. By that time production was already in excess of 13 million tons[117]. Nevertheless in 1950 the Kreditanstalt criticised the ongoing decartelisation and the breaking up of the *Verbundwirtschaft*. It claimed that without the break-up a steel production of 13.9 million tons would have been possible[118]. Of course, this was only another argument to get rid of the production limits and the controls under Military Government Law No. 75.

The steel boom also had a negative side. The increased steel production caused a higher demand for coal which escalated the existing coal shortage and thus backfired on the steel industry. Of the 123 blast furnaces which were operational in the Federal Republic in October 1950, only 78 were in service. But seven of those ran on only 25 to 50 per cent of their full capacity because they were up to a quarter short of their coke supply[119]. The steel plants had no intention to

---

[114]PRO FO 371 93732 CE(w)1104/1105. The plants were the Henrichshütte Hattingen, the Hüttenwerke Hörde, Huckingen, Oberhausen and Haspe, the Stahlwerke Bochum, the Rheinische Röhrenwerke Mühlheim, and the Westfalenhütte.

[115]DBBHA B 330/3338, Anlage 8 zum Protokoll der Kreditbewilligungsausschuß Sitzung vom 16 Dezember 1950. This protocol enclosure shows also the ECA I figures. But those were of lesser importance for the question since that money was already given before the Korean War. No documents concerning ECA III could be found.

[116]Adamsen, *Investitionshilfe*, pp. 94 f.; *Jb* 1950, p. 35.

[117]Abelshauser, *Ruhrkohle*, pp.69 f.; *FRUS* 1950, vol. III, p. 1244, p. 1291.

[118]*Jb* 1950, p. 16.

[119]Abelshauser, 'Korea', p. 302.

lose their (mainly) American customers. However, with not enough dollars to pay for a sufficient supply of US coal, the steel plants were left with only one alternative, to barter their products for American coal. It is pretty obvious that these kinds of deals made no sense for the national economy as a whole since they meant a loss of foreign currency, that is dollar, revenue. For 1000 tons of coal 200 tons of rolled steel had to be exported which created a short supply for the domestic steel processing industries and in manufacturing, many of which produced for exports[120]. But it meant that the steel industry could extend its production further thus creating facts against the Allied production limits and controls.

American policy in 1951 was particularly contradictory with regard to Germany's iron industry. On the one side, ECA delayed the release of ECA III money for the industry, along with the money for mining and the export industries so as to force the Germans to provide a bigger share of investment in the basic industries and because ECA punished suspected East-West trade they had banned by withholding funds. On the other side they demanded the expansion of the steel production to 19 or 20 million tons which was very difficult because of a tight capital market and with decartelisation still under way[121]. In May 1950 Allied High Commission Law No. 27 replaced Military Government Law No. 75. Though the liquidation of large conglomerates like the Vereinigte Stahlwerke was still a possibility the new law for the first time guaranteed compensation for the former owners. Furthermore, the first and second regulation to Law 27 appointed the managers of the companies in question as liquidators[122]. Naturally, the liquidators and all other Ruhr industrialists put up determined resistance against Law 27. This finally paid off. During 1952 and 1953 most companies were released from the law's restrictions while at the same time new, often informal links between the coal and steel plants were established. By August 1952 it had become clear that decartelisation had failed to a large extent and by the mid-1950s re-cartelisation or *Rückverflechtung* was well under way[123].

The Korean War and the sudden need for German iron and steel products helped the Germans to regain control of their industry. Equally important, the money supplied under the AIL strengthened the industry. The iron and steel industry received the biggest share of investment money, some DM 296 million, of which the KfW handled DM 284 million. The large share could only be achieved because the industry had the strongest lobby in the *Kuratorium* which in the end meant a strengthening of its power in general. The AIL also offered an opportunity for the iron and steel industry to rehabilitate its reputation after its involvement with

---

[120]*Jb.* 1951, p. 20.

[121]KfW HA-Prot 10-2, Protokoll der 21. Sitzung, TOP 5; *Jb* 1951, p. 56.

[122]Abelshauser, *Ruhrkohle,* pp. 54 f.; also a table with the actual restructuring and changes of property, pp. 192 ff.; Eberhard Schmidt, *Die verhinderte Neuordnung 1945-1952,* Frankfurt/M 1981 (8th edn.), p. 176; AHC Regulation nos. 1 and 2 under Law 27, reprinted in: Ruhm von Oppen, *Documents,* pp. 513 ff.

[123]Gillingham, *Coal,* pp. 266 ff, pp. 301 ff, p. 312; *Jb* 1952, p. 52; *Jb* 1953, p. 58; Abelshauser, *Ruhrkohle*, p. 82.

the Nazi regime by portraying the 'sacrifices' they were to take on with the AIL. It is also very likely that the iron and steel association was the main player to demand the introduction of article 36 of the AIL which allowed the excessive tax depreciation on investments and profits. A general survey on capital and investment finance and prices carried out by the KfW showed this development.

Even with higher costs than in 1936 and prices still fixed there must have been considerable profits in the iron and steel industry, since coal prices remained also fixed at a low level and foreign demand for iron and steel increased after the summer of 1950. When the prices for rolled steel were freed in 1952, iron and steel could ask for even higher prices[124]. Therefore, the end of price controls has to be seen in connection with the special tax depreciation under article 36 of the AIL in the way that both measures supplemented each other and produced additional self finance capacity for the steel plants. The large-scale investments encouraged by the AIL were necessary because most of the rolling mills were outdated and needed replacement in order to increase productivity which lagged clearly behind that of the investment goods industry[125].

Table 7.2.3
Productivity and Prices of the Steel Industry 1949-1952
(in per cent compared to 1936)

	Lead in productivity of the investment goods industry over the iron and steel industry	Lead in prices of the iron and and steel industry over the investment goods industry
1949	31	6
1950	39	16
1951	63	21
1952	59	55

Source: KfW HA-BA 6, Memorandum Kapitalmarkt und Investitionsfinanzierung in der Bundesrepublik, 28.12.1953, p. 24.

As before with ECA II there is no indication that the eight plants which were able to produce armour plate received a bigger share of AIL investment money than other companies. Two of them actually did not receive any money at all. This fact allows only one conclusion, namely that the profit situation of the companies must have been quite good. There is even the possibility that, with the traditional strict

[124]Gillingham, *Coal*, p. 308.
[125]KfW HA-BA 6, Memorandum 'Kapitalmarkt und Investitionsfinanzierung', 28 December 1953.

discipline within the industry and the feeling of belonging to 'one family', individual plants for this reason did not apply for loans to allow more funding for the others[126].

In 1952, the situation in the German iron and steel industry in general and that of the Ruhr in particular was much better than it might have appeared at first sight. War damage was by far not as severe as had been expected and the Korean War provided large export profits while considerable tax depreciation allowed a high rate of self-finance. The decartelisation had been stopped, a certain level of *Rückverflechtung* took place and output levels were increasing steadily. However, it is worth comparing the development with Germany's main rival. While West German steel output reached pre-war levels again in 1951-52 the figures in its neighbouring countries were even more impressive at first glance. France, Belgium and Luxembourg had increased their pre-war output by 40 to 60 per cent, the USA by a staggering 124 per cent[127]. These figures have to be put into the historical context, though. The expansion of French productivity was the result of a political plan and therefore it was financed to a very large extent by the French government. Nevertheless the target output of 12 million tons was not achieved without the production of the Saar. The 124 per cent increase of the USA requires more detailed explanation. In 1936, while the Nazi armament programme was already underway, the USA was still in its worst recession so that output levels there started from a relative low level before it became the workshop of the post-war world.

The fact remained however, that Germany's competitors on the world steel market had used the post-war years, in the case of the USA even the war years, to modernise and to rationalise their industries. The Ruhr therefore had to follow suit in order to keep or regain its market share. Since the reorganisation of the Ruhr coal and steel industry was more or less completed in 1952 and Allied controls had been either lifted or become a formality, the political obstacles for large-scale modernisation had vanished. The costs for this modernisation programme were estimated at about DM 4 billion for the next four years, with an outside capital requirement of DM 500 million in 1953 and 1954. Modernisation was necessary for the Ruhr, both to compete on an international market which had become increasingly tough in the aftermath of the Korean War and to satisfy domestic demand. The economic boom which followed the Korean War made the steel consumption within the Federal Republic rise well above the domestic output, so steel had to be imported from 1952 onwards[128].

---

[126]KfW HA-VS 201, table 'Investitionshilfe Eisen und Stahl' 31 December 1952. Due to German archival laws, individual applications are treated as banking secrets and cannot yet be accessed so that this must remain speculation.
[127]KfW HA-Prot 10-2, Protokoll der 25. Sitzung, TOP 3.
[128]*Jb* 1952, pp. 21, 56.
[129]*Jb* 1953, p. 23.

Table 7.2.4
Ingot Steel Production in France and Germany 1936-1952
(in million tons)

	1936	1938	1945	1947	1948	1949	1950	1951	1952
Dt Reich	19.2	22.6							
FRG	14.2		0.3	3.0	5.5	9.1	12.1	13.5	15.8
France	6.7	6.2	1.6	5.7	7.2	9.1	8.6	9.8	10.9
Saar			0.7	1.2	1.7	1.9	2.6	2.8	n.a

Source: KfW HA-Prot 10-2, Protokoll der 25. Sitzung, TOP 3, Anlage 2.

The end of the war brought a worldwide steel surplus and it became cheaper for German manufacturers to import foreign steel than to buy the domestic product, which confirmed the need for rationalisation[129]. The KfW tried to use the iron and steel industry's need for long-term investment money for its own purpose when it proposed that DM 100 million of its scheduled new 5.5 per cent bond should go to the aid of the industry[130]. The way the Kreditanstalt changed the beneficiaries of the proposed bonds indicated that their main interest was not with the iron and steel industry although during the process the proposed share for the industry remained at DM 100 million but with its own interests of issuing a new series of bonds. This is confirmed in a KfW letter to Karl Bernard, the Central Bank Council president[131]. Using the large investments the French had made in their steel industry as a pretext, Bernard was asked to support the Anstalt's request for the issue of bonds in order to start a similar investment programme.

Although the bonds were not issued at the time there were considerable sums of money for the industry in 1954 and 1955 as Table 7.2.5 shows. The Federal Government had another reason besides the improvement of the German iron and steel manufacturers' competitiveness. The Federal Republic was preparing to re-enter the military arena with its planned participation in the European Defence Community. That is not to say that all DM 100 million the government provided from the sale of its own 1953 bond issue went into new armaments factories, since the federal government still had to give money to compensate for dismantled plants but the money certainly helped to rebuild military production[132].

1954 brought another new task for the Kreditanstalt which was part of the legacy of the Great Depression and the World War. In 1926 and 1927, the Vereinigte Stahlwerke had issued dollar bonds on the American market to the face value of more than $95 million. While most of these securities were redeemed before the war some $21.5 million remained. During the negotiations on the

[130]KfW HA-VS 192, KfW letter to BMWi, 28 July 1953.
[131]DBBHA B 330/3152, KfW letter to President Bernard, 23 November 1953.
[132]*Jb* 1955, p. 50.

London Debt Agreement the Americans insisted on the repayment of this sum. Abs convinced the Americans that this could only be done if the Vereinigte Stahlwerke's successor companies were allowed to split the debt amongst them. On this the Americans only agreed if a third party was going to give a guarantee for the whole sum and it was consented that the KfW was a suitable guarantor. In its 24th meeting, the BoD accepted in principle that the successor companies would have the necessary money to buy the dollars for the repayment of the bonds. In case the companies were unable to raise the money the KfW had to step in and provide the money instead.

Table 7.2.5
Confirmed KfW Loans to the Iron and Steel Industry 1954-1960
(in million DM)

	1954	1955	1956	1957	1958	1959	1960	Total
ERP/MSA	64.1	123.8	7.0	21.8[2)]	48.8[2)]	28.3[2)]	78.0	371.8
KfW bonds	11.2							11.2
AIL	38.9							38.9
Fed. budget					5.0	94.0		99.0
KfW funds	3.0				70.8	98.6[4)]	61.0	233.4
Others	18.5	58.7[1)]	48.6	61.5[3)]				187.3
Total	135.7	182.5	55.6	83.3	124.6	220.9	139.0	941.6
(included money for the Saar)				(40)	(59.4)	(70)	(78)	

1) Including DM 10 million for Auftragsfinanzierung Berlin.
2) Including iron and steel processing companies.
3) Confirmation partly for 1958 and beyond.
4) Including ECSC and Kapitalsammelstellen.

Source: *Jb* 1954-1960, passim.

There were three reasons for Abs and the Kreditanstalt to take part in the deal: it would help to spread the KfW's name and reputation on the New York Stock Exchange which was regarded as being helpful to the Anstalt's long-term interests. Secondly, redeeming the bonds returned the successor companies' credit worthiness which was important for their long-term planning. And, of course, Abs was chairman of the supervisory board of the biggest successor company, the

Dortmund-Hörder-Hütten-Union[133]. While the BoD decision had already been taken in 1952, the KfW had to take on the guarantee only two years later. Abs had managed to get the same long running terms of repayment for the successor companies as were agreed for German public debts but the profit situation of the companies was so good that already by the end of 1961 Herbert Martini could inform the BoD that the guarantee had been transformed into a normal loan and that it was redeemed prematurely[134].

In 1955 West German ingot steel output reached a record level of 21 million tons[135]. The August-Thyssen-Hütte which had been largely dismantled in the late 1940s could pay a dividend on its shares of 8 per cent that year. It is fair, then to speak of the end of *Remontage*, and when Thyssen received a $10 million loan from the Ex-Im Bank the following year one could argue that the reconstruction process, at least in the iron and steel industry, was nearing its completion[136]. Companies could again borrow on the international money markets. For the Kreditanstalt a new field of operation emerged that year. In the aftermath of the so-called *Saarstatut* referendum on the 'Europe-isation' of the Saar in the framework of a European Union, which had been rejected by the population, France and Germany finished their negotiations on the region's return to Germany in October 1956. According to the Saar treaty, the region would become part of the Federal Republic on 1 January 1957 with a maximum transition period of three years in which legal and economic matters could be settled[137]. Since the Saar economy as a whole had lacked the large-scale investment programmes which had taken place in the Federal Republic, its industries faced a considerable disadvantage in competitiveness compared to the West German firms. In particular the coal and iron industries which employed more than half of the Saar's industrial workforce was faced with serious competitive disadvantages if it did not receive additional help. The Saar government estimated the necessary sum to close the investment gap just in the iron and steel industry to be 45 billion French Francs, or about DM 540 million for the next three years[138]. The West German government was put on the spot since Adenauer himself had spoken in favour of the rejected Saar Statute so now he had to regain lost political territory by aiding the investment process. Money for the Saar industry also made economic sense. If West Germany was

---

[133]KfW HA-VS 10, paper by Otto Neubaur for the BoD, 6 December 1952; KfW HA-Prot 10-2, Protokoll der 24. Sitzung, TOP 4; Kurt Pritzkoleit, *Bosse, Banken, Börsen*, München, Wien, Basel, 1954, p. 136.

[134]KfW Ha-Prot 10-2, Protokoll der 28. Sitzung, TOP 3, Anlage 8; KfW HA-VS 10, paper by Otto Neubaur for the BoD, 6 December 1952; KfW HA-Prot 10-3, Protokoll der 43, Sitzung, TOP 2.

[135]*Jb* 1955, p. 24.

[136]Gillingham, *Coal*, p. 353.

[137]Herbst, *Option*, p. 179.

[138]KfW HA-VS 111, confidential manuscript, 'Probleme der Rückgliederung des Saarlandes auf wirtschaftlichem und sozialem Gebiet', undated; KfW HA-VS 209, confidential report by the government of the Saarland, 20 November 1956.

neglecting the region, it was going to create its own impoverished industrial and economic backyard, therefore aid had to be given. But with tax authority still in French hands the option of self-finance via high tax depreciation was not available. Loans were the only feasible way and it was once more the Kreditanstalt für Wiederaufbau which took on the task.

Before the first money could be distributed, the KfW saw itself faced with a grotesque problem: although the Saar was to be part of the Federal Republic from 1 January 1957 it was still part of the French economic area so that special permission for all money transactions was needed from the BdL[139]. The Ministry for Ecomomic Co-operation gave the KfW a commitment for DM 300 million from the ERP Special Assets for a long-term investment programme of which DM 110 million were scheduled for the Saar's iron and steel industry. The programme was later enhanced to DM 360 million, the iron and steel industry being again the largest single beneficiary. Its share rose to nearly half of the total. In addition to the ERP funds in 1957 DM 260 million federal budget money was provided for the return of the Saar, DM 175 million of which were handled by the KfW[140]. DM 36 million of the budget money went to the steel industry. The money was designated for the biggest steel plant at the Saar, the Röchling Werke, as a government compensation for three billion French Francs which the company had paid to France to avoid dismantling[141]. The money has to be seen as part of the commitment of Adenauer's government to *Remontage* and since money for the purpose had been given to the Ruhr it now had to be given to the Saar as well.

A representative of the new Land took a seat on the KfW's BoD from 1959 to 1982 to look after its interests there. But while KfW money most certainly helped to modernise the Saar's industries it was not possible to change the structural weakness of the region[142]. The Saar's economy was built on coal and steel which caused serious long-term problems when these industries began to decline after 1958 (coal) and in the 1960s (steel).

Table 7.2.5 shows the volume of KfW money for the iron and steel industry in the second half of the 1950s and allows some interesting insights into the industry. Since only about half of the money for 1957 and the following years (the figures in brackets below the table's main body) went into the modernisation of the Saar steel industry, it is clear that, with the exception of 1954-55, only a moderate amount of KfW money went into the Ruhr's iron and steel sector.

---

[139]KfW HA-VS 109, Ministerialblatt des BMWi, Runderlaß 6/57, 29 January1957; KfW note 18 February 1957; BdL letters to KfW, 24 April 1957, 18 December 1957, 9 December 1958, which granted this permission *per se.*

[140]KfW HA-VS 108, KfW note regarding the 300 million programme; KfW HA-VS 110, Sitzungsprotokolle Investitionsausschuß Saar, table 'Belegung der Saarprogramme', undated (24 October 1960); KfW HA-VS 111, subfile Allgemeine Planung, note 11 January 1957; KfW HA-Prot 10-2, Protokoll der 33. Sitzung, TOP 3.

[141]KfW HA-VS 111, KfW letter to H.J. Abs (in his capacity as chairman of the Süddeutsche Bank which held strong interests in the Saar), 28 January 1957.

[142]Harries, *Wiederaufbau*, p. 56.

1954-55 were the years when reconstruction of war damaged and dismantled plants could finally be carried out on a large-scale after the years of planning which followed the release of the industry from Allied control[143]. An armaments industry was re-established following West Germany's entry into NATO, though not necessarily by the old armaments companies such as Krupp. The relatively small amount of money after 1955 for the plants outside the Saar shows that the industry could rely on profits or on tax depreciation for its investments. The basis for this had been laid during the Nazi years when gross fixed capital rose as a result of the armaments and war production. But it shows also that war damage due to bombing or ground fighting and dismantling, for which in any case companies were compensated, were not as bad as contemporaries thought or claimed. The Ruhr industry in particular, if one exaggerates the situation a bit, had only to clear up the rubble and wait for production limits to be lifted before they could start investing in new and better plants. In addition to its loans the Kreditanstalt supported the process with non-cash aid by taking on sureties for the plants, mainly for ECSC loans which ran in tens of millions each year.

7.3 The Electricity Industry

The electricity industry constitutes a special case amongst the basic industries. It was the sector which received by far the largest amount of money out of the GARIOA and ECA funds and it was the only basic industry which did not experience decartelisation and dismantling. Allied plans in this direction were never put in action[144].

Electricity companies had experienced their first boom in the decade before the First World War. The war saw the industry expanding considerably to satisfy the power demands for armaments production. This was accompanied by increased state intervention, state regulation of and state participation in electric power companies[145]. This trend continued during the 1920s and up to 1935, along with first attempts to link up various power stations to establish a *Verbundwirtschaft* or national grid which was intended to cover the whole Reich. At the same time the electric power generation by 'public' suppliers for the first time surpassed those of industry's self production[146]. The Nazi planning for the electricity industry after 1935 was faced with a dilemma. The centralisation of electric power generation

---

[143]*Jb* 1955, p. 50.

[144]See PRO FO 371 85794 CE 1580, letter by Erhard to BiCO, 16 September 1949.

[145]Gert Bruche, *Elektrizitätsversorgung und Staatsfunktion*, Frankfurt/M., New York 1977, pp. 47 ff.

[146]Bruche, *Elektrizitätsversorgung*, p. 144. Public suppliers include power plants in the ownership of municipalities, the Länder, the Reich and those of mixed ownership in which private investors as well as public authorities had a stake. They supplied public installations, private households and industrial customers alike. The 'private' suppliers were mainly producing for industrial self-consumption.

meant a rationalisation in the process but posed a strategic risk in times of war. Therefore the Nazis took a twin-track approach by trying to extend the *Verbundwirtschaft*, while at the same time new industrial plants like the chemical works in Saxony and south Prussia were constructed with their own huge power stations which could be connected to the grid. The total electricity generation during the Nazi years rose by 84 per cent from 13,000 MW in 1933 to 24,000 MW in 1944, with the main increase of 10,000 MW between 1937 and 1944[147]. At the end of the war productivity of the electric power supply industry had been reduced to half its 1943 level as a result of power plant and grid destruction[148]. Unfavourable weather conditions meant that the remaining hydroelectric power plants could produce only a fraction of their full capacity in the immediate post-war years. Worse, 30 per cent of the thermal power stations' capacity was out of operation in order to service the previous overworking during the war. To ease this strain and to try a better utilisation of the scarce resource the western Allies in 1947 allowed the establishment of a cross zonal *Zentral-Lastverteiler* (central power distributor)[149]. In contrast to the other basic industries, none of the leading managers and technicians of the power industry were removed from their posts and in autumn 1949 a US committee decided that there was no excessive concentration of economic power within the German power industry. Consequently there was no need for decartelisation. That not even the 'Big Four', the Rheinisch-Westfälische Elektrizitätswerke (RWE), the Vereinigte Elektrizitätswerke (VEW), the Preußenelektra and the Bayernwerke were regarded as monopolistic could easily be justified by pointing out the legal ownership of the companies. The Bayernwerk was an enterprise of the Bavarian state, Preußenelektra, as part of the VEBA, a Prussian state company (with the VEBA becoming a West German federal holding company) and the VEW was in the ownership of public bodies, while the RWE was a mixed company with private and public ownership[150].

In the case of the RWE, the majority of shares were in the hands of private investors who held 60 to 70 per cent of the ordinary shares with ordinary voting rights. Another 25 to 30 per cent of shares were preference shares with no voting rights but a guaranteed dividend. Only about 3 per cent of shares were held by municipal and regional authorities as named shares (*Namensaktien*) with a 20-fold voting right so that in theory local government would always be in control of the company. But since the municipalities and local authorities regarded themselves as

---

[147]Wolfgang Löwen, 'Rechtshistorische Aspekte der deutschen Elektrizitätsversorgung 1880-1990', in: *Die Geschichte der Stromversorgung*, Frankfurt/M, 1992, pp. 191, 194; Georg Boll, *Entstehung und Entwicklung des Verbundbetriebs in der deutschen Elektrizitätswirtschaft bis zum europäischen Verbund*, Frankfurt/M., 1969, pp. 97, 99; Abelshauser stated the increase of power by 77 per cent between 1933-43, see, Abelshauser, *Westdeutschland*, p. 45.

[148]Löwen, 'Aspekte', p. 194.

[149]Thomas Herzig, 'Wirtschaftsgeschichtliche Aspekte der deutschen Elektrizitätsversorgung 1880-1990', in: *Geschichte der Stromversorgung*, p. 142.

[150]Bruche, *Elektrizitätsversorgung*, pp. 46, 90, esp. footnote 156.

the real owner (*Eigentümer in letzter Instanz*) they would not act against the commercial interests and the long-term plans of the company and thus the company was a private company (and monopoly) in all but name[151]. The decision not to split up the power companies was therefore a political one because they were needed for the rapid reconstruction of western Germany which is shown in the 'at once' and ECA programmes. This Allied decision was made easy because of the companies' semi-public ownership and the fact that they were not in the limelight as much as the coal and steel companies.

By 1948 power supply in the three western zones had again reached 1936 levels. But since electricity output had grown massively after 1936 it meant that it was still only about half the wartime maximum production. The loss of the big power plants in the area which would become the GDR, as well as the part of the grid which ran through that territory had become a severe handicap for faster expansion. An OECD study estimated the deficit in the Bizone's power supply at about eight billion kWh for 1949 at a current production of 30 billion kWh. At first glance this was due to an inadequate coal supply at the power stations[152]. But because of the lack of power, old plants had to produce electricity as well, even when their coal consumption was up to twice the level of modern power stations thus creating a vicious circle. Furthermore, because of the general shortage of coal, consumers substituted coal with electricity as their energy supply which added to the strain on power supply[153]. For this reason and in an attempt to improve the situation, BiCO gave the highest priority, even before coal production, to the repair and modernisation of old power plants and the construction of new ones.

In its 'at once' programme the KfW proposed financing 44 projects in the power industry with DM 170 million. In its reply on 15 February 1949 BiCO reduced this to only 20 projects involving ten companies in order to concentrate scarce resources. Nevertheless the KfW's proposal was extended by BiCO into a programme of its own, called Energy I, which would stretch for several years until 1954 and amounted to more than DM 600 million for the 20 projects for which BiCO promised the necessary funds. The aim was to produce additional 1236 MW by the programme's completion[154]. For 1949 DM 220 million were scheduled towards Energy I. In the first place the electricity companies themselves were to raise the money by issuing debenture bonds (*Obligationen*) on the open market. In this way it was hoped to stimulate the German capital market for reconstruction finance. But since nobody, not even the Americans, expected the market to be in a shape to provide the money, it was agreed that the KfW would buy the obligations not sold on the open market. The Kreditanstalt raised the money necessary to buy

[151]Pritzkoleit, *Männer*, pp. 390, 394.
[152]Borchard, Buchheim, 'Wirkung', p. 331; Bruche, *Elektrizitätsversorgung*, p. 92.
[153]*Jb* 1953, pp. 26 f.
[154]KfW HA-Prot 10-1, Protokoll der 5. Sitzung, TOP 5 and enclosure to the meeting; KfW HA-BA 1, table 'Aufteilung des Kreditbedarf nach Jahren'; KfW HA-BA 1, copied letter BiCO/Memo(49)13 to the BoD, 15 February 1949. The letter speaks of 1236 MkW which must be a typing error.

them by issuing promissory notes (*Schuldscheine*) which would then be accepted by BiCO and refunded with GARIOA money[155].

Until the end of 1949 debenture bonds with the face value of DM 29.1 million were sold on the market. Because of the lack of GARIOA funds BiCO was able to pay out only DM 110 million to the KfW, leaving a considerable financial gap. Although the money was not released in one instalment but only in accordance with the construction process, the KfW had to pre-finance DM 50 million. They were to be redeemed with ECA I funds which also had to cover for the missing half of the GARIOA funds[156]. For ECA I BiCO had suggested the amount of DM 180 million new money for electricity but the Germans again had different priorities and got the amount reduced to DM 110 million. One reason for the German wish to keep the programme small was the hope that the country would soon be re-united. Then the huge power plants in the GDR would provide cheaper energy and the new construction programmes would have been a waste of resources[157]. That the Americans did not consider this option is an indication that they had already accepted Germany's division.

The new money under ECA I was to go completely into the Energy II programme which included also the programme 'French Zone' and amounted to DM 419 million in total. It was planned that Energy II would provide an additional 1220 to 1300 MW, thus doubling the first programme's output[158]. In contrast to Energy I the ECA gave no guarantee for the programme's entire financing. The surprise for the KfW was even bigger when the Marshall Plan Administration declared that they did not feel bound by the Military Government's promise to finance Energy I to its completion. The reason for the retreat was political rather than financial. The VfW had sent a long-term plan to the ECA Mission in Paris in which a capacity increase of 8225 MW was scheduled up to 1958. This had caused strong French protests for fear of a new stage of German rearmament and the Americans were forced to screen all projects once again before they could finally adhere to the Military Government's commitment[159].

ECA II provided another DM 133.7 million for the electricity industry. The problem the KfW faced this time was the lack of commitment by the ECA. The

---

[155]KfW HA-BA 1, draft 'Spezialprogramm Energiewerke', reply to BiCO/Memo(49)13, 7 March 1949; KfW letter to BiCO, 17 March 1949.

[156]*Jb* 1949, p. 22. In the 1950 Annual Report the KfW gives a figure of DM 82.1 million for 1949-50 which had to be given to supplement Energy I, see *Jb* 1950, p. 22.

[157]KfW HA-Prot 10-1, Protokoll der 9. Sitzung, TOP 6; KfW HA-VS 40, KfW note 'Offene Fragen', 1 August 1949.

[158]KfW HA-BA 1, KfW note 'Finanzierung der Elektrizitätswirtschaft durch die KfW', 28 June 1950; *Jb* 1950, p. 44.

[159]KfW HA-BA 1, note 5 December 1949; KfW note 'Finanzierung der Elektrizitätswirtschaft durch die KfW', 28 June 1950.

Kreditanstalt therefore had to plan on a monthly basis and had to pre-finance the money until new counterpart funds were released[160].

While the ECA at first wanted to reduce ECA III money and then delayed its release, in particular for utilisation in coal and steel, in order to put pressure on the Germans, the funding for the power industry did not seem to have been affected. Whether this was because the ECA thought the electricity supply still central to German reconstruction or because they, too, were shocked by the power cuts which appeared in the aftermath of the outbreak of the Korean conflict is not clear[161]. Anyway, it was once more ECA which suggested a bigger proportion of money for the electricity industry, DM 275 million as compared to the BMWi's DM 190 million. Although the power cuts were due to the lack of coal (output between April 1950 and April 1951 had risen only by 11 per cent compared to a 32 per cent rise by all industry and 23 per cent by electricity) it made sense to invest in new power plants[162]. New power stations consuming hard coal would need less coal for higher output thus reducing the strain on coal production; and since brown coal was easier and cheaper to mine, it also made sense to build new plants near the brown coal fields. On this occasion the Americans achieved their aim. They not only released the money they had scheduled for electrical power but extended the funds to DM 356 million. The Auxiliary Investment Law poured additional investment money into the sector and by the end of 1953 the Kreditanstalt had confirmed nearly DM 1.2 billion to the industry as Table 7.3.1 shows. It is somewhat astonishing that nearly a quarter of all counterpart funds, including MSA funds and reinvested repayments and interests, went into the electricity industry thus making it the biggest beneficiary of the funds[163]. Nothing demonstrates more clearly the importance of the electrical power industry for the Americans, if only by building new plants as a coal-saving measure. Initially this appears to be in contrast to American interests in coal exports but they knew that they did not have enough shipping capacity to transport all the coal necessary and that it was a very uneconomical way of producing electricity.

Out of a total of DM 241 million of AIL funds scheduled for the electricity industry only DM 161 million were distributed by the Kreditanstalt to complete previously begun projects.

By the end of 1952 nearly the whole programme for the construction of new power plants was completed, adding a total of 2800 MW. About 70 per cent of the increase had been in public power supply, financed with ECA funds. In terms of the total of the national power supply, that is including industrial self-supplier, ECA money helped to build still about 60 per cent of the increase[164].

[160] *Jb* 1950, p. 24; *Jb* 1951, pp. 29, 53 f.; KfW HA-BA 1, KfW letter to the Direktorium der Bank deutsche Länder, 1 February 1950.
[161] Abelshauser, 'Korea', p. 288.
[162] KfW HA-Prot 10-1, Ergänzende Niederschrift zur 17. Sitzung, TOP 1; Protokoll der 18. Sitzung, TOP 4; Adamsen, *Investitionshilfe*, p. 84.
[163] *Jb* 1952, p. 32; *Jb* 1953, pp. 39, 61.
[164] *Jb* 1951, p. 54; *Jb* 1952, p. 55; Borchard, Buchheim, 'Wirkung', p. 335.

Table 7.3.1
Confirmed KfW Money to the Electricity Industry 1949-1953
(in million DM)

	1949	1950	1951	1952	1953	Total
GARIOA	110					110
ECA I		(	(	(	(	(
ECA II		(354	(355	(75.2	(13.3	(842.3
ECA III		(	44.8	(	(	(
MSA					20.5	20.5
AIL			44.2	114.8		159.0
KfW funds			22.4	21.6	4.5	48.5
Others					10.0	10.0
Total	110	354	466.4	211.6	48.3	1180.3

Source: *Jb* 1950, passim; *Jb* 1953, p. 61[165].

In 1951 electricity consumption was estimated to grow by 15-20 per cent every year so that a long-term plan was required to control and direct the development. By the end of the year future investment into electricity was estimated by the KfW to be a minimum DM 1 billion per year to enable the industry to expand its annual production by 1000 MW. DM 635 million of this money was to be spent on new power plants, the rest was needed to rebuild and extend the national grid. These figures, presented to the BoD by Neubaur, showed the areas to which the KfW lent its money. Loans for the extension of the electrical grid were only given in two exceptional circumstances, as usually KfW loans went only into power plant construction or modernisation[166]. From the economic point of view this restriction made sense. Electricity was desperately needed therefore the construction of new power plants was prioritised. The power companies could then finance the grid extension on their own, using the forthcoming profits generated by their new power plants. The handling of the finance in this way was advantageous for the electricity companies, too. They received cheap, long-term loans to build their future source

[165]Once again, the various Annual Reports are not very clear and sometimes even inconsistent, with the same money apparently named in different programmes. The 1951 and even more so the 1952 Annual Reports are especially unclear. This table is therefore based on the KfW table in *Jb* 1953, p. 61 and on *Jb* 1950 which do not allow an accurate picture of how the three ECA tranches were utilised in the various years.
[166]*Jb* 1951, p. 20; KfW HA-VS 10, 'Finanzierung der Elektrizitätswirtschaft', 23 October 1951; *Jb* 1952, p. 54; Borchard, Buchheim, 'Wirkung', p. 334.

of income. This was most striking in 1951 when all new constructions were financed with counterpart funds via the KfW. The biggest single beneficiary was certainly the RWE. Until the end of 1952 they received loans amounting to DM 241 million which enabled them to finance their whole capacity increase of 517 MW[167]. This was not (only) due to the fact that Abs was chairman of the RWE's supervisory board but because the company was located and had its main customers in North Rhine Westphalia, where the Ruhr industry constituted a huge consumer of electricity. And there was another reason to favour the RWE's expansion of plants. The company owned the largest brown coal fields in West Germany. Although the energy output was not as high as that produced by hard coal, brown coal had various advantages compared to other sources of energy. First, it was more readily available than hard coal and was much cheaper to mine. Unlike hydroelectric power it was available all year round and, of course, a brown coal power plant could be built much more quickly than a hydroelectric plant. Consequently the share of brown coal in electricity production rose from 4.8 billion kWh or 14 per cent in 1948 to 21 billion kWh or 21 per cent in 1958 reducing hard coal's share by 5 per cent to 58[168].

Although the Kreditanstalt financed industrial power plants as well there was a general trend away from industrial self-sufficiency in electrical power. The new, huge public power plants built in the 1950s meant lower production costs so that electricity could become cheaper for large-scale customers. Thus it became cheaper for industry to buy power from the public companies than to produce their own electricity. The share of industrial self-supply dropped from 40 per cent in 1950 to less than 20 per cent in 1970[169].

Apart from the ERP funds it was the AIL which increased the power companies' economic strength. In March 1952 an ordinance issued by the economics ministry lifted the price controls in all but name before they were officially abolished one year later[170]. The effect on the sector can be seen in the gross capital investments made in electricity during these years and the part the counterpart fund played in it (Table 7.3.2). The sharp drop in the ERP's share in gross capital investment in 1952 shows both the decline in available ERP funds and the impact of the Auxiliary Investment Law which allowed a rise in profits and higher tax depreciation. The distribution of ERP funds reached its climax of uneven distribution in 1951 when 37 per cent of all counterpart funds went into electricity. Nevertheless, the ERP's share in investment remained high during 1952 and 1953 despite the overall reduction of funds. This was because of the winding-up of the previous investment programmes which went on for some time. The still impressive

[167]Borchard, Buchheim, 'Wirkung', pp. 337, 355.

[168]Boll, *Entstehung*, p. 111.

[169]KfW HA-BS 59, passim; KfW HA-VS 188, table by the BMWi 'Zur Vorfinanzierung der Elektrizitätswirtschaft aus der Investitionshilfe', 10 August 1951; Borchard, Buchheim, 'Wirkung', p. 335; Herzig, 'Aspekte', p. 145.

[170]Brochard, Buchheim, 'Wirkung', p. 341; Bruche, *Elektrizitätsversorgung*, p.94.

share in investment it provided underlines again the importance of power supply in the critical years of the Korean War.

It is perhaps surprising that the ERP's share in GCI reached 'only' 27 per cent in the year when nearly all new power projects were financed with Marshall Plan funds. This was due to the large amount of their own money which companies had to use for the construction of the electrical grid. They had to rebuild the damaged old 110 kV (main) supply line and parts of the already existing 220 kV grid. In addition they drew on pre-war plans to set up a new 380 kV *Verbundnetz*. This idea was put into practice after the re-establishing of the Deutsche Verbundgesellschaft under the leadership of the RWE in 1949[171]. This indicates that there were considerable funds available within the companies.

Table 7.3.2
Gross Capital Investment in the Electricity Industry 1949-1954 and the Share of ERP Funds
(in per cent)

	1949	1950	1951	1952	1953	1954
ERP share of GCI in electricity	18	25	27	6.2	4.9	2.0
Share of ERP funds for electricity	18.1	20.3	37	17	13	8.6

Source: Baumgart, pp. 124 f.

The MSA strongly criticised the previous practice of finance. The Agency pointed out that one particular company which profited from tax depreciation of some DM 68 million on power plants alone between 1948-1951, (that is before the special depreciation under the AIL was introduced) still received DM 222 million counterpart funds until July 1952. The MSA concluded that a much bigger financial contribution by the company would have been possible. The situation with other power companies was certainly similar and the KfW did its best to improve it further by extending the validity of the loans considerably. Hence, Buchheim's argument of the essential importance of the counterpart funds to the power industry's recovery requires some adaptation[172].

---

[171]See Herzig, 'Aspekte', p. 138, p. 146 for maps of the grid, and Boll, *Entstehung*, p. 92; Löwen, 'Aspekte', p. 195.

[172]KfW HA-VS 118, MSA Special Mission, Report No. P 11, Procedures and Controls Applicable to the Release and Utilisation of ECA Counterpart Funds in the Power Sector,

The mid-1950s saw a new task for the Kreditanstalt für Wiederaufbau in regard to the electricity companies. With the lifting of the Occupation Statute in 1955 the German power companies were allowed research in atomic power. In its 1955 Annual Report the KfW held the view that atomic energy in the near future would not substitute fossil fuels or hydro-electrics but that it would be a supplement for those countries without proper and sufficient resources. There would also be severe consequences in the Federal Republic and huge structural changes if the country were to turn away from its coalmines. Since atomic power technology was still in its infancy and not very economical, it was cheaper to produce electricity with local coal although it could not meet the demand[173]. By 1958 however, the situation and opinion had changed. The West German power industry had signed multinational contracts within the framework of Euratom to research into this potential. The US government had provided a loan to Euratom via its Ex-Im Bank[174]. What the KfW did not mention was its own involvement in the deal. The Ex-Im Bank lent $135 million for the construction of six to eight atomic power stations, the total costs of which were estimated at about $350 million. Because the Economics Ministry did not want to give the Americans a chance to look at the accounts of German companies which took the loan, it was decided that all money should once more be channelled through the KfW[175]. Although the Anstalt appeared to be sceptical about the economic value of atomic power, it stressed that an exporting country like the Federal Republic needed the practical experience in the field to remain competitive in the market, for the sake of the export industries and their suppliers[176].

The rising electricity production during the second half of the 1950s and the money provided for it by the KfW is given in Table 7.3.3. It clearly shows how fast capacity grew, although KfW money had been reduced to a trickle. The electricity companies had become fully self-reliant and public money had just become an incentive to take on some less lucrative tasks.

In September 1952 the KfW received a letter from the Marshall Plan Ministry in which it was notified about a DM 6 million programme to improve the electricity supply in the zonal border area, of which the Kreditanstalt should handle two-thirds[177]. The programme had become necessary after the East German authorities had cut the power lines to this region from the large power plants in Saxony and Saxony-Anhalt. The programme was the beginning of the KfW's role in structural investments. It was completed in 1953 and then extended in 1954 to improve and develop the rural electricity supply[178]. It is important to note that German public electricity companies are subject to public law under which they

[173]*Jb* 1955, p. 23; *Jb* 1956, p. 27.
[174]*Jb* 1958, p. 25.
[175]BA B 102/41080, passim.
[176]*Jb* 1959, p. 32.
[177]KfW HA-BS 59 letter by BMP to KfW, 10 September 1959; *Jb* 1952, pp. 54 f.
[178]*Jb* 1953, p. 61; *Jb* 1954, p. 43.

have a *Versorgungspflicht* (duty to supply), and with their profits certainly soaring in the mid-1950s it is surprising that they still received public money to fulfil their legal obligations. Another piece of structural policy, which will be described in detail in Chapter 9, the financing of orders or *Auftragsfinanzierung* for Berlin consumed another considerable amount of money since 1954[179].

The re-integration of the Saarland into the Federal Republic finally brought the last task for the KfW's electricity finance in the period under investigation. The Saar government wanted to build a new power plant and improve already existing facilities, both to increase the sale of coal which was handicapped by a relatively bad transportation situation and to cover the Saar's electricity demand. The sum necessary for the constructions was estimated at 21 billion French Francs or DM 230 million over three years. Although the KfW provided some money for the purpose, no sum is mentioned in the Annual Reports. But since DM 40 million of the DM 144 million given to electricity between 1957 and 1960 went into rural power supply and another considerable amount went to Berlin, there was certainly less than a quarter of the required DM 230 million provided for the Saar. This only stressed the fact that the electricity industry could now look after itself.

Table 7.3.3
KfW Money to the Electricity Industry and the Installed Public and Industrial Output Capacity 1954-1961
(in million DM and MW)

	1954	1955	1956	1957	1958	1960	1961	Total
KfW money	17.1	28.6	10.2	42.8	44.1	57.9	n/a	200.7
of which for rural areas	2.3	15.7		15	18.8	6.3	n/a	58.1
Publ. Cap.	9830	11530	11940	13380	14320	17200	17800	
Ind. Cap.	5500	6050	6430	7220	7660	9570	10400	
Total	15330	17580	18370	20600	21980	26770	28200	

Source: *Jb* 1954-1960, passim; *Statistisches Jahrbuch* 1959, p. 203; 1963, p. 251.

None of the other basic industries, in fact none of the other sectors regained its viability as quickly as electricity. But it was to a large extent American pressure which was responsible for the remarkable flow of counterpart funds into the industry during the crucial years 1949-1952. The American demand for higher electricity output to help the reconstruction process and the defence effort in those years made them pour so much money into the sector that even they later regarded

[179] *Jb* 1954 ff, passim.

it as excessive. In this way KfW money up to 1952 helped the industry more than necessary. Following the AIL the power companies were definitely back on their feet and the KfW could begin to finance projects which were motivated by considerations of structural politics or those of a purely political nature.

Chapter 8

Housing Construction

'Der Wohnungsbau ist für uns auf Jahre hinaus das wesentliche Erfordernis, um das deutsche Volk einer politischen, wirtschaftlichen, ethischen und kulturellen Gesundung entgegenzuführen'[1].

This statement by Adenauer during the Parliamentary debate on the first housing act underlined the importance of housing construction in 1950s Germany and outlined the policy of a task which aimed at the rebuilding of destroyed towns and cities and most important of all to create housing for millions of refugees.

Housing shortage was not unknown in 20th century Germany. The First World War had caused a significant reduction in housing construction and although the authorities of the Weimar Republic tried hard to make up the shortage they were hampered, during the Republic's early years, by revolutionary movements and the hyper-inflation and, towards its end, by the Great Depression. Consequently, when the Nazis came to power in 1933 there was a shortage of one million dwellings in the whole of the Reich. Contrary to their propaganda effort, the Nazis were unable to build sufficient new housing to close the gap[2]. The shortfall of one million flats was nothing compared to the damage caused by bombing war and ground fighting during the Second World War. About 2.3 million, roughly one quarter of all dwellings in the area of the future Federal Republic had been destroyed or become uninhabitable by the end of the war. The statistical index of 255.6 dwellings for 1000 people in 1936 dropped to 214.2 in 1950[3]. This statistical average does not tell the whole story since large cities and industrial areas showed a much higher rate of destruction. All big cities had lost more than half their 1939 residential stock. Worst hit was Cologne where only 30 per cent of pre-war dwellings remained intact. Small and medium sized towns which were only bombed from late 1944 onwards when the Allies had supreme command of the air, suffered

---

[1]Chancellor Adenauer speaking in the Bundestag during the first reading of the 1. Wohnungsbaugesetz on 24 February 1950, *Bundestagsprotokolle*, 1. Wahlperiode, 41. Sitzung, p. 1388c, quoted in: Wolfgang Bohleber, *Mit Marshallpan und Bundeshilfe,. Wohnungsbaupolitik in Berlin 1945-1968*, Berlin 1990, p. 59. 'For years to come, housing construction will be the essential requirement for leading the German people towards a political, economic, ethical and cultural recovery'. (Translation AG).

[2]Karl-Christian Führer, 'Anspruch und Realität der Nationalsozialistischen Wohnungsbaupolitik', in: *VfZ* No. 45 (1997), pp. 225 ff.

[3]Schulz, *Wiederaufbau*, p. 33; Statistisches Bundesamt (ed.), *Bevölkerung und Wirtschaft 1872-1972*, (no place) 1972, p. 186.

even more and lost between 70 and 99 per cent of their houses[4]. Although there was less bomb damage, the housing situation in many rural areas was not necessarily better. Refugees and later on expellees from the East had first found shelter in Schleswig Holstein, Lower Saxony, northern Hesse and northern Bavaria. To control the situation, the Allies adhered to the Nazis' method of regulating the housing market by assigning dwellings. However, Allied preference immediately after the war lay with families with many children, the elderly, and with those who had been persecuted under the Nazis. While this was justified and desirable in moral terms it did not take into account the social situation during the immediate post-war years and bore a high risk of social unrest[5]. It had to be kept in mind that the six million expellees and refugees in 1946 felt themselves to be victims of the war as well and therefore to have a right to decent housing, too[6]. The political potential of this group became visible after the first Bundestag election in 1949 when the demagogic 'Wirtschaftliche Wiederaufbau Vereinigung', due to a large share of refugee votes gained 12 seats in Bavaria[7]. The social and political problem the Allied and German authorities were faced with in the housing sector was huge. The shortfall of dwellings amounted to six million in 1950, resulting from war damage, the influx of the refugees, the pre-war shortage and the setting up of new families[8].

In contrast to other European countries housing reconstruction in West Germany did not begin on a significant scale before 1949 which made the county's social and economic situation more difficult. Lack of housing or bad quality housing had a direct detrimental impact on workers' productivity while prioritising some sections of the workforce with housing carried the risk of social dissatisfaction and political radicalisation amongst the less fortunate, the refugees in particular. The reasons for the delay in housing construction were manifold. First of all, there was no central government which could have co-ordinated the effort. Only the British in their zone tried to organise a centrally planned reconstruction programme, but with little success. Otherwise local authorities had to deal with the problem and this was simply beyond their capability. With the establishment of the Bizone, responsibility was concentrated with the *Länder*, but they had to defend their new authority soon against Erhard's VfW[9]. In the first post-war years supply of building materials was extremely limited and the little that was produced was

---

[4]Schulz, *Wiederaufbau*, p. 350.

[5]Georg Wagner, *Sozialstaat gegen Wohnungsnot. Wohnraumbewirtschaftung und Sozialer Wohnungsbau im Bund und in Nordrhein-Westfalen*, Paderborn 1995, p. 79.

[6]Schulz, *Wiederaufbau*, p. 36. By 1950 the number had risen to 7.8 million with an additional 1.5 million fleeing from the Soviet zone of occupation and from Berlin so that the share of expellees and refugees made up 20 per cent of the Federal Republic, that is without Berlin and the Saar.

[7]Benz, *Gründung*, p. 132.

[8]Schulz, *Wiederaufbau*, pp. 39 f.

[9]Schulz, *Wiederaufbau*, pp. 49 ff.

often enough requisitioned by the occupying forces[10]. In addition, Nazi economic policy and the war had reduced the number of qualified masons. While there were 1.3 million men employed in the construction sector in 1939, the number had dropped to 617,758 in 1944 less then half the pre-war figure. Of these only half were Germans, the rest were either drafted foreigners or POWs[11]. Although it is very likely that the number of skilled masons rose again after the end of the war, productivity remained below normal levels, which was mainly due to malnutrition of the workforce and, ironically, the lack of housing which all to often caused squalor. Finally, while there was a shortage of building materials prior to June 1948, the currency reform changed things. Now the materials could be bought but neither public authorities nor other organisations or individuals had enough money to build on a large scale.

The dire housing situation was taken into consideration during the legal process of the KfW's establishment. A representative of the housing industry (*Wohnungswirtschaft*) could take a seat on the KfW's Board, and the Anstalt itself immediately established a Committee for Loans to Housing Construction. The appointment of the housing industry's representative opened the political question of how housing construction should be carried out and financed in the future. There were certainly occasional disagreements on the Board and even bitter rows over factual questions, but housing construction provided the cause for the first ideological disagreements. Before the political dimension of housing construction is discussed, it is necessary to examine the most pressing problems in the late 1940s that is miners' housing and the role the Kreditanstalt played in it.

Miners' Housing

Before the war, there were more than 1.22 million houses in the Ruhr area. Air raids and ground fighting destroyed 450,000 and damaged another 560,000, leaving less than 200,000 dwellings, or 16 per cent, undamaged. Miners' houses were slightly less severely affected, out of a quarter of a million homes 50,000 remained undamaged while 65,000 were completely destroyed. Figures by the DKBL speak of 311,000 pre-war dwellings which were reduced to less than 74,000 by the end of the war. Not all of the losses were complete destructions and in February 1948, there were already 220,800 dwellings habitable[12]. Despite the increase in available flats living space per head dropped. In Bochum, for example, it fell from more than

[10]Jeffery M. Diefendorf, 'America and the Rebuilding of Germany', in: Jeffrey Diefendorf, Axel Frohn, Hermann J. Rupieper (eds), *American Policy and the Reconstruction of West Germany 1945-1955*, Washington 1993, p. 334. For example in the first quarter of 1947 US forces in Bavaria requisitioned 83 per cent of the brick production, 90 per cent of the cement and 50 per cent of all roofing felt.

[11]Schulz, *Wiederaufbau*, p. 38.

[12]Roseman, *Ruhr*, p. 95; KfW HA-BA Sch 85c, DKBL graphic 'Bergarbeiterwohnungsbau Ruhrkohlengebiet', January 1951.

14 square meters in 1939 to 5.6 square meters in July 1945 and to only 4.1 square meters by the end of 1947[13]. This reduction after the war was due to the return of evacuees and former soldiers or POWs as well as a result of British attempts to increase coal production by hiring more miners and bringing in workers from outside the Ruhr. During the winter of 1946-47 this created a housing crisis in the Ruhr for all the new miners had to be housed in face of the severe shortage of dwellings. Traditionally, Ruhr miners experienced better housing conditions as a compensation for their hard work underground and many of the new miners had taken on the job only to improve their living conditions. Large numbers left the pits again when the promised improvements did not materialise. Those who remained were often housed in emergency accommodation in which no family members were allowed. Indeed, frequently members of the families of new miners' were not even allowed to move into the Ruhr area at all, which, of course, had a very bad effect on workers' morale[14]. The British Military Government was aware of the situation and the need for more accommodation. A special housing programme called 'Ruhr 47/48' drafted by the German *Siedlungsverband Ruhrkohlenbezirk* (SVR) was implemented by BiCO to tackle the problem at its roots and to supply the necessary housing. Unfortunately, the scheme was based on completely false assumptions concerning the availability of the necessary building materials and manpower. Only if the rest of the Bizone had been stripped bare of all material and builders could the programme have succeeded. The plan did not survive its first year and was axed in late October 1947 by the VfW. Indeed, it would take until 1949-50 before a large-scale construction programme began which both repaired damaged houses and built new ones. The delay was in part due to quarrels about who had to pay for any construction and partly due to the question where to build the new houses. The Americans insisted that the houses should not be owned by the pits because they feared the miners might become too dependent on the collieries, but in the end the Americans had to compromise on the situation[15].

In order to improve the situation the Military Government demanded a DM 400 million emergency programme for miners' housing construction for 1949. DM 160 million from the Bizonal budget were to be channelled via the KfW. As so often the Military Government failed to achieve its goal. The only money the Kreditanstalt could provide for miners' housing construction was part of the DM 135 million 'at once' programme, although the BoD did not know at first whether they were allowed to utilise any 'at once' money for the purpose at all[16]. Ultimately, DM 23.5 million were used to build, or support the building, of 18,000 dwellings of a scheduled programme of 113,000 units. While the KfW urgently appealed for more money for miners' housing, the Americans expected a bigger

[13]Abelshauser, *Ruhrkohle*, p. 34.
[14]Roseman, *Ruhr*, pp. 97, 121 f.
[15]Roseman, *Ruhr*, pp. 101 ff., 115 ff; DKBL graphic, see footnote 14.
[16]KfW HA-VS 66, BIB/P(49)43, (translation) 'Bericht über finanzielle Probleme in der Kohlenindustrie', 16 March 1949; KfW HA-Prot 10-1, Protokoll der 5. Sitzung, TOP 5.

financial contribution from the collieries and ECA I money was only made available for other housing projects[17].

Already in 1948 the DKBL had estimated its share in miners' housing construction up to 1951 to be more than DM 500 million which was only one-third of the total money necessary to reach building targets. In addition the DKBL had to find the pits another DM 1.5 billion for the same period for scheduled modernisation. Attempts to solve the financial problem often got stuck in the jungle of federal and regional government quarrels over responsibility and jurisdiction, and the southern *Länder* showing little interest to pay for housing in North Rhine-Westphalia[18]. Once more it was the Korean War which determined and changed developments.

The coal shortage which followed the outbreak of the war in Korea made the vicious circle visible to everybody. The lack of miners' housing was the main reason for the insufficient number of miners, which was in part to blame for the inadequate coal output which had an impact on the economy as a whole including production for the construction industry. In the autumn of 1950 the Germans still quarrelled over competence on miners' housing, so the Americans increased their pressure on them to find a solution. At the same time they put forward their own idea how to ease the situation with ECA III money. The Americans wanted to invest DM 90 million directly into the pits and to use the same amount of money exclusively for miners' housing construction. The German plan suggested DM 45 million for miners' housing and DM 80 million for the pits and an additional DM 135 million for housing in general which was not mentioned in the US proposal[19]. In doing so the Germans tried to address the general housing situation in the country. They feared strong social tensions in case the bombed-out and the refugees were not housed adequately in the near future. It seems that the Germans at first were able to push through their ideas but later in 1951 had to realise that they were running out of money. In October 1951 Marshall Plan Minister Blücher began negotiations with ECA chief Harris about the release of the ECA III reserve for miners' housing. Harris agreed in principle but it took another five months to agree on the details under which the money, DM 100 million, was to be released and the KfW was not pleased about some of the conditions. As before in the DM 45 million programme the money had to be used not for the repair of damaged houses but only to build new dwellings which was part of the American propaganda strategy to improve the standard of living in the Ruhr. The ECA insisted on authorising every single building project which delayed construction considerably[20]. The Americans further demanded that the new dwellings should be given only to those miners who

---

[17]*Jb* 1950, pp. 43, 53.

[18]Roseman, *Ruhr*, pp. 129, 135 ff.

[19]KfW HA-Prot 10-1, Protokoll der 18. Sitzung, TOP 4.

[20]KfW HA-BA Sch 85a, Zeittafel 100 mio Bergarbeiterwohnungsbau, undated, presumably mid-1952; KfW HA-BA Sch 85c, Sachstandsbericht by the BMWo, 2 February 1951; KfW note, 21 May 1951.

showed a high performance and work attendance. Top priority had to be given to miners working at the coalface and who had the highest level of work qualification but had to live separated from their families because of the existing insufficient housing capacity. Second came miners who had to live with their families in emergency accommodation[21]. While the allocation of dwellings was intended to boost miners' morale and make them stay with the pits, it limited the German authorities' room for manoeuvre. The ECA insisted that the DM 100 million also had to be used to pay for the developing costs and to provide temporary capital for the residents' *Eigenkapitalanteil*. This was a necessary measure to provide the building constructors with a low interest loan to finance the works. Unfortunately, it meant that DM 21 million were no longer available for housing construction itself. The loss of funds cut the number of new houses by 1,300 out of 6,300 scheduled originally. To compensate for some of these cuts the ECA proposed to increase the interest rate the miners had to pay for their borrowed share to 3 per cent. KfW officials had considerable doubts about this idea because they were not sure about the miners' ability to pay the higher interest. Since other projects for example the one financed with the coal levy, had a lower rate the Kreditanstalt saw it as a clause which would cause dissatisfaction and trouble with the disadvantaged miners. The DKBL and the miners' union held the opinion that the miners could cope only with a rate of 1.4 or 1.5 per cent. The matter was settled in the usual way when the North Rhine Westphalian government stepped in and gave an interest guarantee of 2 per cent[22].

Although ECA III money accelerated housing construction in the Ruhr the federal government, still under pressure from the Americans, and the Land government of North Rhine-Westphalia had to realise that more had to be done and that more money was needed for miners' housing. Finally, in October 1951, the Bundestag passed a law for that purpose. For a period of three years a special levy of DM 2 per ton of hard coal and of DM 1 per ton of brown coal sold was raised to finance miners' housing construction. With the help of the programme some 90,000 new dwellings were built until the end of 1954. Then the levy was reduced by half, but extended until 1959. As the extension of the levy indicates, housing problems for the miners and the ensuing staffing problems at the pits persisted throughout the 1950s[23].

The increasing demand was in part due to the need for 70,000 additional dwellings for surviving dependants of miners, assignments of dwellings to non-miners and to miners who had become unfit for work, or for those who were retiring and those who had retired. Housing for the latter group was very important,

---

[21]KfW HA-BA Sch 85c, KfW letter to Siedlungsverband Ruhrkohlenbezirk, 18 April 1951.

[22]KfW HA-BA Sch 85a, letter by BMP to KfW, 9 February 1952; KfW telefax to BMP, Oberregierungsrat Goedecke, 29 January 1952; note by BMP, 'Finanzierungsstand des 100 mio Bergarbeiterwohnungsbaus', 6 February 1952.

[23]*Bundestagsprotokolle*, 1. Wahlperiode, 164. Sitzung, p. 6658; Abelshauser, *Ruhrkohle*, p. 85; Roseman, *Ruhr*, pp. 140, 147 ff, esp. pp. 149 f.

as it showed new and younger miners that they would be cared for in retirement or illness. This, too, was designed to convince new hands to stay in the pits.

The KfW provided about 10 per cent of the money for miners' housing construction[24]. Due to the usual scheme of part-financing, that is the KfW never provided the whole loan necessary for a project, its involvement in miners' housing construction in the years 1949-1953 can be estimated to be about double the size of its actual financial contribution. This is not to say that without the KfW 20 per cent fewer houses would have been built: because of their importance, other sources of finance would have been found. Nevertheless, money from the KfW provided a source of long-term money at an extremely low interest rate and only this kind of money made large-scale construction projects possible without even bigger participation of public authorities. KfW loans also enabled both the ECA and the federal government to influence housing construction along their own ideas. The ECA was thus able to press for modern housing standards, developed and built on a mass production basis and whenever possible outside the pits' ownership[25]. The federal government in its turn would favour the increase of private ownership of housing; both aims will be dealt with below in more detail.

Demand for Ruhr coal increased throughout the 1950s not least because of the ECSC. The pits tried to cope with the growing demand by taking on new miners. As before, they were to be attracted to the pits by modern housing with cheap rents while at the same time the collieries tried to make old miners to stay on by providing them with more modern housing. Therefore, the demand for new dwellings did not cease during the mid-1950s. In contrast to the late 1940s and early 1950s it was now no longer the Americans and the federal government who were most keen on higher coal output, although there were still considerable federal loans and subsidies for the coal industry. The body now most interested in German coal was the ECSC and it began to provide loans for miners' housing construction. The first ECSC funds came at a time when due to a rise in the price of coal the abolition or at least reducing the coal levy was considered. The termination of the levy would have opened a financial gap of DM 200 million and threatened the construction of 36,000 new dwellings over the next three years. The KfW declared itself unable to cover such a sum and the abolition of the levy was consequently cancelled. Instead, the KfW received DM 50 million on a trustee basis from the ECSC[26]. The Anstalt's credit committee had refused to participate in the financing of the ECSC's housing scheme on the grounds that the ECSC's operation was too ponderous and inefficient. The *Treuhänderschaft* was therefore a compromise by the KfW's Board of Directors. Yet it is possible that the Kreditanstalt simply did not wish to raise another DM 100 million to top up the money from Brussels or that

---

[24]KfW HA-BA Sch 85b, KfW note on 'Bedarf und Finanzierung von Bergarbeiter-wohnungen', 29 December 1953.
[25]Roseman, *Ruhr*, pp. 191 ff.
[26]KfW HA-BA Sch 8, KfW note on a meeting with the BMWo, regarding loans for miners' housing, 25 April 1955; *Jb* 1955, pp.42, 54.

the KfW feared that the ECSC might get too much of an insight into the books of German companies. The projects financed by the loan were nevertheless completed in 1956, providing nearly 10,000 new dwellings and 16 hostels[27].

The following year the Kreditanstalt took full part in the ECSC's second housing programme. The DM 18 million the KfW received from the High Authority were supplemented by DM 27 million from ERP funds. This time the KfW accepted the loans even if they did not like the conditions. Coal production in 1957 had fallen and the Ruhr needed the money more urgently then ever. In 1958 the ECSC launched its third housing programme. It was reduced to DM 5 million and no German supplements were given. This was a sign that the High Authority had realised the collapse in demand for coal and the resulting structural changes in coalmining. From now on, the ECSC no longer financed housing projects but instead paid for the growing stockpiles of coal[28].

Refugee Housing, Special Programmes and *Sozialer Wohnungsbau*

For economic reasons miners' housing had high priority amongst housing construction programmes during the 1950s. But in face of a shortage of six million dwellings, social tensions, unrest and political radicalisation seemed to loom amongst non-miners who were looking for new accommodation. The likelihood of 'ordinary' persons or families moving into a new dwelling or at least a rebuilt flat were very slim indeed. During the inter-war period the whole of the former Reich never managed to build more than 350,000 new units per year[29]. Experts therefore estimated the building capacity of the western zones to about 250,000 units annually so that it would take up to 25 years for the unlucky ones to get a new home. Occasionally, even the Americans seemed to lose heart when faced with this situation. During a meeting of the Military Governors, General Clay stated that in the present state of their economy, the Germans could at best afford to clear rubble but not to build houses. He went on to say that he was no longer prepared to give housing construction in the Ruhr any priority over construction in the American zone[30]. Clay's outburst was a sign of frustration about the slow developments in housing, especially in the Ruhr, after the currency reform had caused a real fall in completed constructions due to lack of money. Shortly before the meeting, Clay had warned about the social consequences and possible political radicalisation of

---

[27]KfW HA-Prot 10-2, Protokoll der 29. Sitzung, TOP 2; *Jb* 1956, p. 57.
[28]*Jb* 1957, pp. 23 f., 39, 45; *Jb* 1958, pp. 41, 46; KfW HA-BA4, Amtsblatt der Europäischen Gemeinschaft, 14 November 1958.
[29]Schulz, *Wiederaufbau*, p. 267; in 1936 the number of new dwellings in the whole Reich was 310,000, the 1937 figure for the area of the Federal Republic, that is without the Saar and Berlin, was only 177,000, see *Statistisches Jahrbuch*, 1952, p. 224; *Jb* 1950, p. 17.
[30]PRO FO 944 799, BiCO telegram to FO, 31 March 1949, regarding BiB meeting 30 March 1949.

the homeless[31]. To avoid these he wanted to see housing construction everywhere in the Bizone, not only in the economically important Ruhr. The major handicap was of course the lack of money to finance any large-scale construction projects.

Despite the lip-service to housing construction in the first draft of the 'at once' programme, it was not a German priority. Of the DM 400 million nearly half was scheduled for the power sector. The KfW even gave a statement about the top priority of energy and stressed that it was unable to utilise any money for housing and consequently asked for additional funds that it could use in order to satisfy political and social concerns arising from the lack of housing[32]. When the 'at once' programme was eventually extended to DM 555 million, DM 90 million were scheduled for housing construction. But due to the lack of GARIOA funds the programme in the end had to be cut to DM 81.5 million. The KfW's handling of the affair suggests that they did not want to sacrifice any of their major projects but tried to obtain additional funds with reference to the desperate housing situation.

The first funds, DM 34 million, the Kreditanstalt actually handled in March 1949 were indeed for housing construction but it is somehow ironic that the money was not used for German purposes but to build houses for American service personnel and their families involved in the airlift. Money under the 'at once' programme went to the KfW only in September 1949 although housing construction had been declared a key sector for the reconstruction[33]. It was hoped that the DM 90 million, respectively the 81.5 million remaining, would act as the starting point of a construction boom with considerable spin-offs to other sectors of the economy. The total costs for housing construction were estimated by the VfW to be DM 1.1 billion in 1949-50 and it was hoped that 125,000 to 150,000 dwellings could be repaired or built with the money, 50,000 of which should be new constructions[34]. The Americans imposed tough conditions on the use of the money. First, building from scratch was allowed only for multi-storey buildings. Secondly, the completion of those constructions projects which had run out of money before finishing was sanctioned. The reconstruction of buildings, although much cheaper than new constructions, received only money if new living space was created. Building sites had to have a minimum number of dwellings under construction to prevent the split up of resources, the total building costs per cubic meter interior area was limited, the building sites had to be in areas of vital production and should be assigned only to workers with a limited income. It was partly because of these conditions that the KfW received the money only in

---

[31]KfW HA-VS 67/II, BiCO Finance Group, Memorandum FIN 26563/1 on Problems in Housing Construction, 6 May 1949; Schulz, *Wiederaufbau*, p. 154.

[32]KfW HA-VS 38, KfW letter to Fisher-Freeman, OMGUS Finance Adviser, 28 January 1949; PRO FO 944 799, KfW letter in appendix 'A' to BiB/P(49)21, 11 February 1949.

[33]NA RG 260, OMGUS, BiCO, BiPartite papers, box 67, folder 1 (390/50/35/5), letter by General Clay to the Chairman, Bizonal Executive, 13 March 1949; KfW HA-BA Sch 80a, KfW press note, 13 September 1949.

[34]Schulz, *Wiederaufbau*, pp. 156, 159.

September 1949 when the building season was already approaching its end and only DM 18 million could be passed on to borrowers[35].

Despite the late start of the KfW building programme the overall results were impressive with more dwellings built or rebuilt than the VfW had hoped for. The available figures for 1949 housing construction vary. The Cabinet spoke of about 200,000, the KfW of 215,000 and the Statistical Office estimated the figures to be 194,000[36]. The number of building permits is better documented. Both KfW statistics and Schulz speak of 315,000 requested permissions that year so that the 1950 construction figures profited from the surplus of houses half-finished in 1949.

Lack of money remained the biggest problem for the construction process. With rents still fixed, housing construction for letting would have caused net losses for landlords since the rents were too low to cover the interests and repayments of mortgages. In other words, the housing industry was not able to provide the necessary housing as long as the rents remained fixed. Rent increases were only possible on a scale insufficient to cover the costs since '... der Mietpreis genauso wie der Brotpreis ein politischer Preis sei ...'[37]. The only solution to the problem was large-scale state intervention. Eventually 50 per cent of all money for housing construction came from public sources and this sector of the economy was the prototype of state intervention[38]. The money was raised from four main sources. The first, indirect, way was the reduction in the rate of property tax for those clients who were able to build or rebuild small dwellings (*Kleinwohnungen*) since it left more money with the potential clients. The Bundesministerium für Wohnungsbau (BMWo) often gave guarantees for loans while the *Länder* could draw on repayments of the *Hauszinssteuer*, a public subsidy which was given for private housing construction during the Weimar Republic. The last source was the *Umstellungsgrundschuld* (property debt conversion) which arose during the currency reform[39]. During the reform not only savings but also mortgages were converted on a 1:10 basis, or, in other words, cut by 90 per cent. Since this reduction would have put house owners in a very advantageous position, it was agreed by the Economic Council that the 90 per cent had to be transferred to a

---

[35]KfW HA-BA Sch 83 b, KfW note 'Richtlinien für die Gewährung von Hypotheken Darlehen für Wohnungsbaukredite aus dem Sofortprogramm', 15 September 1949; KfW HA-BA Sch 80d, letter from the Direktorialkanzlei des VWG to Martini, 29 July 1949; *Jb* 1949, pp. 29 f.

[36]*Kabinettsprotokolle*, vol. 1, p. 122; KfW HA-BA Sch 2, Vermerk für Herrn Martini betr. Wohnungsbau in der Bundesrepublik, 4 May 1955; *Statistisches Jahrbuch* 1954, p. 260. The *Jahrbuch* gives a figure of 973,200 for 1949-51, of which approximately 20 per cent were built in 1949.

[37]Schulz, *Wiederaufbau*, p. 272, the quote from a trade union official during a 1951 campaign to prevent rent increase. '... the cost of rents is a political price in the same way as the price of bread ...' (Translation AG).

[38]Baumgart, *Investitionen*, pp. 92, 94. Baumgart's figures cover only the period from 1949 to 1956, later on the public share was somewhat smaller.

[39]Schulz, *Wiederaufbau*, pp. 217 f.

trustee account on which the *Länder* could draw to pay for war damage and provide funds for housing construction. Until 1952 DM 2.4 billion out of a total of DM 6.8 billion raised for the *Umstellungsgrundschuld* went into housing construction[40].

Of all the projects the KfW was concerned with, housing construction had the strongest and the longest lasting (political) influence although it varied in form over the years. This political influence can be divided into three categories, ECA involvement, early 1950s German political discussions on housing, and the late 1950s housing programmes.

Already with the 'at once' programme OMGUS had given guidelines along which GARIOA money could be used for housing construction. When the DM 81.5 million for housing construction had to be re-financed with ECA I money, the agency added new restrictions on the money's utilisation. The funds, disbursed to the *Länder* via the KfW on a previously agreed distribution plan were to be used only to build dwellings for workers who could find no living space near their workplace. The workers had to be refugees, expellees or war victims and employed in a sector regarded as 'productive' under Marshall Plan guidelines. Furthermore, a modern standard of building and living was required by the ECA, so that the new dwellings had a high propaganda value as well. However, the ECA's assignment criteria could hardly ever be met and only half a year later the ECA had to accept other tenants for their housing projects when no 'first choice' candidates could be found. In September 1950 the ECA mission demanded that all building sites which received ERP money had to be sign-posted as sponsored by the Marshall Plan[41]. This measure, designed purely for propaganda reasons, proved to be very successful. The German population began to believe even more in the Marshall Plan and a new myth about the volume of American aid emerged, while in reality the share of American funds for housing was fairly small[42]. Despite the limited size of the funds, the psychological effect of the measure could hardly be overestimated. It demonstrated to the public once again America's willingness to help but, perhaps more importantly it raised people's hopes for a new home, perhaps even for an *Eigenheim*.

Behind the scenes, things were more difficult. As part of the work creation scheme the federal government had pledged DM 250 million for a special programme for housing construction. From this sum DM 115 million should be funded from ECA II, the rest from ECA III. Two-fifths was scheduled for a refugee housing programme in the three most affected *Länder*, the other DM 150 million

[40]Schulz, *Wiederaufbau*, pp. 149, 151.

[41]*Jb* 1950, p. 53; KfW HA-BA Sch 83b, letter by the BMWo to Länder Wohnungsbauminister, 19 June 1950. Productive sectors were, among others, investment goods industry, mining, agriculture, and export trade; KfW HA-BA Sch 83d, letter by the Rheinland-Pfalz Sozialminister to Landräte und Bürgermeister, 4 January 1951; KfW letter to all Realkreditinstitute, 23 September 1950. For examples of the sign-posts see: *Hier half der Marshallplan*, a KfW exhibition catalogue on the Marshall Plan, Frankfurt/M. 1997. My gratitude to Frau Dr. Köchling.

[42]Diefendorf, 'America', p. 331.

were spread over the whole of the republic for the *Sozialer Wohnungsbau*[43]. At first, controversy arose about interest rates. OMGUS and the ABC had insisted on an interest rate of 5.5 per cent for the KfW. The Kreditanstalt strongly opposed this rate in the construction sector since it would mean too high an interest rate for the final borrowers, causing a problem similar to the one in agriculture. While the ABC insisted on 5.5 per cent rate and suggested a reduction by subsidising it with federal or *Länder* funds, the ECA already called a rate of only 4 per cent usury. Following the Bilateral Agreement when the counterpart funds came under German control, the federal government lowered the rates and changed the terms of previous loans[44].

In late April 1950 the ECA Special Mission to Germany had agreed to release the DM 115 million for housing with the reservation that ECA Paris and Washington agreed on it and that the money would be used only for such projects which were specifically authorised by the ECA but the conditions imposed on the loans, especially the size of new dwellings and the average building costs delayed the construction process[45]. By the end of the year, the Americans threatened to refuse funding for half of all new dwellings, in particular for the Bavarian refugee housing programme, because they had surpassed the DM 10,000 limit per unit. For Bavaria, the ECA withheld nearly DM 21 million of the DM 30 million because the average building costs were DM 9,936 as compared to DM 8,500 in the other *Länder*. The Minister for Housing Construction, Wildermuth, justified the higher costs in Bavaria with the delayed start of construction, with the need for larger dwellings because of larger families and higher wages in construction. High wages were blamed for the higher construction price index which was 174 in Munich as compared to 159 in Kiel. Furthermore, a higher standard in building, such as double-glazing was necessary in Bavaria which increased costs further. Wildermuth ended his letter by stressing the growing disappointment and dissatisfaction amongst the affected refugees and hinted at the serious consequences of any further delay. The situation had deteriorated not least because the ECA in late 1950 had introduced new and tougher guidelines on construction without informing the German authorities[46]. According to a KfW survey the Germans had followed the earlier guidelines quite well. DM 134 million out of DM 150 million had been used in accordance with the instructions, helping to build nearly 50,000 new dwellings and using on average DM 2,775 of ERP money per dwelling unit. The ECA

---

43 *Jb* 1950, p. 53.

44 KfW HA-BA Sch 80a, KfW letter to ABC, 6 July 1949; ibid., ABC letter to KfW (ABC/670/6), 18 July 1949; KfW HA-Prot 10-1, Protokoll der 15. Sitzung, TOP 5; KfW HA-BA Sch 80a, KfW letter to banks involved in housing construction and agriculture, 1 November 1949.

45 KfW HA-BA Sch 83b, letter by the ECA Special Representative to Germany to BMP, 25 April 1950; *Jb* 1950, p. 53.

46 KfW HA-BA Sch 83b, note by Poprawe, 19 December 1950, regarding a meeting with Mr. Butler, ECA Housing section; KfW HA-BA Sch 83c letter ECA Special Mission to Germany to BMP, 16 October 1950; letter by BMWo to BMP, 13 December 1950; KfW HA-Prot 10-1, Protokoll der 19. Sitzung, TOP 3.

tightened the conditions to raise money for its own projects. The Administration had started a programme of so-called *Demonstrationsobjekte* in the magnitude of DM 20 to 25 million, known in the KfW as the ECA's *Steckenpferd* (hobby horse) which should be financed with the money refused for general constructions[47]. This time the Americans accomplished their aim despite strong German resistance. In spring 1952 the KfW was informed by the BMP that for the construction of *Entwicklungsbauten* (development buildings) as they were now called DM 9.1 million of ECA II and DM 27.9 million from ECA III would be provided[48]. The Americans regarded the programme, which was entirely designated for refugees, as important for propaganda purposes since it helped to demonstrate their superior technology and advanced living standards. The dwellings were usually pre-fabricated and provided a high standard of living for the time. Although the dwellings did not necessarily comply with German building style, they helped to ease the social pressure.

In 1953 the USA donated $ 15million worth of agricultural surplus goods for the Federal Republic with the condition that the counterpart funds from its sale were used for housing construction for GDR refugees only. Despite strong German protest, the MSA insisted that DM 20 million had to be used for housing construction in Berlin. The remaining DM 43 million were given to GDR refugees already in West Germany. Loans were given interest free with just an annual administration fee of 0.5 per cent so that refugees could easily be resettled in their own houses in the Federal Republic. The KfW provided DM 6,000 for a single dwelling, more than double the amount of normal ECA programmes[49]. The large share of interest free loans for this building project was because most refugees had little or no money. Helping them to settle into the Federal Republic, even with a house of their own, provided for good propaganda during the Cold War.

The strife over housing policy amongst the Germans largely went along party lines[50]. It was not possible to run housing construction within the market economy, instead the German administration relied on *Sozialer Wohnungsbau* to provide the necessary housing. Neither the idea nor the name was new. An active public housing and building policy had been practised in Germany since the beginning of the Weimar Republic. The term *Sozialer Wohnungsbau* had been introduced by the Nazis in 1940. It only meant that housing construction was supported with the aid of public funds. Nowadays it means publicly supported housing construction for socially weaker sections of the population[51]. In 1950, the Housing Construction Act demanded the construction of dwellings affordable for

---

[47]KfW HA-BA Sch 83b, apendix to KfW letter to BMWo, 3 January 1951; note by Poprawe, 19 December 1950; KfW HA-Prot 10-1, Protokoll der 19. Sitzung, TOP 3.

[48]KfW HA-BA Sch 83c, letter BMP to KfW, 7 April 1952.

[49]*Jb* 1953, p. 32; *Jb* 1954, p. 52.

[50]For a very detailed account from a slightly conservative point of view see Schulz, *Wiederaufbau*.

[51]Wagner, *Sozialstaat*, pp. 5 f.; *Gablers Wirtschaftslexikon*, Wiesbaden 1988 (12th edn), p. 1543.

the majority of the population. It will be shown that during the 1950s due to the way housing construction was financed the opposite was the case.

The question was who was going to build the new homes, private owners and private landlords or *Gemeinnützige Wohnungsbaugesellschaften* (non-profit housing construction associations), but also whether the houses should be built for private ownership or for rent. The SPD favoured a centrally planned housing construction programme which was carried out by the non-profit making building associations. Their aim was cheap rented flats in small blocks of flats or in a house for several families which would provide a modest but modern living standard. The left wing of the CDU backed a controlled market solution in order to avoid unnecessary hardships. Owner occupied houses built in small settlements by the *Gemeinnützige* was seen as ideal. The right wing of the party, represented by Handschumacher demanded a preference for the private housing market and complete deregulation of all rents, an end to all regulations on the housing market (*Wohnraumbewirtschaftung*), tax reductions for house owners and an end to all real or supposed privileges of the *Gemeinnützige*[52]. These demands were so unrealistic that not even the threats to vote against the CDU in case of non-compliance could help to push them through.

Chancellor Adenauer's ideals were those of a man whose values were still rooted in bourgeois imperial Germany. He was in favour of owner-occupied small houses in the suburbs or medium or small size towns in order to create a consolidated small-town population, or to turn people of a working class background into middle class (*verbürgerlichen*) by giving them their own home[53]. Adenauer's appointment of Handschumacher to the KfW's Board of Directors, although it did not have an immediate influence on politics or building programmes, nevertheless constituted a political decision on the direction housing construction was going to take.

The creation of a separate Ministry for Housing Construction in the first post-war government demonstrated the severity of the construction problem. On the party political side, the new post helped the Chancellor to balance the 'coalition arithmetic' since he could offer one more ministerial post to his coalition partners. Christian Democrats and Liberals quarrelled over which party should get the post. Both were hoping for the propagandistic boost which a flourishing building programme would bring. This was despite the fact that final responsibility for housing construction lay still with the *Länder* and that the federal Ministers for Economics, Agriculture, Justice, Refugees, and for the Interior all had a say in the subject.[54] Although the main task for the new ministry was one of co-ordination and of establishing the principles (*Richtlinien*) of housing policy the quarrels were more than a coalition wrangling. It was an attempt by all parties involved to gain politically from successes in housing construction.

---

[52]Schulz, *Wiederaufbau*, pp. 70 ff., 84 f.
[53]Schulz, *Wiederaufbau*, pp. 108 f.
[54]Schulz, *Wiederaufbau*, pp.179 ff., 186.

One of the first pieces of legislation the new government passed was the Housing Construction Law (1. Wohnungsbaugesetz), enacted on 24 April 1950[55]. In it public authorities were committed to build 1.8 million flats within six years as *Sozialer Wohnungsbau*. The government received the authorisation to make the *Kapitalsammelstellen* to contribute a certain proportion of their funds to the finance of housing construction[56]. The clause in section one which asked for the construction of dwellings which were '... für die breiten Schichten des Volkes bestimmt ...' (designated for the general population) however, was contradicted in a later section of the law. At a time when the average monthly gross pay of an industrial worker was just DM 304 the upper income limit of a person to benefit from social housing was fixed at DM 7,200 per year or DM 600 per month. In accordance to the law, landlords were allowed to choose 40 per cent of the tenants when a new dwelling was constructed with public aid, the other 60 per cent were chosen by the housing administrations (*Wohnungsämter*). Since housing administration had a strong interest in viability, they chose only such tenants which in the long run could pay a high rent and were able to provide at least 20 per cent of their annual income as a contribution towards the building costs. In early 1954 only 4.2 per cent of the income group earning DM 500-DM 750 a month were registered as *Wohnungssuchende* while the share of civil servants, white-collar workers (*Angestellte*) and self employed earning less then DM 500 was at 25.5 per cent and those of skilled workers at 30 per cent respectively. Thus, social housing in the 1950s, despite its name, became available mainly for the better off. Middle- income earners occupied about two-thirds of all dwellings built under *Sozialer Wohnungsbau* with a very strong overrepresentation of civil servants and white-collar workers[57].

While in general the political parties (with the exception of the SPD) and the building associations including the non profit organisations paid little attention to social housing construction for the lower income groups there was one exception from this rule. GDR refugees, *per definitionem* regarded as a low-income group, received special treatment, even in cases where they earned a medium or high income. In their case up to 80 per cent of the building costs were covered by public authorities. Their own share of construction costs of about 15 per cent could normally be covered by a *Aufbaudarlehen*, a special loan provided from the federal equalisation office (*Bundesausgleichsamt*). The amount they were entitled to was laid down on the basis of the funds necessary to cover a client's own share for housing construction. Between 1953-58 more than 324,000 dwellings for GDR refugees were built in 12 special programmes. The construction figure for 1958, 147,000 dwellings, was the result of an agreement reached the previous year, according to which the federal government had to pay half the construction costs

[55]BGBl 1950 (I), pp. 83 ff.

[56]*Kapitalsammelstellen* were Social Insurances, private insurance companies, building societies and saving banks.

[57]Wagner, *Sozialstaat*, pp. 39, 356, 363 ff.; Schulz, *Wiederaufbau*, p. 282.

per head. Since each dwelling would typically house four people, the federal share per unit was on average only 12.5 per cent. Special preference for these dwellings was given to new arrivals who were usually young, highly skilled and fit for work while elderly refugees who had already lived for some time in the camps received less preferential treatment[58].

The preferential treatment given to GDR refugees is in stark contrast to that experienced by the lower income groups in the Federal Republic at a time when large numbers of refugees from the eastern territories and those bombed-out were still living in emergency accommodation. It can only be explained in terms of Cold War propaganda. The federal government was determined to demonstrate its superiority over the East German system by providing new dwellings for all refugees, thus encouraging more people to flee the GDR. In their case consideration of economics and viability were not applied in the same way it was done with the lower income groups in West Germany

The Housing Construction Law was also the first step to penetrate fixed rents and rent control. Landlords who built dwellings without public funds, but who still received tax reductions, could set their rents at will. Only out of consideration for refugees did private housing construction not receive preferential treatment in the law. They usually could not afford an *Eigenheim*, especially not when they lived in a bigger town or city where land for housing was more expensive[59].

Soon after the housing law had been passed, there was criticism from the CDU's right-wing and the Catholic Church. The figurehead of the movement was Paul Lücke, the CDU's spokesman for housing affairs. Motivated by Catholic social teaching (*Katholische Soziallehre*), strong anti-Communist sentiments and a conservative worldview which was based on the *Verwurzelung im Vaterhaus*, he propagated the increased construction of *Eigenheime* instead of rented dwellings. During the 1951 Catholic Diet demands were voiced to dedicate all public funds to the construction of owner occupied houses. Furthermore, funds for housing construction should be on equal terms with the funds for rearmament which was expected to begin in the near future, since private ownership meant 'moral armament'. This lobbying did have some effect. From 1953 onwards at least 20 per cent of all social housing construction was carried out as *Eigenheimbau.* In the spring of that year Chancellor Adenauer had demanded an early fulfilment of the set targets for housing construction. Since it was an election year he was very keen on using the construction figures to his own political advantage. Although all previous planning had been brought into disarray by the growing numbers of refugees from the GDR, the influx of which prevented the housing gap from closing, the construction figures were easily matched[60]. The Kreditanstalt für Wiederaufbau itself knew about the propaganda effect of the construction

---

[58]Wagner, *Sozialstaat*, pp. 135 ff., 197.
[59]Schulz, *Wiederaufbau*, p. 238.
[60]Schulz, *Wiederaufbau*, pp. 255 ff. 265, 275 f.; Wagner, *Sozialstaat*, pp. 55f.; *Jb* 1953, p. 27.

programmes. The KfW's proud presentation of the annual construction figures, which are shown in Table 8.1, read almost like a totalitarian state's announcement of the latest 'production battles'.

Social housing construction usually had three sources of money. The so-called *1. Hypothek* (first mortgage) was money raised by public or semi-public credit institutions, the *Kapitalsammelstellen* and made up 20-30 per cent of the total. The 2. *Hypothek*, 40-50 per cent in size was provided by public funds of all kinds, the rest was subsumed under *Restfinanzierungsmittel.* These 10-15 sometimes up to 20 per cent of the total had to be provided by the client[61].

Table 8.1
Housing Construction 1949-1956, Costs and Share of Clients

	I New dwellings	II Total costs in bn DM	III % of Social housing	IV Built by private[3]	V Built by Gemein[3]	Share of col. V over col. IV (%)
1949	200,000	3.0	69.1	n.n.	n.n	
1950	340,000	3.8	68.6	148,478	88,990	59.9
1951	350,000	4.7	69.5	n.n.	n.n	
1952	400,000	6.3	68.9	206,060	169,910	82.4
1953	475,000	7.8	56,4	250,060	194,650	77.8
1954	520,000	9.0	54[1]	304,896	172,032	56.4
1955	540,000	9.5	50.8[2]	323,226	154,024	47.6
1956	560,000	11.0	50	340,047	160,597	47.0

[1] Plus another 17 % for miners, resettlers, refugees.
[2] Plus another 10 % for miners, resettlers, refugees.
[3] Figures from *Statistisches Jahrbuch*, Baufertigstellungen, Normalwohnungen. These figures do not add up to those in column 1 (KfW figures which are similar to *Statistisches Jahrbuch*, section 'Reinzugang an Wohnungen') since public construction is not mentioned, neither is the conversion of buildings.

Source: *Jb* 1949 -56; KfW HA-BA Sch 2; *Statistische Jahrbücher* 1952-58; Schulz, *Wiederaufbau*, p. 351.

By the end of 1952 the KfW stated that its loans to housing construction constituted DM 636 million[62]. Although this was only 3.5 per cent of the total money spent on housing since 1949, the actual impact was three to four times bigger because of the way the schemes were operated. The share of counterpart funds in Gross Capital Investment in housing was only about 1.2 per cent between 1949-1956, although

[61]Wagner, Sozialstaat, pp. 105 f.
[62]KfW HA-Prot 10-2, Protokoll der 26. Sitzung, Anlage 2.

about 10 per cent of all counterparts went into housing during the period. The question of whether it made sense for a national economy to put such large sums into one sector where they would be tied up for a very long time has to be answered positively, nevertheless. The largest part of KfW money for housing went into special programmes like miners' housing and refugee housing which both helped to ease an economic bottleneck and social tensions[63].

Two more particulars emerge from the table. First, the *Gemeinnützige* were never in a position to control the market for housing construction as Handschumacher claimed. On the contrary, the share of non-profit building organisations in housing construction declined year after year. Secondly, a large proportion of dwellings under social housing schemes were built by private companies. They benefited twice by receiving public money to help with the construction and by cashing in on the higher rents, unaffordable to average workers and their families.

Schulz's statement that housing construction remained determined by social policy and not by market forces, because the CDU's and the SPD's political co-operation in the field is difficult to sustain[64]. It was the fact that large numbers of refugees and war victims could easily decide an election that made the CDU look after this group. At the same time, thanks to the social housing programmes, they were able to satisfy their supporters in the private house and property owner's association who received huge state subsidies.

1956 proved to be a significant year for West German housing policy. First, in February, the FDP quit the coalition government with the CDU in North Rhine Westphalia, partly because of differences in housing policy. Some 'young Turks' among the Liberals thought that without enough cheap rented dwellings, the lower income groups would lose out as a result of the home ownership policy favoured by the CDU and the Liberal Minister for Housing, Emanuel Preußker. The second event was the passing of the 2nd Housing Construction Law, which expressly favoured the construction of owner-occupied houses, relaxed the control of rent prices and reduced the federal funds for housing step by step over the next couple of years[65]. As in all previous years, it was argued that housing construction carried out by the non-profit organisations was 'collectivism' and 'not suitable for families'. However, these were only political labels. The real reason was Lücke's belief in the Catholic social philosophy and the stability in value of housing property in particular in times of crisis, which would help to *verbürgerlichen* new homeowners of working class background. Of course, the growing number of homeowners was also a perfect instrument in the propaganda struggle with East Germany[66].

---

[63]Baumgart, *Investitionen*, pp. 95 f.
[64]Schulz, *Wiederaufbau*, p. 324.
[65]Wagner, *Sozialstaat*, pp. 46 f., 212 ff, esp. pp. 216 f. Schulz, *Wiederaufbau*, pp. 288 ff.
[66]Günther Schulz, 'Eigenheimpolitik und Eigenheimförderung im ersten Jahrzehnt nach dem Zweiten Weltkrieg', in: Axel Schild, Arnold Sywottek (eds), *Massenwohnung und*

The year 1956 was also the first year in which the *Kapitalsammelstellen* were not asked to give a written pledge on how much money they would contribute towards housing since they had always exceeded their promise in previous years[67]. The move was very much in the spirit of market economy, but the situation on the financial markets suddenly changed for the worse and threatened the reintroduction of the written pledge. It is not without some irony that the reason for the situation to worsen was with the construction sector itself. Housing construction had to compete for funds, building material and labour with industry and the public administrations, from the federal government down to the local authorities. All of them had authorised major construction works. The KfW had already warned in its 1955 Annual Report that construction other than social housing should be reduced in order to prevent the economy from overheating[68]. The federal government eventually implemented a programme to slow down the economy in 1956. The Bank deutscher Länder reacted more decisively and raised interest rates in two quick steps from 3.5 to 4.5 and 5.5 per cent. This coincided with the expiry of tax reductions for construction which resulted in a sharp drop in demand for debentures[69]. The measures had an immediate impact. The number of new dwellings completed in 1956 could only be sustained because a considerable surplus of unfinished flats was brought forward from 1955 and it was feared that there would not be enough *1. Hypotheken* to keep the level of construction in 1957. In August 1956, the KfW warned the BMWo once more about the danger and proposed to use public funds to substitute the dried up capital market. These funds were, of course, to be handled by the KfW itself due to its experience in the field[70]. The Cabinet responded by drawing up a DM 200 million programme. The BMWo and the Defence Ministry would each provide half the money to be given to the Kreditanstalt. The KfW in turn would lend the funds to the *Realkreditinstitute* which then would organise the final distribution. The money was given with a repayment date of 31 March 1959 which marked it clearly as an interim measure until the capital market recovered. The Defence Ministry's money was scheduled to vacate barracks of local residents or GDR refugees who had found emergency accommodation there and for housing construction for soldiers of the new German army. In the end, the programme's payout rate was reduced to 95 per cent so that the total value of the scheme rose to DM 208 million, but the direct involvement of the Defence Ministry was no longer mentioned. The 1956 Annual Report outlined the use of the funds and stressed once more that they were only a means of pre-finance and would be redeemed very quickly[71].

Eigenheim. Wohnungsbau und Wohnen in der Großstadt seit dem Ersten Weltkrieg, Frankfurt/M. 1988, pp. 416 ff.

[67]KfW HA-BA Sch 8, minute on a meeting of the representatives of the *Kapitalsammelstellen* with the BMWo, 5 December 1955.

[68]*Jb* 1955, p. 27.

[69]*Jb* 1956, p. 22; Deutsche Bundesbank (ed.), *Deutsches Geld*, p. 276.

[70]*Jb* 1956, p. 31; KfW HA-BA Sch 102, KfW letter to BMWo, 16 August 1956.

[71]KfW HA-BA Sch 102, various drafts of credit agreements; *Jb* 1956, p. 56.

Thanks to this intervention, construction figures dropped only slightly in 1957 and 1958. But by then the situation on the capital market had been solved and the KfW was able to repay half the money prematurely. In his reply Staatssekretär Wandersleb called the programme virtually terminated and thanked the KfW for its work. Once more he said, the Kreditanstalt had proved itself '... als die wirtschaftspolitische Feuerwehr des Bundes ...'[72].

The Federal Republic's building boom during the 1950s surpassed all similar previous booms in Germany by far. It was also top on an international scale. Between 1950-57 West Germany had built 99 dwellings per 10,000 heads, compared to 57 in Great Britain, 63 in the Netherlands, 35 in France and Italy and only 24 in the GDR and the boom continued. In 1959-1961 547,500, 530,270 and 523,260 residential units were built. The KfW for its part took on a new task from 1959 onwards by providing cheap loans for the renovation and modernisation of old houses. The official idea behind it was to increase the number of building contracts during the winter months[73]. But it was also a step to support and anticipate political developments. Paul Lücke, since 1957 Minister for Housing, introduced the *Gesetz über den Abbau der Wohnungszwangswirtschaft und über ein soziales Miet- und Wohnrecht* in June 1960. Since the name of the law was too long even for German taste, it became simply known as the 'Lücke Plan' or the *Abbaugesetz*. As its name indicates, the law deregulated rent controls for flats in old houses where controls had remained in place. With the deregulation, Lücke went a step further. Housing experts had always argued that the housing market was in equilibrium when there was a surplus of 3 per cent over actual demand. Lücke simply turned this rule upside down and declared the housing market in equilibrium if there was a 3 per cent deficit of flats and houses. He could justify this because for him the lack of housing was not an indicator of the situation on the housing market. Lücke believed that this was only determined by the viability of old housing stock[74]. By enacting the law he could allow the increase of rents for old houses and, in the next step in 1961, declare the end of the housing shortage during a ceremony in which the six millionth new dwelling was handed over to its new occupants. Since 1961 was again an election year it is of little surprise that the new dwelling was an owner-occupied house and not a rented flat. And, sticking to the ideology of private housing construction, no other group involved in post-war construction, like the *Gemeinnützige* or the building societies was invited to the celebration[75].

The building of six million new flats in 12 years, less than half the time originally estimated, was the real economic miracle in post-war Germany. It is too

---

[72]The *Jb* speaks of 500,000 each year, the 1957 numbers exceptionally include Berlin dwellings as well, *Jb* 1957, p. 23, *Jb* 1958 p. 30. The *Statistisches Jahrbuch* gives a figure of 524,000 in 1957 and of 483,950 in 1958; KfW HA -BA Sch 102, KfW letter to BMWo, 14 May 1958; letter by Staatssekretär Wandersleb to KfW, 16 May 1958. '... the Federal Government's fire brigade for economic policy matters.' (Translation AG).

[73]Schulz, *Wiederaufbau*, p. 336; *Statistische Jahrbücher* 1961-63, passim; *Jb* 1959, p. 50.

[74]Wagner, *Sozialstaat*, pp. 90 ff.

[75]*Der Spiegel*, 1961, no. 36, pp 23 f.

often forgotten that this miracle did not conform to a market economy but had its origin in massive public subsidies. For ideological and political reasons the Adenauer government tried to keep out or at least to limit the influence of non-private building associations. Profit-oriented construction firms on the other hand gained two-fold from government policy. They received huge sums of public money without which they would hardly have been in a position to build so many dwellings in such a short time. Secondly, they could also profit from the high rents which they were allowed to charge for new flats under the first housing construction law. Therefore, and as demonstrated above, it is fair to argue that contrary to its intentions the *Sozialer Wohnungsbau* in the 1950s largely benefited the better-off. Only in the late 1960s, when the demand for housing for middle-income groups was satisfied did lower income groups have a chance to improve their living conditions. This is confirmed by the fact that by 1970 there were still 800,000 people housed in accommodation with inadequate standards[76]. By mid-1961 the Kreditanstalt für Wiederaufbau had channelled DM 1041 million into housing construction. According to its statistics most of the money went into projects like miners' housing and refugee housing, in other words into sectors which needed low interest rates and therefore offered only a low rate of return, if any at all, but which were vital for the economic, the social and the political recovery and therefore stability, of the Federal Republic[77]. Despite their relatively small proportion of the total number of housing construction in the post-war years these projects were more than a side show. For economic and political reasons, the work of the KfW in these fields was crucial.

[76]Wagner, *Sozialstaat*, p. 27.
[77]KfW HA-BA Sch 2, table 'KfW Abteilung Wohnungsbau, Kreditprogramme bis 30.6. 1961'.

Part IV
Fighting the Cold War: Exports and Development Aid

Chapter 9

Berlin, the Cold War's Foremost Front

The Kreditanstalt für Wiederaufbau's provision of loans for West Berlin was motivated by political considerations more than any other of its activities. The city's geopolitical location put it in a unique position. West Berlin's importance as a political symbol in the Cold War, but also in terms of propaganda, intelligence gathering and psychological warfare can hardly be overestimated. As the main focal point of the ideological battles between East and West in Europe any money spent in support of West Berlin's economy was as much a political statement as it was an economic subsidy and consequently massive amounts were poured into the city after the end of the blockade in 1949[1]. The KfW began its support for the city immediately after the blockade had ended with a loan to a Berlin power plant, an investment project which was of crucial importance. After this project the bank's direct involvement in the city ceased for some years because there was already another *Hauptleihinstitut* in the city, the Berliner Industrie Bank (BIB). It was only due to changing political circumstances and declining US subsidies during the second part of the 1950s that Kreditanstalt once more became directly involved in loans and subsidies for Berlin.

KfW aid for the city was motivated by the impact of the war and its legacy even more than this was true for the Federal Republic. The establishment of Greater Berlin in 1920 had created a metropolis larger in size than New York, London, or the Ruhr area, in which 4.2 million inhabitants lived in 1939[2]. Berlin was not just an important road, rail, and canal hub but also a major industrial area which was home to about half of Germany's electrical industry, a quarter each of textiles and precision engineering and optics and about 20 per cent of the country's mechanical engineering industry. Approximately 1000 air raids and severe fighting on the ground when the Red Army conquered the city altered this profoundly. About 25 per cent of the industrial capacity was destroyed. Two-thirds of the remaining industrial plants and installations fell prey to Soviet dismantling between May and June 1945. Within the remaining 25 per cent of capacity some sectors were reduced to as little as 10 per cent of their 1936 level. An American newspaper summed up

[1]Armin Grünbacher, 'Sustaining the Island: Western Aid to 1950s West Berlin', in: *Cold War History*, vol. 3, no. 3 (April 2003), pp. 1-22.
[2]Benz, *Gründung*, p. 9.

the situation by stating that the problem of German post-war industry in Berlin had been solved because there was no industry left[3].

During the blockade in 1948-49, West Berlin's survival in terms of commodities was guaranteed by the airlift. The transport costs, about $200 million, were paid by the US and British governments while the commodities flown into the city were paid for by the West German Wirtschaftsrat. In addition the West German administration had to subsidise, to the tune of DM 53 million per month, the rising social costs in Berlin, in particular unemployment benefit. With the total annual budget of the Bizone amounting to only DM 500 million the Americans allowed the Economic Council to draw on the GARIOA counterparts. In addition the Wirtschaftsrat introduced the *Notopfer Berlin*, which was a 2 Pfennig surcharge on all posted mail in Germany and a 1 per cent special tax on all salaries and wages. This measure was necessary because unemployment during the blockade had risen above the crisis level of 1932-33 and many of those who kept their jobs had their working week reduced to half[4]. Contrary to expectations Berlin's economic situation deteriorated further when the blockade was lifted in May 1949. Once free access was restored to the city the Americans reduced their financial support for Berlin quite drastically and as a consequence the Berlin government had to cut subsidies for many public orders which had kept the economy alive. Even more severe was the impact on work-creation programmes most of which had to be terminated. The situation of the city's trade and industry deteriorated as well. During the blockade they had run out of all stocks of raw materials and supplies and were now unable to buy new ones due to the lack of money[5]. Shortage of raw materials proved to be a major disadvantage in competition with West German companies. The latter had stockpiled as much as possible of their basic materials already before the currency reform which allowed them a head start in production and DM profits which could then be used to acquire new stocks. Trade and industry in Berlin had lost this opportunity with devastating effects on output and employment figures. The Allies realised that they had to take action if they did not want to run the risk of losing the psychological war and the propaganda battle after they had won such an overwhelming victory with the airlift.

One of West Berlin's strategic problems was the electrical power supply. The Soviets had dismantled boilers and turbines with an electrical production capacity of 618,000 kW in the western zones of the city, much more than in their own zone[6]. The British, in whose zone the power plants had been located had plans to rehabilitate the plants as early as 1946 but their reconstruction efforts were hampered, first by a lack of funds and then by the blockade itself. Nevertheless

---

[3]Cited in: Peter G. Rogge, *Die amerikaniscche Hilfe für Berlin*, Tübingen 1959, pp. 23 ff.
[4]Benz, *Gründung*, p. 30; Rogge, *Hilfe*, p. 76; Gunther Gerhardt, *Das Krisenmanagement der Vereinigten Staaten während der Berliner Blockade (1948/49). Intentionen, Strategien und Wirkungen*, Berlin 1984, p. 100.
[5]Rogge, *Hilfe*, pp. 90 ff, p. 94.
[6]Rogge, *Hilfe*, p. 26.

some work and certainly a lot of planning to improve the situation continued throughout the blockade[7]. One month before it eventually ended, the Kreditanstalt began its assistance by preparing the ground in discussions with the Berliner Elektrizitäts und Licht Werke AG (BEWAG). In a meeting with Berlin officials on 8 April 1949 Abs was asked by an American observer how the Bizone could financially assist the city. He replied that it was not a question of whether there should be financial aid but only how it should be organised. However, the issue of support for Berlin and the BEWAG was of such a highly political character that it was well beyond BiCO's Finance Group to decide. Instead the matter was most likely to be settled in Washington itself[8].

Abs was right in his assessment but it took the Americans three months to organise any help and another two months were lost in the bureaucratic jungle of US authorities in Europe. On 19 May BEWAG had applied for financial assistance with the Military Governors. On 12 July they instructed BiCO to ask the KfW to begin negotiations with the BEWAG on the terms of a loan. DM 55 million was the estimated cost of the new power plant and the KfW was expected to provide 20 per cent or DM 11 million from German sources while the US Military Governor was prepared to provide the other DM 44 million from StEG funds which were under his control[9]. But as StEG funds had been used to pay for the housing of American service personnel involved in the airlift, the funds which remained were not sufficient. In any case BiCO had to look for new sources of money and asked the ECA to release the DM 44 million to the KfW[10]. By mid-August ECA was eventually prepared to give the Kreditanstalt a grant of DM 44 million but with conditions attached. First, the money had to be used only for the BEWAG project and had to be supplemented by DM 11 million KfW funds, just as BiCO had suggested before. Secondly, although the money was a grant to the Kreditanstalt it would be part of America's claim against Germany. The bank was only bound to use repayments and interest on the loan as a revolving fund or as a reserve fund[11]. Therefore, it has to be stressed that the DM 44 million as part of the DM 94 million grant to the KfW was not intended to improve its ability to issue bonds as Abs told the BoD[12].

---

[7]NA RG 260, OMGUS, Records of the High Commissioner for Germany, Records of the ABC, box 8, BiCo letter (BiCO/Memo(49)81) to Norman Collinson, ECA Mission Chief in Germany, 1 August 1949.
[8]KfW HA-VS 66, note dated 8 April 1949.
[9]PRO FO 371 76984 CE 3417 letter by the Bipartite Board to BiCO, 12 July 1949.
[10]NA RG 260, OMGUS, Records of the High Commissioner for Germany, Records of the ABC, box 8, BiCO letter (BiCO/Memo (49)81) to Norman Collinson, ECA Mission Chief in Germany, 1 August 1949.
[11]KfW HA-BA 1, translation of a copy of a Bipartite Board letter to Norman Collinson, 31 August 1949.
[12]KfW HA-Prot 10-1, Protokoll der 10. Sitzung, TOP 2; Pohl, *Wiederaufbau*, p. 66.

Detailed negotiations between the Kreditanstalt and the BEWAG went on until late October 1949 when the KfW paid out the DM 44 million. The payout of its own share of DM 11 million provided from the energy companies' obligations did not happen before spring 1950[13]. Quite some time before this, on 2 December 1949 the first block of the new BEWAG power plant, producing 110 MW, started generating electricity and ended West Berlin's dependence on Soviet controlled power supplies[14]. It was partly the KfW's insistence on a federal guarantee both for the DM 44 million and the DM 11 million which had delayed the release of the money. The claim that its own share could be taken from the electricity obligation, too, was first opposed by BiCO, but the Military Government in the end gave in to the Anstalt's insistence[15]. Those demands were the bank's own insurance policy against the economic, and even greater, political risks which were attached to the loans. There was still the fear that the Soviets would blockade the city again, or even worse, occupy it.

Less than six months later it became clear why it was important that the KfW had given the BEWAG loans from its 'own' means. The mayor of West Berlin, Ernst Reuter, requested a reduction of the interest rates for the BEWAG from 6.5 per cent to 5 per cent to ease the company's economic situation. The KfW stated in a meeting of the government's ERP Committee that it could take on the responsibility for such a step on its own since it concerned its own funds and that it would agree to Reuter's request[16]. In spite of the BEWAG's overall importance for West Berlin the ECA would not have allowed such a reduction since, as in the case for agricultural credits, it would have set a precedent for other ERP loans.

The BEWAG loan would remain the Kreditanstalt's only direct involvement in Berlin affairs up to 1954 but the Americans and the Federal government continued to pour massive amounts of money into the city. Initially, after the blockade had ended the Americans had their subsidies to the city cut heavily which had a devastating impact on the unemployment situation and by October 1949 they had to reverse their decision. Now West Berlin was incorporated into the ERP with ECA funds allowing the development of a long- term investment plan. GARIOA funds, which were not subjected to the tough ECA restrictions, were used to cover some of Berlin's budget deficit and pay for large- scale work creation schemes, rubble clearing and reforestation of the city's parks. With GARIOA due to expire in spring 1950, the US administration developed a plan to keep the funds flowing. The State Department, in charge of the ERP, signed an agreement with the Department of the Army (in charge of GARIOA), according to which 25 per cent of all Marshall Plan counterpart funds which appeared in Germany after 1 July 1950 had to be transferred to GARIOA accounts. These funds could then be utilised by

---

[13]*Jb* 1949, p. 23.
[14]PRO FO 371 76984 CE 5142.
[15]KfW HA-VS 55, KfW letter to BiCO, 27 August 1949; KfW letter to BiCO 22 September 1949; BMF letter to KfW, 19 October 1949, confirming the guarantees.
[16]KfW HA-VS 54, minute of a meeting of the ERP Ausschuß, 28 February 1950, TOP 8.

the US High Commissioner (in his capacity as successor to the Military Governor) to finance politically desirable projects without being restricted by the strict ECA guidelines[17]. It was a simple way of redirecting ERP funds away from their economic purpose into the politically motivated aid to Berlin.

A further measure to improve Berlin's situation came with the signing of the (second) Bilateral Agreement by the Federal Republic in December 1949. The Americans had inserted a new clause according to which West Germany had, in consultation with the city's administration, to support West Berlin to the maximum amount possible. The article had caused strong reservations within Adenauer's cabinet. It was feared that the Americans could withdraw from the city and that the young Federal Republic would be financially burdened by an area which legally did not belong to West Germany. Indeed, throughout the 1950s the city received more than one billion DM annually in direct subsidies from the Bonn government. Most of the West German funds ended up covering both Berlin's persisting budget deficit and the gap in the city's unemployment benefits fund. Although most subsidies in 1949-50 came from the Americans West German contributions to Berlin were bigger than the amount West Germany received during the same period under the Marshall Plan[18].

In addition to the direct subsidies 10 per cent of all ECA tranches had to be used for the benefit of the Berlin economy. The KfW transferred these funds to Berlin without any legal obligation[19]. There was, however strong opposition to this aid within the Kreditanstalt. In June 1950 a KfW board member inquired whether these 10 per cent, which would ultimately add up to nearly DM 400 million, was not too large an amount to be spent sensibly in the city. Abs replied that the volume of aid was determined by strong political motives and that they had to expect even further cuts in the Federal Republic's share of ECA III for the sake of Berlin[20]. In spite of this KfW managers voiced strong protest against the Americans scheduling DM 150 million for Berlin under ECA III. The Board of Managers believed that the Berlin economy at this time was only able to absorb a maximum of DM 100 million in loans. Any money given beyond this amount could not be deployed in a way that made economic sense[21]. Eventually it was the Korean War which made the ECA reduce the third tranche to Berlin to DM 135 million but the BoD upheld its 'justified doubts' about the size of the aid. Again, the importance of the city overruled economic considerations and continued American support for Berlin on such a scale.

An important reason for the Kreditanstalt's opposition to those loans was, although this may sound paradoxical, the negative effect they had on Berlin companies. With the money the firms could obviously rebuild and expand much

[17]Grünbacher, 'Sustaining', pp. 5 ff.
[18]Grünbacher, 'Sustaining', pp. 7 f., 14 ff.
[19]See for example *Jb* 1950, pp. 22, 24, 31.
[20]KfW HA-Prot 10-1, Protokoll der 16. Sitzung, Ergänzende Niederschrift TOP 2 and 3.
[21]KfW HA-VS 68/I, KfW letter to BMWi, 19 October 1950.

faster than otherwise possible. But on their balance sheets it had a very negative effect. With all the investments made on borrowed money, they began to lack *Eigenkapital*. Since the firms had already mortgaged everything possible to secure ERP and GARIOA credits they lacked securities for any future loans and the good American intentions had led them into a vicious circle[22]. The natural way to solve the problem would have been to increase their profits by boosting orders and sales but with Berlin's handicap of long and constantly endangered supply routes and the resulting lack of competitiveness this could not be achieved in the usual way. It was the Korean War which brought some relief to the city's troubled economy, with orders for armaments contracts coming in from the Americans and the British. British orders, in particular to West Berlin's optical industry amounted to about £1.35 million by January 1951. But with the Treasury's deficit within the European Payment Union rising further contracts to Germany had to be cancelled in the summer of that year[23]. The Americans also placed armaments contracts in the city. But of greater significance was their establishment, with the help of the GARIOA funds, of the *Berliner Auftragsfinanzierung* (Financing of orders to Berlin). Under the scheme any customer from West Germany received a medium to long-term loan for its orders to Berlin of up to 80 per cent of the order value. Up to 60 per cent of the contract's total could be borrowed from GARIOA funds with another 20 per cent being given by Berlin banks so that the customer had to pay only 20 per cent for the orders in the first place, the rest was credited. The rules for those loans were quite tight to ensure that only customers who would otherwise not have placed a contract in Berlin could receive them. With the help of the scheme additional orders to the total value of DM 330 million could be attracted to the city until the end of 1955[24].

Still, the problem of under-capitalisation was severe especially in the early 1950s. To ease the financial strain somewhat ECA developed a new scheme. In June 1951 Jean Cattier, the ECA Mission Chief wrote to Minister Blücher expressing his wish that the KfW's BEWAG loan should be handed over to the Berliner Industrie Bank in order to strengthen the bank's financial basis[25]. The discussion raised by the letter went on for more than two and a half years in which various attempts were made by the BMP to delay the transfer of the money. It is therefore likely that the transfer was deferred for political reasons. Increased funds for the BIB would have enabled the city of Berlin to conduct its 'own' economic policy which was not always in line with that of the government in Bonn, as future events would show.

In mid-June a meeting took place between representatives of the KfW, the US High Commission and ECA Mission Control in which the Americans demanded the transfer, in full, of the DM 55 million BEWAG loan to the BIB, claiming that it

---

[22]Rogge, *Hilfe*, p. 274.
[23]PRO FO 371 93725 CE(w) 1104/6; FO 371 93730 CE(w) 1104/95.
[24]Rogge, *Hilfe*, pp. 284 f.
[25]KfW HA-VS 55, letter Cattier to Blücher, 8 June 1951.

comprised ECA money. The KfW representatives explained that they were going to transfer the money as soon as they were compensated since the money was part of the ECA's special allotment and belonged to the Kreditanstalt. To make their point perfectly clear, the KfW wrote a letter to the ECA controller in which they stated the facts once more. ECA, however, did not give up. By the end of July the agency's chief Harris himself wrote to Blücher asking for the transfer, this time even offering compensation for the Kreditanstalt which was prepared to agree to the deal. Now it was Blücher's turn to block the transfer by pointing out that there would be a loss of interest payments amounting to DM 660,000. While the argument about who was to bear the cost of the transfer went on in 1952 and even drew in the *Bundesrechnungshof* (Federal Audit Office), and although the MSA as the ECA's successor improved the offer, it was the FOA which saw the transfer finally completed a year later by shifting various loan programmes around. In this way the ECA and its successor agencies respectively could kill two birds with one stone. The KfW was able to keep its special allocation while at the same time money could be made available for the BIB without violating the ECA's stringent rules and Congressional controls on how the money was spent. The whole episode was officially concluded in March 1954 when the KfW confirmed to the BMwiZ that the transfer had taken place[26].

Like everything else concerning 1950s Berlin, the affair was of a political nature. The American idea was to increase the BIB's capital and at the same time to use the bank to get *Kapitalbeteiligungen* (stakes) in Berlin companies thus increasing their working capital. It was only in 1954 after the BEWAG transfer was completed that this practice began[27]. For Blücher's ministry on the other hand the transfer of the money meant more than just the loss of capital. The DM 55 million made Berlin and more so the BIB as a *Hauptleihinstitut* more independent of financial and political pressure from Bonn. After all, apart from a brief spell West Berlin was governed by the SPD and they had different views on various political issues than the CDU in Bonn.

While all three parties involved, the Berlin Senate, the Americans and the Federal Government had a common goal, that is an economic viable or at least stable West Berlin in order to keep the Communists out, their motives and habits were quite different. The Berlin Senate's main aim was to keep subsidies coming, regardless if they were German or American, and at the same time try to keep their political independence from Bonn as far as possible. The Americans tried to stabilise the social and economic situation with short-term and long-term investment programmes in an attempt to bring down unemployment in the city

---

[26]KfW HA-VS 55, KfW note 19 June on the meeting on 18 June 1951; KfW letter to ECA Mission Controller Binkley, 18 June 1951; letter Harris to Blücher, 28 July 1951; letter KfW to Blücher, 4 October 1951; letter Blücher to KfW, 22 October 1951, letter Michael Harris to Minister Blücher, 19 December 1952; FOA letter to BMZ, 7 December 1953; letter BMZ to KfW, 18 December 1953; KfW letter to BMZ, 16 March 1954.

[27]Carstens, *Bund*, pp. 242 f.

which they saw as a potential breeding ground for Communism. At the same time they tried to make the Germans pay an ever-increasing share of the costs. The Adenauer government, finally, wanted to increase its influence over affairs in Berlin, use western successes in the city for propaganda against the GDR and tried to limit their direct financial engagement in and for the city, although the indirect aid, such as tax concessions, increased constantly, especially at times when the GDR tried to achieve some kind of diplomatic recognition by means of limiting access to the city[28].

The Kreditanstalt's entanglement with the BIB would come up again in 1956 when the government tried to increase its influence on Berlin affairs. The BIB was a joint foundation in 1949 of the Industriekreditbank and Berlin companies, set up to supply loans suited to the special conditions in Berlin[29]. To support the bank's development, the Berlin Senate, the government of the three western zones, became a majority shareholder. With Berlin's inclusion in the ERP, the BIB in 1950 became a *Hauptleihinstitut* to handle the counterpart funds designated for the city. In 1953, during the row over the BEWAG loans, Blücher's ministry bought BIB shares in the name of the ERP Special Assets with a face value of DM 5 million when the bank increased its capital[30]. Of course, the BMwiZ's intention was not only to increase the BIB's capital but also to gain more control over it and its use of counterpart funds. Despite the ministry's increased influence on the bank's supervisory board, Blücher was not happy with the conduct of business. In April 1956, when a high ranking ministry official paid a visit to Frankfurt he confidentially informed the KfW that the ministry was going to withdraw the BIB's status as a *Hauptleihinstitut* and the KfW should take over the task[31]. This would have enlarged the Kreditanstalt's business considerably and eliminated one of its rivals for counterpart funds in one stroke. For the ministry such a step would have meant a better control over the Berlin Senate's economic policy via the KfW. By the summer that year the ministry had stepped up its pressure. The ministry's Staatssekretär complained about the unsatisfactory situation in Berlin. The wishes of the ministry were disregarded by the BIB and the bank refused to take up supervisory board seats in companies in which it held shares. Although the BIB gave most credits as direct loans without using any other bank as intermediates it had still asked for a higher interest margin for the loans[32]. There were certainly several members on the Kreditanstalt's Board of Directors who disliked the idea of direct loans. It meant that the credit institutions they represented did not get involved in any of the transactions and therefore could not profit from the interest rates. The Staatssekretär and the KfW manager discussed possible ways of

---

[28] The most striking cases were the so called 'little air-lift' in 1952-3, the 1955 increase in transit tolls and after Khrushchev's 1958 ultimatum, see Grünbacher, 'Sustaining', p 16 f.
[29] Harries, *Wiederaufbau*, p. 56.
[30] Carstens, *Bund*, pp. 220 ff.
[31] KfW HA-VS 120, subfile Allgemeine Vermerke, note on Dr Thissen's call, 6 April 1956.
[32] KfW HA-VS 4, subfile Berlin, confidential note for Martini regarding a meeting with Staatssekretär Dahlgrün, 3 August 1956; BA B 126/7421, passim.

controlling and directing the flow of capital after the BIB's role was reduced or even eliminated. But since the ministry was not able to gain more influence by buying more of the bank's shares – they were special name shares (*vinkulierte Namensaktien*) the voting rights of which could not be transferred – the possibility of establishing a KfW branch office in Berlin without changing the KfW law was considered[33].

Despite the BMwiZ's annoyance with the unruly Berlin bank it had to take political considerations into account, as well. A public dispute between the federal government and the Berlin Senate about the running of a bank would have been very bad publicity. The ministry, therefore, decided to avoid further public quarrels with the Senate. Instead they tried to bring in the KfW through new aid programmes for Berlin[34]. But this was a difficult route as well. The Federal Government, that is the BMwiZ, could not easily work against the BIB since it was one of the bank's shareholders. It was therefore decided that Blücher's ministry would get rid of its shares as soon as possible by selling them to the KfW. The ministry was prepared to take this course of action '... selbst wenn dies dem BM[wi]Z etwas kosten würde ...'[35]. However, political events granted the BIB a delay. In the general election in September 1957 Adenauer's CDU gained an overall majority in Parliament and FDP minister Blücher lost his job. His successor, Hermann Lindrath, had to deal with a different agenda, the KfW's establishment as development aid bank, which kept him busy from 1958 onwards.

It was only in 1961, 'on request of the Federal Government' that the KfW became a shareholder in the BIB[36]. As part of the BIB's second capital increase, the Kreditanstalt acquired DM 10 million worth of shares. The ERP Special Assets, instead of selling its holdings increased its stake to DM 34 million. At the same time the special rights of the remaining DM 5 million shares were abolished[37]. Given this new constellation of influence, it was no longer necessary to withdraw the status of *Hauptleihinstitut* from the BIB. The erection of the Berlin Wall also made it a political imperative to keep both institutions working for the Berlin economy. It was only in 1991, a year after Germany's reunification and the privatisation of the BIB that it lost its status as *Hauptleihinstitut* and the KfW took over its task[38].

Not every task the KfW carried out in or with regard to Berlin had to do with political intrigue as the early example of financing the BEWAG power plant has shown. The city was much too important in the political calculations of both Bonn and Washington and usually matters were dealt with the necessary

[33]KfW HA-VS 4, subfile Berlin, confidential note for Martini.

[34]Ibid., note dated 10 August 1956.

[35]Ibid., note regarding meeting with the BMZ, 27 February and 6 March 1957, dated 8 March 1957, '... even if it were to cost the ministry...'(translation AG).

[36]Harries, *Wiederaufbau*, p. 56, p. 102.

[37]Becker, *ERP*, p. 72.

[38]Harries, *Wiederaufbau*, p. 51.

pragmatism. The city's significance had been stressed repeatedly, so in a MSA report which stated that '... Berlin is important to US aims not only in Germany but throughout the free world as a symbol of victory in the Cold War. It is a show window of democracy behind the iron curtain.'[39] The city's importance for the Americans is evident in the amount of money spent there. Of the DM 6.15 billion German ERP and GARIOA counterparts DM 2.1 billion went to West Berlin[40]. Similarly, for the Federal Republic West Berlin was a showpiece of the superiority of the capitalist system in the West over its communist counterpart in the East. A constant flow of between 150,000 and 200,000 refugees left the GDR in the years between 1949-52[41]. With the tightening and eventual sealing off of the inner-German border more and more of these refugees had to take the route to the west via Berlin. The flow of refugees increased significantly in 1953 with the forced introduction of collective farming, the economic centralisation and the increased labour norms. While in the long-run the constant influx of mostly young and highly qualified people from the eastern zone meant an increase of 'human capital' for the Federal Republic which was worth some DM 30 billion over the period, it was a strain in the short-run[42]. The refugees had to be housed and competed in Berlin in particular for rare employment. Unemployment figures in West Berlin between 1950-52 never fell below 265,000 more than a quarter of the workforce[43]. The German mission to the MSA gave a gloomy picture of the problem in Berlin and asked for further aid. Adenauer did the same in April 1953 when he went for talks to Washington in a public relations stunt prior to the general elections in Germany. The Americans told the Chancellor that aid to Berlin was high on the MSA's agenda, not least because of the refugee situation. But no commitment could be given since a global review of the Agency's work was under way and Congress first had to agree any new aid[44]. In the end Congress decided that the Federal Republic should receive a gift consisting of agricultural surplus commodities worth some $15 million. The counterpart proceeds of this aid, DM 63 million, were solely designated for the building of dwellings for GDR refugees, with DM 43 million spent in the Federal Republic and the rest in Berlin itself[45]. But whilst

---

[39]NA RG 469, Records of the US Foreign Assistance Agencies 1948-1961, Office of European Operations, German Division, subject files, box 3, folder briefing papers, Germany, 6 February 1953.

[40]Ibid., box 4, letter by the German Mission to the MSA, Dr Fitzgerald, 2 March 1953.

[41]Cristoph Kleßmann, *Zwei Staaten, eine Nation. Deutsche Geschichte 1955-1975*, Bonn 1988, p. 558.

[42]Abelshauser, *Wirtschaftsgeschichte*, pp. 95 f.

[43]NA RG 469, Office of US Foreign Assistance Agencies 1948-1961, Office of the European Operations, German Division, subject files, box 4, letter by the German Mission to the MSA, Dr Fitzgerald, 2 March 1953.

[44]NA RG 59, General Records of the Department of State, Records of the Political Planning Staff 1947-1953, box 16, folder Germany, minutes of US-German talks (Dulles-Adenauer) on 8 April 1953.

[45]*Jb* 1953, p. 32.

unemployment there was still above 25 per cent it was close to 5 per cent in West Germany and, with an expanding economy, expected to fall further. Accordingly the Federal Government wished to resettle as many refugees as possible from Berlin to West Germany and hence reduce Berlin's share of the money but the FOA insisted on the given quotas[46]. The most obvious reason for the Americans to decline the German wish was propaganda. With the money they could demonstrate that they were not giving up on Berlin and that housing construction in West Berlin was working better than in the east of the city. And of course, the programme itself would create new job opportunities.

East German repressive measures in 1953 had increased considerably the number of refugees to West Berlin and hence unemployment remained a serious problem. West German and American efforts to strengthen the job market sometimes took indirect routes. In order to encourage West German companies to 'buy Berlin' the Adenauer government introduced several tax refund and tax rebate schemes for the city. From 1954 onward, West Berlin companies received a 20 per cent reduction in income tax and corporate tax, which was increased to 30 per cent in 1961 in an attempt to boost the city's exports[47].

Auftragsfinanzierung was another way to support Berlin exports and the city's labour market. Prior to 1954 it was paid for by GARIOA funds only but that year the KfW developed a programme of its own to finance orders and to support the existing Berlin scheme. Although only DM 4.4 million were provided for the purpose in the first year, the sum confirmed in 1955 was already DM 67 million[48]. Similar to the *Auftragsfinanzierung* financed with GARIOA funds through the BIB there were strict conditions imposed on any borrower. All orders financed under the scheme had to improve the situation on the Berlin labour market that is they had to be labour intensive. They had to be additional contracts which would not have been placed without the public funds and they had to be projects which helped to improve the national economy[49]. In contrast to the BIB loans, a KfW credit covered only 60 per cent of a contract's total value. The sectors to benefit were Berlin's traditional industries, rail carriage construction, telecommunications and electrical engineering, machine tool manufacturing and shipyards. At first, most of the money was lent to the federal railway and to the federal mail[50]. Since they were state owned they could easily be requested to support the scheme by placing their orders with their pre-war main supplier companies. Private response to the programme seemed more restrained so that the West Germans initiated some schemes to increase the 'buy Berlin' drive[51]. For this reason the KfW also changed its lending

---

[46]BA B 146/241/h, notes regarding meetings on 2 September 1953 and 7 December 1953.

[47]Grünbacher, 'Sustaining', p. 15.

[48]*Jb* 1955, p. 43.

[49]KfW HA-BS 52, Ergänzende Mitteilung an alle Kreditabteilungen, 24 June 1957.

[50]*Jb* 1957, p. 46; *Jb* 1955, p. 43.

[51]KfW HA-BS 71, KfW letter to the BMBes, 7 November 1957, Grünbacher, 'Sustaining', p. 15.

practice in 1957. It now actively 'encouraged' West German companies to place contracts in Berlin and even linked credits to the steel industry to the condition of ordering from the Berlin industry[52]. In the official history of the KfW Harries calculates the *Auftragsfinanzierung's* total value up to the end of 1960 to be DM 728 million, of which two-thirds were supplied in 1959 and 1960[53]. The boost was a political reaction in West Germany to Khrushchev's Berlin Ultimatum of November 1958 but was still only a supplement to direct federal subsidies of more than DM 1.2 billion annually since the early 1950s[54]. In addition to increased public subsidies after the ultimatum the president of the Federation of German Industry, Fritz Berg, called on his associate members to support the Berlin economy and his appeal produced a very positive response as well[55]. The reduction of interest rates for *Auftragsfinanzierung* by the KfW to four or five per cent, depending on the kind of contract, certainly helped to increase the financial interest in orders to Berlin, while Berg's request initiated additional contracts. In economic terms Khrushchev's ultimatum clearly backfired and gave West Berlin's economy an additional boost although the city never achieved viability on its own and continued to depend on western subsidies.

1961 marked the end of an era but not the end of aid to West Berlin. The building of the Berlin Wall finally stopped the flow of East Germans into the West. 2.7 million people had fled since September 1949[56]. The building of the Wall meant that no more skilled labour from the East would enhance the workforce in the West which had been short of qualified workers for years. It also meant that West Berlin was completely sealed off, except for the transit routes. But the various patterns of aid continued to flow in. Berlin was the biggest single beneficiary of subsidies in all forms in post-war German history. It is debatable whether the aid made economic sense since West Berlin's importance was a political one. All the aid given by the KfW, the Federal Government and the Americans since the financing of the BEWAG power plant had had one main objective, to keep the city alive economically so that it could remain a political thorn in the flesh of the communist governments in Moscow and East Berlin. Even if the western part of the city was no longer accessible from the east, it remained a showcase of the western economic system and its successes. It was an important base for western intelligence services and a platform for propaganda as well as a political symbol to the world of America's determination to oppose Communism.

---

[52] *Jb* 1957, p. 46.
[53] Harries, *Wiederaufbau*, p. 57.
[54] Grünbacher, 'Sustaining', p. 14.
[55] Gerard Braunthal, *The Federation of German Industry in Politics*, Ithaca, 1965, p. 288.
[56] Kleßmann, *Zwei Staaten*, p. 558.

Chapter 10

Exports

The aid the Kreditanstalt für Wiederaufbau provided in support of West Germany's export industries was a small-scale version of the bank's other major tasks and its development. It runs parallel to the various stages of West German recovery from the painful beginnings under full Allied control to the complete economic self-determination and the Kreditanstalt's participation in international development aid projects in the late 1950s. The process of West Germany re-entering the world market was strongly influenced by the Cold War, where from the very early stages both Americans and Germans often had the same or at least similar aims for different reasons. The examples of KfW export subsidy in the trade with Yugoslavia and India demonstrate this clearly.

Even before 1948-49 it had been clear to many German politicians that the easiest way for Germany to lose its pariah status after the Nazi atrocities and to rejoin the international community would be by utilizing the country's industrial capacity and economic potential which was badly needed for the reconstruction of Europe. This assumption was verified on two occasions. The first was the 1950 Schuman Plan which was among others the French acknowledgement of West Germany's growing economic potential. The second was Germany's return in late 1951 to a positive balance of payments within the European Payment Union thanks to ever increasing export figures after the country had suffered a short but severe crisis in its balance of payments. It proved that German goods were still highly sought after on the world market. But while German exports were essential to, and competing successfully on, the European markets there was a slightly different picture on the global scale. Since the late 19th century Germany had always been an exporter of highly sophisticated capital investment goods while it imported its raw materials and much of its foodstuffs. After the Second World War it had become imperative to boost exports to the rest of the world, in particular to the dollar area, in order to earn hard currencies to pay for the raw materials and the increased amount of foodstuffs necessary to compensate for the lost eastern territories. But boosting exports was more than just a tool to survive in the short term; it was also a crucial long-term investment in the viability of the national economy which lacked a large enough domestic market to sustain economic growth and which therefore depended on selling abroad and regain markets lost during and after the war.

The American's were at first interested in increased German exports for very much the same reasons. The income and hard currencies derived from these exports did help to close Germany's dollar gap and by virtue of supplying the European market with its goods helped to close the Old Continent's gap as well. Later, from the mid-1950s onward, when German exports created a constantly growing surplus in hard currency and gold at the Bundesbank the Americans would ask for Adenauer's support and money in paying for development projects in third world countries, which had become the latest battlefield of the Cold War. Beyond these practical reasons there was also a political-ideological one. It was easier for the Americans and the whole of the western camp to have a Germany on their side that had some of its prestige restored and was no longer the international outcast. Here too, German and American interests were identical.

On the other side of the coin, foreign policy and the Cold War had a direct negative impact on West German foreign trade. Prior to the Second World War Germany had conducted a significant share of its foreign trade with countries which were now behind the Iron Curtain. While initially the Military Governments in the immediate aftermath of the war had signed bilateral trade treaties with those countries on Germany's behalf, the Cold War led to their termination or non-renewal after 1948. Only in one case the opposite effect, that is increased trade and aid resulted from the superpowers' confrontation. Financing exports to Yugoslavia would cause serious problems and a lot of trouble for KfW managers during the first half of the 1950s.

US-Soviet tensions also had a direct impact on German Marshall aid. Companies which were suspected of bypassing any of the tough regulations regarding East-West trade were blacklisted by the ECA and were barred from receiving any ERP loans in the future. Here American political principle did not allow for the German economy to benefit from its traditional export markets in East and South-east Europe.

Finally, post-Stalinist Soviet policy and President Eisenhower's reaction to it transferred some of the Cold War policies into the developing countries. Exports or the withholding of aid became a weapon in the ideological struggle. During these years, the Adenauer government developed and enacted its own foreign policy dogma, the Hallstein Doctrine. It would determine West German foreign policy for more than a decade after its declaration in 1955. In particular aid to India in the late 1950s would be heavily influenced by the doctrine as will be demonstrated below.

10.1 Exports as a Means of West German Political Rehabilitation

Prelude: The Years of Total Allied Control 1945-1949

Following the unconditional surrender of Nazi Germany the Four Powers had taken over all state authority including the responsibility for Germany's foreign trade. The Americans had hoped to revitalise German industrial production within a couple of weeks to a level which would allow them to cover their occupation costs with any resulting export proceeds. When in summer 1945 the Americans realised the severe disruptions the war had caused in the former Reich, they increased their economic control even more by introducing a dollar clause for all foreign trade which established that all exports from Germany had to be paid for in dollars. This clause was introduced for three main reasons. First, it should protect German industry from losses caused by hidden reparations taken from ongoing production. This step was also welcomed by the British, although they saw it much more as a temporary measure[1]. Secondly, the Americans foresaw that they would become the only source of food supplies for Germany and expected to be paid for those in dollars which they hoped to raise with the export proceeds. Finally, the dollar clause was the first step of integrating at least the western part of the old Reich into a future dollar market, respectively a US dominated world market[2]. Later General Clay would defend the dollar clause as necessary to earn dollars for the Bizone in order to buy new raw materials to keep the industries going and thus support the European economies in the long-run, instead of, as he put it, bartering valuable German machine tools for Italian fruit and vegetables[3]. But the American calculations did not add up. Foreign trade figures for the western zones lagged behind other economic performance and it became clear from summer 1946 onward that the dollar clause was a severe handicap, not a protection for Germany's struggling economy.

The reconstruction process which had begun in the liberated European countries immediately after the war demanded huge amounts of money to buy or repair machines, equipment and other kinds of investment goods. Traditionally, Europe's main supplier for these goods had been Germany. In 1936, already under the Nazis economic restrictions the Reich's trade share with the future OEEC countries in key sectors like electrical products, machine tool manufacturing and rolled steel products was 43 per cent, 40 per cent and 37 per cent respectively[4]. Prior to the Second World War, trade was usually conducted on the basis of bilateral trade agreements amongst the various European countries. When the USA insisted in 1945 on dollar payments for German exports this kind of bilateralism became impossible. Worse, with dollars in short supply in Europe in the immediate post-war years and most of the essential food supplies to Europe coming from the USA, the European countries had to consider carefully on what goods to spend their scarce dollars. For most governments it was politically impossible and economically undesirable to spend the little dollar reserves they had on trade with the former enemy. Their only other source of investment goods were the United States. Spending their small amount of American currency on US foodstuffs and

[1]Christoph Buchheim, *Die Wiedereingliederung Westdeutschlands in die Weltwirtschaft 1945-1958*, München, 1990, pp. 13 f.
[2]Hardach, *Marshallplan*, p. 20.
[3]Clay, *Decision*, pp. 196 f.
[4]Kretzschmar, *Auslandshilfe*, p. 189.

US machinery meant that the dollar shortage increased rapidly to create what became known as the 'dollar gap'. Although American economy benefited from the situation and to some extent, as in the case of US farming, even depended on it, most other actions taken by the Truman administration and by OMGUS in regard to Europe and Germany indicate that the prime aim of the Americans was not to profit from the European situation in the short-term but to rebuild the Old Continent to mutual benefit in the long-run[5].

On the other side, there was little or no incentive for German manufacturers to sell their goods abroad. Apart from the fact that the war and its aftermath still kept the output down, there were several organisational problems facing the German exporters. Their supply of raw materials did not necessarily increase when they dealt with customers abroad, and of course, they did not receive the dollar proceeds of their goods sold abroad. Instead the German exporters were paid the equivalent of the dollar value of the sale in RM and later in DM. There was no proper single exchange rate but various rates for different goods were in place. To make matters worse, quite often the Americans and the British did not agree on a common exchange rate for similar commodities. The rate oscillated overall between RM 1.25 and RM 3.57 per dollar in the American zone and between RM 1.74 and RM 10 per dollar in the British zone[6]. It was only after the establishment of the Combined Economic Area, the Bizone, in January 1947 that at last the administration and control of German foreign trade was centralised with the Joint Export Import Agency (JEIA), but it would take another 15 months until a single $-RM exchange rate was established in March 1948[7].

By the end of 1946 it had become obvious that Allied expectations to cover their occupation costs with the dollar earnings of West German exports could not be fulfilled[8]. On the contrary, the dollar clause, in the words of Robert Murphy, the US political adviser to OMGUS, had become a 'dollar fence' which strangled European trade[9]. Reluctantly, JEIA was forced to change its policy in early 1947 to allow and to sign bilateral trade treaties on behalf of the Bizone with other European countries. This was only an emergency measure since the treaties ran for no more than 12 months and then had to be renewed[10]. The treaties were relatively small in size and allowed only the trading of an exactly defined range and amount of goods the size and value of which were calculated on a dollar basis. These bilateral trade treaties were more a measure to supply essential goods for the Bizone's survival than an attempt to increase European trade.

Although by 1947, Europe's trade based on bilateral agreements had surpassed 1938 levels the continuing exclusion of Germany as the continent's

---

[5]See Daniel, *Dollardiplomatie.*

[6]Friedrich Jerchow, 'Der Außenkurs der Mark 1944-1949', in: *VfZ* No. 30 (1982), pp. 264 f.

[7]Buchheim, *Wiedereingliederung*, pp. 16 f.; Jerchow, 'Außenkurs', p. 275.

[8]Buchheim, *Wiedereingliederung*, p. 20.

[9]Hardach, *Marshallplan*, p. 91.

[10]Buchheim, *Wiedereingliederung*, pp. 43 ff; *Monthly Reports*, various months 1947/48.

major importer and exporter accelerated the economic crisis which arose from the dollar gap[11]. The Truman administration reacted to it in two ways. The Marshall Plan allowed the purchase of goods in dollars on a large scale and therefore acted as short-term relief. The easing of JEIA restrictions on Bizonal foreign trade from 1948 onward was the long-term route to the reintegration of West Germany into the European market. The climax came in mid-1949 in form of a new trade treaty with Switzerland. It was agreed that both countries could conduct trade in their own currencies. This meant the end of the dollar clause since other European countries wanted to conduct their trade with Germany on the same kind of terms[12]. By that time the political decision to integrate West Germany into the western community and treat it as an equal was already well under way.

The Way Back: OEEC and GATT

German politicians and industrialists had realised quite early that the easiest way for the country to re-enter the international community was via economic recovery and international trade[13]. One of the most radical views on the matter was held by Ludwig Erhard to whom exports were first and foremost a means to regain economic growth, strength and prosperity[14]. But there was another important reason to increase the Bizone's exports. While the area of future West Germany had traditionally been strong in exports, selling about 43 per cent of its total production abroad in 1936, some 36 per cent used to go to the area which now comprised the GDR. This previously internal trade ceased as a consequence of the growing East-West tensions, cutting off the western part of Germany from an area which had consumed more than half of its output (if one considers the combined territories of the GDR and those which came under Polish administration). It proved relatively easy for the western zones to replace the commodities which had been produced in the East. Those were mainly light industry and consumer goods, the factories for which could be built fairly quickly from scratch in the Federal Republic. For the western investment goods industries on the other hand new markets had to be found[15]. The political necessity and the economic pressure for international trade and co-operation soon found a valve with the emergence of the Marshall Plan. Although Germany was at first not mentioned as a participant of the programme out of political considerations towards France there is no doubt that the US State Department planned for German participation right from the beginning, not least because they anticipated the benefits this would bring[16].

---

[11]Kolko, *Limits*, p. 337; Milward, *Reconstruction*, p. 13.
[12]Buchheim, *Wiedereingliederung*, pp. 48 f.
[13]Bührer, Schröder, 'Revival', pp. 174, 180.
[14]See Ludwig Erhard, *Deutschlands Rückkehr zum Weltmarkt*, Düsseldorf, 1953.
[15]Hankel, *Kapitalverteilung*, pp. 23, 25.
[16]Bührer, Schröder, 'Revival', p. 181.

The Federal Republic received its first international recognition when it gained full membership in the OEEC on 31 October 1949, an event with wide-ranging consequences. It meant that the Federal Republic could determine its own (foreign) policy within the organisation. This constituted a violation of the occupation statute which did not allow Germany a foreign policy of its own.[17]. Although German economic experts who at first acted merely as advisers to the Military Governors had gained more and more influence and responsibility in the weeks prior to full membership they could not take any decisions on their own[18]. The fact that the French Republic, although hesitantly, accepted Germany on equal terms in the organisation was a significant development which helped to pave the way for future co-operation.

It was only about one year later, within the framework of the work creation scheme that the Kreditanstalt für Wiederaufbau got involved in export finance for the first time. As part of the ABP DM 100 million were scheduled to support exporting industries, especially world renowned firms of the optical industry such as Zeiss or Leika. The money, which was extended to DM 110 million in December 1950, was provided from a special line of credit from the BdL under the condition that it had to be redeemed with ECA III funds. In addition to this programme, which was called by the Kreditanstalt one of the most valuable schemes for the national economy, there was another DM 300 million for the financing of export orders[19]. In its first meeting after Parliament passed the ABP, the KfW's Board of Directors discussed the matter for the first time after having conducted intensive behind the scenes consultations and talks. The initiative for the KfW's participation in export finance seemed to have originated within the BdL itself. At a meeting with banking representatives in January 1950 at the Land Central Bank of North Rhine Westphalia during which the establishment of an export bank was discussed, BdL members suggested that the KfW should take on this task based on bills of exchange. Not surprisingly, the banking representatives resented the idea. They feared that the KfW could establish itself in this market and take away some of their business. They argued the KfW had neither the personnel nor the infrastructure for the task and export financing was not at all in the Kreditanstalt's field of operations[20]. The BdL countered this by stressing the risk which the additional but crucial export finance would place on the already stretched banking apparatus. For the BdL there was an additional advantage in assigning the task to the Kreditanstalt. The Central Bank could ensure its influence and control over export business via the BoD. Involving the KfW in export finance reduced the risk of a single bank with its limited assets becoming overburdened or even insolvent if

[17]Milward, *Reconstruction,* p. 383.
[18]Werner Bührer, 'Erzwungene oder freiwillige Liberalisierung?', in: Werner Bührer, Ludolf Herbst, Hanno Sowade (eds) *Zwischen Marshallplan und EWG,* München 1990, p. 147.
[19]*Jb* 1950, p. 28; *Jb* 1951, p. 35.
[20]DBB HA B330/3337, minutes on a meeting at the Landeszentralbank Nordrhein-Westfalen, 21 January 1950.

an export deal failed, as this would have had severe consequences for the whole of Germany's banking system. The KfW itself stated great interest in export financing and regarded itself suitable to do the job both in legal terms and in matters of organisation. However, they made it clear that a special export bank should be established as soon as export finance reached a certain volume[21]. Both the Kreditanstalt's interest in export finance and its call for the establishment of a separate export bank at a later stage can most certainly be attributed to H.J. Abs and his own banking experience throughout the 1930s and 1940s when he became an expert in the field of export and currency trade. When the BoD finally discussed the matter, Abs stressed that the ECA was not prepared to release any money for the purpose of export financing although money for the reestablishment of export industries would be made available. Since the BdL was not allowed to give loans directly to private customers, the BoD decided that the KfW would provisionally step in as an intermediary and carry out the task of export financing. For this purpose the BdL would provide a special credit line of DM 300 million on a revolving basis that is the KfW could lend the money again as soon as it had been repaid by a client[22]. In addition the BdL waived the right to demand federal guarantees for those export loans for which it had previously provided funds without asking for such guarantees[23].

The actual programme ran similarly to the financing of the coalmines. Exporters wrote bills of exchange which received the endorsement of a foreign trade bank (*Außenhandelsbank*) before being passed on to the KfW. The Kreditanstalt then paid out cash for the exchange bills which in turn it received from the Bank deutscher Länder's special DM 300 million credit line. The loans given to the exporters in this way were long or medium term with an interest rate of 5.5 per cent and exempted from the bill of exchange tax[24]. The loans were given to allow German exporters to extend their customers' period of payment thus making them more competitive on the world market. Since German companies still lacked sufficient working capital the KfW money provided the exporters with liquidity until the customers finally paid. In practice not everything ran so smoothly. Only three months after this procedure had been agreed Abs criticised the *Außenhandelsbanken* and accused them of incompetence. Many of them offered normal loans at a rate of 9 per cent interest instead of the much cheaper BdL/KfW credits at 5.5 per cent. To solve the problem and to clarify the situation, he suggested and called a meeting of all foreign trade banks[25].

On top of these credit subsidies, exporters could rely on federal export guarantees, the so-called *Hermes Bürgschaften* which covered up to 90 per cent of a contract's value. A bigger incentive still were the tax reductions granted for

[21]Ibid., KfW letter to BdL Directorate, 3 February 1950.
[22]KfW HA-Prot 10-1, Protokoll der 14. Sitzung, TOP 3.
[23]KfW HA-VS 29/I, letter BdL to KfW, 14 March 1950.
[24]*Jb* 1950 p. 28.
[25]KfW HA-Prot 10-1, Protokoll der 16. Sitzung, TOP 5.

exporters. In addition to a rebate on the turnover tax for exported goods, there was a 3 per cent tax reduction on the companies' profits gained from exports. Revenue losses due to these subsidies were estimated to have amounted to something between DM 850 million and DM 1 billion between 1950-55 when both tax reductions were abolished, the first due to British pressure, the second because of Finance Minister Schäffer's intervention[26].

The tough British reaction against export subsidies in form of tax concessions took some time to develop. Ludwig Erhard had consistently and vehemently denied any subsidies for the German export industries. That he could do so was only possible because he chose a very narrow definition of the term 'subsidies' which did not include Hermes guarantees, tax reductions, or loans under special conditions[27]. In particular the British had apparently a misperception of German export finance in late 1950. When asked by the Treasury how German export finance was conducted and if the German government was involved in it, the Foreign Office replied that this was not the case. Instead, the Foreign Office thought that the Germans either used 'wrong calculations' when they undercut competitors' prices or that they used the high domestic profits to subsidise their exports. It was even thought that they abstained from their profits for one or two years in order to regain markets in the long run[28]. The Foreign Office also missed the point when it stressed that the KfW export finance was only granted to gain foreign currency revenues or to re-enter foreign markets since most German exports fell into one of these two categories. At this time, only the lack of funds prevented the KfW from a much larger involvement in export finance and Germany regaining more of their old markets, partly to the detriment of the British.

Funds to support export industries were indeed limited in these first years. No money was scheduled for the purpose with ECA I and only DM 2.3 million were provided under the ECA II programme[29]. Most of this money was used to promote German goods abroad, in particular in the dollar area, and it helped to increase the number of trade links and contracts. It was only with the ECA III programme that a larger sum of money, DM 50 million, was provided for the rehabilitation of the export industries[30].

However, in some special situations money had been given to at least a few exporting companies before. The most striking example was the case of the Zeiss optical plant. Originally located in the area which would become the GDR, American troops took with them some machinery, personnel and know-how when

---

[26]Alan Milward, *The European Rescue of the Nation State*, London 1995, p. 148.
[27]Erhard, *Rückkehr*, pp. 233 f.
[28]PRO FO 944 697, letter by D.R. Serpell, Treasury Chambers, to R.S. Crawford, FO, 31 October 1950; reply by C.F. Farlane, FO, to Serpell, 25 November 1950 with enclosed memorandum on German stockpiling and export finance.
[29]*Jb* 1950, pp. 22, 24.
[30]KfW HA-BS 73, unmarked paper (signed by Dr Grießbach of the BMWi), dated Frankfurt 7 August 1950; *Jb* 1951, p. 31.

they withdrew from Jena and resettled them in their own zone[31]. Although the resettled firm could offer no securities, no company capital and was at first housed only on a temporary basis, Abs supplied them with large loans from the KfW which then encouraged other banks to give money as well[32]. Not least with the help of risk capital like this German exporters regained a share in world trade of 3.6 per cent in 1950, starting from literally nil in 1945. The figure did not compare badly with France's share of 5.6 per cent, 11 for Great Britain and 18.2 for the USA[33].

The hitherto moderate recovery received a big boost in 1950 and 1951. As in the other sectors, the Korean War massively accelerated exports although it initially had caused a crisis. The conflict in East Asia increased German export orders by a large factor but caused a sharp rise in world raw material prices as well. This meant that German exporters and any other businesses had to buy more goods and raw materials to satisfy their demand for exports but they had to pay higher prices. With some of the raw materials even going in stockpiles in anticipation of further price rises West Germany ran into a serious balance of payment crisis and consequently had to suspend much of its liberalised trade within the EPU[34]. The BdL successfully countered the crisis with tight monetary policy and foreign currency restrictions. The Central Bank's measures imposed tough conditions on companies' profitability and forced them to achieve the highest competitiveness on the international markets. With the fall of raw material prices in 1952 and the continuing tough BdL policy the DM became *de facto* undervalued which helped the export industry's competitiveness all through the 1950s, not only during the export boom at the time of the Korean War[35].

Table 10.1.1 shows the development of the Kreditanstalt's loans for export finance from 1950 to 1951. Even without the Korean War there would certainly have been an increase in the Kreditanstalt's export business. But the fact that by late 1951 the BdL increased the KfW's credit ceiling for the purpose to DM 600 million and then added another DM 126 million especially for exports to Yugoslavia indicates clearly that the export boom resulting from the war played a decisive role in trebling the size of export financing within one year[36].

It is interesting to note that the largest share of these exports subsidies went to contracts outside the EPU, the dollar and the sterling area and the rest of the world although the EPU area was Germany's biggest market. The Kreditanstalt claimed that the total value of contracts subsidised by its loans was DM 1 billion and that the goods were sent to nearly 100 different countries or dependencies all

---

[31]For the official company history see Armin Hermann, *Nur der Name war geblieben*, Stuttgart 1989.

[32]See for example DBB HA B 330/3338, Protokoll zur 6. Sitzung des (KfW) Kreditbewilligungs-Ausschusses, TOP 1.

[33]Buchheim, *Wiedereingliederung*, p. 177.

[34]Hardach, *Marshallplan*, pp. 297 ff; Buchheim, *Wiedereingliederung*, pp. 126 ff.

[35]Hölscher, *Westdeutschland*, pp. 43, 47, 60.

[36]KfW HA-VS 29/I, BdL letter to the KfW directorate, 10 November 1951.

over the world. This suggests that exports to EPU countries could do without subsidies as Germany's growing EPU balance of payment surplus shows. As mentioned earlier, the Federal Republic's European exports were large enough to turn a debt of $457 million to the Union in February 1951 into a surplus of $43 million in December. It was only the exports to dollar countries which stagnated and caused some concern in 1951. All this suggests that the KfW was financing West Germany's return to the wider world markets while there were only relatively little subsidies needed for the European market[37].

Table 10.1.1
Breakdown in Areas of KfW Loans for Export Finance 1950-1951
(numbers of loans; amount in million DM)

	1950		1951		Total	
	Nos.	Sum	Nos.	Sum	Nos.	Sum
EPU countries	137	27.2	87	99	224	126.2
Sterling area	14	2.2	56	57.5	70	59.7
Dollar countries	33	35.7	21	39.1	54	74.8
Other countries	54	9.6	238	297.9	292	307.5
Var. countries as part of *Globalkredite*	56	51.6	186	204.5	242	256.1
Total	294	126.3	588	698.0	882	824.3

Source: *Jb* 1951, p. 68. The total exceeds the DM 726 million granted by the BdL due to the revolving use of interests and repayments.

Two other important events had a strong impact on German foreign trade that year. On 6 March Chancellor Adenauer in a letter to the Allied High Commission acknowledged in principle Germany's pre-war debts[38]. Secondly on 1 October the Federal Republic became a member of the General Agreement on Tariffs and Trade (GATT) treaty[39]. The first led to the London negotiations on Germany's foreign debts and the subsequent signing of the London Debt Agreement. It restored the

[37]*Jb* 1951, pp. 22, 67; KfW HA-VS 53, Anlage 1 to a report by the BMWi on export guarantees, 26 April 1952; Hardach, *Marshallplan*, pp. 317 ff.
[38]PRO FO 371 93728, CE 1104/58.
[39]Harald Gudin, 'Außenwirtschaftspolitische und außenpolitische Einflußfaktoren im Prozess der Staatswerdung der Bundesrepublik Deutschland', in: *Aus Politik und Zeitgeschichte (APuZ)* B32/87 (1987), p. 19.

young republic's international credit worthiness and helped to bring foreign investments into the country[40]. The acknowledgement of Germany's foreign debt was the basis of the country's international financial rehabilitation while joining the GATT symbolised the even more important political restoration of the country. The Occupation Status which had been enacted in September 1949 preserved the High Commissioners' rights to control Germany's foreign trade and foreign currency transactions[41]. This clause gave the Americans a chance to force West Germany into the role of a pacemaker in European trade liberalisation. Replacing the predominant system of bilateral trade was the crucial steppingstone to their aim of introducing a system of multilateralism in international trade[42]. In a first step they made the western zones agree on multilateral trade liberation and tariff reductions and made them sign a most favoured nation clause with 13 GATT member states in September 1948 without receiving that status for themselves at the same time. During the GATT's Annecy meeting in summer 1949 the latter was extended to all GATT nations[43]. This marked an important step in the process of West Germany's integration into the western camp. West Germany's ascension to the GATT during its 1951 Torquay conference, which took place in the wake of Germany's suspension of its trade liberalisation in the winter of 1950-51, indicated the country's importance as a trade partner of the western world. But it was not all plain sailing. The initial agreement to join GATT was declined by both the Bundestag and the AHC, which was still nominally in charge of Germany's foreign trade. Several changes and amendments to the treaty were necessary before an agreement was finally reached. The patience the other participating countries displayed in this process can only be explained with the importance Germany had regained on the European and world markets. One of the most important aspects for Germany joining the GATT was article XXXIII of the GATT agreement which stated that only sovereign states could join. But by the summer of 1951, due to the Occupation Statute and the control by the AHC, the Federal Republic could be called semi-sovereign at best. Consequently, after West Germany became a full GATT member the AHC in October 1951 transferred to Adenauer's government some of the powers they had previously reserved for themselves. Most important among the controls handed over were those on foreign trade and currencies. Thus, with the exception of all trade with Eastern Europe, over which the AHC retained the final say, due to the CoCom restrictions, West Germany had regained sovereignty over its foreign trade affairs[44].

With the political and economic situation improved in these ways the KfW in 1952 handed over export financing to a newly established export bank, the

---

[40]See Abs, *Entscheidungen;* Christoph Buchheim, 'Das Londoner Schuldenabkommen', in Ludolf Herbst (ed.), *Westdeutschland 1945-1955*, München 1986, p. 227.

[41]Gudin, 'Einflußfaktoren', p. 3.

[42]See Bührer, 'Liberalisierung'.

[43]Gudin, 'Einflußfaktoren', p. 7.

[44]Gudin, 'Einflußfaktoren', p. 18 f.

Ausfuhr Kredit AG (AKA). In the first place it had never been the KfW's intention to be responsible indefinitely for general export finance. After all there were enough bank managers on its board who had an interest of getting a slice of the cake for their own institutions. Consequently by early November 1951 negotiations on what kind of institute was to conduct any future export financing had proceeded much further[45]. One week later, the Kreditanstalt received the BdL's permission to split the DM 726 million credit line in two, creating one line of DM 126 million for weak loans for Yugoslavia and a line of DM 600 million, to be taken over by the new institution as soon as it was established[46]. On 28 March 1952 the AKA was officially founded by a banking consortium under the leadership of one of the Deutsche Bank's successor banks. It began work on 1 April[47]. Since the BdL was not prepared to extend further its already stretched lending frame, the DM 250 million initially provided by the AKA's subscribers provided a considerable extension to the DM 600 million which the KfW handed over to the new bank gradually until March 1953[48]. The transfer of money was not the end of close co-operation between the two banks. There remained close personal links and the AKA actually took office in the same building as the KfW[49].

Despite this close co-operation the Kreditanstalt realised the limitations the AKA was under in terms of its business conduct and soon issued a warning that the Federal Republic lacked an institution which was able to handle both large scale and long-term contracts running more than five years. From this warning the conclusion could be drawn that, since neither the AKA nor any other bank was capable or willing to take on such loans the KfW as the only alternative solution would be back in the export financing business sooner or later[50].

On Equal Terms

Soon after the revised occupation statute had been enacted in March 1951 and after West Germany had joined the GATT, an argument within the German administration broke out. The revised occupation statute allowed West Germany to take control over its foreign affairs. The Auswärtige Amt (AA), which was re-established soon after, demanded to regain control over foreign trade policy, which had been taken charge of by Erhard's Economic Ministry. Although the *Außenwirtschaftsabteilung* (foreign trade section) was returned to the AA with a

[45]DBB HA B330/3337, note regarding a meeting on 3 November 1951.
[46]KfW HA-VS 29/I, BdL letter to KfW, 10 November 1951.
[47]Ibid., KfW letter to BMWi, 3 April 1952; Holtfrerich, 'The Deutsche Bank', p. 379.
[48]KfW HA-Prot 10-2, Protokoll der 24. Sitzung, TOP 6; Holtfrerich, 'The Deutsche Bank', p. 504;
[49] KfW HA-VS 17, KfW draft letter 'An alle Außenhandelsbanken', 3 April 1952; *Jb* 1952, p. 69.
[50]*Jb* 1953, p. 71.

loss of staff and prestige for Erhard the quarrel went on[51]. The reason for this was not only power politics within the cabinet, Erhard's economic 'ideology' was an equally strong motive. For Erhard, *Außenwirtschaftspolitik* (foreign economic policy) meant that, in spite of all justified political aims, it had to serve first and foremost the expansion of the German (export) industry[52]. Following this basic principle, BMWi officials produced sometimes quite dubious arguments for financial aid to exports. For example, in early 1952 at a time when the KfW's BoD had serious doubts about Argentina's solvency, a BMWi official supported the granting of an export deal to sell tractors to that country. In support of the deal he argued that without the tractors Argentina's agriculture would falter. Germany would not be able to import enough grain from the South American country and would have to reintroduce ration cards which could all be prevented if the deal was approved[53].

Other than tradition there were two more reasons for Adenauer to return responsibility for foreign trade policy to the AA. Obviously it meant a reduction in Erhard's power and prestige, which in itself was reason enough for Adenauer to do it, perhaps in anticipation of the clashes the two would have later on, but there were also important political reasons. In contrast to Erhard, the Auswärtiges Amt and Adenauer, who at this time acted as Foreign Minister as well, regarded foreign trade as a means to support politics and this line became much more important in 1955 when the Hallstein Doctrine came into effect and negotiations on the EEC began. It is therefore no surprise that from this year onwards, German commercial policy in particular vis-à-vis developing countries became more systematic while before it was based on private initiative backed with government support[54]. The establishment of the EEC was not only motivated by the idea of a politically united Europe but also out of national self interest of various kinds, often based on economic advantages[55]. For West Germany the EEC meant the ultimate recognition by the other European countries and an important if not dominant role in political and, even more so, in economic affairs[56]. The Treaty of Rome was the final guarantee to Western European countries and in particular the other five founding members of the EEC that the West German industrial potential was integrated into a wider European economy thus preventing it from becoming a threat to them once more in the future.

---

[51]Hans-Jürgen Küsters, 'Adenauers Europapolitik in der Gründungsphase der Europäischen Wirtschaftsgemeinschaft', in: *VfZ* No. 31 (1983), p. 653.

[52]Hans-Jürgen Spanger, Lothar Brock, *Die beiden deutschen Staaten in der Dritten Welt*, Opladen 1987, pp. 282 f., quoting from a 1954 BMWi paper.

[53]KfW HA Prot 10-2, Protokoll der 22. Sitzung, TOP 6; KfW HA-VS 28/II, note on a meeting of the Interministerieller Ausschuß für Ausfuhrgarantien, 20 February 1952.

[54] Bührer, Schröder, 'Revival', p. 192.

[55]See Milward, *Rescue*.

[56]Küsters, 'Europapolitik', pp. 672 f.

The strength of the German export industry in Europe and North America in the second half of the 1950s is reflected by the work of the KfW which named not a single loan for Canada, the USA or a European Community country[57]. As in the early 1950s the KfW's export operations concerned either the non-western world market or non-EEC country loans. Nevertheless, as the KfW had predicted there were problems developing in export financing as early as 1954. They arose from the AKA's unwillingness to give loans for more than five years duration and not totally unexpected, the Kreditanstalt had to step in. To enable the KfW to finance the project, the construction of a steel plant in India by Krupp, the bank received an early confirmation that it could refinance the loan with counterpart funds in 1958-59. But by that time the Kreditanstalt was fully involved in export deals and had found new ways of financing these long-term export loans[58].

In the 1955 Annual Report, published in March 1956, the KfW stressed more than usual its participation and its importance in export finance: 'Während des Berichtsjahres hat sich die K[f]W mit relativ erheblichen Beträgen an der langfristigen Finanzierung von Ausfuhrgeschäften ... beteiligt, womit sie den Wünschen der Bundesregierung, der Banken und der interressierten Industriekreise nachkam ...'[59].

This strong worded statement was chosen to demonstrate the KfW's role in export finance and was a response to a ten-page memorandum by the influential BDI on how to improve export finance[60]. The memorandum directly raised the question of whether or not a special institute for (long-term) export financing should be established. The BMWi asked the Kreditanstalt für Wiederaufbau to comment on the memorandum. The KfW, keen to stay in business, gave a couple of good reasons why there should be no new institute, especially not one which was state owned. The main argument was that Germany's competitors would regard a state owned export bank as state sponsored discrimination of their exports and would act with countermeasures. The KfW concluded that it had the personnel, the funds and the experience to do the job, and most importantly, since it had to fulfil other major tasks besides export financing, foreign complaints about unfair trade would not arise[61]. A similar line was struck by Otto Rieck, Deputy Managing Director (*stellvertretendes Vorstandsmitglied*) in a letter to an AA official. Rieck

---

[57]*Jb* 1957-1961; furthermore, no indication of such a loan could be found in the archives. There was only a case of a loan to Greece in 1954, see *Kabinettsprotokolle*, vol. 7, pp 96 f., but Greece not being an EEC member at that time.

[58]KfW HA-Prot 10-2, Protokoll der 28. Sitzung, TOP 1; *Jb* 1954, p. 62.The Krupp deal will be investigated in detail in chapter 10.2.

[59]*Jb* 1955, p. 44. 'During the year under review the KfW participated with considerable amounts in the financing of long-term export deals. In doing so it followed the wishes of the Federal Government, the banks and the interested industries'. (Translation AG).

[60]BA B 102/25449, BDI letter to BMWi, 17 February 1956.

[61]Ibid.; KfW HA-VS 32, KfW letter to BMWi, 29 February 1956.

stressed the need for a *geräuschlose* (silent) export finance, that is one without the involvement of the press, and that the KfW could offer a guarantee on this[62].

Soon after, the KfW's lobbying paid off when it was agreed that it should carry out the long-term export financing to less developed countries. But it was emphasised by the economics ministry that no political loans or grants whatsoever should be made to those states[63]. This declaration proved to be wishful thinking at best or naivety at worst. The AA was already investigating the political effects the Eastern Block's economic offensive had in developing countries and how it could be countered[64]. Since it was able to operate quietly, the KfW was the perfect instrument for any such countermeasures, even more so because it had already gained experience in the economic Cold War.

Towards the end of the 1950s the KfW's volume in foreign and export business increased strongly. Until 1957 it had provided about DM 1 billion for such deals in which loans to Yugoslavia and Turkey featured very prominently. For the domestic economy on the other hand, loans amounting to DM 9 billion were on the books. In 1958-59 KfW credits within the Federal Republic amounted to DM 2.5 billion and those for export finance or loans to other countries had risen to DM 1.2 billion, more than half of which, DM 700 million, had been given as direct loans, either to foreign companies or governments[65].

By this time the KfW had got involved in five types of foreign business. Amongst those only the loans to German exporters and the passing on of federal loans were fully covered by the KfW law. The conversion of foreign debts against German exporters might have constituted a grey area, but loans to foreign importers or banks to allow them to buy German goods and even more so unconditional loans (*ungebundene Finanzkredite*) abroad were certainly outside the scope of the law[66]. Also, direct loans to foreigners were definitely not covered by the KfW law. A change of the law to legalise some parts of the bank's operations was imminent.

10.2 Exports and the Cold War in the 1950s

Exports in the 1950s had a much wider impact than just enabling the re-establishment of West Germany on the world market and on the political scene. Trade or its prevention had been a form of war at least since the time of Napoleon. Apart from covert operations and propaganda, foreign trade was a major weapon in

---

[62]KfW HA-VS 32, subfile 'Allgemeine Korrespondenz', letter by Rieck to Legationsrat Harkort, 5 March 1956.

[63]BA B 102/25449, note by BMWi, Abteilung VI on a ministerial meeting, 9 March 1956.

[64]Ibid., note on an inter-ministerial meeting at the AA on 'Zusammenarbeit mit unterentwickelten Ländern', 12 March 1956; report of the AA on the topic, 24 April 1956.

[65]Hankel, *Kapitalverteilung*, pp. 158 ff.

[66]BA B 102/2531, KfW memorandum regarding foreign business, 5 November 1959.

the Cold War[67]. The granting of aid or the withholding of trade could strongly influence a political or economic decision in particular, but not only, in a third world country. The problem for the Federal Republic was that its export trade was squeezed between US embargo policy and the Hallstein Doctrine.

Before the second half of 1948 even the post-war economic superpower, the USA, depended on a large scale on the import of various strategic raw materials from the Soviet Union and therefore had to consider its foreign policy in regard to economic matters as well. In 1947 in the face of the upcoming Cold War one-third of the USA's supply in strategic metals such as manganese and as much as half of its platinum and chrome supply came from the Soviet Union so the US had to be very careful with its own blockade policy[68]. In regard to the Bizone, the US authorities after 1946 had signed several bilateral trade treaties with Eastern European countries to improve the zone's economic situation, especially in view of food supplies. The last treaty to be signed with a country within the sphere of Soviet influence was with Czechoslovakia, as late as February 1949[69]. This was nearly one year after the USA had drawn up and implemented two lists of export commodities which should be withheld from the Soviet Union and its satellites. The immediate reason for American restrictions had been the Soviets blockade of Berlin to which the western Allies introduced a counter blockade. For the Bizone JEIA supervised the blockade which interrupted nearly all trade between the eastern and the western parts of Germany. When, after the signing of the Jessup-Malik agreement the Berlin blockade was lifted and all trade restrictions on both sides of the inner German border were supposed to be lifted, the Americans ignored the treaty and continued to prevent most exports from the West going behind the Iron Curtain[70].

American policy soon showed effects. In 1938 the share of East-West trade in total world trade was 6.4 per cent. Ten years later, it was down to 2.6 per cent only to drop further to half this figure in 1953. Since the American share in trade with the Soviet Union and Eastern Europe had been insignificant, it was easy for them to implement this kind of policy at home[71]. It was the Europeans who had to bear the brunt of the embargos. Their share in exports to the East had dropped from 33 per cent in 1938 to 13 per cent in 1948. At the same time, western European imports declined from 25 per cent to 9 per cent and finally to 4 per cent in 1951[72]. With the Marshall Plan the United States had a sharp instrument to convince not only its former allies but also European neutrals to go along with the embargo policy. Although they could not impose too harsh sanctions in case of non-

[67]Gunnar Adler-Karlson, *Western Economic Warfare 1947-1967*, Stockholm 1968.
[68]Daniel, *Dollardiplomatie*, p. 164.
[69]*Monthly Reports*, No. 44 (February 1949), p. 101.
[70]Hardach, *Marshallplan*, pp. 185 ff.
[71]Karl-Heinz Schlarp, 'Das Dilemma des westdeutschen Osthandels und die Entstehung des Ostausschusses der Deutschen Wirtschaft', in: *VfZ* No 41. (1993), pp. 226 f.; Hardach, *Marshallplan*, p. 185.
[72]Schlarp, 'Dilemma', pp. 226 f.

compliance with the embargo policy out of consideration to European public opinion, the hint that they might withhold or cut Marshall aid was a strong incentive for the Europeans to comply. Formal consultations between the USA and the Europeans about the embargo lists were officially taken by the notorious Co-Ordination Committee, or CoCom, but these restraints were barely necessary in occupied West Germany[73].

When in early 1950 the Federal Republic committed itself to participate in the embargo it happened on the basis of the full restriction list for American companies which was about 20 to 30 per cent longer then the list of the other OEEC countries[74]. The Adenauer government conceded to the tougher conditions not least to prove its value as a reliable ally. But for West German exporters it amounted to a severe handicap compared to their European competitors. It has to be kept in mind that in the early 1930s some crucial sectors of German industry such as mechanical engineering had sold up to 50 per cent of their products to the Soviet Union. In 1950 alone German export losses were estimated to be about DM 1.15 billion with another loss of DM 1 billion due to non-realised imports[75]. Contrary to government policy the BDI considered in its first major initiative on foreign trade policy during a confidential meeting in early May 1950 to revive those good years of German eastern exports. In doing so they followed their own traditional trade patterns which concentrated on exports to western and eastern Europe. Dollar deals and business with the USA were seen at this time with much scepticism and not as an alternative to the traditional trade links and markets[76]. However, the BDI had to change their minds in face of the actual political facts created by the Americans. In the aftermath of the passing of the Battle-Act in July 1951, the ECA suspended ERP money to companies suspected of conducting East-West trade and even set up black lists with the names of such companies which made the BDI realise that it had to change its policy[77]. While they had already supported Adenauer's policy of *Westintegration* in the political field they now had to accept it in economic terms as well because with the embargo in place countries in the western hemisphere had become the only place where West Germany could find large enough markets[78]. Although both the government and the BDI stuck firmly to their pro-western course neither of them gave up the idea of trading with Eastern Block countries, in particular the Soviet Union. Small West German trade contracts with Eastern European countries, although severely restricted by the

[73]Hardach, *Marshallplan*, pp. 186 ff.

[74]Reinhard Neebe, 'Optionen westdeutscher Außenwirtschaftspolitik 1949-1953', in: Bührer, Herbst, Sowade, *Zwischen Marshallplan und EWG*, p. 178; Schlarp, 'Dilemma', p. 229.

[75]Schlarp, 'Dilemma', pp. 231, 236.

[76]Neebe, 'Optionen', p. 175.

[77]Nebe, 'Optionen', p. 182, Hardach; *Marshallplan*, p. 191.

[78]Bührer, Schröder, 'Revival', p. 187.

CoCom list, were signed throughout the 1950s[79]. Furthermore, during the GATT negotiations the Federal Republic would make the claim that its trade with the GDR was domestic, even if it concerned some strategic commodities[80]. The assertion was made for the political purpose of supporting the *Alleinvertretungsanspruch* (sole representation claim). 1952 saw a final attempt to revitalise the old trade links to Russia on their previous scale which demonstrated the ambivalence between economic and foreign policy decisions. In the aftermath of the Moscow Economic Conference in April 1952, but only after the signing of the *Generalvertrag* in May the Adenauer government established the *Ostausschuß der deutschen Industrie* (Industrial Committee on the East) with the help of the BDI[81]. But in the face of the Cold War even this committee failed to increase West German-Soviet trade to a significant level.

Some British intentions and policies in the early 1950s appear to have been similar if not identical to those in Germany. When in February 1950 Switzerland started trade negotiations with the GDR, the Foreign Office was alarmed. They feared that those negotiations might lead to the recognition of East Germany by Switzerland which in turn would trigger a cascade of recognitions of the GDR by other countries. British pressure on the Swiss helped to cause the breakdown of the official negotiations, thus sustaining the Federal Republic's claim of sole representation[82]. Britain also strongly supported Adenauer in the attempt to increase West Germany trade with Eastern Europe and co-operated with him to get some goods off the embargo list. This move was borne out of self interest since German goods sold in the Soviet Union meant less competition for British goods on the world market[83]. However, since the old European trade patterns had been disrupted, British attempts to keep German goods from western markets were unsuccessful and West German competition for British goods increased further.

Political developments in 1953, in particular the end of the conflict in Korea marked the beginning of a new era in the economic warfare. The Federal Republic had established itself on the world markets and began to ascertain itself within the western economic, political and military structures. The latter meant a lessening but not a total end to US influence and control over German external trade, while the end of the Korean War brought about a reduction of the CoCom list. Soviet policy after Stalin's death changed as well. The new leaders in the Kremlin began to pay much more attention to Third World countries and their needs, a development which would have a major impact on the KfW's task[84].

---

[79]See Robert Mark Spaulding, *Osthandel and Ostpolitik. German Foreign Trade Policies in Eastern Europe from Bismarck to Adenauer*, Oxford, New York 1997.
[80]Friedrich von Heyl, *Der innerdeutsche Handel mit Eisen und Stahl 1945-1972. Deutsch-deutsche Beziehungen im Kalten Krieg*, Köln, Weimar, Wien 1997.
[81]Neebe, 'Optionen', pp. 190f; Braunthal, *Federation*, p. 310; Schlarp, 'Dilemma', passim.
[82]PRO FO 371 85122, passim.
[83]Neebe, 'Optionen', p. 184.
[84]Burton Kaufman, *Trade and Aid. Eisenhower's Foreign Economic Policy 1953-1960*, Baltimore 1982, pp. 58 f.

In September 1955 Adenauer achieved one of his biggest political and personal victories when he travelled to Moscow to successfully negotiate the release of German POWs and establish diplomatic relations with the Soviet Union. However, in taking up diplomatic relations with the Kremlin he created a dilemma for German foreign policy which would last for the next one and a half decades. With the Soviet Union the Federal Republic had for the first time diplomatic relations with a state which recognised the German Democratic Republic as a sovereign state. The government in Bonn now had to fear that other states outside the communist block would take this as an invitation to take up top-level contacts with East Germany, a possibility which would have shattered Adenauer's claim for sole representation. To avoid this, a new political guideline which became known as the Hallstein Doctrine was developed already during Adenauer's flight home from Moscow. The Doctrine was named after Staatssekretär Hallstein of the Auswärtiges Amt and reaffirmed West Germany's *Alleinvertretungsanspruch* and threatened to terminate diplomatic relations with all countries which recognised the GDR. Although there was only one country during the period under investigation on which the Hallstein Doctrine had to be applied, Yugoslavia, the Federal Republic became prone to blackmail and had to pay an economic price for the upholding of the doctrine. Exports and economic aid to Third World countries were to become an increasingly important tool in the ideological struggle of the late 1950s and the Federal Republic and in particular the Kreditanstalt got more and more entangled in it. Especially after the Suez Crisis, when western credibility in the developing countries had hit an all time low, the Eisenhower administration began to rely more and more on West Germany and pushed it towards a steadily growing engagement of economic aid out of Cold War considerations. The two case studies, loans to Yugoslavia and aid to India will illustrate how Cold War economics changed during the 1950s, both in regard to the motivation of aid and the results it produced.

The German-Yugoslav Trade Treaties

The German-Yugoslav trade treaty which was signed in April 1950 and the subsequent arrangements were among the KfW's most politically motivated deals. The material gains for the Federal Republic were small though financial complications were enormous. The actual German-Yugoslav treaty was signed out of Cold War considerations in 1950, its roots lay further back. Since 1947 BiCO had been signing bilateral trade treaties on behalf of the Bizone[85]. Apart from Western European countries, these treaties were concluded with states east of the Iron Curtain despite the fact that American policy in 1947-48 was turning more and more anti-communist. Communist activities in Eastern and South-Eastern Europe

[85] *Monthly Report,* Nos. 37, 38 and 39 (July, August and September 1948).

gave rise to concern in the West. Especially Tito's active support for the communist rebellion in Greece during 1947 worried the Americans. General Clay, in a cable to his deputy, Draper, expressed concern and disapproval over the planned restitution of silver to Yugoslavia which had been looted by the Nazis. In Clay's eyes this silver would be used for anti-western actions and although the worth of the whole shipment was only $25,000 the Americans saw it as a potential danger[86].

Following the communist coup in Czechoslovakia in April 1948 General Clay suspended reparation deliveries not only to Czechoslovakia, but to Yugoslavia and Albania as well[87]. This negative attitude changed, however, within two months following Tito's break with Moscow. Now Yugoslavia began to receive strong US support and by mid July 1948 both countries had settled their mutual commercial disputes concerning the nationalised former US property in Yugoslavia and frozen Yugoslav assets in the USA[88]. The Truman government realised that they had to increase their support for Tito even further to keep the country viable. In January 1949 the US embassy in Belgrade sent a telegram to Secretary of State Acheson, claiming that the United States should even grant Yugoslavia aid for the establishment of an industrial infrastructure. The American aid necessary for this could be given either directly or indirectly via countries participating in the ERP. Those countries were in particular Italy, Britain and the German Bizone. The embassy stressed the necessity for aid in whatever form as being the only way for the USA to acquire Yugoslav ores and metals some of which were strategic materials[89]. Under the circumstances the US government opted for a mixed solution of direct help and aid given via countries participating in the ERP. This method could guarantee a broader base for aid in the short-run and would draw in other countries which would lead ultimately to aid by these countries and independent of the USA. However, even America's most loyal ally, the British, who were under heavy economic strain at the time, were cautious and quite concerned about the size of loans intended for Yugoslavia[90]. But in the end they too participated in the scheme. In the case of Germany the situation was easier for the Americans. The US Military Government did not have to take German reactions into account. By 23 March 1949 the Joint Export Import Agency had signed a trade agreement with Yugoslavia on behalf of the Bizone and had relaxed the Bizone's strict regulation of East-West trade for this purpose.

The treaty signed by JEIA would become the basis for the German-Yugoslav trade agreement. JEIA's treaty ran until 31 December 1949 and amounted to $35 million. The Bizone had to ship electrical equipment, machine

---

[86]Lucius D. Clay, *The Papers of General Lucius D. Clay: Germany 1945-1949*, edited by Jean Edward Smith, 2 vols., Indiana University Press 1974, p. 565.
[87]*FRUS*, 1948, vol. II, p.751.
[88]*FRUS*, 1948, vol. IV, p. 1093.
[89]*FRUS*, 1949, vol. V, pp. 854 f.
[90]*FRUS*, 1949, vol. V, pp. 889 f.

tools, chemicals, coke and vehicles worth some $18.9 millions to Yugoslavia, which in turn was going to give agricultural goods, raw materials and some semi-finished products to West Germany[91]. After the establishment of the Federal Republic direct German-Yugoslav talks on the continuation of the agreement took place, starting in December 1949 but Adenauer himself delayed the signing of the treaty[92]. In doing so he hoped to put pressure on Tito in order to gain concessions regarding German Prisoners of War still held in Yugoslavia. Tito was not at all impressed by the German tactics. In a meeting with the American Ambassador in March 1950 he threatened to publish a 'white book' on German war crimes committed in Yugoslavia should the treaty be delayed further[93]. Neither the delayed signing of the agreement nor Tito's threats pleased the Americans but disrupted their political concept. The delay threatened the economic stability in Yugoslavia, thus carried the risk of losing the country again to the Soviet block, either as a result of a direct Soviet invasion after economic turmoil or simply because Tito would be forced to compromise over the economic situation in his country. The threat to publicise German war crimes would have had a negative effect on US attempts to integrate West Germany into the western camp. So US Secretary of State Acheson had to take quick action. He informed his Ambassador in Belgrade that he and his British and French colleagues should intervene on behalf of the German POWs but without linking their fate with economic matters. At the same time the Allied High Commissioners in Germany were ordered to put pressure on Adenauer to sign the treaty. This strategy seems to have worked and on 18 April 1950 the agreement was finally signed[94]. Similar to the treaties signed before by JEIA, the German-Yugoslav agreement of April 1950 worked on a compensation basis i.e. that payments made for deliveries were made through a special offset account and probably even balanced in US dollars, thus there was no need for the KfW to get involved[95].

Although the British supported the German deal they felt uneasy about it. In January a Foreign Office paper showed surprise at the fast growth rate of German-Yugoslav trade and warned of the risks of losing the Yugoslav market to the revived German competition[96]. The British were alarmed when on 20 April, just two days after the signing of the German Yugoslav trade agreement they received some unofficial information from the US section of the Allied Banking Commission. According to this source, West Germany and Yugoslavia were going to negotiate a further trade agreement with an even bigger credit for Yugoslavia. This was to be done without giving the compulsory notification to the Allied Bank

---

[91]*Monthly Report,* No. 46 (April 1949), p. 114.
[92]PRO, FO 371 85755, CE 108.
[93]*FRUS,* 1950, vol. IV, p. 1388.
[94]*FRUS,* 1950, vol. IV, p. 1395.
[95]*Monthly Report,* No. 38 (August 1948), pp. 81 f.
[96]PRO, FO 371 85755, CE 108.

Commission[97]. Indeed, the Yugoslav Minister for Trade had approached Ludwig Erhard for a new loan. The German Minister for Economics, although he knew about Yugoslavia's bad economic and financial situation and poor terms of trade agreed in principle[98]. But while the Yugoslavs hoped for a loan of $80 to 100 million over the next two years which they could repay in commodities between 1952 and 1957, the Germans thought only of $20 to 25 million on similar terms[99]. On 17 May 1950 German experts, including KfW staff, met with Yugoslav officials to negotiate on a credit agreement. The KfW representatives seemed extremely sceptical about the whole deal and declared that all the bank's funds designated for export financing had already been earmarked for specific projects. When, in spite of this, they promised to find new financial sources it may have not been only a kind of loyalty to Erhard but also an attempt to stay in the export business in the longer term. The BdL members in the German delegation were even more cautious. They said that the only way for the Federal Republic to raise a loan of that size was by printing the money, thus triggering inflation. Only Erhard appears to have been in favour of the loan without any hesitation[100].

During the spring and summer of 1950 France and Britain voiced strong opposition against a credit agreement that size. Apart from the immediate loss of export markets to Germany both countries were even more concerned with the long-term threat of Germany re-establishing its pre-war trade dominance in South-East Europe. By this time, however, the USA was pressing for the signing of the treaty, regarding it as 'a matter of tripartite principle' thus leaving its Allies little choice[101]. Although the British themselves gave a $20 million loan to Yugoslavia they did so only out of political considerations which arose out of the American pressure and because they hoped that West Germany would then drop the idea of an $80 million loan, knowing full well that Yugoslavia was not solvent[102]. By mid-1950, for this very reason, the British called further financial concessions to Yugoslavia 'sheer madness' but they seemed to realise that Adenauer was under heavy American pressure to go ahead with the loans[103]. Under these circumstances they accepted that the deal had become unavoidable.

By June 1950 the Kreditanstalt für Wiederaufbau was already involved in two programmes to increase German exports. The *Investitionsprogramm Exportintensive Industrie* (investment programme for export industries) was encouraged by the ECA administration in order to improve West Germany's foreign currency balance. For this the KfW had received a special line of credit from the BdL of DM 110 million in advance of the third tranche of ERP money[104].

[97]PRO, FO 371 85755, CE 1789.
[98]Erhard, *Rückkehr*, pp. 129 f.
[99]*FRUS*, 1950, vol. IV, pp. 1432 f.
[100]PRO FO 371 85755, CE 2282, CE 2723.
[101]*FRUS*, 1950, vol. IV, pp. 1437 f.
[102]PRO, FO 371 85755, CE 2444.
[103]PRO, FO 371 85755, CE 3189.
[104]*Jb* 1950, p. 28.

The second programme, bigger in size and more important, was part of the federal government's work creation scheme of February 1950. The KfW was given temporary control of financing export loans. Another special line of credit worth some DM 300 million was established for this with the BdL for the purpose. The line was extended to DM 400 million when the KfW began its involvement in the Yugoslavia treaty[105]. The Board of Directors discussed the proposed trade agreement and the KfW's part in it at its 17th meeting on 31 August 1950. It was planned that West Germany would export equipment worth some DM 126 million, equivalent to $30 million, to Yugoslavia within two years. The repayment in raw materials and foodstuff was scheduled to begin in 1953 and be completed within five years. It was stressed during the meeting that the agreement was strongly motivated by political reasons and that there were considerable economic arguments against it. In particular the long period of validity for this kind of deal was a cause for concern, but even more so was Yugoslavia's political situation. Two months into the Korean War, Soviet intentions both in regard to Western Europe and even more so to Yugoslavia were unknown. A Soviet invasion of Tito's People's Republic seemed possible, even likely. In the face of this political risk it is somewhat surprising that the Board of Managers declined Allied requests for information on the size of the export loans. The BoM justified the decision on the grounds that the loans were solely a German affair and that the Allies had no right to ask for the information. This view was shared by the Board of Directors and once more showed the determination of the KfW's executives to assert their independence, especially against the Allies[106].

By early September 1950 the treaty had still not been signed although most of the disputed points including the size of the loan had been resolved. Furthermore, under American pressure the British had changed their official stance on the project. They had agreed not to veto a German loan up to $65 million, but would advise the Germans that a loan of this size would be 'economically unsound'[107]. Once more in the process of German reconstruction the British had to put aside their own interests and give in to the Americans.

The next meeting of the KfW's BoD on 3 November 1950 nearly coincided with the signing of the German-Yugoslav Export Treaty on 1 November. Once again, Abs stressed the political background of the treaty in particular that it should help to bring home German POWs still held in Yugoslavia. West Germany agreed to supply machinery and equipment for mining, chemical, electrical, iron, and crude oil industries. The value of the deliveries was some DM 147 million or $35 million. Of these the KfW had to supply DM 126 million for the next five years for which the bank received a guarantee from the federal government. In his statement to the BoD Abs was more candid than before when he said that under normal

---

[105]Ibid.
[106]KfW HA-Prot 10-1, Protokoll zur 17. Sitzung, TOP 4.
[107]*FRUS*, 1950, vol. IV, p. 1447.

circumstances the Kreditanstalt would have turned down the project and used the money otherwise. The Yugoslav economy and especially the agricultural sector, which was to be the main source of the repayments, gave cause for the greatest concern[108]. The entire agreement must have given Abs a feeling of unease and not only for economic reasons. In 1945 he had been sentenced to death in absentia by a court in Zagreb for alleged war crimes[109].

Abs highlighted the real state of the Yugoslav economy. Because of two consecutive crop failures the situation was so desperate that the USA was forced into an aid programme which was somewhat of an embarrassment to them: the USA made Italy buy 238,000 tons of wheat in the Soviet Union for which Italy paid in commodities. The USA in turn compensated the Italians for those commodities at a later date. In addition to this West Germany had to supply 10,000 tons of flour on a weekly basis to Yugoslavia. They would later be given compensation for the deliveries through extra Marshall Plan funds[110]. In their justification for supporting Belgrade the Americans displayed true Cold War mentality: Tito received aid *because* he was a communist, and not in spite of the fact that he was a communist. The existence of Tito's communist regime outside the Soviet bloc was a propaganda victory for the West because it weakened the Kremlin's claim for worldwide communist leadership. This was the underlying reason for American aid. However, with their support for the communist government in Belgrade, the USA broke their promise not to help any country which did not grant the four liberties of the Atlantic Charter[111]. Cold War realities had overruled once more idealistic declarations.

The technical procedure for the KfW's loans to Yugoslavia followed the already well-established pattern under which the bank operated. The exporters wrote bills of exchange which received the endorsement of a foreign trade bank. Those were then accepted by the KfW which in turn got the cash from the above-mentioned special BdL credit line. The loans given to the exporters in this way were again quite cheap with an annual interest rate of only 5.5 per cent[112].

The processing of export loans to Yugoslavia had hardly begun when it was stopped again. As early as 26 January 1951, in its 19th meeting, the Board of Directors had to deal with the first serious problem: DM 40 million designated for an advanced loan could not be given to German applicants because loans given in

---

[108]KfW HA-Prot 10-1, Protokoll zur 18. Sitzung, TOP 5 and Ergänzende Niederschrift, TOP 5.

[109]Tom Bower, *Blind Eye to Murder. Britain, America and the Purging of Nazi Germany: A Pledge Betrayed,* London et al. 1981, p. 408. Holtfrerich speaks only of ten years imprisonment and hard labour. See Holtfrerich, 'The Deutsche Bank 1945-1957', p. 374. Abs' crimes were related to his leading role on the Board of a Croatian bank. The difference in the sentence certainly is due to a reduction in the original death sentence. The sentence was eventually lifted by the Yugoslav government just before Abs visited Belgrade in 1956.

[110]*Der Spiegel,* No. 48, 4. Jg. (1950), p. 23; No. 50, 4. Jg. (1950), p. 28.

[111]*Der Spiegel,* No. 8, 4. Jg. (1950), p. 18.

[112]*Jb* 1950, p. 28.

early 1950 had already gone bad and it had become imperative first to negotiate with the Yugoslavs about those loans which affected contracts amounting to anything between $10 to 15 million[113]. On the German side emergency talks were held at the BdL in February as well. During these discussions the representative of the Economic Ministry declared that the Germans themselves were partly to blame for the troubles: since Adenauer had refused to sign the contract unless the question of the German POWs was settled, the loans were delayed which had worsened the Yugoslav trade position and in the end helped to let the loans go bad altogether. To solve the problems the BdL suggested that the ECA should give a guarantee of up to $15 million for the bad loans. The member of the Allied Banking Commission present at the meeting did not refuse this straight away, instead he promised to examine the idea further. The KfW interpreted this as another sign that the Americans had put pressure on Adenauer in the first place to agree to the loans[114].

Although the immediate problems were solved in the course of this meeting, a long-term solution had to be found. It was against this background that the KfW tried to divide its export loans in two parts. During the course of 1951 the BdL had increased the special credit line for export finance to DM 600 million[115]. Now the KfW was trying to separate the Yugoslavia loans from the other export business. The Kreditanstalt did this not least in anticipation of the establishment of the AKA which was scheduled for 1952. On 10 November 1951, the Bank deutscher Länder granted permission for the separation of the loans and increased the whole credit line to DM 726 million. This enabled the KfW to split the lines in two, one of DM 600 million solely for financially sound export finance and one of DM 126 million for the critical Yugoslavia deal[116].

Just after the KfW had split off the export finance loans from the Yugoslavia loans, new problems arose. On 28 November 1951 the three Allied High Commissioners sent identical letters to Adenauer. The letters said that Yugoslavia was almost insolvent and the High Commissioners hoped

> '... daß sich die Bundesregierung vor Augen halten wird, wie wichtig es für die westlichen Länder im allgemeinen ist, der jugoslawischen Wirtschaft dabei zu helfen, ohne Hilfe von außen stabil und lebensfähig zu werden, und daher Anträge der jugoslawischen Regierung auf Schuldenaufschub verständnissvoll aufnehmen wird.'[117]

---

[113]KfW HA-Prot 10-1, Protokoll zur 19. Sitzung, TOP 4.

[114]KfW HA-VS 29, subfile 'Jugoslawienkredit 126 mio.', note 13 February 1951.

[115]KfW HA-VS 29, letter BdL to KfW, 16 May 1951.

[116]KfW HA-VS 29, subfile '600 mio Rediskontkredit'; *Jb* 1951, p. 69.

[117]DBB HA-B 330/52, Zentralbankratssitzungen, annex to a letter from Schäffer to Bernard, 2 February 1952. '... that the Federal Government is aware of how important it is for the western countries in general to help the Yugoslav economy to become stable and viable without help from outside and that because of this the Yugoslav government's application for debt referral will be treated with sympathy.' (Translation AG).

The High Commissioners' letters were an indication of what might happen if Yugoslavia was not granted an extension to the loans. The plea was a warning that West Germany (and with her all the other western countries) risked not only losing the money already given but also and more seriously, a possible Soviet invasion of Yugoslavia if Tito's experiment failed. The American position was to provide outside help to avoid losing Yugoslavia to any 'help' from the Soviets. The High Commissioners' letters marked the successful end of a year-long campaign by the Yugoslavs. As early as January 1951 they had asked the Americans to intervene on their behalf with the Germans to extend the loans to $40 million and prolong those already given[118].

The Allied request caused problems, even a dilemma, for the Adenauer government. It was essential for the Germans to avoid any kind of disharmony with the Allies because at the time negotiations concerning West German defence contributions were well under way. A straightforward decline of the Allied demand would have upset the Americans and in consequence worsened the German position in those talks. On the other hand, direct governmental involvement or, even worse, a governmental loan had to be avoided at all costs. A loan given by the German government would have had to be discussed in Parliament first, thus bringing the government into a position in which it had to explain not only the reasons for the problems in Yugoslavia but also its own actions[119]. It may just have been acceptable for the Bundestag to pay for the freedom of the POWs by giving loans to Yugoslavia. The fact that those loans were given due to American pressure was certainly not. It would have discredited further chancellor Adenauer as the 'Allies' Chancellor' [120].

In this situation the West German government played for time. After lengthy negotiations with Yugoslav government officials an agreement was reached on 11 June 1952[121]. The outcome of the talks took the Kreditanstalt für Wiederaufbau completely by surprise since it had not been involved in the negotiations. Furthermore, the Board of Managers received word of the agreement only after it was signed and from a member of the BdL directorate. West Germany did extend its loans to Yugoslavia by DM 38 million (approximately $ 9 million), to be repaid by 1955. The BdL was to give another special line of credit to the KfW, amounting

[118]*FRUS*, 1951, vol. IV, part 2, p. 1679.
[119]DBB HA-B 330/52 Zentralbankrats-Sitzungen, Annex to the 113th meeting of the Zentralbankrat, note 28 January 1952 regarding a meeting with Yugoslav officials on 26 January 1952.
[120]This probably most famous remark in modern German parliamentary debate was made by the Social Democrat leader Kurt Schumacher on 25 November 1949 while debating the Petersberg Protocols, see *Bundestagsverhandlungen, 1. Wahlperiode*, 18. Sitzung, p. 525.
[121]KfW HA-VS 10 Otto Neubaur, Vorträge im Verwaltungsrat 1949-1956, note 5 December 1952.

to DM 31 million, or 80 per cent of the sum, bringing the total lent by the KfW to Yugoslavia to DM 157 million[122].

In his immediate answer Herbert Martini told the BdL member that the Kreditanstalt did not want to become involved in any new contract[123]. The KfW had no intention of becoming further entangled in politically motivated loans which were financially so unsound that the AKA had refused them. The KfW's official reaction to its late information was quite a strong one. In a letter to the Economic Ministry the bank complained fiercely about the loan agreement and the way the Kreditanstalt had been drawn into it. The KfW stressed that as a corporation which could act in its own sovereignty (... *eine in eigener Entschließungsfreiheit handelnde Anstalt...*) it regarded the way it was drawn into a new contract without any prior consultation as an 'unfriendly act' by the Ministry. However, in spite of the ministry's improper action, the KfW agreed to participate in the new agreement once more but emphasised that it did so very reluctantly. The KfW managers stressed that they were doing this only to avoid compromising the Ministry of Economics. If similar incidents were to happen again, the KfW would simply refuse to co-operate[124].

In his reply and justification Staatssekretär Westrick stressed once more the political dimension of the whole deal. The new arrangements, he underlined, came about only because of urgent personal intervention by the Allied High Commissioners with Adenauer[125]. As in the previous cases, Adenauer was hardly in a position to refuse their request without threatening his foreign policy.

The Kreditanstalt's objections, however, soon proved justified. By the end of 1953 about DM 100 million out of the DM 157 million were agreed for loans but only 42 million were actually paid out[126]. A mere six months later it had become clear that the Yugoslavs were unable to repay even their reduced loans and that the re-negotiation of the treaty was necessary. In its 21st meeting the *Kreditbewilligungsausschuß* suggested a prolongation of the repayments. The DM 164 million which Yugoslavia wanted to utilise in full was to be paid back in six-month instalments in 1958, 1959 and 1960. The new arrangements also changed some contracts which were due for repayment in cash in 1953 and 1954. Those contracts, amounting to DM 17.5 million, were credited until 1955. The prolongation of the loans also made it necessary to increase German government guarantees for the loans to 95 per cent. However, the deal was still not to the liking

[122]KfW HA-VS 10 Otto Neubaur, Vorträge im Verwaltungsrat 1949-1956, note 5 December 1952; *Jb* 1952, p. 67.
[123]KfW HA-VS 29, subfile 'Jugoslawienkredit, 31 mio', note re. telephone call between Benning and Martini, 11 June 1952.
[124]KfW HA-VS 29, subfile 'Jugoslawienkredit, 31 mio' letter to the Ministry of Economics, 21 June 1952.
[125]Ibid., letter from Westrick to Neubaur, 7 July 1952.
[126]*Jb* 1953, p. 71.

of the KfW executives and the 1955 annual report stated with some surprise that the repayment for the year had duly been fulfilled[127].

1957 witnessed a different blow for German-Yugoslav relations. In spite of the Hallstein Doctrine on 15 October that year Yugoslavia recognised the GDR and established diplomatic relations with East Berlin. Adenauer immediately terminated diplomatic relations with Belgrade[128]. The economic contacts, however, continued. The KfW's 1957 annual report gave, in dry language, the state of the German-Yugoslav loan agreement[129]. At the same time, this is the last mentioning of the deal in the reports, indicating that the repayments which went on until the end of 1960 did not cause any further problem. Furthermore, by 1958 export finance and official loans to other countries had reached such a volume that the loan to Yugoslavia was no longer worth mentioning and the official end to this financial adventure became very much an internal affair. In a letter to the Deutsche Bundesbank, dated 19 January 1961, the KfW confirmed that the last instalment had been repaid by Yugoslavia on time on 31 December 1960[130]. By then the Kreditanstalt was already preparing for its new role as Germany's bank for development aid.

The Indian Example

The most striking similarity between KfW export loans to Yugoslavia and India is the fact that in both cases the Americans had asked for German support. Other than that self-interest played an important role in the German government's decision for action. The most prominent difference is that the KfW's participation began with a loan to a private company which had been contracted by the Indian government. Eventually, KfW aid for exports to India and ultimately direct aid to the Indian government itself was as much motivated by the competition between the capitalist and the socialist system as it was by German foreign policy doctrine. In this way German aid to India is the first major example of how the Federal Government was held at ransom over the Hallstein Doctrine and with the help of the KfW paid in order to sustain its claim for sole representation.

Following the country's independence, the Indian government in 1951 had launched the first five-year plan to modernise the country. It was envisaged that during the second five-year plan a modern steel plant would be built by German companies under the leadership of Krupp near the town of Rurkela. The German government supported the project and had discussed it several times, mainly to

[127]KfW HA-VS 29, Exportfinanzierung, note for the 21st meeting of the Kreditbewilligungsausschuß, 18 June 1954; *Jb* 1954, p. 62; *Jb* 1955, p. 45.
[128]Herbst, 'Option', p.147.
[129]*Jb*. 1957, p. 49.
[130]KfW HA-VS 29, subfile 'Jugoslawienkredit, 121 mio.'.

tackle the problem of how to finance it[131]. The companies involved had not enough cash capital to finance such a big project and the AKA refused to give export loans with a validity over five years. The government therefore agreed by the end of 1954 that the Kreditanstalt in 1958 should receive DM 100 million from the ERP Special Assets to help Krupp finance the project[132].

Between 1954, when the government had authorised KfW money for Krupp and the others, and 1957-8, when it was supposed to be paid out the international political landscape had changed. Soviet policy after Stalin's death with its ideology of self-containment had been replaced by a new strategy of propaganda in, and economic aid towards, Third World countries. This development in world affairs presented India, apart from Yugoslavia the most influential member of the non-aligned movement, with a cheap option to improve its infrastructure and also to demonstrate its independence from the West since India no longer had to rely solely on western aid and technology. As a result of the new Soviet policy, India and the Soviet Union in February 1955 signed a contract for another steel plant, to be constructed by the Soviets at Bhilai[133]. The 1956 Suez Crisis meant another setback for the western containment policy. The French and British invasion of the Suez Canal zone convinced many people in the developing countries that the Europeans still had not given up their colonial attitudes. The USA on the other hand was seen by many as the 'new' colonial power and therefore was not very popular within the non-aligned countries, either. This view was held in particular in India, not least because of America's policy of military alliances which included India's arch-enemy Pakistan. The anti-American attitude changed only for a brief time after the US had stopped the invasion of the Suez Canal zone[134].

These developments made the Americans look for ways to improve their and their allies' standing in the Third World and an opportunity arose when India's second five-year plans ran into financial difficulties in 1957. The Indians were facing a shortage of $930 million in foreign currencies and hoped for help from President Eisenhower who was prepared to set up an international consortium to bail India out. In addition, the Indian government approached Adenauer to help them with a three-year moratorium for West German companies to whom they owed DM 660 million[135]. There were several reasons why Adenauer could not decline the Indian request. First, he would have alienated his friend Eisenhower who had already put considerable pressure on him to participate with DM 168 million ($40 million) in the international bailout package. Since the US Congress

---

[131]Armin Grünbacher, 'Profits and Cold War – Politically Motivated Export Finance in West Germany during the 1950s: Two Case Studies', in: *German Politics*, vol. 10 no. 3 (Dec. 2001), p. 150.
[132]KfW HA-Prot 10-2, Protokoll der 28. Sitzung, TOP 1, TOP 3.
[133]Kaufman, *Trade,* p. 64.
[134]BA B 136/3637, letter by Günter Henle during a trip to East Asia to Chancellor Adenauer, 10 May 1957.
[135]*Jb* 1958, p. 49.

had cut American foreign aid for the 1958 budget by $1 billion to $2.7 billion, the Eisenhower administration depended on the help of its allies to fill the gap. West Germany was to play an important part in American aid planning since the country had no significant colonial past which made it the most suitable country to provide aid without arousing suspicion of political intention of any kind. Furthermore, the experts in Washington expected West Germany, at least in the long run due to the country's economic success, to provide the biggest share in aid second only to the USA[136].

There were other reasons for Germany to follow the American call and participate in the relief effort. The German government was concerned about the financial situation of the German companies involved in trade with India. If India could not repay its debts to them, these companies would face severe financial problems which in turn could lead to strong repercussions for the rest of the economy. Furthermore, since the Soviet Union was building a steel plant in India as well, West German companies and their reputation in plant construction (*Großanlagenbau*) stood in direct competition to Soviet technology and engineering. National prestige dictated that the German plant could not come second to the one the Soviets built. The ultimate reason however, was the Hallstein Doctrine. With the recent experience of Yugoslavia recognising the GDR, Adenauer could not risk that India would take a similar decision. Its high reputation amongst the non-aligned countries and its position as a role model to developing countries could have triggered an avalanche of further recognition of the GDR, thus destroying Bonn's claim for sole representation. The fact that German-Indian negotiations on the deferment of the repayments of the DM 660 million, which after all were private capital, could be completed by the end of February 1958 signifies the importance Adenauer attached to the matter.

Under the agreement the Federal Government asked the German companies involved to accept Indian government promissory notes instead of money payments. The notes with the face value of DM 660 million were valid for three years and could be cashed in by the companies with the Kreditanstalt für Wiederaufbau. For the purpose the KfW had to raise DM 360 million, to which the government provided additional DM 240 million from budget funds of the 1957-60 budgets. For the remaining DM 60 million the government obtained a full moratorium agreement from the companies[137]. Although budget funds were used in the arrangement, it is unlikely that the government became directly involved in it, instead the money was lent to the KfW. In this way a full parliamentary debate on the aid could have been avoided. The statement in the KfW's annual report further supports this theory since it indicates that it was the Kreditanstalt which physically bought the promissory notes.

---

[136]Kaufman, *Trade*, p. 184, Werner Bührer, 'Der BDI und die Außenpolitik der Bundesrepublik Deutschland in den 50er Jahren', in: *VfZ* No. 40 (1992), p. 256.

[137]Politisches Archiv des Auswärtigen Amtes (henceforth quoted PAAA) 411/106, Aufzeichnung des AA für den Handelspolitischen Ausschuß des Bundestages, 9 April 1958.

> '... An der Finanzierung der gestundeten Zahlungen von insgesamt 660 Millionen DM beteiligen wir uns in der Weise, daß wir die den deutschen Lieferanten an Stelle der mit ihren indischen Auftraggebern ursprünglich vereinbarten Zahlungen gegebenen Promissory Notes der indischen Regierung ankaufen.'[138]

To raise its share of money the KfW issued its new bonds, the *Kassenobligationen*, at first in the face value of DM 80 million[139]. The Board of Directors actually had authorised the issue of DM 160 million for this purpose in the first place with a possible increase to DM 250 million if necessary[140]. The first issue was limited to DM 80 million because the KfW did not need all the money at the same time since the German companies redeemed their promissory notes only slowly. The management even had to tell the BoD by the end of 1958 that a large part of the *Kassenobligationen* was not used for the Indian deal. Instead, the money provided for new loans to medium-sized German companies. It was suggested during the board meeting that the remaining part of the DM 250 million that was not to be used for the redemption of the promissory notes should instead be utilised for export finance in general. Former Minister for Housing Preußker, now on the Board as representative of the housing industry, and Finance Minister Etzel at this point sharply criticised the deal with India and the volume it had reached. Erhard's deputy, Staatssekretär Westrick, dismissed the criticism and pointed out the political dimension of the deal. He stressed that the money was needed to cover for otherwise endangered German investments. Abs, in support of Westrick emphasized that the KfW had taken action on the request of the federal government and that the government expected an even larger engagement in the future[141].

The government intervention in the moratorium and West Germany's participation in the international aid package for India was a visible turning point in German foreign aid policy. The basis for the changes had been prepared as early as 1953 when the Economics Ministry had lost the *Außenwirtschaftsabteilung* or Foreign Trade Section to the AA where it had been located traditionally. In contrast to Erhard, who was interested in exports for their own economic sake, the AA and Adenauer himself saw foreign trade as a tool to serve a country's wider political interests. After the overall supervision of foreign trade had been given to the AA in 1956 the India problem had become the test case for the new allocation of responsibilities within the German administration[142].

---

[138]*Jb* 1958, p. 49. 'We participate in financing the deferred payments of DM 660 million in the way that we buy the promissory notes which the Indian government had given to the German suppliers instead of the promised payments'. (Translation AG).
[139]*Jb* 1958, p. 39.
[140]KfW HA-Prot 10-3, Protokoll der 34. Sitzung, TOP 4.
[141]KfW HA-Prot 10-3, Protokoll der 37. Sitzung, TOP 3.
[142]Grünbacher, 'Profits', p. 152.

Despite the decision the BMWi managed to incense the Indian government with an attempt to boost German exports. The Economics Ministry demanded that DM 60 million of the DM 660 million package had to be used as a 20 per cent instalment of new Indian orders to Germany. In other words, India had to buy new goods from Germany worth some DM 300 million just to get a moratorium on its previous debts. Demands like this helped the German export industry but inevitably provoked sharp Indian protests and were dropped eventually. Similar interventions on behalf of the German economy were made by the Bundesministerium für Verkehr (BMVk, Ministry for Transport) which asked the AA to agree that any further loans to India were conditional that at least half of the commodities were shipped on German vessels[143].

Despite these setbacks political relations between India and West Germany remained on a good footing. The situation at the construction site at Rurkela was quite different. Bad organisation and mismanagement had delayed the completion of the plant for several months and the official opening had to be postponed several times. Eventually, the first tap at the steel plant was scheduled for 3 February 1959[144]. Although Krupp finished the plant some days before the Soviets completed theirs and despite the fact that the plant was regarded as the most modern steel plant on the Asian continent, the Germans at best achieved a draw in the propaganda battle. The lack of sufficient numbers of properly trained Indian staff to operate the plant meant that Rurkela never reached its output capacity. The Soviet plant, on the other hand was less sophisticated but did its job much better, even with less well trained personnel. Management failures which were in part to blame for the delays did not improve the German reputation, either. Worst of all, rudeness of German staff, racial segregation on the construction site and even 'master-race' attitudes damaged the German reputation. The Russians on the other hand who were building the plant at Bhilai handled their information policy brilliantly and managed to keep up appearances in the face of the local population[145].

The KfW's involvement in aid to India had begun as a support for private German firms had transformed into a matter of pure trade policy and Cold War strategy. Under pressure from Eisenhower, Adenauer had agreed to participate in the international rescue package by contributing DM 168 million before the end of March 1959, a first instalment of a total German contribution of DM 420 million[146]. An agreement between Germany and India on the matter of these loans was finally signed on 6 January 1959, after the AA had accepted a draft agreement devised by the KfW in autumn 1958. Since there were no funds for foreign loans scheduled in

---

[143]PAAA 411/106, letter by the BMWi to the AA's *Handelspolitische Abteilung*, 7 May 1958; PAAA 411/108, letter BMVk to AA, 17 October 1958.
[144]PAAA 411/108, letter German Embassy in India to AA, 26 January 1959.
[145]*Der Spiegel*, No. 14, 14. Jg. (1960), cover story.
[146]PAAA 411/128, AA note 7 September 1959.

the federal budget, the government had to rely once more on the good services of the KfW to raise the money[147].

Then, in May 1959, just three months after the opening of the Rurkela plant the Indian Trade Attaché asked for more German money. He explained that the third five-year plan had a volume of DM 88 billion as compared to DM 63 billion for the second plan. To achieve it India estimated the need for foreign currencies to be DM 15 billion and expected especially German aid to cover the shortfall. The Attaché pointed out that 28 per cent of India's total trade deficit, DM 1 billion per year, was due to its trade with West Germany. If the deficit remained at such a high level, India would expect German loans in the volume of DM 2 to 2.5 billion to balance its books. Otherwise they would be forced to introduce trade restrictions which could cost Germany up to DM 1 billion in lost exports[148]. This warning helped the Germans to increase their efforts to find funds for the second tranche of DM 126 million ($30 million) under the multinational agreement after the KfW had ruled out the possibility of raising the whole sum all by itself as the government had expected. An agreement was reached only in spring 1960 after the KfW received additional funds from the *ERP Sondervermögen.* Only now was the Kreditanstalt prepared to raise the missing DM 70 million on the market[149].

Parallel to its negotiations with Germany, India since late 1957 and early 1958 had been in loan negotiations with several other countries which raised the fear in Bonn that parts of the Indian market could be lost in the long-run if they did not lend a helping hand. But before the Germans could reach an agreement with India the government in New Delhi had already begun negotiations with the Soviet Union on a loan of 1.8 billion Rupees, or DM 1 billion[150]. Although it is most likely that this was just an expression of Indian independence, or at worst, a sign of see-saw policy, it alarmed Bonn. There was always the risk that the Soviet Union would ask for political favours in return for favourable loans and the Federal Republic acted with various means including unofficial warnings, towards India. In one such case Klaus Mehnert, an influential conservative political scientist, writer, and commentator with excellent knowledge of and contacts in the Soviet Union, met with the Indian Permanent Secretary of State for Foreign Affairs. Mehnert made it quite clear that he and many other influential people in Germany would press for the termination of diplomatic and even of economic relations between both countries if India was to recognise the GDR. He stressed that he and his political friends were prepared to accept, for the sake of the political principle, the economic

---

[147]PAAA 411/108, KfW letter to the AA, 8 October 1958; copy of the treaty, signed 6 January 1959; *Jb* 1958, pp. 49 f.

[148]PAAA 411/128, letter by BMWi to various ministries and the KfW regarding meeting with the Indian Trade Attaché, 13 May 1959.

[149]KfW HA-Prot 10-3, Protokoll der 39. Sitzung, TOP 3; Protokoll der 40. Sitzung, TOP 5. No reason is given why the KfW did not take on the commitment in the first place.

[150]PAAA 411/106, passim, and various press articles on India's negotiations; PAAA 411/128 letter by the German Embassy in India to AA, 15 September 1959.

disadvantages such a step would bring for West Germany[151]. It is difficult to say whether comments like this prevented India from recognising the GDR at the time or if India was aware of the long-term negative effects of such a step. After all, the reliance on western technology and economic strength was an important building block in the country's drive for modernisation and not easily forsaken in a demonstration of political independence. The comments showed the Indian authorities that there were influential pressure groups within the German public which would have demanded the implementation of the Hallstein Doctrine if India did indeed recognise the GDR. Mehnert made it clear to the Indians that there was not only the German government's reaction to be considered if they, or for that matter, any other country, had any intention of taking up diplomatic relations with the GDR. The existence of powerful conservative pressure groups made the implementation of the Hallstein Doctrine and even economic sanctions more likely.

Despite this, the Germans must have perceived a remaining risk, however small, that India would recognise the GDR. Therefore Adenauer's negotiating position vis-á-vis India was in some respect worse than that of India. Although such a step appeared unlikely, there remained always the possibility that India might take up diplomatic relations with East Berlin because of Soviet presure or out of an irrational step by the government in Delhi to demonstrate its independence from the major ideological camps. Consequently, the West Germans had to keep India 'happy' by providing the requested loans and development aid projects. But it appears that until the end of 1961 Bonn was only committed to interest protection in the way that it was reacting to Indian requests (and increasingly those of other countries). Such behaviour instead of an active forward-looking policy in the face of Soviet activities in the Third World provoked strong American criticism. From at least mid-1959 onward President Eisenhower had tried to start a new economic offensive against the Soviet Union in Third World countries for which he needed West German money[152]. US attempts to gain German support and money went on all through 1960 and reached its climax in October that year with a personal letter by Eisenhower to Adenauer. Although Adenauer in his reply made no commitments at all, hardly referring to the matter, West Germany's engagement in development aid projects increased considerably[153]. By the end of 1961 loans for this purpose had reached DM 2.3 billion (some $548 million) with another half billion available. Of the money already lent, more than half, DM 1.2 billion, had been given to India[154]. These loans were also used by West Germany to help reduce the massive balance of payment surplus the country had acquired because of its export-led economy.

---

[151]BA B 136/3637, letter by the CDU/CSU Fraktion to Adenauer, 16 January 1960, attached Mehnert's report on the meeting.

[152]See, for example FRUS 1958-60, vol. VII, part I, pp. 196 f., memorandum of conversation between US Undersecretary of State, Dillon, and Chancellor Adenauer, 10 December 1959.

[153] FRUS 1958-60, vol. IX, pp. 666 f., 674 f., 692 ff.

[154] KfW HA Prot 10-3, Protokoll der 43. Sitzung, Anlage 1.

By the end of 1961 the KfW had provided the last tranche of Germany's share of the multinational aid package for India. By that time the Kreditanstalt's development aid credits amounted to DM 2.3 billion of which DM 1.2 billion had gone to India for new loans or refunding old ones[155]. By then three facts had become clear: first, if the West German government wanted to sustain its claim of sole representation, which they did until there was a change in government in 1969, they had to be prepared to pay for it. In other words, they had become the prime target for political blackmail. They paid for projects in Third World countries although those were sometimes useless or even a foolish waste of money, such as provisions in countries' infrastructure which went well beyond their needs. It proved to be an expensive way to keep the Hallstein Doctrine in place but no other state except Cuba, in 1963, recognised the GDR[156]. Secondly, in the process the KfW had once more proved itself to be the long arm of the government. As in other cases before, the Kreditanstalt raised loans when the BdL, since 1957 the Bundesbank, refused to provide the necessary funds[157]. And of course, the KfW could act on behalf of the government in a way which de facto bypassed Parliament in budget matters. Finally, it had become increasingly evident that the country's trade surplus began to show negative effects like revaluation pressure and that these had to be countered by capital export. Political considerations in the ongoing Cold War now fully combined with new German economic needs as well as the drive for exports. Development aid on a new, larger scale would be the answer to these issues.

[155]KfW HA-Prot 10-3, Protokoll der 43. Sitzung, Anlage 1.
[156]Spanger, Brock, *Staaten*, p. 287.
[157]PAAA 411/106, letter by the Deutsche Bundesbank to the AA, 26 March 1958.

Chapter 11

Towards the Development Aid Bank and Beyond

The experiences drawn from the Kreditanstalt für Wiederaufbau's involvement in export finance and loans to India, both in terms of Cold War politics and financial requirement, called for an amendment and update of the existing laws. The changes in the wider political and economic situation in the second half of the 1950s necessitated such a move as well. In too many fields the KfW was operating, at best, in legal no-mans-land while at the same time the government began looking for a way to reduce the country's ever-growing foreign currency surplus. Both of these requirements would lead to the KfW's establishment as West Germany's development aid bank in 1961. In the process a number of changes in the political administration were made which would have an impact on the KfW's day-to-day running. And, of course, the bank's operational remit was widened in order to give it more freedom when taking on new tasks for the government.

Technical Assistance and Economic and Political Requirements

Although the discussion within the ministerial bureaucracy about large-scale development aid or the establishment of a special bank for such a purpose began in earnest only in 1958, aid had been given long before. Under the term 'Technical Assistance' the Economics Ministry had provided DM 500,000 per annum from the *ERP Sondervermögen* since 1953[1]. Of course, DM 500,000 was not a great deal of money to make available on the spot aid for several countries. Indeed, the funds were not used to support any projects in the developing world but merely to finance business trips for German company representatives to those countries in order to negotiate export deals and explore future business opportunities. Even for this relevant small brief the funds were not enough and in 1955 the sum was increased to DM 700,000 and even further in 1956. Now DM 3.5 million were included in the Economic Ministry's budget for classic export finance and a further DM 2 million for the Ministry of Economic Co-operation, the former Marshall Plan

[1]Spanger, Brock, *Staaten,* p. 279.

Ministry, in order to pay for experts' travels[2]. As already stated, the BMWi saw the technical assistance in the first place as a long term means of boosting West German foreign trade and not so much as an instrument of politics. The view on the matter within the AA was quite the opposite. The AA certainly acknowledged that technical assistance could help to improve exports but the main reason why aid was given was to facilitate propaganda for West Germany and its political position vis-à-vis the GDR and the Soviet Union. This view was confirmed by an internal AA memorandum, *Grundsätze für die Verausgabung des Fonds*, which dealt with the fundamental questions of development aid against the background of the Soviet economic expansion, which was yet again stressed as a threat to the West[3].

1956 saw the final victory for the AA over the BMWi in the struggle of who controlled foreign aid and with it a big increase in the AA's budget. It was a clear signal that from now on foreign policy had priority over economic policy. The East-West conflict and ideological and political competition with the GDR were one strong reason for Adenauer to decide in such a way, not least because this competition was fought increasingly on a worldwide scale. But there were domestic reasons as well. Chancellor Adenauer had been his own Foreign Minister until June 1955. In setting the priorities as he did and at the same time providing the AA with an additional fund of DM 50 million annually for technical aid he strengthened further the position of the new Foreign Minister, Heinrich von Brentano[4]. At the same time he undermined the position of his most likely successor as Chancellor, Erhard, by reducing the latter's political portfolio.

Nevertheless, by the mid-1950s KfW's complete programme of export finance and by and large its technical aid had the sole purpose of supporting German exports and delivering propaganda; real aid to Third World countries was at best a positive side effect. This is clear from an article by Herbert Martini in the AA's journal *Germany* on the advantages of the KfW's involvement in exports to developing countries. From today's point of view, the article appears to be somewhat patronising and cynical in the way that Martini stressed the advantage developing countries could gain from the KfW's export finance. They did not have to bother themselves with any detail of the contract[5]. They only had to pick up the bill. The article's underlying message is that development aid in the mid-1950s had to develop the German economy, not the developing country.

Following the general trend, project financing became more and more politicised as the example of the construction of Egypt's Aswan High Dam shows. The Kreditanstalt's considerations on the project were based on the facts that the Federal Government regarded the venture as one of the highest priority on grounds

---

[2] PAAA 400/12, note by Referat 400 on 'Wirtschaftliche Unterstützung unterentwickelter Gebiete', 18 February 1956; BMWi survey 'Technische Hilfeleistung der Bundesrepublik Deutschland', 1 September 1956.

[3] PAAA 400/12, undated draft, but written after the Suez Crisis.

[4] Spanger, Brock, *Staaten*, pp. 279, 282.

[5] PAAA 400/12, undated manuscript by Herbert Martini on export financing.

of trade and general policy. With the loans for the dam, West Germany would have been able to regain some political ground in Egypt after the Federal Republic previously had signed the Compensation Agreement with Israel. Therefore the government was prepared to abandon other lucrative plans for export financing. The administration's political interest had to be transformed into federal loan guarantees and a declaration that the political risk could be accepted[6].

In order to establish a financial basis for any (political) export financing, the KfW in 1957 suggested the establishment of a revolving fund for that purpose. It was proposed that over a period of five years, starting from 1958, a DM 250 million fund should be established by redirecting interest payments from ERP Special Assets loans. The fund should be used in particular to finance exports to politically important developing countries[7]. The KfW's suggestion went well beyond any previous plans and announcements by the BMZ. The ministry had planned on the basis of DM 50 million from 1958-60 interest and repayments on ERP loans[8].

In 1958 the USA experienced a drain of its gold reserves amounting to nearly $2 billion[9]. Partly as a result of this the major European currencies were in a position to introduce full convertibility of their currencies by the end of the year. The booming export market allowed the Federal Republic to achieve a trade surplus of DM 5 billion. Although West Germany had to repay its debts under the London Debt Agreement amounting to a total of DM 14 billion and made contributions to Israel also in the order of several billion as compensation for the holocaust, the country in 1960 had a surplus in gold and foreign currencies amounting to DM 32.8 billion[10]. With such an impressive economic performance the DM immediately came under revaluation pressure. However, a revaluation of the DM would have increased the prices for German exports and resulting from this, perhaps a decline in their volume altogether so that this solution was fiercely opposed *in uniso* by the BDI and Abs[11]. When the revaluation finally took place in March 1961 the BDI suspended its monthly donations of DM 100,000 to the CDU out of political protest and disappointment[12]. The decision to revaluate had not been taken lightly and there had been many proposals of how to avoid it. One way to keep the rise of capital surplus in check was to redirect internal investments away from 'productive' sectors such as investment goods industry into export neutral ones such as mining or agriculture. Spending money on the infrastructure such as road construction or water supply and social investments in schools and

[6]KfW HA-BA 80, memorandum by the KfW, 4 March 1955.
[7]PAAA 407/32, KfW letter to BMZ (copy) dated 6 August 1957.
[8]Ibid., BMZ letter to various ministries and the KfW, 11 July 1957.
[9]Kaufman, *Trade*, p. 177.
[10]Buchheim, *Wiedereingliederung*, pp. 166 ff, esp. p. 170; Bundesbank (eds), *40 Jahre Deutsche Mark*, pp. 4 f.; Abelshauser, *Wirtschaftsgeschichte*, pp. 155 ff.
[11]Harries, *Wiederaufbau*, p. 65.
[12]Braunthal, *Federation*, p. 200.

hospitals had a similar effect and was done as well. But it was still not enough and a feasible alternative, large-scale capital export in the form of development aid, had to be pursued[13].

The Kreditanstalt für Wiederaufbau from about 1957-58 onwards became the first and until the late 1960s the only bank in Germany to be concerned with capital export. The long term refinancing of India's debts was one of the ways the KfW conducted this task. In 1959 the KfW developed a new method in co-operation with the relevant ministry. The traditional way of financing exports had been the so-called *Lieferantenkredite* (supplier loans), given to the German export companies by the banks. These loans had the major disadvantage of inflating the firms' balance sheets so that they had difficulties finding outside money for other purposes, especially when the *Lieferantenkredite* were for crucial loans with a validity of more than five years. To avoid this handicap, the Kreditanstalt switched to *Bestellerkredite* (customer loans)[14]. These loans were contract bound credits, that is, they were given to customers to enable them to buy German goods which had been specified beforehand in the loan agreement. Although lending for such a purpose was not sanctioned by the KfW law, more than 50 per cent of the money confirmed for export finance in 1960 were customer loans, a situation which increased the pressure for a change in the law[15].

Although the KfW's activities in capital export of various kinds increased considerably up to 1960 it was by far not enough to balance the faster expansion of the trade surplus which in turn fostered speculations about the revaluation of the Deutschmark. At the same time the German government came under increased pressure from the Americans to expand its share in the 'economic defence' of the West[16]. But with the budget already under a heavy strain from rearmament, debt repayment and the German support for the Allies' costs in stationing troops in the Federal Republic it was difficult to find an adequate source for the money. Even tax increases were considered to finance the foreign aid although only as a last resort[17]. When industrialists, business leaders and banking representatives saw themselves confronted with the possibility of tax increases or revaluation of the DM, they did not like either option and in a bid to avoid both they came up with the idea of a voluntary loan by the business community of DM 1-1.5 billion. Despite the bad experience with the AIL, banks, insurance, and most of all, industry itself did indeed raise DM 1.2 billion without any compulsion, just through urgent pleas by the top associations[18]. This so-called *Entwicklungsanleihe* (development loan) became better known as *Blessing Milliarde*, named after former industrialist turned head of the Bundesbank, Karl Blessing. Similar to the case of the AIL, the BDI in

[13]Hankel, *Kapitalverteilung*, pp. 98 ff., 105 ff.
[14]Harries, *Wiederaufbau*, pp. 59 f.; Hankel, *Kapitalverteilung*, pp. 106 ff.
[15]Harries, *Wiederaufbau*, p. 60.
[16]Spanger, Brock, *Staaten*, p. 277.
[17]BA B 102/25352, Vermerk über Resortbesprechung, 25 May 1960.
[18]Adamsen, *Investitionshilfe*, p. 21.

particular was not prepared to hand over the money to the government for fear it could disappear in the normal budget. Instead they wanted the funds to go directly to the KfW on the condition that industry would get a bigger say within the bank's Board of Directors[19].

Soon the industrialists' had to realise that they would fail in their attempt to prevent the revaluation of the DM and they began negotiations with the government on how the *Blessing Miliarde* was to be utilised. The talks went on until after the revaluation took place. On 21 March and 28 April 1961 respectively the BMF and the KfW finally signed the contract permitting the latter to borrow from the *Blessing Milliarde* for use in development aid finance[20]. By the end of the year the fund made up more than 40 per cent of the KfW's commitment in development finance and enabled it to lend on a large scale before already scheduled federal funds actually became available[21].

Yugoslavia's recognition of the GDR had considerably increased the pressure on the Adenauer government in terms of foreign policy. More money for Third World countries had to be provided to buy their political friendships so that West Germany's claim for sole representation of Germany could be sustained although it took some time to raise funds and set up a programme. In 1958 the pressure had been further increased by the Americans who demanded German aid to satisfy their own political aims. Already a year before when Congress had cut back US foreign aid by $1 billion, the Eisenhower administration began to look for help in Europe for its 'economic defence programme'. In a statement on US policy towards Germany the US National Security Council was highly critical of West Germany. Washington disapproved in particular of Germany's limited interest in the developing countries which saw them only as a platform for export expansion. The lack of significant long-term lending and aid policy by the Federal Republic was also criticised, although it was conceded that greater willingness to expand credits abroad had been demonstrated recently, including $2 million for Iceland which were channelled through NATO. Of course, the military nature of the aid was not mentioned in the KfW's Annual Report, which speaks of a loan to finance investments for the Icelandic economy[22].

Nevertheless, in the second half of 1958 the State Department felt that little progress had been made in convincing Adenauer to use public funds for development aid and continued its complaints about Germany's apparent narrow interests on exports only[23]. But at the time there were actually only limited public resources in Germany. The introduction of a dynamic pension system in 1957 together with other 'election gifts', the green plan and not at least the ongoing

---

[19]BA B 102/25352, internal BMWi letter by Abteilung VI to Minister Erhard and the Staatssekretär, 21 September 1960.
[20]PAAA 403/275 copy of the signed treaty.
[21]KfW HA-Prot 10-3, Protokoll der 43. Sitzung, Anlage 1.
[22]*FRUS* 1958-60, vol. IX, pp. 631 ff, here pp. 640 f.; *Jb* 1958, p. 49.
[23]*FRUS* 1958-60, vol. IX, pp. 649 ff.

rearmament had plundered the *Julius Turm* that had been built up by Finance Minister Schäffer prior to his demotion to Justice Minister[24]. It was the events in Cuba in 1959 which helped to change the Germans' mind. Following Castro's takeover of power on the island, the Americans came up with the idea of German financial aid to Third World countries of DM 3-4 billion per year, in order to help prevent a similar experience elsewhere. While events in the Caribbean might also have had an influence raising the *Blessing Milliarde*, the German government in principle agreed to support US global policy financially but it took two more years to find a solution the size of which satisfied the USA[25].

American eagerness to take West Germany as a non- colonial power along its own foreign economic policy was evident again in 1960, first when Adenauer in March that year visited Washington and later in October when Eisenhower wrote a personal letter to the Chancellor. The US President, as in his previous visit to Bonn in August 1959 asked Adenauer for more aid to underdeveloped countries. Adenauer tried to evade the point although the legal process for the establishment of a development aid bank was already under way. He agreed to and stressed the need of using aid more as a political tool instead of just providing humanitarian aid. But beyond this he was not prepared to put any figures to a German commitment. The story was similar when the two Foreign Ministers met the same day. Secretary of State Christian Herter pointed out that although there were considerable private German investments in developing countries, public funds still lagged well behind those of France and Britain, in spite of their recent increase. Foreign Minister Brentano, too, used delaying tactics and referred to ongoing planning in Germany. Adenauer's reaction to Eisenhower's personal letter in October 1960 was perhaps even more disappointing for the Americans. The US President referred to Marshall aid which he contrasted to the present drain of US currency reserves, of which the Federal Republic was one of the greatest beneficiaries, but Adenauer's reply was mainly concerned with German internal affairs and on the ongoing German election campaign[26].

Despite Adenauer's hesitation there was progress behind the scenes, not least because the various German ministries had their own reasons to support the establishment of a development aid bank. And thanks to the inter-ministerial rivalry each ministry tried to get its say in, and influence on, the proposed bank as soon as its establishment was on the cards. Karl-Heinz Sohn, Staatssekretär in the newly established Ministry for Economic Co-operation as the Development Aid Ministry was called[27], commented about the situation in 1961:

---

[24]The term which describes the revenue surpluses accumulated by Schäffer to finance the expected rearmament of West Germany derives from a tower in the Spandau Citadell, where the Prussian war treasure used to be kept.

[25]Spanger, Brock, *Staaten*, pp. 279 f.; Adamsen, *Investitionshilfe*, p. 21.

[26]*FRUS* 1958-60, vol. IX, pp. 666 f.; pp. 674 f.; pp. 692 ff.

[27] The 'old' BMZ from 1953-57 received its name from the English translation of 'Economic Co-operation' from the Bilateral Treaty to show the continuation of its work after the Marshall Plan had expired. The task of the 'new' Bundesministerium für

> Das Auswärtige Amt benutzte sie, um der Hallstein Doktrin Nachdruck zu verleihen; das Wirtschaftsministerium sah in der Kapitalhilfe ein zusätzliches Instrument der Exportfinanzierung. Das Landwirtschaftsministerium wiederum versuchte, Agrarüberschüsse als Entwicklungshilfe loszuwerden, ... das Presse- und Informations-amt der Bundesregierung sah in der Entwicklungshilfe ein vorzügliches Propagandainstrument, um über Rundfunk- und Fernsehprojekte deutsche Politik in der Dritten Welt zu verkaufen. Das Bundesverkehrsministerium wurde aktiv, wenn die deutsche Schiffahrt ... bedroht schien.[28]

The Kreditanstalt was to play a role in financing projects abroad which grew more and more in size and significance. The increase of loans to foreign countries or foreign companies which doubled to more than DM 2 billion in 1958-59 also made it inevitable that the KfW's work was put on a new legal basis. By mid-1961, when the development aid bill was finally passed, the KfW was engaged, among others, in projects in Mexico, the Sudan, Pakistan, Chile, Spain, and Guinea[29]. A loan to Liberia of DM 208 million as part of a US-Swedish consortium was given by the KfW as the first credit purely motivated by commercial interests. Even the federal government was only informed about the deal when it was asked to guarantee the loan under the Hermes scheme, which of course, caused some serious trouble for the KfW[30].

Three main aspects have been identified which led to the establishment of the Kreditanstalt für Wiederaufbau as development aid bank. On the economic side Germany's growing foreign currency reserves caused pressure to revaluate the DM and, in order to avoid this, the need for large-scale capital export. The first political reason to establish a bank for development finance was US pressure on Germany to support American global policy and the western defence with economic means at a time when the Soviet Union had started an economic and propaganda offensive in Third World countries. The second political reason was West Germany's own foreign policy doctrine. It made inevitable the creation of an institution with which

---

wirtschaftliche Zusammenarbeit was to establish a real co-operation with, and help to, developing countries.

[28]Karl-Heiz Sohn, *Entwicklungspolitik. Theorie und Praxis der deutschen Entwicklungshilfe*, München 1973, (2nd edn), p. 21. 'The Auswärtiges Amt used it to give vigorous effect to the Hallstein Doctrine; the Economics Ministry regarded financial aid as an additional instrument for export-finance. The Agricultural Ministry tried to get rid of agricultural surpluses as developing aid ... the Federal Government's Press and Information Office regarded development aid as a perfect propaganda instrument to sell German politics in the Third World with the help of radio and television projects. The Ministry for Transport became active when German shipping seemed to be under threat'. (Translation AG).

[29] *Jb* 1960, pp. 57 ff.

[30] Harries, *Wiederaufbau*, pp. 61 f.

the government was able to pay the 'ransom' to Third World countries in the form of development aid without having to ask Parliament's permission for funds each time. Aid to India is a striking example of this. At the same time, development projects and development aid were used as an additional weapon in Cold War propaganda in developing countries. It is therefore clear that, although economic matters played a role, the decision to establish a development aid bank was first and foremost a decision with roots in German foreign and domestic policy.

The Legislative Process

While some of the most important changes of the 1961 amendment of the KfW law have already been discussed in Chapter 2, here a closer look is taken at how these changes had come about in their political context and what importance the *Entwicklungshilfegesetz* (Development Aid Law) had for the KfW's work[31].

Apparently, it was the AA which started to think about a change of the 1951 KfW law. A draft from 24 January 1959 already featured the new and extended task of the Kreditanstalt very much as it would be cast in law two and a half years later[32]. Not surprisingly it was the AA which took the lead in the legislative process since it was the ministry in charge of foreign trade policy and foreign aid and at the same time the one which would benefit most from the bank's new tasks. The AA would get a seat on the KfW's Board of Directors from where it had a better and more direct influence on financial decisions necessary to support the Hallstein Doctrine. When the Finance Ministry as the body which ultimately had to supply the funds for the new task, began to work on the matter, it was stressed that an amendment of the old KfW law was overdue in order to cover legally all the new tasks the Kreditanstalt had taken on in the second half of the 1950s. Obviously, the BMF's intentions were different from those of the AA. Their prime concern was to strengthen the influence of the Federal Government on the BoD vis-à-vis the *Länder* and the Trade Unions. If the latter's presence on the board could be reduced or even eliminated, the KfW's transformation into the sole instrument of government economic and foreign policy would be much easier. This last objective was to be achieved with the introduction of some new far reaching clauses which would allow the bank to intervene whenever a deal seemed beneficial to West Germany in economic or political terms[33]. Erhard and his Economics Ministry on the other hand seemed to have been mainly concerned with the problem of how to find more money which could be used for the increase of exports. The reduction of

[31] *BGBl* 1961 (II), pp 577 f.
[32] PAAA 403/275, changes to the KfW law, 24 January 1959, copy.
[33] BA B 126/7451, note by Referat VA 3 to the Finance Minister, 6 August 1959.

Länder and Trade Union influence played only a minor role in their considerations[34].

There were three major problems facing the ministries involved in the preparation of the new law. The most important one was how and from where to raise the expected large sums of money needed for the task. Budget funds could be expected only on a small scale, for the federal budget was, as usual, under strain. Another matter concerned the KfW's basic capital, as the original DM 1 million simply had become totally insufficient for the expected increase in the bank's balance sheet. The question was therefore by how much the basic capital should be increased and from where the money would come. The third problem concerned the ownership and the balance between the federal and *Länder* institutions. Should the *Länder* be allowed any say on the new BoD at all and if so to what extent? One obvious solution for the funding problem was to rely once more on the ERP Special Assets. Although it was hardly possible to cover all expected requirements with the Special Assets they could provide a large proportion of the development fund. Hermann Lindrath, Minister für den wirtschaftlichen Besitz des Bundes (BMBes, Minister for Federal Commercial Assets) agreed to increase Special Assets funds for export finance to developing countries from the previously promised DM 260 million to DM 600 million. However, the money would be provided only in instalments over a ten-year period. To raise additional funds, Erhard proposed to Finance Minister Franz Etzel the utilisation of DM 600-800 million of the expected proceeds from the ongoing sale of the hitherto state owned Volkswagen (VW) company. The money should be lent to the ERP Special Assets which then in turn could lend it to the KfW. In this way the government would have remained the owner of the funds. During the last days of 1959 and the first weeks of 1960 the prospects of utilising ERP money or VW proceeds diminished. During a meeting of the BMWi's heads of sections it became clear that while the KfW's capital requirements for exports and development finance were going to exceed the expected DM 1 billion, the situation on the capital markets had taken a turn for the worse. It had also become doubtful whether the now expected DM 400 million from the VW sale would become available. The situation seemed so serious that Abs felt it necessary to write to Adenauer personally to ask for all cuts in funding to be prevented[35].

The increased financial demands for the KfW and the need to establish a large fund for development aid made inevitable the introduction of a new bill, the *ERP-Entwicklungshilfegesetz*, to secure the financial basis[36]. A draft bill took

[34]BA B 102/25351, passim. The name of the file 'Entwicklungsfond für Refinanzierungen' (Development Fund for Refinance) underlined these intentions.

[35] BA B 102/25351, BMB letter to various ministries, 15 December 1959; letter by Erhard to Etzel, 13 November 1959; BMWi note on a 'Resortbesprechung' on 22 February 1960; letter by Abs to Adenauer, 26 January 1960.

[36]*BGBl* 1961(II), p. 577 f., 'Gesetz über die Finanzierungshilfe für Entwicklungsländer aus Mitteln des ERP-Sondervermögens'.

account of Abs's demand for more money and allowed DM 1.5 billion to be spent for aid to developing countries. Two-thirds would be provided from the ERP Special Assets, the rest would be covered with the proceeds of the VW sale. A previous BMWi draft had partly followed the proposals made by Lindrath, suggesting that the Special Assets would provide annual instalments for the development fund until 1966. The proposed utilisation of VW proceeds, on the other hand should only happen indirectly by borrowing the necessary amounts from the VW Foundation[37]. These essential points appeared eventually in the ERP Development Aid Law but a contract with the VW Foundation regarding borrowing was signed only in September 1963, two years after the law had been passed[38].

To enact the Development Aid Law and to avoid a violation of other regulations, further legal amendment of the ERP Administrative Law was necessary. This happened together with the introduction of a corresponding clause in the Development Aid Law. Although it was stated neither in the Development Aid Law nor in the new KfW Law, all development aid funds were handled by the Kreditanstalt[39]. While the political debate on how to raise funds was going on, the KfW itself in April 1960 demanded money from the budget for development aid[40]. For this demand the BoD found allies within the Economics Ministry. Erhard's experts asked the minister to call for DM 800 million for development aid in the 1961 budget. The request was justified, they argued, on the grounds that '... development aid has at least the same priority as rearmaments ...'[41]. It was another attempt by the BMWi to take advantage of the geopolitical situation in order to receive more funds for export finance. This contrasts with the BMWi's inability throughout the 1960s to provide proper guidelines on what principles development aid should be given[42]. There was only one internal ministerial paper which stressed that control of all development aid should be with the federal government regardless of whether it was funded from ERP sources or the KfW. In order to achieve overall control and efficiency, better co-operation between government agencies and the KfW was necessary. The BMWi experts suggested giving the KfW's Board of Directors an advisory capacity on the inter-ministerial committee on development aid but at the same time strengthening the government's position on the BoD with a seat for the Foreign Minister. Furthermore, a new committee for the approval of development aid loans (*Kreditbewilligungsausschuß für Entwicklungshilfe*) should be established in which the ministries had a majority[43]. To counter such far-reaching demands, the Kreditanstalt announced its own

[37]BA B 102/25352, draft bill, 11 May 1960; draft bill, 29 April 1960.
[38]Becker, *ERP*, p. 62.
[39]Becker, *ERP*, pp. 60 ff.; also for all legal details.
[40]KfW HA-Prot 10-3, Protokoll der 40. Sitzung, TOP 3.
[41]BA B 102/25352, letter by Abteilung VI to Erhard, 23 June 1960; the quote is underlined in the original.
[42]KfW HA-Prot 10-3, Protokoll der 41. Sitzung, TOP 2.
[43]BA B 102/25352, note by Abteilung VI, 'Vorschläge beim Verfahren bei der bilateralen Finanzhilfe für Entwicklungsländer', 1 September 1960.

principles for development aid during its first BoD meeting in 1961. The KfW managers suggested raising most of the necessary funds on the capital market but they insisted on full control of the financial and banking aspects of any loan in an attempt to limit the government's control over their business. At the same time such a solution would have turned the available state funds into an emergency reserve. The KfW managers happily conceded the political decisions which countries and which projects would be supported to the government. In doing so the KfW made it clear that they continued to regard themselves only as a governmental tool in economic and political affairs[44].

The question of how to finance development aid and what kind of responsibilities the Kreditanstalt would have in the process was settled by mid-1960[45], the matter of company capital and *Länder* participation proved more difficult to settle. The first AA draft for an amendment of the KfW Law in early 1959 did not tackle the question of company capital and it therefore remained at DM 1 million. The BMF was apparently the first to suggest a capital increase[46]. Then, in December 1959 during a meeting of the BMWi's section heads, a full scale reform of the KfW Law including capital and board membership was proposed within the framework of development aid. The viable argument was that since most funds came from federal sources, the federal government should have more influence than the *Länder*. Herbert Martini who was present at the meeting suggested for this reason to declare the famous DM 94 million plus the interest they had yielded up to the end of 1958, DM 54.3 million, a federal asset, thus changing the financial balance in favour of the federal government. Already three days later Martini's idea had been picked up by the BMWi but more as a means of exerting pressure on the Länder. If they did not agree to a reform of the Kreditanstalt law in the way Bonn wanted it, the abolition of the KfW and its subsequent re-establishment as a federal institute would be considered[47]. However, it soon became obvious that Erhard did not regard the exclusion of the *Länder* as a serious option. During a ministers' meeting the increase of the KfW's *Grundkapital* to DM 150 million by transforming the DM 94 million plus interests was on the agenda. But the Economics Ministry did not like a suggestion by the BMF which proposed to pay off the *Länder* with three times their initial capital[48]. To Erhard, *Länder* with strong export industries were natural allies in his pursuit to increase exports with the help of a newly shaped Kreditanstalt für Wiederaufbau. The ministerial meeting did at least help to settle the legal status of the DM 94 million. According to the

---

[44]KfW HA-Prot 10.3, Protokoll der 42. Sitzung, TOP 3.

[45]See Becker, *ERP*, p. 63.

[46]PAAA 403/275, changes to the KfW law, 24 January 1959, copy; BA B 126/7451, note by Referat VA 3 to Finance Minister, 6 August 1959.

[47]BA B 102/25351, note on a 'Resortbesprechung' regarding Finanzhilfe für Entwicklungsländer on 19 December 1959, TOP 3; draft letter by the BMWi to various ministries, 22 December 1959.

[48]Ibid., note by Abteilung VI, 6 January 1960 on the scheduled meeting on 7 January 1960.

KfW they were not federal assets but KfW capital. Only in the case of the Kreditanstalt's dissolution were the federal agencies entitled to claim it first[49]. Of course, when federal representatives met with their Länder colleagues, the latter strongly denied the federal claim on the 94 million and demanded a 50:50 split. But since the Länder had different opinions on the usefulness of a development aid bank, the BMWi saw a possibility for compromise. Especially export-driven Baden-Württemberg and North Rhine-Westphalia were interested in the project and even favoured an increase of their own capital to a quarter or a third of the total[50]. Three weeks later it was decided at the highest levels that the *Länder* should remain on the KfW's supervisory board. The fact that the KfW was designated to continue financing domestic projects as well was the main reason for this decision[51].

In due course a compromise was reached on the question of the DM 94 million and on the company capital. The interest yielded on the money, by the end of 1960 some DM 63 million, was to be shared between both parties while the federal government could claim the DM 94 million. The paid-in basic capital was to be increased to DM 150 million, of which DM 30 million had to be provided by the *Länder*. It was agreed that there should be a further but only nominal increase that is, the money had not actually to be paid in. A very important accord was reached on any future profits and reserves respectively. The decision was taken that no proceeds would be paid out. Instead all profits were to be used *ad infinitum* to set up two reserve funds consisting of a *ordentliche Reserve* (normal reserve) of DM 150 million and once this amount was reached a *Spezialreserve* (special reserve) into which all additional profits should go[52]. The special reserve was devised to cover any loss the federal government might suffer as a result of development aid projects. It is therefore very likely that the clause was introduced after a meeting of bankers and KfW representatives with officials of the Economics Ministry after the banks had previously complained that the federal guarantees for export deals were not big enough[53].

On 10 February 1961, Fritz Schäffer as Minister for Justice acting on behalf of the Chancellor, sent the cabinet draft bill of the new KfW Law to the *Bundesrat*, the second chamber, to start parliamentary consultations on the bill[54]. Despite all the tough negotiations or because of them the *Bundesrat* put up resistance against the bill. This unexpected reaction made the BMWi seriously reconsider its plans to establish a new federal institute for development aid, similar in structure to the

[49]Ibid., minutes of ministers' meeting on 7 January 1960, annex 5, note by KfW, 24 January 1956.

[50]Ibid., note on a meeting with *Länder* representatives on 25 March 1960.

[51]BA B102/25353, note on a 'Chefbesprechung' (ministers meeting), 12 April 1960.

[52]*Jb* 1960, annual balance sheet; BA B 102/25352, note by Abteilung VI, Vorschläge zur KfW Reform, 1 September 1960.

[53]PAAA 403/277, telefax by Pferdmenges to Staatssekretär Scherpenberg, 15 July 1960, regarding a meeting in the BMWi in late June.

[54]PAAA 403/275, letter from the Chancellery to the *Bundesrat*, 10 February 1961.

KfW[55]. Of course, such a solution was not at all in the Kreditanstalt's interest and new negotiations in which Abs seemed to have played a major role reached a compromise. Now both the federal government and the *Länder* took an equal share of DM 29.5 million out of the existing reserves and transformed it into *Grundkapital*. The federal government, in order to reach its 80 per cent share in the capital furthermore transformed a claim of DM 90 million from the ERP Special Assets into basic capital as well. In this way the new capital could be underwritten without using any additional budget funds from either side, while the KfW could keep its DM 94 million special reserve[56].

On 25 May the amended bill went into Parliament for consideration and was finally passed on 16 August 1961. The law made the Kreditanstalt für Wiederaufbau officially what it *de facto* had already been for about four years, West Germany's development aid bank. Certainly more important than the legal adaptation to existing circumstances were the new extended tasks for the bank. While the KfW took on these new tasks one paradox remained for the next eight years. Although it was now officially the development aid bank and a new ministry was created for the purpose in September 1961 the minister got a seat on the Board of Directors only in 1969 when the law was again redrafted[57]. Until then, the minister only had an advisory role at best in 'his own' bank.

The KfW after 1961

There are several events in or around 1961 which support the argument that West Germany's reconstruction process had been completed. The revaluation of the Deutschmark in 1961 and the completion of the six-millionth new dwelling demonstrated the economic muscle the Federal Republic had built within just more than a decade. Even with the end of the reconstruction the existence of the 'Reconstruction Loan Corporation' was not terminated by the German government, the bank even keeps its name right up to the present day. It survived not only the main purpose it was set up for, reconstruction, it also outlasted the second big development which had such a strong impact on its work, the Cold War and probably even helped, to a small extent, to overcome it. Whenever it became active the bank did so either with the consent or on the more or less explicit wishes of the federal government.

When the Berlin Wall went up in 1961, the Kreditanstalt increased its aid for the island of West Berlin. When the Cold War ended with the fall of the Berlin Wall in 1989-90 the KfW expanded its operations into Berlin and the former GDR, taking over in the process the task of its former fellow *Hauptleihinstitut*, the

---

[55]Ibid., letter by the BMWi to the Staatssekretär in the Chancellery, 21 March 1961.
[56]Harries, *Wiederaufbau*, p. 67.
[57]Spanger, Brock, *Staaten*, p. 284; Harries, *Wiederaufbau*, p. 69; *BGBl* 1969 (I), pp. 573 ff.

Berliner Industrie Bank in 1992. Under the motto 'Our Name is our Programme' the KfW helped within the former GDR to finance the establishment of new businesses, the complete refurbishment of many of the GDR's high-rise tower blocks, the *Plattenbauten* and provided considerable funds for the restoration of historic buildings and monuments and other national treasures previously badly neglected by the GDR regime. The KfW's work in the aftermath of the Cold War went even further when it got involved in the financing of housing construction in the former Soviet Union for Soviet military personnel which had to withdraw from the East of Germany under the 'Two Plus Four' agreement on German re-unification. DM 13.5 billion was provided by the federal government in total, DM 7.8 billion for housing construction, by far the largest single loan the KfW had ever given and despite the chaos which ensued in the aftermath of the Soviet Union's collapse[58].

The changing situation and demands on the capital market made the Kreditanstalt one of the first German financial institutions to seek admittance to the New York Stock Exchange in 1985. The necessary rating carried out by both Moody's and Standard and Poor was passed successfully with the award of the triple 'A' status. Two years later, the KfW was the first German financial institution which received the approval of the Securities Exchange Commission, the American authority in charge of vetting any potential emitter of public bonds. Then, in 1988 a subsidiary company, 'Kreditanstalt International' was set up especially to deal on the New York market[59].

Not everything was such plain sailing and the Kreditanstalt was involved in some dubious, even illegal, transactions which caused some scandal. The most infamous incident happened in October 1988 when it was leaked to the press that the KfW was going to finance the sale of Tornado fighter planes to Jordan. Under German law, weapons export into crisis areas were strictly prohibited and by that time the Middle East and Jordan fell into this category. After a huge public and political outcry the bank had to withdraw its involvement and the deal was cancelled[60].

A more successful operation was began in 1997 when the German government privatised the previously state owned Deutsche Telecom and sold its shares on the open market. In the process some 24 per cent of Telecom's shares were taken on by the KfW to be 'parked' there[61]. Also, one of the more spectacular successes in export finance was achieved during the 1990s when the KfW was involved in the financing of the construction of the Shanghai metro, a project in which some leading German exporters were involved. Finally, on 1 January 2003 the Kreditanstalt für Wiederaufbau created the *KfW Bankengruppe* when it took over the Deutsche Ausgleichsbank, formerly the Lastenausgleichsbank, the

---

[58]Harries, *Wiederaufbau*, pp. 176 ff., 187 ff.
[59]Ibid., pp. 160 f.
[60]*Die Tageszeitung* (*TAZ*), 24 October 1988, pp. 1f.
[61]*Financial Times*, 8 July 2003.

remaining other *Hauptleihinstitut* which had dealt originally with compensation claims of refugees under the equalisation of burden scheme before it had begun to carry out *Mittelstandsförderung* as well. With this step the KfW had outlived any other financial institution established during the early reconstruction period except for the BdL/Bundesbank. This in itself is proof of the bank's significance and influence. We can expect to see it continue its work in years to come.

Conclusion

The reconstruction process in post-war West Germany has been closely linked to, and influenced by, Cold War developments. The area of what would become the Federal Republic, due to its economic potential, was the crucial cornerstone in the process of European economic rehabilitation. After the political decisions had been made in Washington for West German reconstruction, two crucial factors were missing before the process could begin: money and an institution that could efficiently channel funds into the most needy of the strategic economic sectors. After some hesitation and because they had no feasible proposal of their own the Americans in summer 1948 took on an idea the British had developed in their attempt to provide funds for the reconstruction of the Ruhr area and charged the Germans with the drafting of a law for a Reconstruction Loan Corporation. The Germans eagerly took up the request which gave them the opportunity to gain back some more authority over their affairs from the Allies. The product of German deliberations was a very German institution, the Kreditanstalt für Wiederaufbau. In the process of its establishment the Americans, who by this time were calling the tune amongst the three western powers, had to make several concessions to the Germans, in particular in regard to the running of the bank and its personnel. This confirms Gimbel's wider theory that the Americans needed German co-operation in cases where they wanted to implement a certain policy or were faced with failure of this policy.

The well documented delay of Marshall Plan funds reaching needy German industries in 1948-9 and the increasing Cold War tensions as well as General Clay's personal interest in the reconstruction of the Bizone made him kick-start direct American aid through the provision of GARIOA funds. The Kreditanstalt received GARIOA funds and began the reconstruction process months before the more famous ERP counterpart funds became available. Although quite limited in size GARIOA funds set the pattern of the reconstruction process and the continuing argument between the Americans and the Germans, in particular Economics Minister Ludwig Erhard, as on which economic sectors the reconstruction focus should be placed. When the first Marshall Plan money eventually became available in late 1949 the ECA widened Clay's reconstruction focus which had been on Germany only in the wider European context. With the ERP the Americans had a tool in their hands with which they continued to intervene in the Federal Republic's economy. Projects favoured by the Americans, such as the electricity industry, received continuing funding even to an extent that the Americans by about 1952 began to regard as excessive. In other areas the Marshall Plan helped to enforce American policy towards the Eastern European countries by withholding ERP funds from companies they suspected of illegal trade with the East. US Marshall

Plan policy in Germany therefore had three main aims which in many respects were overlapping. First, it was to stop the spread of communism, secondly to help European recovery as a whole and thirdly, it intervened in the German economy, partly to support the first two aims. After the outbreak of the Korean War American reconstruction aid became increasingly militarised as the very specific conditions applied to MSA funds demonstrated. From here, a direct line can be drawn to American insistence on German participation in development aid in the second half of the 1950s.

The story of German funds raised for use by the Kreditanstalt is a tale similar to the wider economic developments in the late 1940s and 1950s. It begins with an extremely disappointing result in the KfW's first attempt to raise money through the issue of bonds. The generally poor situation on the German capital market in the early years made it necessary instead to rely on some questionable book balancing exercises involving unsold bonds and, even more criticised, a small-scale re-run of the Mefo bills of exchange scheme. The inadequacy of some of Erhard's political planning came to the fore during the Korean crisis when some of the basic industries proved unable to meet the increased demand. The resulting Auxiliary Investment Law turned out to be the most important step back into positions of influence for German heavy industry and business associations and demonstrated the limitations of Erhard's market economy. In the process, and as before during the work creation scheme, the KfW proved itself to the federal government as a surrogate to the Bank deutscher Länder, providing or at least handling funds the administration did not receive from the BdL or which the central bank did not like to give directly to the government for reasons of monetary stability. The role of surrogate central bank became politically more important throughout and especially towards the end of the 1950s. What had changed during that period was the KfW's source of funds which shifted gradually away from almost complete reliance on the ERP Special Accounts to funds which the bank itself raised on the capital market once Finance Minister Schäffer had been replaced in his post. The long-term development would turn KfW issued bonds into highly sought after and well-referred financial papers.

Loans by the Kreditanstalt in its early years of operation had first and foremost the purpose of enabling West Germany's economic recovery but in doing so, other issues came to the forefront. Germany's economic strength was important for the wider European reconstruction and at the same time offered the country a relatively easy way back into the western community. Mainly from the American point of view an economically recovered Germany – and Europe – seemed to be the best insurance against the spread of communism. The investment finance into strategic bottleneck sectors of the economy that was carried out with the help of KfW loans brought some desperately needed financial relief and compensation to the basic industries thus enabling Economics Minister Erhard to stick to his policy of preference of the consumer good industries. Towards the second half of the 1950s, when most of the big companies in the basic industries were able to raise their own finance loans were given instead to small and medium sized companies, the *Mittelstand*, which held an important position in the German economy in an attempt to bolster their productivity and competitiveness.

Support for agriculture, on the other hand, which began on a relatively small-scale, was driven by the need to improve the desperate situation in the food supply. If Germany could enhance primary production it could not only improve the population's food supplies which was important in regard to the long-term health of the population, especially children. At the same time precious foreign currencies used for imports of foodstuffs could be saved and perhaps even yielded through the export of some sought after products such as sugar beet or processed sugar. In the longer run KfW loans in agriculture were used to improve rural infrastructure including water and electricity supply, roads and, in a wider sense, the re-parcelling of land. The resulting huge increases in farming productivities were a precondition for the structural changes which appeared during the 1950s and 1960s and helped to increase German farmers' competitiveness within the newly established EEC.

If there was any achievement miraculous in the context of the 'Economic Miracle' then it was West Germany's ability to build six million dwelling houses within the space of a dozen or so years. Providing housing for the huge number of refugees and people who had lost their homes as a result of the war was the largest social challenge the Federal Republic faced. Housing was essential in the Ruhr to improve miners' labour productivity and it was politically vital for refugees, otherwise they could have turned into a politically dissatisfied group, leaning towards political extremes either on the left or the right. The loans the Kreditanstalt provided for refugee housing on ridiculously cheap interest rates has therefore to be seen as one of the bank's most important political and social task. The building programmes that went on all throughout the 1950s were also a strong weapon in the propaganda war between East and West.

The link between reconstruction and Cold War is nowhere more visible than in the case of West Berlin and the aid the city received throughout the 1950s. After its initial involvement in the financing of the BEWAG power plant in 1949-50, the KfW took up its support for the city again towards the middle of the decade, partly to replace the diminishing American funds. The co-operation which happened between the various US agencies, the city of West Berlin and (every so often under a lot of US pressure) the Federal Republic, the latter sometimes in the form of the KfW, is perhaps the best example of successful Cold War economic warfare throughout the whole period of the conflict. The KfW's great contribution here has to be the financing of the BEWAG project and its subsequent success in convincing the ECA to reduce interest rates for loans to Berlin.

The other large area where the Cold War played a very important role was export finance. Here, too, the first important step was to restore the capacity to export, to earn hard currencies and to re-enter the world markets. The latter concerned especially Germany's traditional markets in Latin America but also and increasingly the penetration of new markets in Asia. American policy towards

Yugoslavia demonstrated how quickly US attitudes could change, with a significant impact on Adenauer's policy and action. Although at best only partially successful, Adenauer for the first time tried to use West Germany's economic muscle in his attempt to achieve the release of German POWs. The precariousness of loans to Yugoslavia which soon forced the Kreditanstalt into several rescue missions brought again to the surface the value the bank had for the government by carrying out semi-official duties and providing funds for those without needing parliamentary approval. It must have come as quite a shock to the West German government that after all the hassle it was Yugoslavia which recognised the GDR. The subsequent application of the Hallstein Doctrine for the first time opened a new chapter in West German foreign policy and in the work of the KfW. Although it started out as support for the exports of private companies, export finance and eventually loans to India were more and more dominated by the Cold War and the Hallstein Doctrine. A combination of American demands for increased German participation in the 'economic defence' of the West in the Third World, an ever increasing commitment by the KfW in export finance and loans and the precarious situation the Hallstein Doctrine as well as the legal loopholes under which the KfW had to operate more and more eventually let to its transformation into West Germany's development aid bank.

If one looks at the establishment of the Kreditanstalt für Wiederaufbau and the composition of its supervisory Board of Directors, its original source of funds and its semi-official tasks one has to agree that it is a very German institution in the best traditions of the country's 'corporate economy'. The size of its success is best demonstrated by the fact that the KfW is the only organisation from the Bizonal era which has survived up to the present day (the BdL was founded eight months earlier but became the Bundesbank in 1957 but with a new legal basis). With reserves of over €3.2 billion in 2001 and a net profit of €264 million in 2002 as the KfW banking group it is easy to understand why it has outlived and taken over its former fellow *Hauptleihinstitute*[1].

[1] *Jb* 2002, pp. 117, 122.

Glossary of German Financial, Legal and Economic Terms

Außenhandelsbanken: banks which until 1956 had special authorisation to operate foreign currency transactions necessary for import and export trade.

ECA I-III: name of the three (originally scheduled: four) instalments which were made from the ERP counterpart funds to the KfW to provide a source of finance for the reconstruction process; continued with MSA IV and FOA V programmes.

Eigenkapital: comprises of *Grundkapital* plus all profits and all reserves of a company.

Eigenkapitalanteil: share of the total costs of a dwelling under the social housing construction programme a tenant had to provide in order to rent the property.

Flurbereinigung: re-parcelling of small agricultural plots, mainly in the west and south-west of Germany; due to the inheritance law prevailing there, the land was divided amongst all children, thus creating over the generations unprofitable and unworkable small fields; the re-parcelling worked usually by exchanging small plots so that larger segments were created; another task of *Flurbereinigung* was the building of a better agricultural infrastructure, mainly roads to the fields.

Grundkapital: the basic capital with which a company begins its operations; it remains fixed unless increased by a formal act and does not indicate the real value of a company.

Hauptleihinstitut: literally main lending institute; a bank which is authorised by the Federal Government to borrow money from the ERP Special Assets; only two banks other than the KfW (the BIB and the Lastenausgleichsbank) received this status which is based on a *Rahmenkreditvertrag*.

Hauptverteilungskonto: literally main distribution account; account at the BdL onto which the BMP transferred money from the ERP Special Assets. The *Hauptleih-institute* were authorised to withdraw the money in accordance to the development of confirmed projects.

Hauszinssteuer: the repayment of public loans for housing construction which had been given during the Weimar Republic. The money was mainly used to support the social housing construction.

Kapitalsammelstellen: collective term for institutions which receive large pay-ins as a result of their business and accumulate large financial reserves. Examples are insurance companies, social insurance and building societies (Bausparkassen).

Kassenobligationen: medium-term bonds with fixed interest, sold by the Bundesbank on the order of a (semi) public institution.

Lombardfähigkeit: the right to use ones bonds as a mortgage for bank loans.

Obligationen: long-term debenture bonds with fixed interest.

öffentlich-rechtliche Anstalt or *Anstalt des öffentlichen Rechts*: German legal term describing an institution which carries out public tasks which are not part of the actual state administration but which is supervised by the public administration.

Pfandbriefe: bonds issued by *Realkreditinstituten* which can themselves be given as securities for loans.

Rahmenkreditvertrag: contract between the *Hauptleihinstitute* and the Federal Government (represented by the BMP or the successor ministries), in which the legal details for borrowing money from the ERP Special Assets are laid down.

Realkreditinstitute: credit institutions which usually provide mortgages. They raise their money by issuing long-term bonds (*Pfandbriefe*) and have an important role in the financing of housing construction and agricultural finance.

Remontage: term used in Germany to describe the rebuilding of dismantled plants and factories.

Rückverflechtung: process in the coal and iron industry in the aftermath of the outbreak of the Korean War which re-established in principle the old *Verbundwirtschaft*, only on a less monopolistic scale.

Schiffshypothekenbanken: literally shipping mortgage banks; banks which provide loans for ship owners; properly registered ships are mortgaged as securities for the loans; the banks themselves raise the money by issuing long-term bonds.

Ungebundene Finanzkredite: unconditional loans; loans to foreign countries which were not bound to the purchase of exactly defined commodities from the debtor country. These loans allowed a creditor country to purchase commodities from the cheapest supplier country.

Verbundwirtschaft: term used (a) in the electrical power industry where it describes the operation of an integrated national or international grid for power supply, and (b) in the iron and coal industry, where it describes a horizontally and vertically integrated company, that is one that owns both coal mines which supply the own blast furnaces with coal and coke as well as metal processing facilities. The Americans tried to abolish *Verbundwirtschaft* in the coal and iron industry since it supported the existence of monopolistic cartels.

Verpflichtungsschein: financial commitment to pay; usually given when debenture bonds are issued which need, but do not have, a public authorisation.

Bibliography

1. Primary Sources:

1.1 Archival Sources

Bundesarchiv Koblenz (BA)

B 102 Bundeswirtschaftsministerium
B 109 Stahltreuhandverwaltung
B 126 Bundesfinanzministerium
B 136 Bundeskanzleramt
B 146 Bundesministerium für den Marshallplan
NL 5 Nachlaß Pünder
NL 168 Nachlaß Schäffer
Z 3 Wirtschaftsrat
Z 4 Länderrat
Z 13 Direktorialkanzlei des Vereinigten Wirtschaftsgebietes
Z 14 Berater für den Marshallplan
Z 45F OMGUS

Deutsche Bundesbank, Historisches Archiv (DBBHA)

Bestand B 330

Deutscher Bundestag, Parlamentsarchiv (BTPA)

Bestand 2

Historisches Archiv der Kreditanstalt für Wiederaufbau (KfW HA)

Bestand Prot
Bestand BA
Bestand BS
Bestand VS

National Archives, Washington, DC (NA)

RG 59 General Records of the Department of State
RG 260 OMGUS
RG 466 Records of the US High Commissioner for Germany
RG 469 Records of the US Foreign Assistance Agencies 1948-61

Politisches Archiv des Auswärtigen Amtes (PAAA)
Referat 400
Referat 403
Referat 407
Referat 411
Referat 412

Public Record Office, Kew (PRO),
Foreign Office Files (FO) 371 General Records
944 Control Office for Germany and Austria
1005 Control Commission for Germany

1.2 Printed Sources

Akten zur Vorgeschichte der Bundesrepublik Deutschland (eds Christoph Weisz et al.), vol. 4, München, Wien 1983.

Amtsblatt der Europäischen Gemeinschaft, 1958.

Bundesgesetzblatt, various years.

Foreign Relations of the United States (ed.), US Department of State, various years and vols.

Gesetzblatt der Verwaltung des Vereinigten Wirtschaftsgebietes, 1948, 1949.

Die Kabinettsprotokolle der Bundesregierung 1949-1956, (eds Hans Booms et al.), München 1982-98.

Kreditanstalt für Wiederaufbau (ed.), *Jahresberichte für die Geschäftsjahre,* various years, Frankfurt/M.

Monthly Report of the US Military Governor, OMGUS, 1948-49.

Ruhm von Oppen, Beate (ed.) *Documents on Germany under Allied Occupation 1945-1954,* London, New York, Toronto 1955.

Statistisches Bundesamt (ed.), *Statistisches Jahrbuch für die Bundesrepublik Deutschland,* Wiesbaden, various years.

Statistisches Handbuch von Deutschland 1928-1944 (ed.), Länderrat des Amerikanischen Besatzungsgebietes, München 1949.

United States Strategic Bombing Survey, Report # 3, The Effects of the Strategic Bombing on the German War Economy, Washington, DC 1945, reprinted New York 1976.

Verhandlungen des Deutschen Bundestages und des Bundesrates, 1. Wahlperiode 1949-1953, Verhandlungen des Bundestages, Microfilm edition, München (no year).

Wörtliche Berichte und Drucksachen des Wirtschaftsrates des Vereinigten Wirtschaftsgebietes 1947-1949 (eds), Institut für Zeitgeschichte and Deutscher Bundestag, vols. 2 , 3, 4, München, Wien 1977.

1.3 Periodicals

Financial Times
Europa Archiv 1948, Oberursel.

Die Neue Zeitung
Der Spiegel
Der Volkswirt
Die Tageszeitung
Die Zeit

2. Literature

Abelshauser, Werner, *Wirtschaft in Westdeutschland,* Stuttgart 1975.

Abelshauser, Werner, 'Probleme des Wiederaufbaus der Westdeutschen Wirtschaft 1945-53', in: Heinrich August Winkler (ed.), *Politische Weichenstellungen im Nachkriegsdeutschland 1945-53,* Göttingen 1979, pp. 208-253.

Abelshauser, Werner, 'Korea, die Ruhr und Erhards Marktwirtschaft: Die Energiekrise von 1950/51', *Rheinische Vierteljahresblätter* 45 (1981), pp. 287-316.

Abelshauser, Werner, 'Ansätze 'korporativer Marktwirtschaft' in der Koreakrise der 50er Jahre. Ein Briefwechsel zwischen dem Hohen Kommissar John McCloy und Bundeskanzler Adenauer.', *VfZ* 30 (1982), pp. 715-756.

Abelshauser, Werner, *Wirtschaftsgeschichte der Bundesrepublik Deutschland 1945-1980,* Frankfurt/M. 1983.

Abelshauser, Werner, *Der Ruhrkohlenbergbau seit 1945. Wiederaufbau, Krise, Anpassung,* München 1984.

Abelshauser, Werner, 'Schopenhauers Gesetz und die Währungsreform', *VfZ* 33 (1985), pp. 214-218.

Abelshauser, Werner, 'Kohle und Marktwirtschaft. Ludwig Erhards Konflikt mit dem Unternehmensverband Ruhbergbau am Vorabend der Kohlekrise', *VfZ* 33 (1985), pp. 489-546.

Abelshauser, Werner, *Die langen Fünfziger Jahre. Wirtschaft und Gesellschaft in der Bundesrepublik Deutschland,* Düsseldorf 1987.

Abelshauser, Werner, 'Hilfe und Selbsthilfe. Zur Funktion des Marshallplans beim westdeutschen Wiederaufbau', in: Hans-Jürgen Schröder (ed.), *Marshallplan und Westdeutscher Wiederaufstieg,* Stuttgart 1990, pp. 150-178.

Abs, Hermann Josef, *Entscheidungen 1949-1953. Die Entstehung des Londoner Schuldenabkommens,* 2nd edn, Mainz 1991.

Adamsen, Heiner R., *Investitionshilfe für die Ruhr. Wiederaufbau, Verbände und Soziale Marktwirschaft 1948-1952,* Wuppertal 1981.

Adler-Karlson, Gunnar, *Western Economic Warfare 1947-1967,* Stockholm 1968.

Agartz, Victor, and Heinrich Deist, (eds), *Gesetz 75 und Ruhrstatut,* Köln 1949.

Bauer, Franz-Josef, 'Der bayrische Bauernverband, die Bodenreform und das Flüchtlingsproblem 1945-1951', *VfZ* 31 (1983), pp. 443-482.

Bauernkämper, Arnd, 'Landwirtschaft und ländliche Gesellschaft in der Bundesrepublik in den 50er Jahren', in: Axel Schildt and Arnold Sywottek (eds), *Modernisierung im*

Wiederaufbau. Die Westdeutsche Gesellschaft der 50er Jahre, Bonn 1993, pp. 188-200.

Baumgart, Egon, *Investitionen und ERP-Finanzierung,* Berlin 1961.

Becker, Wolfgang, *Das ERP-Sondervermögen. Entstehung und Verwaltung,* Göttingen 1968.

Benz, Wolfgang, *Die Gründung der Bundesrepublik. Von der Bizone zum souveränen Staat,* 3rd edn, München 1989.

Bohleber, Wolfgang, *Mit Marshallplan und Bundeshilfe,* Berlin 1990.

Boll, Georg, *Entstehung und Entwicklung des Verbundbetriebes in der deutschen Elektrizitätswirtschaft bis zum europäischen Verbund,* Frankfurt/M 1969.

Borchard, Knut, and Buchheim, Christoph, 'Die Wirkung der Marshallplan-Hilfe in Schlüsselbranchen der deutschen Wirtschaft', *VfZ* 35 (1987), pp. 317-347.

Bower, Tom, *Blind Eye to Murder. Britain, America and the Purging of Nazi Germany: A Pledge Betrayed,* London et al., 1981.

Braunthal, Gerard, *The Federation of German Industry in Politics,* Ithaca 1965.

Bruche, Gert, *Elektrizitätsversorgung und Staatsfunktion.,* Frankfurt/M, New York 1977.

Buchheim, Christoph, 'Das Londoner Schuldenabkommen', in: Ludolf Herbst (ed.), *Westdeutschland 1945-1955. Unterwerfung, Kontrolle, Integration,* München 1986, pp. 219-229.

Buchheim, Christoph, *Die Wiedereingliederung Westdeutschlands in die Weltwirtschaft,* München 1990.

Buchheim, Christoph. 'The Nazi Boom: An Economic Cul-de-Sac.' Paper given at St. Anthony's College, Oxford, February 1997.

Bührer, Werner, Herbst, Ludolf and Sowade, Hanno (eds), *Zwischen Marshallplan und EWG,* München 1990.

Bührer, Werner, 'Erzwungene oder freiwillige Liberalisierung?', in: Werner Bührer, Ludolf Herbst and Hanno Sowade (eds), *Zwischen Marshallplan und EWG,* München 1990, pp. 139-162.

Bührer, Werner, and Schröder, Hans-Jürgen, 'Germany's Economic Revival in the 1950s. The Foreign Policy Perspective', in: Ennio Di Nolfo (ed), *Power in Europe II ? Great Britain, France, Germany and Italy and the Origins of the EEC 1952-1957,* Berlin, New York 1992, pp. 174-196.

Bührer, Werner, 'Der BDI und die Außenpolitik der Bundesrepublik Deutschland in den 50er Jahren', *VfZ* 40 (1992), pp. 241-261.

Carstens, Dieter, (ed.), *Der Bund als Finanzier. Kredite, Leistungen und Bürgschaften des ERP-Sondervermögens,* Bad Godesberg 1960.

Clay, Lucius D., *Decision in Germany,* 2nd edn, New York 1970.

Collins, Michael, *Money and Banking in the UK,* London et al., 1988.

Conze, Werner, and Lepsius, Rainer M. (eds), *Sozialgeschichte der Bundesrepublik. Beiträge zum Kontinuitätsproblem,* Stuttgart 1983.

Daniel, Ute, *Dollardiplomatie in Europa. Marshallplan, Kalter Krieg und US-Außenwirtschaftspolitik 1945-52,* Düsseldorf 1982.

Deist, Heinrich, 'Organisationsprobleme der Eisen- und Stahlindustrie', in: Victor Agartz and Heinrich Deist (eds), *Gesetz 75 und Ruhrstatut,* Köln 1949, pp. 15-37.

Deutsche Bundesbank (ed.), *Deutsches Geld- und Bankenwesen in Zahlen 1876-1975*, Frankfurt/M 1976.

Deutsche Bundesbank (ed.), *40 Jahre Deutsche Mark*, Frankfurt/M 1988.

Di Nolfo, Ennio (ed.), *Power in Europe II? Great Britain, France, Germany and Italy and the Origins of the EEC 1952-1957*, Berlin, New York 1992.

Dickertmann, Dietrich, *Öffentliche Finanzierungshilfen. Darlehen, Schuldendiensthilfen und Bürgschaften als Instrumente des finanzwirschaftlichen Interventionismus*, Baden-Baden 1980.

Dickhaus, Monika, *Die Bundesbank im westeuropäischen Wiederaufbau*, München 1996.

Diefendorf, Jeffry M., Frohn, Axel, and Rupieper, Hermann-Josef (eds), *American Policy and the Reconstruction of West Germany, 1945-1955*, Washigton, DC, Cambridge 1993.

Diefendorf, Jeffry M., 'America and the Rebuilding of Urban Germany', in: Jeffry M. Diefendorf, Axel Frohn and Hermann-Josef Rupieper (eds), *American Policy and the Reconstruction of West Germany 1945-1955*, Washington, DC 1993, pp. 331-351.

Dohrn, Klaus, *Meine Zeit. Erinnerungen eines Bankiers*, Pfullingen 1991.

Edinger, Lewis J., *Kurt Schumacher. A Study in Personality and Political Behaviour*, Stanford, Cal. 1965.

Edward Smith, Jean (ed.), *The Papers of General Lucius D. Clay: Germany 1945-1949*, 2 vols. vol. 2, London 1974.

Erhard, Ludwig, *Deutschlands Rückkehr zum Weltmarkt*, Düsseldorf 1953.

Führer, Karl-Christian, 'Anspruch und Realität der nationalsozialistischen Wohnungsbaupolitik', *VfZ* 45 (1997), pp. 225-256.

Gall, Lothar, et al., *The Deutsche Bank 1870-1995*, London 1995.

Gall, Lothar, 'A Man for all Seasons? H.J.Abs in the Third Reich', *Financial History Review*, vol. 6, no. 2, (Oct. 1999), pp. 147-202.

Gablers Wirtschaftslexikon, 12th edn, Wiesbaden 1988.

Gerhardt, Gunther, *Das Krisenmanagement der Vereinigten Staaten während der Berliner Blockade (1948/49). Intentionen, Strategien und Wirkungen*, Berlin 1984.

Gillingham, John, *Coal, Steel, and the Rebirth of Europe 1945-1955. The German and French from Ruhr Conflict to Economic Community*, Cambridge, New York 1991.

Gimbel, John, 'Byrnes' Stuttgarter Rede und die amerikanische Nachkriegspolitik in Deutschland', *VfZ* 20 (1972), pp. 39-62.

Gimbel, John, 'Amerikanische Besatzungspolitik und deutsche Tradition', in: *Westdeutschland 1945-1955. Unterwerfung, Kontrolle, Integration*, edited by Ludolf Herbst, pp. 147-150, München 1986.

Grünbacher, Armin, 'Profits and Cold War – Politically Motivated Export Finance in West Germany during the 1950s: Two Case Studies', in: *German Politics*, vol. 10, no. 3 (Dec 2001), pp. 141-158.

Grünbacher, Armin, 'Sustaining the Island: Western Aid to 1950s West Berlin', *Cold War History*, vol. 3, no. 3 (2003), pp. 1-22.

Gudin, Harald, 'Außenwirtschaftspolitische und außenpolitische Einflußfaktoren im Prozess der Staatswerdung der Bundesrepublik Deutschland 1947-1952', *Aus Politik und Zeitgeschichte,* no. B32/87 (1987) pp. 3-20.

Hankel, Wilhelm, *Die zweite Kapitalverteilung. Ein marktwirtschaftlicher Weg langfristiger Finanzierungspolitik,* Frankfurt/M. 1961.

Hardach, Gerd, *Der Marshallplan. Auslandshilfe und Wiederaufbau in Westdeutschland 1948-1952,* München 1994.

Harmsen, Gustav, *Am Abend der Demontage. Sechs Jahre Reparationspolitik,* Bremen 1951.

Harries, Heinrich, *Wiederaufbau, Welt und Wende. Die KfW - eine Bank mit öffentlichem Auftrag,* Frankfurt/M 1998.

Henning, Friedrich-Wilhelm, 'Soziale Marktwirtschaft und Landwirtschaft 1948/49-1955', in: Dietmar Petzina (ed.), *Ordnungspolitische Weichenstellungen nach dem Zweiten Weltkrieg,* Berlin 1991, pp 101-121.

Hentschel, Volker, *Ludwig Erhard. Ein Politikerleben,* München, Landsberg/L 1996.

Herbst, Ludolf, 'Krisenüberwindung und Wirtschaftsneuordnung. Ludwig Erhards Beteiligungen an den Nachkriegsplanungen am Ende des Zweiten Weltkrieges', *VfZ* 25 (1977), pp. 305-340.

Herbst, Ludolf (ed.), *Westdeutschland 1945-1955. Unterwerfung, Kontrolle, Integration,* München 1986.

Herbst, Ludolf, *Option für den Westen. Vom Marshallplan zum deutsch-französischen Vertrag,* München 1989.

Herlemann, Hans-Heinrich, 'Vertriebene Bauern im Strukturwandel der Landwirtschaft', in: Eugen Lemberg and Friedrich Edding (eds), *Die Vertriebenen in Westdeutschland. Ihre Eingliederung und ihr Einfluß auf Gesellschaft, Wirtschaft, Politik und Geistesleben,* Kiel 1959, pp. 53-165.

Hermann, Armin, *Nur der Name war geblieben. Die abenteuerliche Geschichte der Firma Carl Zeiss,* Stuttgart 1989.

Hersch, Burton, *The Old Boys. The American Elite and the Origins of the CIA,* New York 1992.

Herzig, Thomas, 'Wirtschaftsgeschichtliche Aspekte der deutschen Elektrizitätsversorgung 1880-1990', in: *Die Geschichte der Stromversorgung,* pp. 123-166, no place (Frankfurt/M) no year (1992).

Heyl, Friedrich von, *Der innerdeutsche Handel mit Eisen und Stahl 1945-1972. Deutsch-deutsche Beziehungen im Kalten Krieg,* Köln, Weimar, Wien 1997.

Hofmann, Walter, *Private Bank in öffentlichem Besitz. Kleine Geschichte der Reichskreditgesellschaft,* Mainz 1980.

Hogan, Michael J., *The Marshall Plan. America, Britain and the Reconstruction of Western Europe 1947-1952,* Cambridge, New York 1987.

Holtfrerich, Carl-Ludwig, 'The Deutsche Bank 1945-1957. War, Military Rule and Reconstruction.', in: Lothar Gall et al., *The Deutsche Bank 1870-1995,* London 1995, pp. 357-521.

Horstmann, Theo, *Die Alliierten und die deutschen Großbanken. Bankenpolitik nach dem Zweiten Weltkrieg in Westdeutschland,* Bonn 1991.

Hölscher, Jens, *Entwicklungsmodell Westdeutschland. Aspekte der Akkumulation in der Geldwirtschaft*, Berlin 1994.

Hüttenberger, Péter, 'Wirtschaftsordnung und Interessenpolitik in der Kartellgesetzgebung der Bundesrepublik 1949-1957', *VfZ* 24 (1976), pp. 287-307.

James, Harold, 'The Deutsche Bank and the Dictatorship 1933-1945', in: Lothar Gall et al., *The Deutsche Bank 1870-1995*, pp. 277-356, London 1995.

Jákli, Zoltán, *Vom Marshallplan zum Kohlepfennig. Grundrisse der Subventionspolitik in der Bundesrepublik Deutschland 1948-1982*, Opladen 1990.

Jerchow, Friedrich, 'Der Außenkurs der Mark 1944-1949', *VfZ* 30 (1980) pp, 256-298

Kaufman, Burton I., *Trade and Aid. Eisenhower's Foreign Economic Policy 1953-1961*, Baltimore 1982.

Kleßmann, Christoph, *Zwei Staaten, eine Nation. Deutsche Geschichte 1955-1970*, Bonn 1988.

Kluge, Ulrich, 'West German Agriculture and the European Recovery Program 1948-1952', in: Jeffry M. Diefendorf, Axel Frohn and Hermann-Josef Rupieper (eds), *American Policy and the Reconstruction of West Germany 1945-1955*, Washington, DC 1993, pp. 155-174.

Knapp, Manfred, 'Deutschland und der Marshallplan', in: Hans-Jürgen Schröder (ed.), *Marshallplan und Westdeutscher Wiederaufstieg*, Stuttgart 1990, pp. 35-59.

Kolko, Joyce, and Gabriel Kolko, *The Limits of Power. The World and United States Foreign Policy*, New York 1972.

Köhler, Henning, *Adenauer*, Berlin, Frankfurt/M 1994.

Kötter, Herbert, 'Die Landwirtschaft', in: Werner Conze and Rainer M. Lepsius (eds), *Sozialgeschichte der Bundesrepublik Deutschland Beiträge zum Kontinuitätsproblem*, Stuttgart 1983, pp. 115-142.

Kramer, Alan, 'British Dismantling Politics, 1945-49: A Reassessment', in: Ian D. Turner (ed.), *Reconstruction in Post-War Germany. British Occupation Policy and the Western Zones 1945-55*, Oxford, New York, München 1989, pp.125-154.

Kreditanstalt für Wiederaufbau (ed.), *Die KfW - 1948 bis heute*, 2nd edn, Frankfurt/M 1997.

Krengel, Rolf, *Anlagevermögen, Produktion und Beschäftigung der Industrie im Gebiet der Bundesrepublik von 1924 bis 1956*, Berlin 1958.

Kretzschmar, Winfried W., *Auslandshilfe als Mittel der Außenwirtschaft- und Außenpolitik*, München 1964.

Krieger, Wolfgang, *General Lucius D. Clay und die amerikanische Deutschlandpolitik 1945-49*, 2nd edn, Stuttgart 1988.

Küsters, Hanns Jürgen, 'Adenauers Europapolitik in der Gründungsphase der Europäischen Wirtschaftsgemeinschaft', *VfZ* 31 (1983), pp. 646-673.

Leitende Männer der Wirtschaft, 3rd, 8th edn, Darmstadt, Berlin, Essen 1955, 1960.

Lemberg, Eugen, and Edding, Friedrich (eds), *Die Vertriebenen in Westdeutschland. Ihre Eingliederung und ihr Einfluß auf Gesellschaft, Wirtschaft, Politik und Geistesleben*, 3 vols., Kiel 1959.

Loth, Wilfried, *The Division of the World 1941-1955*, London 1988.

Löwen, Wolfgang, 'Rechtshistorische Aspekte der deutschen Stromversorgung 1880-1990', in: *Die Geschichte der Stromversorgung,* no place (Frankfurt/M), no year (1992).

Magnus, Kurt, *Eine Million Tonnen Kriegsmaterial für den Frieden. Die Geschichte der StEG,* München 1954.

Milward, Alan, *Der Zweite Weltkrieg,* edited by Wolfram Fischer. vol. 5, *Geschichte der Weltwirtschaft im 20. Jahrhundert,* München 1977.

Milward, Alan, *The Reconstruction of Western Europe 1945-1951,* London 1984.

Milward, Alan, 'Entscheidungsphasen der Westintegration', in: Ludolf Herbst (ed.), *Westdeutschland 1945-1955. Unterwerfung, Kontrolle, Integration,* München 1986, pp. 231-245.

Milward, Alan, *The European Rescue of the Nation State,* London 1992.

Neebe, Reinhard, 'Optionen westdeutscher Außenwirtschaftspolitik 1949-1953', in: Werner Bührer, Ludolf Herbst and Hanno Sowade (eds), *Zwischen Marshallplan und EWG,* München 1990, pp.163-202.

Nonn, Christoph, *Die Ruhrbergbaukrise. Entindustrialisierung und Politik 1958–1969,* Göttingen 1999.

Petzina, Dietmar (ed.), *Ordnungspolitische Weichenstellungen nach dem Zweiten Weltkrieg,* Berlin 1991.

Pohl, Manfred, *Wiederaufbau. Kunst und Technik der Finanzierung 1947-1953,* Frankfurt/M 1973.

Pritzkoleit, Kurt, *Bosse, Banken, Börsen,* München, Wien, Basel 1954.

Pritzkoleit, Kurt, *Männer, Mächte, Monopole,* 13 edn, Düsseldorf 1963.

Pünder, Tilman, *Das Bizonale Interregnunm. Die Geschichte des Vereinigten Wirtschaftsgebietes 1946-49,* Waiblingen 1966.

Rischl, Albrecht, 'Die Währungsreform von 1948 und der Wiederaufstieg der deutschen Industrie', *VfZ* 33 (1985), pp. 136-165.

Ritter, Gerhard A., Merith Niehaus (eds), *Wahlen in Deutschland 1946-1991,* München 1991.

Rogge, Peter G., *Die Amerikanische Hilfe für Westberlin.,* Tübingen 1959.

Roseman, Mark, 'The Uncontrolled Economy. Ruhr Coal Production 1945-48', in: Ian D. Turner (ed.), *Reconstruction in Post-War Germany. British Occupation Policy and the Western Zones 1945-55,* Oxford, New York, München 1989, pp. 93-124.

Roseman, Mark, *Recasting the Ruhr, 1945-1958: Manpower, Economic Recovery and Labour Relations,* New York, Oxford 1992.

Roskamp, Karl, *Capital Formation in West-Germany,* Detroit 1965.

Schildt, Axel, and Sywottek, Arnold (eds), *Massenwohnung und Eigenheim. Wohnungsbau und Wohnen in der Großstadt seit dem Ersten Weltkrieg,* Frankfurt/M, New York 1988.

Schildt, Axel, and Sywottek, Arnold (eds.), *Modernisierung im Wiederaufbau. Die Westdeutsche Gesellschaft in den 50er Jahren,* Bonn 1993.

Schlarp, Karl Heinz, 'Das Dilemma des westdeutschen Osthandels und die Entstehung des Ostausschusses der Deutschen Wirtschaft 1950-52', *VfZ* 41 (1993), pp. 223-276.

Schmidt, Eberhard, *Die verhinderte Neuordung 1945-1952,* 8th edn, Frankfurt/M 1981.

Schröder, Hans-Jürgen (ed.), *Marshallplan und Westdeutscher Wiederaufstieg,* Stuttgart 1990.

Schulz, Günther, 'Eigenheimpolitik und Eigenheimförderung im ersten Jahrzehnt nach dem Zweiten Weltkrieg', in: Axel Schild and Arnold Sywottek (eds), *Massenwohnung und Eigenheim. Wohnungsbau und Wohnen in der Großstadt seit dem Ersten Weltkrieg,* Frankfurt/M, New York 1988, pp. 409-439.

Schulz, Günther, *Wiederaufbau in Deutschland. Die Wohnungsbaupolitik in den Westzonen und der Bundesrepublik von 1945 bis 1957,* Düsseldorf 1994.

Schwarz, Hans-Peter (ed.), *Die Wiederherstellung des Deutschen Kredits. Das Londoner Schuldenabkommen, Rhöndorfer Gespräche* vol. 4, Stuttgart 1982.

Shonfield, Andrew, *Modern Capitalism. The Changing Balance of Public and Private Power,* London, New York, Toronto 1965.

Sohn, Karl-Heinz, *Entwicklungspolitik. Theorie und Praxis der deutschen Entwicklungshilfe,* 2nd edn, München 1973.

Spanger, Hans-Joachim, and Lothar Brock, *Die beiden deutschen Staaten in der Dritten Welt,* Opladen 1987.

Spaulding, Robert Mark, *Osthandel and Ostpolitik. German Foreign Trade Policy in Eastern Europe from Bismarck to Adenauer,* Oxford, New York 1997.

Statistisches Bundesamt (ed.), *Bevölkerung und Wirtschaft 1872-1972,* (no place) 1972.

Steininger, Rolf, *Deutsche Geschichte 1945-1961. Darstellung und Dokumente,* 2nd edn, 2 vols., Frankfurt/M 1989.

Stern, Susan, *The Marshall Plan 1947-1997. A German View,* Frankfurt/M 1997.

Thiemeyer, Guido, *Vom 'pool vert' zur Europäischen Wirtschaftsgemeinschaft. Europäische Integration, Kalter Krieg und die Anfänge der gemeinsamen Europäischen Agrarpolitik 1950-1957*, München 1999.

Trittel, Günter, 'Hans Schlange-Schöningen. Ein vergessener Politiker der 'ersten Stunde', *VfZ* 35 (1987) pp. 25-63.

Tröger, Heinrich, *Interregnum. Tagebuch des Generalsekretärs des Länderrats der Bizone 1947-1949,* eds Wolfgang Benz und Constantin Goschler, München 1985.

Turner, Ian D. (ed.), *Reconstruction in Post-War Germany. British Occupation Policy and the Western Zones 1945-55,* Oxford, New York, München 1989.

Ullmann, Hans-Peter, *Interessenverbände in Deutschland,* Frankfurt/M 1988.

Wagner, Georg, *Sozialstaat gegen Wohnungsnot. Wohnraumbewirtschaftung und Sozialer Wohnungsbau im Bund und in Nordrhein-Westfalen 1950-1970,* Paderborn 1995.

Wandel, Eckhard, *Die Entstehung der Bank deutscher Länder und die deutsche Währungsreform 1948,* Frankfurt/M 1980.

Warner, Isabelle, 'Allied-German Negotiations on the Deconcentration of the West German Steel Industry', in: Ian D. Turner (ed.), *Reconstruction in Post-War Germany. British Occupation Policy and the Western Zones 1945-55,* Oxford, New York, München 1989, pp. 155-188.

Warner, Isabel, *Steel and Sovereignty: The Deconcentration of the West German Steel Industry 1949-1954,* Mainz 1996.

Weisz, Christoph (ed.), *OMGUS-Handbuch. Die amerikanische Militärregierung in Deutschland 1945-1949,* München 1994.

Winkler, Heinrich August, (ed.) *Politische Weichenstellungen im Nachkriegsdeutschland 1945-53,* Göttingen 1979.

Index

For Product Safety Concerns and Information please contact our EU representative GPSR@taylorandfrancis.com Taylor & Francis Verlag GmbH, Kaufingerstraße 24, 80331 München, Germany

Batch number: 10726007

Printed by Printforce, the Netherlands